Created and Directed by Hans Höfer

INSIGHT GUIDES

TURKEY

Editorial Director Brian Bell
Executive Editor Andrew Eames
Updated by Canan Silay and Lale Apa

HOUGHTON MIFFLIN COMPANY

APA PUBLICATIONS

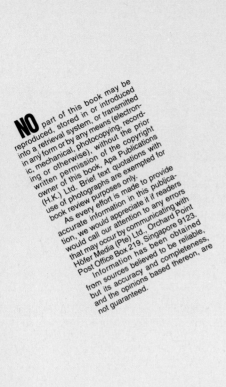
TURKEY

Fourth Edition
© 1994 APA PUBLICATIONS (HK) LTD
All Rights Reserved
Printed in Singapore by Höfer Press Pte Ltd

Distributed in the United States by:	Distributed in Canada by:	Distributed in the UK & Ireland by:	Worldwide distribution enquiries:
Houghton Mifflin Company	**Thomas Allen & Son**	**GeoCenter International UK Ltd**	**Höfer Communications Pte Ltd**
222 Berkeley Street	390 Steelcase Road East	The Viables Center, Harrow Way	38 Joo Koon Road
Boston, Massachusetts 02116-3764	Markham, Ontario L3R 1G2	Basingstoke, Hampshire RG22 4BJ	Singapore 2262
ISSN: ISBN: 0-395-66252-4	ISBN: 0-395-66252-4	ISBN: 9-62421-068-3	ISBN: 9-62421-068-3

ABOUT THIS BOOK

Standing astride the watery border between Europe and Asia, between east and west, Turkey is a country of unending fascination. Its history is as rich as ancient Byzantium and its culture and personality are unique. It has received visitors for centuries and has sent its emissaries around the world. Asian and European conquerors have crossed its soil but it has nevertheless remained proudly independent.

This is the kind of subject that lends itself best to Apa Publications' *Insight Guides*. Combining rich history, objective reporting, outstanding photography and fine writing, *Insight Guide: Turkey* exemplifies this new concept of travel publishing originated by **Hans Höfer**, Apa's founder and publisher. Born in West Germany, Höfer's first book, *Insight Guide: Bali*, won international honors and reflected Höfer's training in the Bauhaus tradition.

This is now the fourth edition of what has become a best-selling title to a best-selling destination. Tourism to Turkey has changed enormously, increasing from three million visitors in the late 1980s to seven million in the early 1990s. This book has had to change frequently to keep abreast of the changes.

The Original Team

To create the first edition of this book, Höfer appointed a single, expert project coordinator to assemble the best available journalists, scholars and photographers who lived and worked in Turkey.

His choice of project editor for the original edition was **Thomas Goltz**. Goltz was born in Tokyo but raised in North Dakota. A graduate of New York University with an MA in Middle East Studies, he lived in Turkey for many years, and has worked for many international press organizations.

An editor with the *Financial Times* in London, **David Barchard** is a graduate in history from Oxford and the author of *Turkey and the West*. A keen student of late Roman history as well as an acknowledged expert on 20th-century Turkish history, Barchard drank his first *rakı* (aniseed-based liquor) in Ankara at age 16 and has identified with the country ever since.

A doctoral candidate at George Washington University in Washington, DC, **Nur Bilge Criss** has lectured widely in the USA. Besides writing the chapters on "Turkish Women" and "Turkish Music", with its bizarre connection to modern jazz and the New Orleans marching bands, Criss also co-wrote the chapter on Turkish history, to the collapse of the Ottoman empire in 1918.

Talat Halman, former Minister of Culture in Turkey and currently a professor of Turkish literature at New York University, chipped in with the article "The Age of Süleyman the Magnificent". Halman is the author of over 30 books and translations on Ottoman and Turkish letters, including the important *Süleyman the Magnificient – Poet*.

Raşit Gürdilek, a student of political sciences, had plenty of time to research the complex nature of Republican Turkey while in prison following the 1971 military coup. He now writes for the German Press Agency DPA as well as *The Times* of London.

Selçuk Bakkalbaşı, who took up the complex issue of the national identity, nearly lost his life for being a Turk, having been gunned down by Armenian terrorists while Press Attaché at the Turkish Embassy in Paris.

Goltz   *Barchard*   *Criss*   *Gürdilek*   *Bakkalbaşı*

Metin Demirsar, a freelance journalist whose articles have appeared in *The Wall Street Journal* and the *Daily Express* of London, wrote the sensitive section on Islam in modern Turkey. Demirsar also edited *Insight Guide: Turkish Coast* and wrote the *Insight Pocket Guide: Turquoise Coast*. Demirsar has also done valuable revision work on this book and on *Insight CityGuide: Istanbul*.

Born in Nottingham, UK, and educated in Wales and Manchester University, **Virginia Penn-Taylor** wrote on Turkish cuisine. A gypsy by birth, Penn-Taylor came to work in Turkey as an English teacher and to write the restaurant column for *Dateline Turkey*.

Marian Ellingworth, who read oriental studies while at Oxford University, put her obsession with Turkish traditional crafts to good use by penning the chapter on "Turkish Carpets and Traditional Textiles", as well as sections on the Ottoman capitals of Bursa and Edirne.

A graduate of the Goodman School of Chicago, **Tony Gillote** wrote the chapters on the "Northern Aegean" and "Izmir" and also helped the production process.

Barbara Samantha Stenzel is an Athens-based journalist who also contributed to the *Insight Guide: Greece* and *City Guide*: *Istanbul*. Stenzel, who wrote the "Southern Aegean" and the feature "Underwater Archaeology", is of German and Czech descent but studied at the University of Illinois and Northwestern University.

Paul Bolding, an editor with Reuters in London, was born in London and educated in Stevenage and Bradford, England. A former Reuters correspondent in Ankara, Bolding has served in such diverse posts as East Berlin, Brussels, Nicosia and Beirut.

An Australian writer and journalist, **Anne Reeves** provided research contributions to the section on the "Turquoise Coast".

Sevan Nişanyan, a graduate of Yale, and **Gabrielle Ohl** of West Germany's primary television channel ARD, teamed up to write the fascinating chapter on the "Turkish Northeast" and the "Black Sea". In doing so, the couple also managed to change Turkish law regarding the ability of tourist class hotels to demand marriage certificates, albeit without too much adventure with the authorities of Erzurum, arguably the most conservative city in the country. Nişanyan also wrote about the Armenians, a delicate subject often neglected by the many writers on Turkey.

Lyle Lawson, who with project editor Goltz wrote the travel chapter on Istanbul, has lived in Turkey. Lawson also contributed many of the photographs in this edition.

Insight Guide: Turkey was illustrated by the superlative photographs of **Şemsi Güner, Albano Guatti** as well as other photographers whose work was provided through the courtesy of the Turkish Ministry of Culture and Tourism.

The Updaters

This edition has been thoroughly updated and carries a new Travel Tips section to keep abreast of the dramatic changes in Turkey's tourism. This work was carried out by Istanbul-based journalists **Canan Silay** and **Lale Apa**. The latter is the publisher of *The Guide*, a series of destination-based English- and German-language magazines and which set the standard for information-gathering about hotels, restaurants and other travel essentials within Turkey. It was produced by **Andrew Eames** at Apa's London office.

Demirsar   *Ellingworth*   *Stenzel*   *Ohl*   *Nisangan*

CONTENTS

History and People

Places

Maps

TRAVEL TIPS

Compiled by Canan Silay

For detailed information see page 329

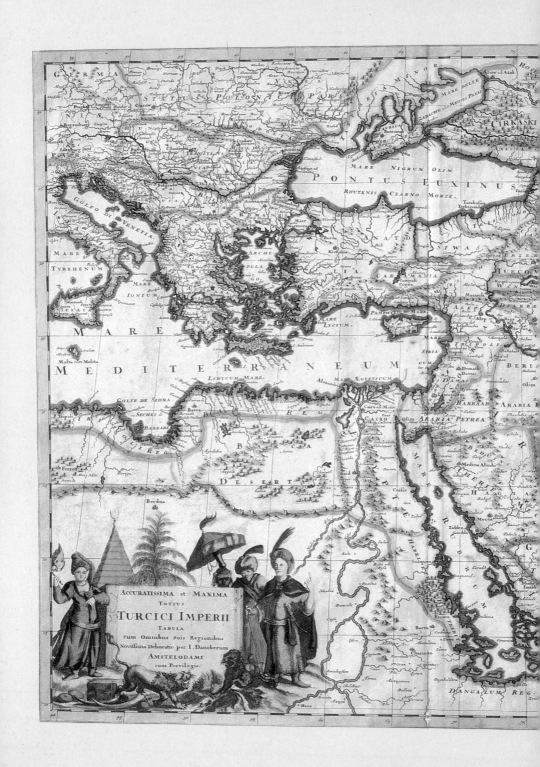

ACCURATISSIMA et MAXIMA
TOTIUS
TURCICI IMPERII
TABULA
cum Omnibus Suis Regionibus
Noviſsima Delineatio per I. Danckerum
AMSTELODAMI
cum Previlegio.

The ancients called it Asia Minor – that landmass protruding from the depths of Asia into the eastern Mediterranean, defined by the Black Sea to the north, the Aegean to the west and the deserts of Arabia to the south.

Since the dawn of time, this land of mountain ranges, high plateaus and fertile rivervalleys has been the dividing line between the Orient and Occident.

The Persian King of Kings Xerxes crossed westwards with his Asian hordes on their way to victory at Thermopylae and defeat at Salamis; Alexander the Great reversed that movement when he led his Macedonians eastward across Anatolia as far as India in pursuit of his world empire, giving the land its indelible Hellenic stamp. The Romans, too, saw in Anatolia a granary and bulwark against their traditional enemies to the east; it was at Zela, east of Ankara, that Caesar uttered his famous words: "*Veni. Vidi. Vici.*" or "I came. I saw. I conquered."

Anatolia was also the nucleus of the 1,000-year Byzantine Empire, with its capital established at Constantinople, and it was here, too, that early Christianity first took root, only to be replaced with the advent of Islam, first under the Arabs, and then under the Seljuk and Ottoman Turks, who pushed the frontiers of their empire from the Persian Gulf to the Atlantic and from the Indian Ocean to Vienna.

Slowly but surely, however, territorial gains were whittled away, until nothing remained but the spirit of the Turks under the leadership of Mustafa Kemal to reestablish modern Turkey in the ancient landscape of Anatolia. Today, the nation looks boldly toward the future, embracing the role not of the dividing line between east and west, but a bridge between them.

"*Hoş geldiniz!*", that is "Welcome to Turkey."

Preceding pages: the man who makes the minaret tops; the Bosphorus in bloom; Roman relief at Ephesus; interior of the St Sophia Museum; view of Istanbul Harbor. **Left**, ancient map of Asia Minor.

Since the time of the Bible, the land and peoples of Anatolia have played a major part in the history of civilization. The Old Testament contains a wealth of references to Anatolia and its peoples, from the Prophet Noah whose ark is said to have landed on Mount Ararat, to Abraham who came from Edessa, the present-day Urfa, and others such as Uriel the Hittite. The rivers which nurtured the great civilizations of the Fertile Crescent, the Euphrates and the Tigris, rise in the mountains of Eastern Anatolia, and the plains of Mesopotamia now lie in the southeast corner of the country.

The story of mankind in Anatolia, however, begins eons before even Noah and Abraham and the kingdoms of the Bible. In a cave at Yarımburgaz, about 20 miles (32 km) from Istanbul, a team of archaeologists working in 1986 and early 1987 discovered the oldest human remains in Turkey or indeed anywhere in the world outside Africa. They go back a million years in time.

Anatolia has been a trail-blazing country in the history of mankind, right from the dawn of time. Some of the earliest towns ever established existed on its soil. The first people in the country of whom we have any remains other than their bones lived in caves at Belbaşı and Beldibi around Antalya in the Old Stone Age, around 10,000 years ago, where a forgotten people painted and carved on walls.

The evolution from a life of hunting and gathering into settled communities seems to have been complete by about 6000 BC when villages existed in western and southeastern Turkey whose residents had domesticated the pig and the sheep, and begun farming crops such as barley.

Çatal Höyük: In 6250 BC, or about 4,000 years after the Beldibi and Belbaşı cave-dwellers, a town sprang into being at Çatal Höyük, south of the present day city of Konya. It was not the world's first city. That honor belongs to Jericho. But it was the first to use irrigation, and may have been the first

to have domesticated animals. It had a population of approximately 5,000 people – a large number to support with a primitive economy. Its inhabitants lived crowded together in houses which ran directly onto one another, there were no streets between them, and the only way to gain entry was by climbing through their roofs.

The major discoveries made so far at Çatal Höyük (only about a sixth of its area has been excavated to date) can be seen in the the Archaeological Museum in Ankara.

Most striking are the shrines with their paintings and statuettes, showing bulls and what seem to be fertility rites.

This was a community which already knew how to make textiles. It had its rich and its poor citizens, and there were even luxury goods. There is a likelihood that the wealth of the town came from obsidian, the black glass-like mineral which is found not very far away and which was widely prized in the Stone Age for the making of axes, daggers, and mirrors. There was long distance trade too. The flint in some of the axes used at Çatal Höyük comes from Syria.

This was not the only settled community

of its time, however. Far away in Eastern Turkey, at Çayönü near Diyarbakır, Turkish archaeologists have uncovered remnants of another settled community which – it seems – were astonishingly far advanced for its time and may even have been making some use of iron as early as 5000 BC.

Around 5400 BC, its inhabitants left Çatal Höyük and the town was abandoned, one of the reasons why this site has survived untouched into modern times.

A few hundred years later, at Hacılar – 135 miles (220 km) to the west of Çatal Höyük – were found the first houses with doors and streets. The people who lived in them were fine potters, producing vessels

settles, a series of levels, rather like the skin of an onion is built up. We know the peoples of Bronze Anatolia largely from their pottery, sometimes dark, sometimes red, and sometimes metallic in color.

The most famous mound is that at Troy, where level I – the original city – came into being about 3000 BC. Buried deep under the later levels, it is impossible to glean more than a few details of this earliest city but what has been discovered suggests a community far more advanced than any seen previously in Anatolia. One house was almost 65 ft by 25 ft with a main hall. It is difficult to imagine what life was like in the crowded and jumbled dwellings of Çatal

which have become famous among archaeologists across the world.

The Bronze Age: By now copper had been discovered, and Anatolia – like the rest of the Mediterranean world – was moving from the Stone Age into the Bronze Age. These changes can be traced in the successive levels built up in settlement mounds across Asia Minor.

As many of these mounds can still be seen across Anatolia, where they are called *höyük* (the same thing as a *"tell"* in the Arabian countries). These are the accumulations of successive generations of mudbrick houses on a single spot. As each level crumbles and

Höyük, but by the time of Troy I, we deal with a world we can guess at.

City walls at the time of Troy I indicate that politics and warfare had arrived. But for about a thousand years we still have no written records as such, though during this period, prehistory had come to an end in Mesopotamia and Egypt.

Anatolia seems to have been, according to D.H.Trump, "a country of flourishing independent city states or petty Kingdoms" during the third millennium BC. Sites like Troy and Mersin show continuous occupa-

Procession of Hittite soldiers at Yazılıkaya.

tion, increasing sophistication in house-building and pottery, and growing trade connections between different areas.

To this period belongs the second level at Troy – Troy II – where in the 1870s the father of modern archaeology, Heinrich Schliemann, discovered the remains of an impressive city, and 16 hoards of gold and jewelry which he thought had belonged to Homer's Trojans and their King Priam. Though they have been dated to a much earlier period, they prove that the local kings of Anatolia enjoyed considerable wealth not long after 3000 BC.

Schliemann's Treasure – taken out of Turkey under circumstances which the Ottoman Government subsequently disputed – was recently discovered at the Pushkin Museum in Moscow, after Soviet forces moved it from East Berlin during World War II. The Turkish Government has been carrying out negotiations with the Russians to bring the treasure back to Turkey. Another piece of missing heritage is the Treasures of Dorak, another northwestern site. These were glimpsed on a journey by the British archaeologist James Mellaart in the 1950s but the Treasure – and the people who showed it to him – could never be traced subsequently. Perhaps they were smuggled out of Turkey.

If the Dorak Treasure was genuine, then it is through it that writing entered the story of mankind in Turkey. Among a whole cascade of valuable objects was a fragment of gold carrying the name of Sahure, Pharaoh of Egypt in 2450 BC. Even if it is not certain that the article was found in Turkey, ivory objects in Troy II were evidence of trade with Africa.

Towards the end of the third millennium BC, the prosperous civilization which seems to have been developing across most of modern Anatolia came to an abrupt end. Cities were destroyed. Those that replaced them were poorer and smaller. It looks as if Anatolia was invaded from the northwest, and most of its territory was devastated.

The second millennium: When the darkness lifts again, we can for the first time name some of the people who were living in Anatolia. Were they the descendants of the (presumed) invaders who had sacked Troy II several hundred years earlier? There are no answers and we are left to speculate.

At any rate Anatolia was now inhabited by several groups. There were speakers of native Anatolian languages, sometimes called Hattites (not to be confused with the Indo-European Hittites who later conquered them), and beside them newer arrivals who spoke Indo-European languages, Luwian, in the north and west, and Hurrian, a language on its own, in the south and east. Beyond the Euphrates was the kingdom of Mitanni spreading across southeastern Turkey and Syria. Ruled by an Indo-European military caste, the majority of its population spoke an early version of Aramaic, the Semitic sister language of Hebrew and Arabic which is still spoken around Midyat in southeastern Turkey today by a few thousand people.

We were able to write history with people, places, names and dates during the second millennium because of a series of discoveries of written documents – which were found on clay tablets and seals, or sometimes upon rock monuments. There are still huge gaps in our knowledge. These, it is hoped, will one day be filled by the discovery of new records and archives.

The first records come from Kanesh, the modern village of Kültepe near Kayseri in Central Anatolia, where early this century the records of a colony of foreign businessmen were discovered, written on clay tablets. The merchants came from Mesopotamia and seem to have been in Anatolia, buying metal goods, mostly copper, to sell to the rest of the Near East.

Not long after this period, the city of Hattusas was conquered by one of the Indo-European kings, who ended a dynasty of Hattite native Anatolian rulers who had lived there and in the nearby town of Alacahöyük. He cursed the city and decreed that it should be abandoned forever. Within the space of two centuries, however, Labarnas I had made the city his capital. Boğazköy, the modern name of Hattusas, became the center of strong inland kingdom which gradually grew into a major state, stretching as far away as the Aegean coast and Cyprus.

The Hittites: When the immense ruins of Boğazköy were first discovered by Western travelers in the 19th century, they seemed at first to be a complete puzzle. The memory of the Hittites had not perished completely

– there was after all a famous reference in the Old Testament to "Uriel the Hittite", however he would have come from the much later southern Hittite principalities in Mesopotamia.

Knowledge of the much larger and older Hittite kingdom in the north revived with the discovery of cuneiform and hieroglyphic tablets at Boğazköy. The Sumerian forms could be read at once. Soon after came the realization that the Hittite language was Indo-European and easy to decipher. Some of its words are touching close even to modern English. The Hittite word for water, for instance, was "watar", while daughter was "dohter".

The records reveal that from around 1800 BC down to 1170 BC successive kings and emperors ruled over a feudal patchwork of client kings and princes. They had a sophisticated administrative system, based upon the use of scribes and writing, and they erected great monuments all across Anatolia. These relics are found in the west at Kemalpasa and Manisa outside Izmir, at Eflatunpınar south of Konya, and in Cilicia north of Adana.

But the Hittites had their rivals and hostile neighbors in Anatolia – the Arzawa, the Lukka and the Ahhiyawa. These seem to have been similar but less powerful states (their records are lost) ruled by a warrior class who spoke another Indo-European language, Luwian. It is Luwian from which, it is thought, the place name ending *assos*, found all across Turkey and Greece, may have come. Some familiar examples are Parnassos, Termessos, Sinasos, and the Roman town of Assos itself.

The Ahhiyawa present a more tantalizing puzzle. In the *Iliad*, the word Homer uses for the Greeks is "Achaeans" (Achaioi). Could it be that the Ahhiyawa with whom the Hittites were in contact are the same people? But this is difficult to know for sure for the Hittites have left us no maps, and working out where each of their neighbors lived is not so easy.

The Phrygians: About 1250 BC another onset of invasions began and the civilizations of the Hittites and their neighbors the Mycenaean Greeks, were destroyed so thoroughly that, as we have seen, all memory of them was lost until modern times.

Troy VII seems to have been among the casualties of the earliest wave of raids and most modern scholars equate its destruction with the story eventually told by Homer in the *Iliad*, 300 or 400 years after the event.

It is tempting to compare the Dark Ages which followed the destruction of Troy and the Hittite capital at Boğazköy, with the later Dark Ages which followed the collapse of the Roman Empire in the west. But whereas in the post-Roman period writing was not lost and Christianity acted as a bridge between the old civilization and the new, there are no such continuities in Anatolia from about 1200 BC to 800 BC.

Of the new peoples who moved into Anatolia at this time, the Phrygians are perhaps the most attractive. They seem to have come originally from Thrace and set up a kingdom which at its greatest extent covered most of central and western part of Turkey.

The Phrygians had a written script derived, like that of the Greeks, from the Phoenician alphabet. They seem to have spoken an Indo-European language and used their alphabet on monuments which can still be seen today at Midas City (Yazılıkaya) south of Eskişehir.

Probably they also had written archives, just as the Hittites had, although excavations at the two largest Phrygian capitals – Midas City and Gordium – have failed to uncover any written materials, perhaps because the Phrygians no longer used clay tablets, or at least not to the extent that the Hittites had done. It remains an intriguing possibility, however, that some day archaeology will unearth a caché of Phrygian records, enabling us to write their history.

The Phrygians do not count wholly as a prehistoric people either, for we catch glimpses of them through the eyes of their neighbors the Greeks, who by this time had been settled for several hundred years upon the western coast of Asia Minor and were gradually moving southwards and northwards along the coastline.

Midas and his father Gordius (who gave his name to the capital city about 60 miles west of Ankara), have survived in legend down to modern times, though there is no doubt that they existed. The tomb of Gordius is one of about a hundred vast artificial burial mounds, which can be seen at Gordium today. About 162 ft (50 meters) high and 975 ft (300 meters) across, it was excavated in 1957.

The body of the king, surrounded by gifts, lay at the heart of the mound in a central burial chamber, built of massive cedar logs now almost turned to stone, which it is reasonable to suppose cannot have come from very far away. No trees of this size exist within radius of hundreds of miles today and the implication is that, in this period at least, Anatolia must still have contained some mighty forests. Strangely, in view of the later legends about Midas, no gold was found in the tomb.

The mound which covers the former city at Gordium is built up of many different to these enemies, most notably the Lydians who set up a powerful kingdom with its capital at Sardis in Western Turkey, as a distinct people they survived until well into Roman times, and a large area – from west of present-day Eskişehir in the north down to beyond Denizli in the south and stretching across to the salt lake Tuz Gölü – was still known as Phrygia in Strabo's day (64 BC–AD 25).

In this area people had Phrygian names and probably spoke and even wrote Phrygian until perhaps about AD 300. Their gravestones, carved in the shape of little doorways into the next world, can still be seen in Ankara and other towns of central Anatolia.

levels very much like that at Troy. But nearby is something which points to the Classical civilization which was shortly to emerge: a mosaic comprising of many colored pebbles, the earliest mosaic known anywhere.

The Phrygians were surrounded by hostile neighbors in much the same way that the Hittites had been. Herodotus (484–424 BC) tells of the wars between Gordius and the Cimmerians, and a defeat in 695 BC after which King Midas committed suicide. Though the Phrygians rapidly succumbed

Charioteers: Assyrian relief at Ankara Museum.

Persians and Greeks: For about a hundred years (650–546 BC) the Lydian kings dominated Western Turkey. They were on close terms with their Greek neighbors, whose awe at their wealth survives in the modern expression "as rich as Croesus." Croesus (561–546 BC) was the last Lydian King, however, in 546 BC, the Persians under King Cyrus invaded Lydia and conquered it. When Croesus was taken prisoner, Sardis became the center of one of four Persian *satraps* or governors.

Persian power quickly extended to the coast and Cyrus followed by his successors, Darius and Xerxes, continued to expand towards the west from their capital at Persepolis in present-day Iran. The Ancient Greeks regarded Persian rule as both stifling and repressive.

The cities of Ionia along the western coast which had been centers of early learning – and where Homer was probably born around 700 BC – hated Persian rule. The word "satrap" has come down to us as a byword for a cruel, despotic official.

It is certainly true that monuments from the Persian period which lasted until Alexander the Great invaded Anatolia in 336 BC are few and far between. The best-known survivals are three stelae at Ergili near Lake Manyas, where the local *satrap* ruled in

settled themselves, their culture remained for centuries after Alexander's victory.

Persian rule inhibited the growth of city states but did not stop it entirely. Throughout Anatolia, particularly in the coastal zones, the local population organized themselves into towns with municipal institutions and public buildings, such as theaters and stadiums.

The cultural history of Anatolia between 700 BC and AD 400 is of the advance of Ancient Greek civilization and the gradual disappearance of local languages such as Carian, Pamphilian, Lycian and Phrygian as their people became Hellenized. This process was slow and complex, but it was

what was then known as Dascyleium. These date from about 400 BC and can be seen in the Istanbul Archaeological Museum.

The Persians, rather, were notorious for their destructiveness, as for instance in 494 BC when they wiped out the city of Miletus, said to have been one of the most splendid of the Ionian cities in the early period, after a revolt, as well as their destuction of Xanthos on the Lycian coast, when the inhabitants preferred mass suicide to the Persian yoke.

In the interior, however, the situation may have possibly been different. In Cappadocia, where the Persian nobles had

also voluntary and peaceful – the result of the prestige and appeal to local peoples of Greek culture. Further east, in Syria and Palestine, and what is southeastern Turkey today, Greek culture came up against a rival written language, Syriac, which it was never able to absorb or subdue fully.

The cultural and linguistic tension between the Semitic Syriac speaking Middle East and Hellenism was a problem which bedeviled the Roman Empire and eventually prepared the way for the rise of Islam and Arabic in the region. In most of Anatolia, however, the picture is one of assimilation and integration of indigenous peoples until the region came to consider itself the heartlands of the Roman world.

Alexander and Hellenism: Alexander the Great was one of history's meteors. Only 11 years separate his first setting foot in Anatolia in 334 BC from his death in 323 BC. After his initial victories in Anatolia at Granicus and Issus, he turned his attention farther afield and spent his energies on distant wars. His influence on Anatolia lasted for centuries.

Alexander did more than just liberate the population of Anatolia from Persian rule. He also acted as a catalyst in the spreading of Greek culture to neighboring populations which, until then, had spoken, and in some cases, written other languages. The influence began spreading first along the coasts where Greek colonists had, for centuries, been setting up their own city-states, and gradually spread inland and eastwards. It was, of course, aided by the political situation which had been created by Alexander's conquests, for the entire Middle East was now ruled by Greek dynasties established by the generals in Alexander's army who were also his heirs.

The spread of Greek culture gave its name to the centuries between Alexander and the Romans – the Hellenistic period. Though the political unit of these centuries was the kingdom rather than the city-state, Greek culture spread into Anatolia through the setting up of strong municipal communities which had control over most of their own domestic affairs.

Alexander, a passionate admirer of Homer's poems, ensured the spread of the Greek language and literature as a major part of Hellenistic civilization. The cities of Anatolia in the Hellenistic period built grand city walls, gymnasiums to educate the young, theaters for plays, stadiums for races, and odeons for concerts.

But walls and water, as much as the *Iliad* and *Sophocles*, were the basis of Hellenistic and Roman culture in Anatolia. Pergamun, for example, had a water supply which began 28 miles (45 km) away in the mountains to the north, running through a triple-pipe system of 240,000 sections. Alexander's suc-

cessors developed the life-support system for the Roman world. The spread of Hellenistic civilization into central Anatolia can be traced in stone masonry techniques brought to local chieftains by builders who were hired from the nearby coasts. The end of the Classical world coincides with the destruction of aqueducts by the Arab invaders in the 7th century.

The Classical Age was a period of splendid architecture and public buildings, erected by slaves. Even the most insignificant communities of the Roman period have left their traces in fine columns and carved capitals. In Anatolia, the most magnificent of these was the altar of Zeus at Pergamun, whose superb

friezes are kept in a museum in the former East Berlin.

No indigenous language in Anatolia could rival that of Greek, though in other parts of the Middle East, Syriac, Hebrew, and Egyptian survived as written languages. Phrygian, the language of King Midas, survives only in a few monuments. Along the coast we have inscriptions in other languages such as Lycian and Pamphylian, but these come from the earlier periods. There seems to have been no major literature in these languages to rival that of Ancient Greece and the Anatolian languages faded gradually as first the prosperous classes, and later the peasantry, be-

Left, Urartian tablet inscription. Right, a Greek soldier goes forth – detail from Istanbul Archaeological Museum.

gun to use Greek as a means of communication and for most of their daily purposes.

The Celts in Turkey: For a generation after the death of Alexander the Great and the establishment of rival kingdoms by his successors, the history of Anatolia was one of civil wars between would-be kings. In 279 BC, however, King Nicomedes of Bithynia, invited Celt mercenaries, then moving across central Europe, to enter Anatolia. He let them travel across the west of the country and settle in what had been eastern Phrygia on the west bank of the Kızılırmak river; they called their new land Galatia.

These Celts, "Gauls" as they were known, were kinsmen of the Gauls who settled in

Advent of the Romans: The Gauls were turned back by the King of Pergamun, Attalus I, in 230 BC. Attalus also had to contend with the growing political and trading power of the Romans, on the other side of the Aegean Sea, which were beginning to make inroads into Anatolia during his lifetime.

The rivalry for the Anatolian kingdoms had drawn the Romans into the area. Hard-headed pragmatists, the Romans did not try to acquire territory unless they had strong economic reasons for it. And Anatolia presented that economic package.

Pergamun sided with the Romans but the growth of Roman power was unpopular with the local peoples of Anatolia, and it was a

what are now France, Britain and Ireland. A robust, warrior people, they challenged the wealthy cities of the Hellenistic kingdoms in much the same way that the Germanic tribes would press upon the decaying Roman empire 500 years later.

The Hellenistic kingdoms immortalized their barbaric but valiant invaders in the famous sculpture of the "Dying Gaul." They left little mark on Anatolia, although a kind of Celtic language was spoken for the next 600 years or so. At the end of the 4th century, according to the records of St Jerome, the Celtic of Ankara could be understood in northern Gaul.

severe shock when in 133 BC, Attalus III, the last king of Pergamun, bequeathed his kingdom to Rome, making much of it into a Roman province.

Over the next century, local rulers tried to stem the Roman advance, led by such figures as Mithridates, King of Pontus on the Black Sea. There was an anti-Roman uprising in Pergamun in 88 BC when there and in other cities, a total of 80,000 Romans were massacred. This was quickly countered by a Roman military expedition to quell Mithri-

Left, Corinthian column at Miletus; and **right**, the Library at Ephesus.

dates and consolidate Rome's powerful grip on the province.

A series of Roman generals made their reputations putting down the Anatolian revolts. Mithridates was defeated first by Sulla and, then again 12 years later by Pompeii the Great who ran the cagey old man to the ground in the Crimea in 63 BC. Rather than be dragged in chains to Rome like Zenobia, Mithridates attempted to commit suicide by poison but failed – he had imbibed far too much toxin during his long life as a prophylactic against assassination, and was obliged to have a trusted servant run him through with a sword.

A public holiday of 10 days was declared in Rome upon the news of his death. Pompey, meanwhile, proceeded to clean up the pirate dens in the Mediterranean coastal towns of Alanya and Side, bringing the cult of Mithras with him back to Rome.

A generation later, Julius Caesar completed Pompeii's work in 47 BC at the battle of Zela (the modern Zile near Tokat) where he defeated Pharnaces, the nephew of Mithridates and uttered the famous boast: "*Veni. Vidi. Vici.*" or "I came. I saw. I conquered." The remaining semi-independent kingdoms in central and eastern Cappadocia were gradually absorbed by the Romans over the next 100 years or so, and the eastern frontier pushed back to the Kingdom of Armenia and the Euphrates, though it often fluctuated in the following centuries under continued pressure from the Persians, who held control over the area around lake Van for most of this period.

The Roman centuries: The story of the Romans in Anatolia stretches from the Battle of Magnesia in 190 BC to the fall of Constantinople to the Turks in 1453. During the centuries, the Latin Romans, originally pagans and republicans, were transformed into the Greek-speaking, imperial and Christian Bzyantines. But they continued to call themselves "Romans" which is why the Greeks of Anatolia and Cyprus are known, even today, in Turkish, as *Rum*.

The first few centuries of Roman rule in Anatolia were a mixed affair. The Roman peace brought security and prosperity to the cities across the land which grew in size and splendor. But Roman rule also meant the arrival of the tax farmer eager to squeeze all the money he could out of the province with

which he was awarded in a kind of auction. These administrators had no interest in the welfare of their province and, inevitably, created fierce resentments which helped Mithridates in his wars against Rome.

However, Roman rule brought many advantages to the less developed interior as well. Ankara developed into a significant city due to the Emperor Augustus who made it a tribal and administrative center. Earlier, Mark Antony and Cleopatra had passed along Anatolia's southern coast, where they had first met at Tarsus (an occasion immortalized by Plutarch and Shakespeare), and married a year later, in 40 BC, in Antakya (Antioch).

Living standards in Roman Anatolia must have been well ahead of what they were at the beginning of this century. We know of the people of this period from their gravestones. Some are haughty senatorial families with estates all over Anatolia and the Roman world; others are simple farming folk with rustic names who carved oven, ploughs, looms and other reflections of the daily life on their headstone.

Reflections of imperial politics are also to be found in the surviving monuments. Emperors were at first venerated and, later, worshipped as gods, as many of the Hellenistic kings had been. Temple inscriptions honor the emperors and their family members, like Livia, the infamous wife of Augustus, commemorated at Ephesus, and Britannicus, the son and heir of Claudius I, mentioned on an inscription in Samsun.

The tremors of change: The population of Anatolia was perhaps 12 million under the Romans, and they must have thought that history was coming to a triumphant climax with the civilized world united in a single state. By the 3rd century, however, tremors began to run through the Roman world. Internally, it was challenged by a religion which was consciously opposed to classical civilization and its values – Christianity. Externally, it was menaced and threatened by barbarian invaders.

In AD 258, bands of Gothic tribesmen broke into Anatolia and ransacked many of its cities, including Ankara. They went far into the center of the country, even remote Cappadocian villages, kidnapping local people for slaves. During the same century, the military threat from the Persians revived and a Roman Emperor, Valerian, was actually taken prisoner in battle and later executed.

The Goths were generally repulsed by Claudius II, a capable soldier who took the name of Gothicus. A column which was erected in his honor still stands on the Seraglio Point in Istanbul. Later, emperors such as Diocletian (AD 284–305) had to be energetic and, sometimes, harsh reformers.

Diocletian reorganized the army and the government system and, in addition, tried to combat a more modern problem – inflation. Copies of his famous edict ordering a price-freeze can be seen across Anatolia, most notably at Aphrodisias. Diocletian's two most radical initiatives failed: he had tried to create a new capital for the Roman empire in Anatolia at Nicomedia (Izmit) and in AD 303, he unleashed a ferocious persecution of Christians in an attempt to completely wipe out the religion.

A generation later, Constantine the Great (AD 306–337) tackled the same problems from a different angle and in doing so, set guidelines for the next 1,000 years. In AD 330, the provincial town of Byzantium (Istanbul) was inaugurated as a new capital under the name of Constantinople. Constantine had been working on this project for nearly six years beforehand, and he is said to have astonished his courtiers when marking the bounds of the new capital by striding much farther out from the edge of the old town of Byzantium than any one had expected. Asked why he did so, he replied that he was following an invisible and, presumably, angelic guide.

Anatolia – the cradle of Christianity: The new religion was born in Roman Palestine but it was in Anatolia that it quickly took root. This was, to a considerable degree – the work of St Paul, a native of Tarsus during his early missionary journeys through southern and western Anatolia between AD 45 and 58. Three of his biblical epistles were written to cities in Anatolia and he preached his first sermon at Perge.

Between AD 54 and 57, St Paul lived for 27 months at Ephesus. His travels in Anatolia are vividly recorded in the Bible's Acts of the Apostles and some apocryphal works. The cities he visited are uncannily familiar to the modern traveler in Turkey: Antakya, Perge, Konya, Antalya, Ephesus, Miletus and Assos.

Other apostles followed him into Anatolia. St Philip is said to have gone to Pamukkale (Hierapolis) and was subsequently martyred there. St John the Evangelist spent the later years of his life in the region largely around Ephesus.

Christianity probably spread quickest among the mixed communities of Hellenized Jews and Judaizing Romans who existed in Anatolia at this date. It evolved from a Jewish sect into a Gentile religion in AD 70 when the destruction of Jerusalem caused the dispersion of Christian Jews into nearby lands where the religion gained even more followers.

By AD 100, Anatolia's Christians, banded into communities in the big cities, were among groups stretching across the Roman world. One of the powerhouses of early Christian thought was at Antioch, which had been St Peter's base before he transferred to Rome. It remained the seat of one of the four chief bishoprics of the early church until the Arab conquest in AD 642.

Mentions of Christianity became frequent in Anatolia after AD 110 when the governor of Bithynia, Pliny the Younger, wrote to the Emperor Trajan (AD 98–117) requesting Trajan's advice on how to handle the Christians in his province.

This signaled the start of persecutions against Christians. In AD 115, the bishop of Antioch, St Ignatius, wrote seven letters to churches in western Anatolia as he was taken by guards on a slow journey to Rome to be thrown to the lions in the arena. In AD 155 the 86-year-old bishop of Izmir (Smyrna), St Polycarp, was unfortunately burned alive in the arena, as was his successor, St Pionius, 95 years later.

The really severe persecutions, however, came under Diocletian in AD 303. Ankara was the most vivid place of terror: in three separate trials, the young bishop of the town, St Clement, and his deacons were executed. So, too, was a wealthy citizen called Plato and his brother, a doctor, Antiochus, and an elderly priest, Theodotus, along with seven virgins. All subsequently became famous local saints.

Most towns had similar lists. However, when Constantine converted, the turnabout propelled Christianity from a persecuted faith into a virtual state monopoly religion within two decades.

The horror of heresy: Christians had been at loggerheads with each other from the very beginning. In Ephesus during the 1st century, the Apostle, St John, had been seen making a rapid getaway from the bath house to avoid Cerinthus, a heretic who seems to have believed that Christ was a spirit rather than a man. A generation later, Marcion, a native of Sinop on the Black Sea, was promoting his own idea of Christianity which rejected the Old Testament and its God.

Between AD 160 and 170 in Phrygia, Montanus, a former priest of the goddess Cybele converted to Christianity, and two women friends developed a theory of ecstatic prophecy which held that the Holy

What was the fuss about? Basically, what the new church was forced to do was to thrash out agreed explanations of what it held to be its central truths – against rationalizations of philosophers and communities of diverse cultural and linguistic backgrounds, with their own vested materials, doctrines and interests to defend. The core issue, stirred up by these men, was whether Jesus Christ was God or man, or (as orthodox Christians held) both at once.

The two extremes were Monophysitism and Arianism. Arius, an Egyptian priest, believed that Christ had not been God but something more like a heroic superman. His followers quickly spread across Anatolia in

Spirit was still speaking – and through them. Although the movement was banned by the bishops, it spread rapidly right across the Roman empire.

Thus for most of its subsequent history, the Roman, and later, the Byzantine empire was beset by problems of theology which sapped the energy of emperors and scholars alike, and causing deep, sometimes unbridgeable, political and social divisions. Yet even to practising Christians today, these disputes are often virtually impossible to understand.

Hercules and the Lion: Detail from a sarcophagus.

Constantine's time. The Monophysites arose out of the reaction against them. They stressed the divinity of Christ, saying he had a single Godlike nature. In between the two positions lay every conceivable variation. Christ was of similar substance to God (but not the same) argued the semi-Arians. He had one mind (Apolloninarianism) or one will (Monothelitism). He was born man and became God (Nestorianism). There were many, many more subvariants and by the middle of the 4th century, the controversy became so acrimonious that no Anatolian bishop was quite sure of his own or any one else's orthodoxy.

Constantine and the founding of his city: But the late Classical Age was plagued by more than the problem of heresies. Indeed, before the founding of Constantinople by Constantine the Great, the most pressing issue at that point of time was the struggle between late paganism and the new religion itself. Constantine himself was not entirely immune from the lingering elements of paganism and was only baptized shortly before his last breath.

The major break with paganism came his new city (surprising his advisors by marking out a much larger city than they had imagined), he declared that he was inspired by an angel. This element of holy inspiration was to remain a leitmotiv of the Christian world thereafter.

No sooner was the city established in AD 324 than courtiers and senators from Rome on the Tiber moved to the New Rome on the Bosphorus; dedicated in AD 330 and decorated with the stolen treasures and columns from all over the classical world, the city

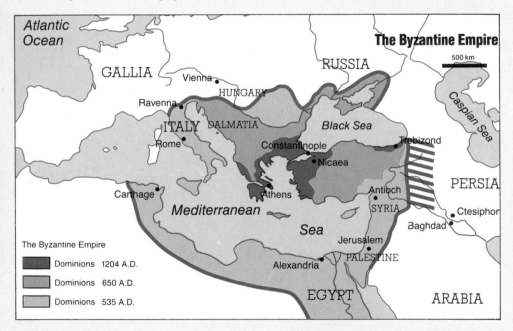

during the civil wars of the early 4th century, when Constantine adopted the cross as his symbol before the decisive battle of Milvisan Bridge in AD 312. A decade later, he made the decision to leave the traditional seat of power (and pagan worship) at Rome and establish a new, Christian city in Asia.

The first area Constantine considered for his new capital, interestingly enough, was the site of Troy on the Dardanelles, replete with Homeric associations; city walls were well on their way to completion when Constantine reconsidered and selected the provincial town of Byzantium on the Bosphorus. Walking the circumference of soon became the seat of Christianity and the venue of the acrimonious fights over the nature of the True Faith.

The Arian movement was countered by a Council of the Church which Constantine held at Iznik (Nicea) in AD 325, resulting in the Nicene Creed, a declaration of faith which is still in use among the majority of Christians. But the Council was questionable: Constantine seems to have prepared the way for it by holding preparatory minor councils the same year to influence the bishops towards his line of thought. There was considerable official pressure to toe the imperial line. Bishops who refused to sign the final documents were given criminal sentences of banishment.

Arianism faded within a few generations. Monophysitism has survived to the present day among the Syriac and Armenian Christians of eastern Anatolia and Istanbul.

Further general councils of the church were held between AD 325 and 787, resolving problems of teaching and discipline. In this way, the early churches of Anatolia laid the basis of Christian belief. The second council at Nicea in AD 787 was the last attended by representatives of both eastern and western churches.

The monks are coming: Around the same time, Anatolia saw a further development which influenced its history until modern times: the rise of monks and ascetics. For the first 250 years of Christianity, there had been no monks. Gradually, however, the "holy man" who set himself apart from the rest of the community by refraining from sex and living a life of fasting and prayer crystalized into the idea of the monk – literally, the *monachos*, or solitary one.

In the year AD 360, Basil of Kayseri (Caesarea in Cappadocia) wrote down a set of rules for the emerging communities of monasteries as they were increasingly called. St Basil's rules are still in force in the Greek Orthodox church and helped form the basis of the Rule of St Benedict in the west.

Monks were part of a cultural revolution whose marks can be seen by every tourist in Turkey today. For at the end of the 4th century and throughout the 5th century, they spearheaded a fierce attack on the survivals of paganism.

Temples were shut down, statues thrown out, and oracles put out of business. The crosses tourists find scrawled on temples such as that of Apollo at Didyma and other classical monuments usually date from this period, a kind of monkish attempt to "disinfect" the great buildings of the pagan religion and convert them for Christian use. Paganism was then gradually forced out of the scene.

Left, map of Byzantine Empire. **Right**, Byzantine icon of the Apostles.

The Emperor Julian (AD 361–363), a great-nephew of Constantine, made an attempt during his brief but remarkable reign to turn the clock back, but was too late: in AD 363, Julian was killed fighting the Persians at Nusaybin, and all subsequent emperors were Christians.

The Byzantine era: While the west was wracked by invading Goths, Vandals, Franks and other sundry barbarians, the eastern realm of the Roman empire thrived, largely unaffected by the chaos in the west. In

Anatolia, by contrast, the 5th and 6th centuries were periods of great splendor under emperors such as Theodosius I (AD 378–395), Theodosius II (AD 408–450) and Justinian I (AD 527–565).

Greek began to replace Latin, though only slowly, as the language of the court and eventually of the administration. The educational system became explicitly Christian. Imperial power grew while municipal traditions waned as town senators cast off their pagan culture and sought careers as monks or bishops.

Holy men on pillars: The figures that the emperors had to defer to were no longer philosophers or senators. Social and political power had shifted to the holy man, who demonstrated his power by extraordinary actions.

Near Antioch, St Simeon the Stylite lived atop a pillar for 30 years. Daniel the Stylite (AD 409–493) passed the last 33 years of his life on a pillar at Rumelihisarı (Anaplous), attracting visitors like Emperor Leo I and his family. Other holy men, called "dendrites", preferred to live in trees; a picture of one can be seen in the Kariye Camii Museum in Istanbul.

The church had now become both the major institution of every city and also its chief builder. When Justinian I rebuilt the

cathedral church of Constantinople, St Sophia, in the middle of the 6th century, he produced one of the architectural masterpieces of all time, but it looked nothing like the older Roman buildings of 200 or 300 years before.

Justinian and Theodora: The Emperor Justinian I has gone down in history as the builder of St Sophia and the codifier of Roman law. These were only parts of a vast imperial program which aimed, among other things, at the reconquest of the western Roman territories lost 60 years earlier to the Germanic chieftains. Justinian's armies conquered north Africa and part of Spain relatively easily, but the reconquest of Italy required a long and enervating war.

To finance it, Justinian squeezed the cities of Anatolia and Greece through his rapacious minister, John of Cappadocia. He weakened what remained of the classical, urban institutions while attempting to finance a strong, centralized empire.

The contradiction was felt acutely by his contemporaries, such as the historian Procopius, who eulogized Justinian in public for the buildings he was putting up across the empire, while privately lambasting him in his *Secret History* as a devil in human form, married to a prostitute, who delighted in humiliating his foremost subjects.

Justinian's legacy did not endure. Within his lifetime, the empire was struck by a great plague which reduced its population. Italy, which he rescued from the Goths, was soon after overrun by the Lombards.

The Slav menace: The northern European provinces of Justinian's empire came under renewed threat at the end of the 6th century. The Danube frontier was attacked by the Avars, a Central Asian people similar to the Huns who had terrified the Romans in the previous century.

Justinian I's successors battled with the Avars, but as the frontier collapsed, a new wave of invaders – the Slavs, a very backward but numerous in population, peoples – flooded the south.

For a generation, the Emperor Maurice (AD 582–602) struggled to contain the challenge from the north. In AD 602, his armies revolted and he was killed by a usurper, Phocas.

For a period, order collapsed in the Roman world. The invasions which were initiated from the north were matched by others from the east. It was at that point of time, the hereditary foes of the empire, the Sassanid Persians, staged their most successful invasion ever, crossing the entire length of Anatolia and seizing Byzantine provinces as far away as Egypt. Also, the Persian armies advanced and reached the shores of the Sea of Marmara at Kadıköy (Chalcedon) in the greatest Persian triumph since Alexander the Great's defeat of Darius.

The middle Byzantine empire: Settled life for the next 100 years was next to impossible. Most cities were destroyed, though Constantinople and Thessalonica survived.

There was an economic and cultural collapse unprecedented since the long forgotten invasions which had destroyed the Hittite empire around 1,170 BC and ushered in an earlier dark age of 400 years.

The classical city of Ankara, for instance, was destroyed by the Persians in AD 622 and the population was massacred or enslaved. The public buildings were either abandoned or pillaged for stone to build new defenses. In half-a-century, Ankara changed, as one writer says, "from a sprawling metropolis to a heavily fortified town on a hilltop."

Remarkably the Emperor Heraclius (AD 610–641) was able to muster his army and expel the Persians by AD 628, but the effort so exhausted both the Persian and the Roman empires that they were unable to resist the sudden appearance of a new enemy on their frontiers – the Arab armies sweeping out of the desert under the banner of Islam.

Islam: The Arab invasions were the beginning of the story of Islam in Anatolia – today the religion of more than 99 percent of its inhabitants. The armies fought in the name of Allah and his Prophet Muhammad. To the Byzantines, the Arabs at first appeared to be only wild and primitive tribesmen. They were quickly stripped of this notion at the battle of Yormuk in present-day Jordan, when the Byzantine host was routed by the Muslim horsemen under Khalid Ibn Walid, the "Sword of Islam."

In AD 654, the Arab armies swept through Anatolia, taking Ankara and other cities. Twenty years later, the Arabs began the first great siege of Istanbul which lasted for 4 years. Thanks, largely, to the walls of the capital, the Arab siege was repulsed, as was the second one in AD 717–718.

The Byzantines lost most of their eastern provinces including eastern Anatolia to the Arabs. Their new frontier stretched from east of Silifke on the south coast, past Kayseri (the great Byzantine frontier defense station of central Anatolia) to a point east of Trabzon on the Black Sea. Tarsus, Malatya, and Erzurum became Arab garrison towns from which annual raids were made on Byzantine territory.

Left, mosaic of Jesus at the St Sophia. Right, the Anastasis mosaic of Jesus, Adam and Eve at the Kariye museum.

Islam brought a different civilization and a different script to Byzantine. It was a radical discontinuity in an area which had been basically Greek-speaking since the days of Alexander. The new religion had some common points with Christianity but it stressed the oneness of God and the supreme importance of His message as revealed in the Quran.

Islam also tolerated people of other Bible-based religions, provided they accepted inferior status and paid special taxes. As a result, those parts of Anatolia under Muslim rule were multi-ethnic and multi-religious until this century.

Byzantium and the Arabs each influenced

the other: in AD 726, for instance, the Emperor Leo III copied the Arab caliph in banning pictures and representations of human beings. The result was a new religious crisis as the Iconoclasts battled with the supporters of images. The leader of the Orthodox party was Mansur, a Christian Arab, and civil servant at the court of the Caliph in Damascus, known to the Greek world as St John of Damascus.

Against the Arab threat, the Byzantines emphasized the cross, on their coins and on their city walls. The unadorned cross can be found in the rock chapels of Cappadocia and in St Sophia as a relic of the emergency period. But by AD 843, the supporters of icons triumphed as images were gradually restored in churches.

Byzantine revival: The turning point was the decade between AD 856 and 866 when Byzantium was ruled by the Caesar Bardas on behalf of the weak Michael III.

On September 3, 863, Bardas's brother, Petronas, defeated the Arab armies of Omer Ibn Abdullah, the Emir of Malatya, at the battle of Poson.

Just at this point, however, Bardas was murdered by the Emperor Michael's homosexual lover and former groom, a peasant from Thrace called Basil. Basil was a penniless youth of Armenian descent who had

empire's sole ruler.

From this sordid beginning emerged Bzyantium's most glorious dynasty, and at the same time, witnessed the immediate revival of the staggering empire. Over the next 200 years, the frontiers were expanded in all directions, with wars fought and won over the Fatamids in Egypt, the Abbasids in Baghdad, as well as the Bulgars and Russians to the north.

Then under the ferocious Basil II ("The Bulgar Slayer"), the late Byzantine state reached the apogee of its glory. With the aid of Varangian soldiers sent by Vladimir of Kiev (in return for which a royal princess was given to Vladmir on his adoption of

drifted from Thrace (Macedonia as the Byzantines called it, hence the name of his dynasty) to the big city as a teenager, sleeping out in churches before he got a job as a groom, first in a wealthy household, and later, in the palace itself where he doubled as a champion wrestler.

He quickly became the favorite of the Emperor Michael, but neither he nor his master were taken seriously by Bardas and the men running the empire. After the assassination, Basil was crowned joint emperor with Michael on May 26, 866. The sequel was predictable: on September 23, 867, Basil murdered Michael III to become the

Christianity), Basil first crushed the revolt of two generals who meant to usurp and divide the empire between them before turning to the Balkans to deal with the Bulgarian Czar, Samuel.

The end came in 1014, when the Byzantine host captured some 14,000 Bulgarian soldiers. They were all blinded and sent back to Samuel, in his last redoubt, in groups of 100, each of which was led by one man who only had one eye put out. When Samuel beheld the gruesome spectacle, he fell into

Artist's conception of the remains of Anadolu Kavaği Fortress on the Bosphorus.

delirium tremens and died within two days. His kingdom was then annexed to the Byzantine state.

Basil II also extended the eastern frontier of the empire to the Armenian kingdom of the Bagratids in the north, and in the south to Amida (Diyarbakır), Edessa (Urfa) and Aleppo. In the west, too, Basil was active in restoring much of Italy to the Byzantine sphere, and was preparing for a decisive campaign against the Muslims in Egypt and Syria when he died in 1025, an unmarried warrior with no heir.

Basil's death in many ways signaled the end of Byzantium, with the ruling house falling into a vortex of complex, sinister intrigues. Basil's aging, younger brother, Constantine VIII next took the purple. He was then succeeded by his aging, spinster daughter Zoe, who was married at his deathbed to Romanus Aryges. The new emperor died in his bath a few years later at the hand of Zoe's young peasant lover, who ascended the throne as Michael IV and attempted to banish his aging wife to a convent. That backfired and Michael IV was blinded and deposed.

Zoe then raised her sister, Theodora, to rule as a joint empress. Zoe, now 63, was determined to wed again and brought Constantine IX Monomachus (along with his young lover, who quickly obtained the official title of Sebaste) to the throne for a bizarre triumvirate, which, if nothing else, drained the treasury.

The final break with the Catholic church in Rome isolated Byzantium from its natural allies in the west, while the civil bureaucracy essentially castrated the Byzantine war machine, leaving the frontier defenses in the hands of local aristocrats and their personal armies of mercenaries and miscreants.

This could not have occurred at a worse time: to the north, Turkish tribesmen ransacked the Danube provinces; far more ominous were the Seljuk Turks who were replacing the Arab threat. After having overrun the Arab lands from Baghdad to Egypt, the new power on the eastern horizon of the empire was now raiding north into Byzantium as far as Cappadocia.

The desperate situation led to the arranged marriage of the widowed Empress Eudocia to Romanus IV Diogenes, who led a host of some 150,000 mercenaries east to meet 14,000 Seljuk horsemen under Alp Arslan on August 19, 1071, on the field of Manzikert north of Lake Van.

It was an utter rout, with large numbers of Armenian mercenaries deserting to the Turks, and Romanus himself falling captive. Although he managed to ransom himself and sign a treaty with the Turks, Romanus's defeat was to turn into a complete disaster: upon his return to Constantinople, he learned that he had been deposed during his captivity. He was subsequently blinded by the new emperor and died of his injuries in 1072.

The freshly signed treaty between Romanus and the Seljuk prince, Alp Arslan was no longer valid. Thus Anatolia lay open to the Turks who began their ineluctable conquest of the country.

The end of the Byzantium: Byzantium struggled on for another four centuries under the new Comneni dynasty, at times appearing to regain the initiative against the Turks, but ultimately doomed to failure as the population decreased and foreign armies – such as the Crusaders – came to play an ever greater role in the affairs of the remnant of Rome on the Bosphorus.

The sacking of the city by the Crusaders in 1204 and the establishment of the Latin kingdom by Baldwin I of Flanders in the capital while the Byzantines retreated to Nicaea was yet another nail in the sarcophagus. The recovery of the city in 1261 by Michael VIII Palaeologus was, in many ways, nothing but an interesting historical detail: the once powerful empire had been reduced to a rump state, in ever greater dependency on the rising power of the Ottoman Turks whose realms slowly but surely surrounded those of Byzantium.

But still the city fought on for life for another 200 years until the sultans, their harems filled with Byzantine princesses taken in exchange for peace, grew tired of the presence of the ancient city of Constantine in their midst. Founded in AD 324 as the capital of the New Rome, Constantinople – and with it, Byzantium – disappeared forever on May 29, 1453, with the last emperor Constantine XI Palaeologus fighting on the walls with his men. Within days it was renamed Islamboul, or the City of Islam.

Somewhere in the vastness of Central Asia, a nomadic people ventured from one dried-up waterhole to the next, fighting drought, the torrid heat and the bitter cold of night. It was almost by a primitive law of nature that when these poor herdsmen came upon cultivated lands they ransacked the riches. And while the names of Atilla the Hun, Genghiz Khan and Tamerlane, riding at the front of their hordes (or ordu in Turkish, meaning army), strike images of horror and blood-thirstiness in the minds of modern man, these figures must be evaluated within the drama of nomads versus settlers, the stirrup versus the plow.

It is from this stock of people that the Turks emerged. Language alone sets them apart from Europeans, Slavs or Semitic peoples. Aside from the modern, western Turkish spoken in Turkey today, millions of Turkic peoples in parts of Iran, the Caucasus in Russia and Chinese Turkestan, speak a form of Turkish or other related languages like Mongolian or Uzbek, which belong to the Ural-Altaic family of languages, along with Finnish, Hungarian, Japanese, Korean and – some say – Navaho.

The word "Turk" was first recorded in Chinese annals as early as 1,300 BC. It appears as *T'u-chueh* or *Durko*. The 8th century BC Orkhon inscriptions found in Mongolia give an account of the ordeal of bringing tribes under a single authority against a major enemy, the Chinese. The inscriptions, written in runic characters, also reveal capital cities of tent-dwellers. An interesting inscription on the east side reads: "If the sky above did not collapse and if the earth below did not give way, Oh, Turkish people, who would be able to destroy your state and institutions?"

One learns more about the lifestyle of these people in the ancient Turkish epic, *Dede Korkut*. Ancient Turks were patriarchal, but monogamous. When the wife was unable to bear children it was accepted as the couple's fate, and taking another woman is not mentioned.

Left, Seljuk Grand Mosque in Sivas. Right, Seljuk "Kümbet" at Ahlat on the shores of Lake Van.

Instead of polygamy, Turks practised exogamy – which is marrying outside one's tribe. In this way they established blood ties with neighboring tribes which won them allies and partially accounts for the confusion surrounding the differences between Mongols and Turks in the various dynasties which arose in Central Asia. The most notable of these was the empire of Timucin or Genghiz Khan – himself half-Mongol and half-Turkish.

Religion: The ancient religion of these

nomads was shamanism, a polytheistic faith with many totems and a lot of magic. Gradually, some tribes like the Uighurs adopted Buddhism, some became Zoroastrians, some Nestorians or Manicheans. The Khazar Turks, whose story is depicted in Arthur Koestler's *The Thirteenth Tribe*, adopted Judaism. Today a small number of Christian Turks, the Gagauz, survive in Poland, in addition to the Jewish Karaim Turks living in Baltic states.

Islam: It was not until the 10th century that Islam penetrated Central Asia and the conversion of the Turks to Islam began. The Abbasid caliphs in Baghdad were well aware of the martial qualities of the Turks and recruited them as paid warriors or as superior slave soldiers in Arab armies. The Arabs, it would seem, had not read their Roman history as regards the hiring and firing of foreigners in the homeguards and by the end of the 9th century, most military command posts of the Empire were held by Muslim Turks.

The Seljuks: In the 11th century, an obscure Turcoman horde called the Seljuks set up a state in Iran, with Isfahan as their capital. The Abbasid Caliph in Baghdad was so taken in by their military prowess, that he sanctioned their leader, Toğrul Bey, with the impressive title "King of the East

Seljuk chieftains had become, the situation on the borderlands between the Seljuks and the Byzantines was anything but peaceful. Turcoman *ghazis* (warriors for the faith, and generally a very motley crew) and Byzantine *akritoi* (mercenaries) were enrolled as private troops for various Armenian-Byzantine landowners but engaged in private looting themselves. The Seljuks and Byzantines constantly accused each other of bad faith and for breaching the general peace. It was not until the third quarter of the 11th century, when the situation reached a critical point that the Byzantines, under Emperor (or *Basileus*) Romanus IV Diogenes, decided to preempt the nascent

and West" thus designating the Seljuk warlord as his temporal deputy.

However, the Seljuks under Toğrul and his successor, Alp Arslan, were not content with controlling only their piece of the disintegrating Arab empire: recent converts to Islam, they saw themselves as the rightful heirs to the lands conquered during and immediately after the time of the Prophet Muhammad, in particular, the heretical lands of the Levant and Egypt. Indeed, in order to secure their own flanks, Toğrul entered into numerous negotiations with the Byzantine emperors of Constantinople.

However, sedentary and acculturated the

Seljuk power on their eastern frontier and reconquer Armenia.

Using ancient Harput (modern Elaziğ) as his base, Diogenes crossed the Euphrates (the classic demarcation of east and west) to confront the Seljuk army on the field of Manzikert, north of Lake Van in 1071. Although they vastly outnumbered the irregular Turkish horsemen, the Byzantine Christian troops could scarcely have selected a worse venue: the light-riding Turks feigned a retreat, lured the main Byzantine force into a loop, and showered the heat-exhausted Christian host with arrows before closing on three sides with the scimitar. The booty for the victors on "that dreadful day" included the vanquished Diogenes himself.

Remarkably, the Seljuks did not drag the beaten Diogenes back home in victory, but released him for a ransom and cession of Byzantine land, and reentered a period of often uneasy peace with Constantinople again. Indeed, the two forces actually stood together against the Mongol invasion of the 13th century. But it was a vain defense as neither Christian nor Muslim were spared the sword as the Mongol hordes rolled across the steppe into Anatolia.

The reigns of Alp Arslan and his son, Malik Shah, were the most glorious years of

the great Seljuks of Isfahan; the death of the latter marked the decline of the great Seljuks and by 1192 the dynasty ended in the same obscurity with which it had begun, unable to cope with the pressures from the Crusaders, the caliph and new Turcoman clans arriving from the east due to the increasing power of the Mongols, who were soon to erupt from the deepest recesses of Central Asia to sack much of the known world before returning just as quickly to the

Left, the dome of the Mevlana tomb in Konya. **Above**, a participant in the "sema" or whirling ceremony of the dervishes.

frontiers of China.

Following the decline of the Great Seljuks and the onslaught of the Mongols, lesser Seljuk clans established their own principalities throughout Anatolia and made the small Christian states in the area their vassals. Through intermarriage, they greatly facilitated the cultural syncretism of the area.

The presence of so many petty Muslim states in east and central Anatolia explains the abundance of Seljuk architecture in modern Turkey, with some of the best examples of this so-called "poetry in stone" to be seen in Erzurum, Divriği, Sivas and Konya. Of these, Konya is perhaps the most impressive. It was where the Sufi mystic, Jelaleddin Rumi, (*Mevlana* or "our master") graced the court of Alaaddin Keykubat, the Sultan of Rum, and initiated the peculiar whirling dervish ceremony in an effort to seek spiritual union with the Creator himself. The cultural effervescence at Konya, however, met with the same abrupt and unhappy end as the others at the hands of the powerful and indiscriminate Mongol hordes of Genghiz Khan (who the modern Turks oddly and often inconsistently claim as one of their own).

Just as they had dealt the Byzantines a decisive blow at Manzikert two centuries before, the now settled Seljuks could not resist the most recent wave of nomads from the steppe. On June 26, 1243, despite Byzantine auxiliaries sent by the Seljuk sultan's "ally" in Constantinople, the once mighty Seljuk army was utterly routed at Köse Dağ, outside the quintessentially Seljuk city of Sivas.

The remaining Turkish clans scattered westwards before being further defeated by the Mongols, until they had no choice but to finally accept their role as mere vassals in the greater scheme of things. But no sooner had the Mongol tide surged over the region than it withdrew once more, leaving behind several unimportant mini-states led by petty chieftains who might well have remained utterly obscure but for one of their number on the fringe of the Byzantine state: Osman, the son of Ertuğrul, the horseman destined to found an empire that stretched from Morocco in the west to Iran in the east, and from the Yemen in the south to the Crimea in the north.

The rise of the Ottomans: As the Mongol forces swept over Anatolia, an exhausted band of retreating Seljuks under the command of Alaaddin of Konya, were cornered unaware by a detachment of the Mongol barbarians from the east. Just as all hope seemed lost for the Turks, a wall of horsemen appeared above the crest of a nearby hill, pausing, it would seem, just long enough to determine the victor and claim his side for a division of the spoils. The chieftain of the horsemen signaled his men forward, drawing his scimitar as he charged.

But instead of joining the apparent victors, the galloping wall of horsemen spurred their steeds toward the Mongol flank, and carved their way through to the surprised relief of Alaaddin, turning the tide of battle with their chivalry. Grateful for his life, the Seljuk commander inquired of the leader of the gallant horsemen as to his name: Ertuğrul, came the answer, father of Osman.

Such is the legend surrounding the emergence of the Ertuğrul Ghazi and his 444 horsemen, and indeed, the entire Ottoman empire. Even if the historical accuracy of this episode is somewhat doubtful, the fact remains that after his gallant interlude during the Mongol invasion, Ertuğrul was in possession of a small fief of land near the town of Eskişehir in western Anatolia, which was to serve as the base from which the Ottoman empire expanded first into Europe, and then over most of the Middle East and Asia.

The prediction of the Ottomans' growth from rustic clan to world power is, likewise, embroidered by legend: upon his succession as clan chieftain, Osman Ghazi happened to spend the night in the house of a pious Muslim who introduced the young warlord to the eternal truths of the Quran. Osman read deep into the night, finally falling asleep on his feet to dream of a giant tree springing from his loins, whose branches grew to such heights as to cover the great

Left, contemporary European oil painting of Sultan Süleyman the Magnificent. **Right**, a Turkish miniature of the "mehter", or Janissary band.

mountain ranges of the known world and whose roots were watered by the great rivers of the day – the Tigris, Euphrates, Danube and Nile. A wind blew through the vision, turning the leaves of the branches into swords, all pointed towards the direction of Constantinople, which appeared as a fabulous, bejeweled ring waiting for the plucking. Thus the legend.

In reality, (and as suggested by the legend itself), the Ottomans were not even Muslim at the time they settled in Eskişehir, and it is

doubtful that they numbered more then 4,000 souls, including women and children – hardly a force to breach the walls of the Byzantine capital. But in the chaos resulting from the Mongolian sack of Anatolia, coupled with the internal confusion of the late Byzantine state itself, no dreams were, perhaps, too wild for credence as the vacuum of power grew, begging for some sort of order. And it was into that power vacuum that the inchoate Ottoman Turks began to be drawn.

Several factors were in favor of the Ottomans. Their fief lay on the march between the Seljuk-Muslim lands of Anatolia and the rump Byzantine state around the Sea of Marmara, and thus presented a convenient frontier to invite the Ghazi (or Holy Soldier) to war with the infidel. Perhaps more importantly, the local population's confidence in Christianity was at an all time low: wrecked by schisms in the faith – the simplest of which was the east-west division between the Roman Catholic church and the Orthodox Byzantine church – the road to piety was confusing and filled with pitfalls. More to the point, it was filled with the *Dhimmi* tax (50 percent of earnings for non-Muslims as opposed to the tithing for believers) on those lands held by the Ottomans, and corvée-labor for serfs on Byzan-

morale and routed the forces of Andronicus II Palaeologus. Not only did the defeat of an imperial army by a still obscure Muslim clan send shockwaves through the recently restored empire, but the reverberations (and suggested promise of further booty) brought Osman increasing numbers of holy warriors and converts from across Anatolia ready to join in the next battle, which was against the Greeks outside Nicomedia 7 years later. The second routing of Byzantium led to a virtual occupation of the entire hinterland of the remaining Byzantine cities in Asia Minor, chief among which was Bursa (Proussa).

Following the slow atrophy of that city by

tine latifundia. Between the rock and hard place, untold numbers of Byzantine peasants had converted their faith to Islam, possibly due to the relative simplicity of belief – one had only to profess belief in the One God and the mission of His Prophet – but more likely as a means to evade the gouging *Dhimmi* tax.

For 12 years, Osman's forces grew from his father's reputed 444 horsemen to over 4,000 men at arms in 1301, when for the first time, the nascent Ottoman state came into direct conflict with Constantinople near Baphaeon. If inferior in numbers, the Muslims easily bested the Christian host in

a 7-year siege, the garrison commander finally surrendered in 1326, and, along with his forces as well as most of the city's remaining inhabitants, embraced Islam. Osman, however, was only able to enter his empire's first capital in a burial shroud, as the eponymous founder of the dynasty died in 1324, but had left his son and successor, Orhan, a firm foundation on which to build. The great tree of Osman's vision was well-rooted, with the branches growing toward the jewel of Byzantium.

Left, 19th-century portrait of Sultan Orhan; and **right**, a miniature of a birth in the Topkapı Harem.

The Ottoman State: The reign of Osman's second son, Orhan Ghazi (1324–59) was marked by consolidation, reorganization, and then expansion. He consolidated the proto-Ottoman state with one religion, Islam: he built mosques and religious schools, as well as promoted Muslim brotherhoods whose members were known as *Akhis*, the Arabic word for "brother." Bursa, in particular, became one large construction site for religious edifices, which have remained the city's primary attraction to this day.

Next, he reorganized the military from being mere waves of religiously inspired horsemen into various discreet units ranging from shock troops to a regular cavalry and infantry.

Finally, Orhan embarked on his multipronged expansion program. He conquered the Muslim Turkish-Seljuk lands to the south and east, after which he either co-opted them as allies or subjected them as vassals or just annexed them. Then he moved towards the Christian region of Thrace across the Dardenelles and Sea of Marmara in Europe. The first step into Europe, oddly enough, was at the invitation of the Byzantine pretender, John Cantacuzene, who married his daughter, Theodora, into Orhan's harem in exchange for aid in his civil war against the house of Palaeologue. This resulted in the peculiar spectacle of Muslim Turks standing shoulder-to-shoulder with Christian supporters of the pretender, besieging the walls of Constantinople as brothers in arms. When peace was finally made by Cantacuzene, marrying another of his daughters to the legitimate Byzantine emperor, Orhan's role as a kingmaker in Constantinople was firmly established along with, at least, a tenuous claim to the crown due to his royal marriage.

Upon his death in 1359, Orhan had witnessed the expansion of his territory from some 5,000 sq miles (8,000 sq km) to nearly 80,000 sq miles (13,000 sq km), and mostly due to the invitation of his rivals and enemies. Twice betrothed to the rulers of Byzantium, Orhan had become a kingmaker/breaker, with the legendary branches of his empire ever closer to the imperial throne. But with the succession of Orhan's son, Murad (at times called Amurath in the medieval chronicles), the policy of expansion-by-invitation was forgotten, as the Ottoman power marched into Europe by force-of-arms and the call of destiny.

Murad I: The second half of the 14th century saw even greater expansion of the Ottoman realm at the expense of Constantinople as well as the would-be heirs of Byzantium in the Balkans. Within 1½ year of his succession, Murad I (1362–89) was in control of all of Thrace, including Adrianople, which, renamed Edirne, was to become the Ottoman's second capital.

Murad I placed equal importance on developing new administrative policies, as on his conquests in Europe. Unlike the Christians of Asia, who had long since been exposed to Islam, and were thus more easily assimilated, the conquered peoples of the Balkans were tenacious of faith and – save putting a garrison in every conquered town to insure their adherence to Islam – had to be treated differently. Thus, slowly but surely the system of *Millets* came into existence. Under this system, minority populations – based on religion – were officially recognized, with their leaders held responsible for the communities' taxes as well as communal and legal affairs.

It should be noted, however, that the recognition of the various minorities came only after conquest and, due to the fact that the Ottoman forces moved forward as a male army save for a few camp followers, the wives and daughters of the conquered instantly became the chattel of the Ottoman forces, eventually resulting in the extremely heterogeneous bloodline of the modern Turk.

The Janissaries: Murad I also began the institution of "taxing" families for their most able-bodied sons, drafting them into corps of "new troops." These candidates, who as new converts to Islam and completely isolated from their origins, insured their absolute and personal loyalty to the sultan himself. Bereft of everything but their own esprit de corps, these *Yeniçeri* (Janissaries) would eventually become the terror not only of Europe, but of the Ottoman empire itself.

Writers, from contemporary historians down through Count von Hammer-Purgstall and Gibbon, have decried the institution of these "slave soldiers" as an affront to human dignity. But there was a fundamental difference between slavery in Islam and the

Christian world. A greater difference existed between standard slavery within the Islamic world and the servant warrior Janissaries of the Ottomans, and the Mamelukes of Egypt and other Arab lands where slave dynasties were formed by the elite praetorian forces. They insured their own legacy by enslaving fresh blood from beyond the *Dar Al-Salam*, (or "abode of peace" as the Muslim world was known) in the *Dar Al-Harb*, ("abode of war," or those lands beyond the borders of the Muslim world).

Murad's end finally came on the field of battle at Kosovo (in today's Yugoslavia) in 1389, when, on the verge of victory over a have his younger brother, Yakub, strangled in order to insure his leadership of the state. This grisly practice of fracticide was to continue through the ages, allowed by Islamic jurisprudence, setting the precedent for all future cases of succession to the power of the Ottoman state. He then took measures to avenge the assassination of his father by massacring all Serbian notables captured. His third act was to accept the hand of Lazar's daughter, Despina, in marriage from her brother, who thus retained a quasi-independent Serbia, although he was forced to supply troops on demand to the Ottoman Sultan in addition to allowing the Muslim settlement in his fief.

Slavic confederation, he was assassinated by Milosh Obravitch, the son-in-law of the Serbian leader, Stephen Lazar, who had accused his relative of treason. Obravitch, apparently trying to prove his loyalty with his life, surrendered to Murad, only to run the 70-year-old sultan through with a dagger as he knelt before him. Obravitch's assassination of the sultan was but in vain as Murad's empire was at that point in near, if still not in actual, possession of the Second Rome.

Beyazıt the Thunderbolt: Murad's son, Beyazıt, was raised to sultan immediately upon his father's death. His first act was to

Beyazıt and the last Crusade: If the Crusades of the first millennium had been inspired by the desire to reestablish the True Faith in distant Jerusalem, the last crusade was a desperate effort to forestall the infidel Turks from knocking down the door to Europe itself. In the summer of 1396, an "international brigade", which had been drawn from all over Christian Europe, assembled in Hungary for the routine of pillage and rape of the lands it was allegedly defending from the Turks. The European Crusaders found little to test their true mettle save the women and children of Nish, who were massacred despite being Christians themselves. Finally, they camped around the town of Nicopolis in present-day Bulgaria, hoping to starve the Turkish garrison into submission. At last, scouts reported that Beyazıt had arrived to relieve the town; while the eastern Europeans urged caution, the western European knights elected for immediate battle. Believing the Ottoman front guard to be the entire battle line, they charged on their armored steeds, wreaking havoc on the Ottoman auxiliaries; dismounting, they carved their way to the crest of a hill, only to find, like Custer at Little Big Horn, that they had merely dealt with the vanguard of an army of over 200,000 highly trained and battle-fresh Janissaries with vengeance in their eyes. The slaughter of the knights – estimated at 10,000 – was complete within hours. Save for a cowering knot of survivors who managed to ford the Danube to safety, Middle Europe was left undefended and open to Ottoman arms.

But Beyazıt did not press through with his victory. Instead, he returned to Constantinople to seize the jewel that had eluded his forefathers for over a century and which laid, as never before, ready for the taking. But as his forces once again set up their blockade-siege of Constantinople, a new and wholly unexpected challenge was heard from the east, delivered by yet another cousin/rival – the limping but iron-willed Tatar, Timur, sometimes referred to in western annals as Timurlenk, but more frequently known as Tamerlane.

Timur the Tatar: Some historians of the Muslim lands refer to "the Big Foot" in central Asia, which periodically kicks out the nomadic elements, sending them in all four directions in search of booty, prosperity and power.

So was it between the established "eastern" power, the Ottomans, and their rivals for hegemony in Anatolia, the Mongul hordes of Timur. At the very moment when the Ottomans, relishing their victory over the combined forces of Christian Europe, were poised to take Constantinople, Timur's mounted archers shattered the late Osman's dream and very nearly extinguished the Ottoman line itself.

The events leading up to the battle of Ankara between Timur's Mongul hordes and the "eastern" force under Beyazıt can be attributed to hubris. Inflated with the success of his European victories, Beyazıt had seized lands belonging to eastern Anatolian vassals of Timur, and then insulted the Tatar ruler by threatening to cuckold him. With personal honor at stake, Timur had no choice but to march against his fellow Muslim. In the summer of 1402, the two armies closed in on the plain northeast of the citadel of Ankara.

But Beyazıt's pride knew no bounds, and, for several days before the battle, he had his troops drive animals in the bush for his

personal hunting pleasure. Timur, meanwhile, positioned himself between Beyazıt's now exhausted forces and the citadel itself, which should have been the Ottoman's bastion of defense. Desertions of his cavalry to Timur insured Beyazıt's doom, and, at the end of the day, the once invincible Janissaries lay dead on the field or in headlong flight, with Beyazıt himself taken Timur's captive.

Bound in chains, Beyazıt was forced to serve as Timur's foot stool; the Ottoman was also obliged to see his favorite wife, Despina, serve the Tatar overlord naked at dinner, and then raped before his eyes.

Marlowe's drama relates how Beyazıt was then dragged through Anatolia in a cage, subject to the insults and ridicule of his former Anatolian subjects, until in utter despair, he took his own life. There was, in any case, precious little left of the Ottoman domains: Bursa had been sacked and Timur's hordes ranged as far as Smyrna (modern Izmir) to uproot the last colony of crusaders on the Mediterranean coast, with the skulls of his victims gathered into a small pyramid to mark the occasion.

Rising from the ruins: Beyazıt was survived by four sons who, as Timur's vassals, were unable to practice fratricide until the old Tatar's disappearance in 1405. Then the

outside Izmir. On both occasions, however, he was obliged to return to Edirne to remove his son from power and to deal with the revolts and aggressions in the Balkans, where the Hungarian king Ladislas and his vassal (and heir) Hunyadi in consort with the Wallachian Prince Vlad Dracul (known popularly as Dracula thanks to his terror tactics of impaling his Muslim enemies in the forests of his realm) plotted against the Turks. Along with the confederate army, the Albanian renegade Iskender Bey managed to inspire sufficient resistance to the Ottomans to insure their collective doom once the Ottoman war machine came against them on the field of Kosova in a replay of

wars of succession began in earnest. After a decade of chaos, Beyazıt's youngest son Mehmet I emerged as the victor, with his siblings dead around him. In 1421, his son, Murad II, succeeded him and the responsibility to re-establish state control fell upon his shoulders.

During his reign, the Ottomans re-expanded in Anatolia, overran Greece and turned the cannons on the walls of Constantinople for the first time. But Murad also had a contemplative turn, and twice renounced the throne in favor of his son Mehmet II, the son of a Christian slave girl, in order to retire to his palace at Manisa

the famous battle enacted there 60 years before. This time, Serbia was absorbed into the realm, thus disappearing from history for the next 400 years.

The siege and conquest of Byzantium: In 1453, Constantinople had a population of scarcely 40,000, a mere shadow of the New Rome founded by Constantine. The hinterland, which once had stretched from France to Ethiopia, had been reduced to a few farms near the city walls. For centuries the city had been little more than a Turkish

Rumelihisarı, the "Throat Cutter" castle built by Mehmet the Conqueror on the Bosphorus.

dependency, allowed to survive in suffering and humiliation, its princesses married off to the harem of various sultans in a desperate attempt to maintain its fragile independence. That the city would eventually fall to the Turks had been a long foregone conclusion. The only question that remained was which sultan would claim the honor of fulfilling Osman's dream. The answer was provided within months of Murad II's death and the subsequent ascension of his oft-wayward son, Mehmet, in 1451.

Mehmet the Conqueror: The young sultan announced the final siege of the imperial city by marching his troops within sight of Byzantium walls and building the castle of *Boğaz Kesen* or "Throat Cutter" on the upper Bosphorus in a mere four months. The castle is now known as *Rumelihisarı* or the Thracian Castle. Paired with the earlier castle of *Anadoluhisarı* on the Asian side of the straits and equipped with heavy ordnance never seen before in eastern warfare, Mehmet had resurrected the ancient usage of the Symphlegades or "clashing cliffs" of Jason and the Argonauts, cutting off any aid to the threatened city via the Black Sea.

The cannons installed were cast for the Muslims by Urban, a Hungarian renegade who had first offered his services to the Byzantines (who had no money to pay him.) So impressed was Mehmet with the cast wonders, that the young sultan made an order for a new cannon twice the size of that mounted at the Bosphorus castle. This new "toy" was of such weight that the bridges between Edirne and Constantinople had to be reinforced before the monstrosity could be lugged around to within firing range of the ancient citywalls.

Such fortifications and new armaments were in direct contradiction to existing treaties; when the government of the last Byzantine emperor Constantine XI Palaeologus protested, Mehmet's had the envoys he sent beheaded. Urban's cannons appeared before the walls of Byzantine, and a Turkish fleet materialized in the Sea of Marmara. With no one like Timur to distract the Ottomans again, it was evident to all that the fall of the city was but a matter of time. Byzantine's only reinforcements to run the blockade of the Turkish navy at that point of time were some 700 Genoese under the command of Giovanni Giustinani, while more than an equal number of able-bodied men who were not willing to stay fled.

The siege itself opened formally, with Mehmet petitioning Constantine for a complete and unconditional surrender. The soon-to-be last Byzantine emperor's reply in equally formal manner, was that it was Mehmet alone who had made the decision to break the peace, and that God would favor the righteous. There was to be neither surrender nor any mercy from any party.

As Mehmet's cannons and siege machinery battered away at the city's walls, teams of oxen dragged boats up from over the hill at Dolmabahçe and down into the Golden Horn, where the Turkish fleet opened up another front against the low harbor walls, thus stretching the limited number of defenders even further. Still the Christians held out. Giustinani and his men performed military miracles by throwing back wave after wave of attackers and patching up gaping holes in the walls as soon as they were formed.

On May 29, Mehmet ordered the final assault, promising his men a 3-day respite from the fighting to boost their flagging morale. Wave after wave of Ottoman soldiers accompanied by the roar of cannons and the crash of cymbals stormed the walls on the promise of spreading the faith. First the shock troops fought and fell back, then regulars, then line after line of the sultan's fresh and rested Janissaries waded through the human debris in their path to test the ultimate resolve of the city's exhausted defenders. A breach here, closed again; a breach there, once again staunched. Finally, the Genoese commander, Giustinani, fell mortally wounded, and with him, the whole resistance collapsed. Alone, among the ruins and flames and cries of the populace, the last emperor of Constantine's city was last seen discarding his purple robe and engaging the advancing Janissaries in hand-to-hand combat like a common soldier. Constantinople, and Byzantium, were no more.

The Turks had conquered Constantinople. Mehmet, the victor, entered the city in imperial style, wearing his majestic turban and riding on a white stallion. The sultan held prayers at Hagia Sophia which the Turks turned into a mosque.

SÜLEYMAN THE MAGNIFICENT: THE OTTOMAN RENAISSANCE

In a chamber of the US House of Representatives, along with the pictures of Hammurabi, Moses, Solon, and Jefferson, stands a likeness of Sultan Süleyman in recognition of his stature as a ruler who promulgated an entire system of jurisprudence.

The title Süleyman saw fit for himself was related to his ideals of justice, *Kanuni*, meaning legislator or lawgiver, and this is how the Turks have always referred to him. Europeans, however, called him "the Magnificent" in the 16th century and the world at large has revered him with that sobriquet ever since.

Prince Süleyman became sultan in 1520 at the age of 26 and reigned 46 years until his death in 1566. The Europe of his decades was an arena in which many prominent figures vied for power – Charles V Habsburg, King of Spain and Holy Roman Emperor; Henry the VIII and Elizabeth I of England; Francis I, King of France and Ferdinand I, Holy Roman Emperor. Ivan the Terrible ruled in Russia. Süleyman excelled as conqueror, statesman, legislator and patron of the arts. A brilliant military strategist, he led his armies into three continents, more than doubling the Ottoman territories he had taken over from his father, Sultan Selim I. His empire embraced all or part of the states which would include present-day Turkey, Iran, Iraq, Egypt, Israel, Syria, Kuwait, Jordan, Saudi Arabia, Libya, Tunisia, Greece, Bulgaria, Sudan, Romania, Hungary, Yugoslavia, Albania, Algeria, Morocco, Czechoslovakia, Ethiopia, Somalia and the Soviet Union. It was one of history's most expansive states and when his navies sailed through the Mediterranean, Ottomania ruled the seas.

Under Süleyman, the Ottomans maintained sovereignty over all of Islam's holiest places, including Mecca and Medina. Holding the title of "Caliph," he declared in an inscription of 1538 at the Citadel of Bender: "I am Allah's slave – and sultan of this world. By the grace of God, I am the head of the community of Muhammad." Following the crushing defeats that his father Selim I inflicted, Süleyman consolidated the Sunni Supremacy over the Shia. His grip over the Islamic world and the success of his expansionist policy gave rise to the last of the great Islamic empires. The Ottoman Empire reached its apogee of power during the reign of Sultan Süleyman. Most historians argue, however, that the roots of Ottoman decline may also be found in this era: the complacency and the pride which fostered neglect of developments in Europe, especially in the technological sphere. Süleyman's granting (to the French and other Europeans) of special rights and privileges, the so-called "capitulations," challenged Turkish sovereignty until Mustafa Kemal Atatürk's Republic ended them. Süleyman's reign as sultan also initiated the start of decisive interference in state affairs by harem women and the succession struggles which killed two of the best-qualified princes and made Selim II the sultan upon Süleyman's death.

Hürrem, *nee* Roxelana, whom Süleyman married (although Ottoman Sultans were enjoined by tradition from matrimony) played a crucial role in his life. During their 25-year marriage Süleyman probably remained monogamous. His earlier concubines and Hürrem gave him eight sons and one daughter. Some of his sons died in infancy or adolescence. He personally gave orders for and witnessed the execution of his heir apparent, Mustafa, a favorite of the armed forces, which almost resulted in a rebellion against Süleyman. Later, Süleyman issued instructions for the strangling of his son Beyazıt and Beyazıt's four sons in order to keep the Ottoman throne for Selim.

Oil paintings, engravings and miniature paintings of Süleyman vary greatly as to his features. Reliable memoirs and historical records are consistent about his appearance: "tall, broad-shouldered...long graceful neck...aquiline nose...dark hazel eyes...fair skin, auburn hair, beetling eyebrows...long arms and hands."

The age of Sultan Süleyman is notable not only for the Ottoman Empire reaching its zenith of military power and economic wealth, but also for the efflorescence of the creative arts. Süleyman's Royal Chief Architect, Sinan (d. 1588), was responsible for building some of the greatest mosques, including the Süleymaniye (the Mosque of Süleyman), baths, bridges and other edifices which represented the apex of the Ottoman architectural achievement. The Palace Studio, where 29 painters (half of them Europeans) worked, produced many albums of miniature paintings depicting Ottoman mili-

tary campaigns and court life and gave new aesthetic direction to the art. It was also during this period that *karagöz* (shadow theater), brought from Egypt by Selim I for his son Süleyman, became a highly popular form of entertainment in Ottoman cities.

Süleyman was an accomplished goldsmith and lavished his generosity on the guild of goldsmiths. Many other arts also flourished during his reign – calligraphy, illumination, weaponry, tiles and textiles, woodwork and metalwork, etc. The 16th century became the

Gilded Ottoman battle axe inscribed with the inscription "Ali".

golden age of Ottoman classical verse for which splendid achievement should be attributed to the romantic mystic Fuzuli, the refined lyricist Hayali and the poet laureate Baki, who is celebrated for his stirring odes which includes his masterly elegy for Sultan Süleyman. Among Süleyman's enduring achievements is his poetry, and although he cannot be ranked with the towering figures of classical verse, he stands nonetheless as a very fine practitioner of the art. His *Divan* (collected poems) gives us insights into his thoughts in greater depth and scope than do his diaries, which consist mainly of his daily entries about battles, travels and politics. Some of Süleyman's poetic lines have become proverbs and are still widely used in Turkey, for example, "the people think of wealth and power as the greatest fate, but in this world a spell of good health is the best state."

Architecture, literary and visual arts, and the strides of history-writing (including the work of verse-chroniclers), sciences, theology and scholarship collectively created an "Ottoman Renaissance" in the age of Süleyman. An important component of the renaissance was jurisprudence: the Codex Süleymanicus made a synthesis of Islamic law and secular law established a full-fledged, comprehensive judicial system with the concept of "justice" as the cornerstone. Its provisions sought to guarantee equal justice before the law and bring a measure of leniency to the penal code. Sultan Süleyman's juridical philosophy, with its humane principles, may be found in a communique he sent to one of his commanders: "Every virtue flows from justice, whatever is done by an unjust person is an evil act. Don't be deceived by the appearance of the officials on your staff – and never employ in an official post anyone who is greedy for material possessions because they are the ones who oppress the common people whom God has entrusted to me. In dealing with my soldiers and subjects whom I have placed in your trust, treat the young as your children, the old as your own father and those your age as your brothers."

JEAN BRINDESI DEL.

21

DECLINE AND FALL OF THE OTTOMANS

The Ottoman empire reached its zenith not only territorially, but also in statemanship, management, culture and arts during the reign of Sultan Süleyman the Magnificient. However, from the end of the 16th century, the Ottoman empire began a slow and steady decline. Systems which once contributed to the glory of the empire could not adapt to internal or external changes.

Deterioration of the empire's internal structure began with the breakdown of the military tradition (i.e. the Janissaries), and of the land-tenure structure. In the past, a fixed number of Christian boys were recruited yearly as "blood tax," since non-Muslims were exempt from military service. The most promising of these boys were sent to Istanbul, converted to Islam, and put through a rigorous Palace School, which insured their absolute dependency and loyalty to the sultan. Afterwards, they built their careers in the bureaucracy or in the military. The rest of the boys were settled with a Turkish family in the provinces, learned a trade and the Muslim way of life before joining the ranks of the elite Janissary corps. Ironically, it was these renegade Christians who as Janissaries became "the scourge of Europe" on behalf of the Turks.

But however revolutionary the initial idea was, the institution of the Janissaries became decadent when these elite soldiers were allowed to marry and become involved in commerce. In addition, their sons, as well as other outsiders, began to be admitted into the ranks. As their numbers swelled, they frequently mutinied to exact more money from the sultan. The "slave soldiers" had in fact become power brokers in the capital, and had the distinction of committing the first regicide which was to taint Ottoman history: Osman II (1618–22), who was unhappy with the less than enthusiastic performance of his troops during his unsuccessful Polish campaign, decided to counter Janissary domination by forming an Asiatic army of conscripts. Upon learning

of the scheme, the Janissaries revolted and beheaded the Grand Vizier. They forced the young sultan to ride on a broken-down nag amid insults, before first raping and then strangling him in the dreaded prison of Seven Towers.

The "Gilded Cage": In addition to the capricious power of the Janissaries over the throne, it must be admitted that the sultans themselves had become weak: previously, succession to the throne had always been macabre, although it generally ensured that

Jhr gericht daran sie Christen Türcken Vnnd Jüden werffen

the best and most popular prince succeeded. After being enthroned, a new sultan practiced legal fratricide to avoid civil strife. This law had been affected by Mehmed II who otherwise was quite a sensitive soul, and an established poet at that. Sometimes sons were killed by their fathers, as was the case with Mustafa, the favorite son of Süleyman the Magnificent, who was strangled with a silk bow (for royal blood was not to be shed) due to the intrigues of Süleyman's second and favorite wife Roxelana. Roxelana had convinced the 60-year-old Süleyman that Mustafa was preparing to dethrone him. This paved the way

Left, European artist's idea of the Janissaries (note different headgear). **Right**, a Janissary's execution according to an European painter.

for the succession of her imbecile son Selim II. But when Mehmed III (1595–1603) had all 19 of his brothers killed (some were still babies), the attitude towards fratricide changed. Due to popular moral and religious outrage, Ahmed I (1603–17), initiated a new custom whereby brothers and sons were to be kept in luxurious captivity after the oldest male of the dynasty ascended the throne, with the other princes kept in what was called "the gilded cage." They were accompanied only by eunuchs, women and an occasional tutor who reported their every move; many potential rulers of the empire became incompetent and even deranged, as was the case with

extent, Vasco da Gama's voyage around the Cape of Good Hope) was thus an unmitigated disaster for the Turks: not only had they lost their control of the trade routes to "distant Cathay," but the shiploads of silver and gold from the New World effectively debased the Ottoman currency. Also, as a result of the daring voyages of the Europeans, naval, geographical and military science took on new importance, and better ships, captains and guns meant better battles: inexorably, the Europeans took control of first the Atlantic, the Indian Ocean and finally even the Mediterranean. The Ottoman victory in Cyprus in 1571 (colorfully treated by Shakespeare in "*Othello*," who was em-

Ibrahim I (1640–48), who personifies the negative image of an eccentric, womanizing oriental despot.

The New World disaster: For centuries, the Ottoman Turks had grown wealthy from controlling the vital trade routes to the east – the Silk Road over land from China, and the sea lanes from India through the Red Sea and from there to the Mediterranean, which in many ways had become a Turkish Lake. Indeed, one of the motivations of the Italian sailor Christopher Columbus in sailing west to China was to find a way around the fleets of such Turkish admirals as Piri Reis. The discovery of the New World (and to a lesser

ployed by the Duke of Venice "against the general enemy Ottoman") only serves to underline the point: within months of the Turkish victory at Famagusta, a grand coalition of Spain, the Vatican and Venice surprised the Turkish fleet at Lepanto in the Gulf of Corinth, effectively destroying Ottoman sea power forever.

On the intellectual level, too, the profound astronomical discoveries with their algebraic and geometrical spin-offs were also a thing of the past, with a strict and rigorous interpretation of Islam preventing further intellectual growth. This attitude corresponded to the period when Europe was fast emerging from the Middle Ages, and intellectuals, free from the dogma of the church, were making rapid advances in scientific discovery, rational thought, technology and industry. The printing press, for example, which had been used for 250 years in Europe, was only allowed by the Islamic clergy in Ottoman lands in 1727.

And as the once glorious empire crumbled from within, its formerly cowed rivals were eager to make it crumble from without: the treaty of Zsitva-Torok put Hungary in the hands of the Hapsburgs, who also stopped paying financial tribute to the Ottomans (1606); the second Ottoman siege of Vienna resulted in failure (1683); Russia

began to make its way into European music, painting and literature. Mozart's opera, "*Abduction from the Seraglio*," as well as his "*Rondo Alla Turca*," appeared. Orientalist painting also gained popularity as trade and colonial expansion led to increased contact with the east. Among the oriental paintings were Jean Baptiste Vanmour's "*A Turkish Hunting Party*" (1711), Eugene Delacroix's "*The Death of Sardanapulus*" (1827–8), J.A.D. Ingres's "*The Great Odalisque*" (1814), and "*The Turkish Bath*" (1862). Overall, the themes involved either sex or violence. Equally significant was the impact of Romantic literature creating eastern fantasies. Byron's exotic harems, sultans,

Left, medieval painting of the skyline of Istanbul. *Above*, map showing the extent of the Ottoman Empire.

gained the Crimea and parts of the north shore of the Black Sea by the treaty of Küçük Kaynarca (1774); and Napoleon invaded Ottoman Egypt (1789), although nominal Ottoman control was reestablished by 1801.

By the 18th century, although still powerful, Ottomans were no longer invincible. Europe, having lost its fear of the "Turk," now became intellectually interested in the east. A Turkish image, mostly fantasized,

cruel pashas; Samuel Taylor Coleridge's *Kubla Khan* (1816), and Edward Fitzgerald's *The Rubaiyat of Omar Khayyam* (1859) presented a romantic if rather misleading view of the Orient.

Capitulations: In the 19th century, the European industrial revolution turned the Ottoman Empire into a supplier of cheap raw materials. In turn, Europe found a vast market for its products. In addition, economic concessions given to the western countries worsened the situation with economic favors ending up as capitulations. "Capitulations" not only meant submitting postal service, street cars, tobacco, electricity, and railway managements to foreigners, it also meant legal privileges. Any legal matter involving a foreigner or a non-Muslim Ottoman who asked for the protection of a foreign consulate on Ottoman lands could not be tried in an Ottoman court. Slowly but surely, the once proud Ottoman Empire became an indispensable market for England and France. So indispensable, in fact, that during the Crimean War (1854) the Muslim Ottomans were saved by Christian England, France and Italy when attacked by the Holy Russian Empire. This war provided inspiration for one Florence Nightingale who established war hospitals in Istanbul. For her services

Bessarabia (1812); Greece became an independent princedom (1827); Moldavia and Wallachia became autonomous principalities (1829); the British occupied Egypt (1882).

Reform attempts: Reform in the Ottoman Empire began in earnest with Sultan Mahmud II (1808–29). In 1826, he abolished the decadent Janissary corps, albeit very violently: after obtaining the support of the clerics and the people, the sultan asked each Janissary battalion to spare 150 men for the new corps he was forming. The Janissaries refused and overturned their camp kettles in the traditional signal of revolt. But Mahmud unfurled the sacred

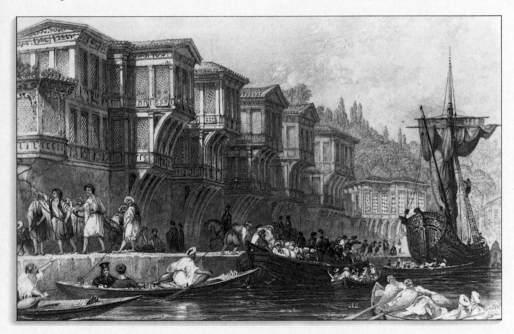

she won the distinction of being the first woman in the world to receive a medal of honor from a sultan. Based on the Crimean War, English literature was enriched by Tennyson's *The Charge of the Light Brigade*, and Russian literature by Tolstoy's *Sevastopol Tales*.

Large-scale borrowings with high interest rates gave rise to state bankruptcy in 1875. The Ottoman Empire came under total western financial control with the establishment of the Ottoman Public Debt Administration in 1881. Despite the various attempts at reform in the 19th century, territorial losses continued. Russia annexed

banner of the prophet and opened fire on his own elite corps from the Seraglio. Four thousand Janissaries were killed in their barracks, with thousands of others slaughtered in the streets of Istanbul and in the provinces as a general purge began.

Mahmud's reforms also gave rise to a generation of French-speaking bureaucrats who were trained in the newly formed translation bureaux. A certain oligarchy in the new bureaucracy desired reform from within, and edicts of 1839 and 1856 attempted orderly tax collection, fair and regular conscription, establishment of banks, public works and commerce.

But "equality," strangely enough, held little attraction for many Ottomans, and was particularly resisted by the non-Muslim population, who, until then, had been exempted from military service. As prosperous tradesmen and farmers – often under the protection of foreign governments thanks to the "capitulations" – they had no intention of interrupting their businesses for the sake of a 5 to 7-year-period of national service. Although paved with good intentions, the road to reform proved very rocky.

First constitution: In 1876, the first Ottoman constitution was adopted and one of the most controversial of the sultans, Abdülhamid II (1876–1909) was enthroned.

and censure. Abdülhamid's autocracy inevitably fomented opposition, and a secret society, the Committee of Union and Progress, began its work to restore the constitution and, eventually, to depose the sultan. In 1908, army officers in Macedonia revolted, forcing the sultan to call for elections and open the parliament. The following year, Abdülhamid II was forced to abdicate in favor of Sultan Mehmed Reshad V (1909–18) who ascended the throne as a mere figurehead. In all but name, the Ottoman Sultanate was a thing of the past.

But dissent from within was matched by intrigue from without, and the European powers vied with each other to establish

Meanwhile, the Pan-Slavic movement in the Balkans was at its height. This culminated in a war with Russia, resulting in an independent Serbia, Montenegro and Bulgaria. Masses of new refugees flooded across the frontiers, leaving some of the Ottomans' wealthiest provinces shorn from the state forever. The crisis prompted Abdülhamid to suspend the constitution and to dissolve the parliament, and for the next 30 years, the empire lived under oppression

Left, the Golden Horn according to Bartlet. **Above**, Sultan Abdülhamid – the first Ottoman ruler to be photographed.

influence on the "Sick Man of Europe," cajoling and threatening by turns. The most successful of the suitors was Kaiser's Germany, which, itself only recently formed as a nation-state, attempted to play catch-up pool with its rivals in the Grand Game of Asia. Military delegations and trade as well as such projects as the Berlin-to-Baghdad railway were the means used to woo the Ottomans to the Imperial German side.

World War I: When war finally broke out in August 1914, the Ottomans equivocated; but the English seizure of two warships being built in dry dock for the Ottoman fleet (collections had been taken throughout the

Muslim world for the payments) finally turned the tide. Two German warships pursued by the English and French navies in the Mediterranean were suddenly "donated" to the Ottomans as they steamed toward the Dardanelles. And with a change of uniform but not of crew, the new Turkish warships proceeded through the Bosphorus and into the Black Sea to lob shells at Russian ports in the Crimea. To the chagrin of many in Istanbul, Ottoman Turkey discovered that it was a Central Power.

But Turkey was scarcely prepared for the war, having still not recovered from its loss of Libya to the Italians in 1911, nor its humiliating defeat at the hands of the Bul-

garians, Greeks and Serbs during the Balkan War, when Istanbul itself was only saved by bickering and internecine war between the Balkan allies. Egypt's nominal loyalty was severed when the British ousted the last Ottoman Khedive in 1914, with the former province serving as a major base for English activities in the Middle East, including the Arab Uprising led in part by the romantic Lawrence of Arabia. The forces of Czarist Russia, with the aid of local Armenians, soon saw the frontiers in the east inexorably rolled back to Erzurum.

Gallipoli: Indeed, the only successful Ottoman military action during the war was the defense of the Dardanelles in 1915, when the combined French, British and Australian-New Zealand (ANZAC) forces landed at Gallipoli. A certain Colonel Mustafa Kemal commanded the defense for the Ottomans, winning a reputation for invincibility and heroism that stood him well several years later when he started the task of building the Republic of Turkey. The colonel was subsequently given the surname "Atatürk." The Gallipoli campaign was instrumental in the fate of other individuals and nations too: Sea Lord Winston Churchill, the architect of the ill-fated invasion, was obliged to resign and join the dough-boys in the trenches in France; Australia and New Zealand acquired a new sense of nationhood as a result of their casualties, and Czarist Russia, unable to export wheat or import weapons – in interesting contrast to the flow of trade today – collapsed in 1917, to resurface as the Soviet Union.

Armenian deportations: While the Ottoman forces held at Gallipoli, on all other fronts disaster followed disaster. The situation in the remote eastern provinces was especially critical, where Armenian nationalists had taken sides with the forces of Czarist Russia on the basis of a promise of future independence.

At the risk of being accused by either the Armenians or Turks for ducking the question of whether a "genocide" was perpetrated against the Armenians or not, suffice it to say that the bare historical facts point to a double tragedy: after the Ottoman government decided to deport the Armenians from their traditional areas of settlement in the eastern provinces of the empire, disease, bandit raids and security excesses resulted in the deaths of tens of thousands of Armenians as they were marched away to "safer" provinces in Mesopotamia. This was indeed a tragedy of the highest magnitude, and one that Armenians the world over bitterly remember to this day. But during the same period, hundreds of thousands of Muslim Turkish civilians and soldiers also perished as a result of combat, disease, malnutrition and attacks by Armenian rebel armies against Turkish villages.

Fighting between the Turks and the Armenians did not in fact end until the signing of the Treaty of Alexandropol in 1920, 2 years after the end of World War I. One historian estimates that 40 percent of the total population in the east died during the war, making it one of the areas of highest mortality for soldiers and civilians in World War I.

The end of the empire: When the Ottomans finally capitulated to the Allies with the signing of the Mudros Armistice in November 1918, the once proud empire was but a pale reflection of its former self, and stripped of many of her former provinces: Iraq and Palestine were ceded to the British, while Syria (including Lebanon) was given to France as part of the new League of Nations' mandate system. Separate Armenian,

Twenty-six "children": The 500-year reign of the Ottomans was over, but everywhere, her "children" sprang up in her wake, and today, we can count 26 nations that owe some part of their heritage to the Turks, be it as banal as military terms, as basic as food or as sublime as architecture: Albania, Bulgaria, the two nations on Cyprus, Greece, Hungary, and Yugoslavia in Europe, (much of the southwestern Soviet Union), with Bahrain, Egypt, Iraq, Israel, Jordan, Kuwait, Lebanon, Oman, Saudi Arabia, Sudan, Syria, the United Arab Emirates and North and South Yemen in the Middle East, and Algeria, Libya and Tunisia in North Africa are indebted to the Turks.

Assyrian and Kurdish states were also envisioned, all of them, oddly enough, to be established in the same eastern provinces. Not even the Turkish "homeland" of central Anatolia was sacred; thanks to various agreements made expediently and secretly by the Allies, Italy was to be given several of the southern provinces as part of an irredentist plan to reestablish the Roman Empire, while the Czarist Russians had been promised Constantinople itself, long regarded as the "key to the Crimea."

Left, a bar girl in Pera before World War I. **Above**, the exhausted Turkish army in defeat.

But the Turks were the last to emerge from the ashes of the Ottoman state and raise their own beacon of nationalism. Their dormant national consciousness was not so easily sparked: it took the ignominy of military defeat, the disgrace of Mudros, the invasion by former subjects (the Greeks), and finally, one man at the right time and place, to establish a national identity along the lines of the modern nation state. The time:May 1919; the place: a harbor on the Black Sea Coast; and the man: Mustafa Kemal, the commander in charge of the defense of Gallipoli, and the only hero the Turks had left.

On October 30, 1918, the Ottoman empire collapsed. Along with millions of lives and huge chunks of territory in battles fought on the side of the losers in World War I.

The victors had little regard for the US-proposed Wilsonian Principles to be the blueprint for peace and a new order in Europe. The Treaty of Versailles stripped Germany of its colonies and dismantled its war machine. But what the Ottomans were forced to sign in 1920 was unlike the "diktat" which the Germans found so unpalatable. The Treaty of Sèvres was literally the death warrant for the pathetic "Sick Man of Europe," a mere redrafting of earlier secret protocols for the empire's dismemberment.

The French and British contented themselves with the patronage of new Arab states created in the strategic and oil-rich Middle East lands they had wrested from the Turks. The Bosphorus and the Dardanelles, sought for centuries by the Russian Czars as the gateway to the warm seas, were put under British occupation along with Istanbul which would nominally remain the Ottoman capital.

The French occupied a few south-eastern Turkish provinces, while the Italians' reward for joining the Allies was the Mediterranean coast and some Aegean islands. The Armenians, who had paid a grim price for siding with the Russian armies in the early stages of the war, were granted their own state in eastern Anatolia under the patronage of the Allies. A Greek minority on the eastern Black Sea coast, meanwhile, was getting a Pontus state.

The prize was much bigger for the mainland Greeks. In fulfillment of the "Megalo Idea" or the restoration of ancient Greece with its Ionian colonies, the kingdom of Greece was granted the eastern Thrace provinces west of Istanbul and, more importantly, the principal Aegean port of Smyrna (now Izmir) with its rich hinterland.

The War of Independence: But the Greek landing at Smyrna on May 15, 1919, was the spark that flamed the latent patriotism of

Mustafa Kemal (Atatürk) at a decisive moment in the War of Independence against the Greeks.

the Turks across the country. Four days later Mustafa Kemal, the brilliant general untainted with defeat and hero of the legendary defense of Gallipoli, set foot on Anatolia at the Black Sea port of Samsun with a brief from the sultan to supervise the disbanding of the eastern armies.

Once safely away from occupied Istanbul, Mustafa Kemal renounced his rank and titles and devoted himself to organizing the nationalist forces. After two preparatory congresses of the ragtag regional defense committees, Kemal convened the Grand National Assembly on April 23, 1920, in Ankara – a sleepy railway junction town of a few hundred homes and shops.

His authority established, Kemal dedicated his efforts to the War of Independence, already underway following operations of the local committees in the southeast which had already mounted against the French. The war-weary French soon came to terms with the Ankara government and withdrew. Mustafa Kemal then sent his troops against the Armenians and Georgians, pushing them back to the boundaries of the present-day Soviet republics. The Italians soon followed the French out of Anatolia, leaving the British as the Greeks' sole allies.

With the rear secure, Kemal turned on the Greek armies in the west which, in the meanwhile, had deployed beyond Smyrna. With Ismet Inönü, a fellow reformist and an accomplished tactician, Kemal first checked the Greek advance and, with the 22-day-long Battle of Sakarya fought almost at the gates of Ankara, turned the tide. The Greeks withdrew and dug in. But Kemal personally commanded a counter-attack the following year. Completely taken by surprise, the bulk of the Greek armies were encircled and annihilated at the Battle of Dumlupınar fought west of Afyon. The Greek commander-in-chief was taken prisoner and the remnants were chased all the way to Izmir in less than two weeks.

The liberation of Izmir on September 9, 1922 – followed by a fire for which each side still blames the other – paved the way for the withdrawal of the British troops from the Dardanelles and the ensuing armistice signed in Mudanya.

Building the nation: Even before the end of the War of Independence, Kemal and his circle turned their attention to the harder task that lay ahead: building the nation which had been ravaged and impoverished by conflicts. Angered by a simultaneous invitation sent by the Allies to the Istanbul government for peace talks and the latter's call for "a joint stand," Kemal announced the abolition of the monarchy on November 1, 1922. A fortnight later Mehmet VI, the ailing last sultan of the house of Osman, sought the protection of Britain and in darkness boarded the *HMS Malaya* for Malta.

29, 1923, the Grand National Assembly unanimously endorsed the proclamation of the Republic of Turkey. Its first president, inevitably, was Mustafa Kemal, now the leader of the newly-founded Republican People's Party (RPP). For the next 58 years, it was to be a teacher of statecraft to generations of politicians, a medium for authoritarian government, and in the end, an experimental laboratory for social democracy until the mark of its closure by a new generation of military tutors.

A clean break: Kemal and his reformist cadre wanted to model the nation after the west. But all the exsiting institutions of the deceased empire were unmistakably east-

On November 20, Ismet Inönü addressed the opening session of the peace conference in Lausanne, Switzerland, covered by, among others, a journalist for the Toronto Star named Ernest Hemingway. Proving himself a match in the unaccustomed game of diplomacy to such eminent adversaries as Lord Curzon, the British Foreign Secretary, Inönü made them sign the peace treaty on July 24, 1923, in a form more in compliance with Turkish terms.

The treaty secured territory for the Turks, and recognised their sovereignty and independence. The time had come for the creation of the new Turkish state. On October

ern. What was more, the Turks were conditioned to see themselves more an *Umma* (Muslim community) than a nation and, unlike the Christian and Jewish minorities, were discouraged from politics, industry, commerce or any other potential source of power that could restrict the absolutism of the Ottoman house.

The dual task of creating a national consciousness and absorbing the western civilization required, therefore. a new interpretation of Islam and Kemal had the Grand National Assembly abolish the caliphate on March 3, 1923, banished all male members of the royal family from the country.

Wrenching changes: The secularization of education was equally radical. In 1925, all the convents run by a host of religious sects were banned and primary school education was made compulsory. The literacy drive gained new impetus in 1928 when the difficult Arabic script was discarded and replaced by the Latin alphabet more suited to the Turkish language.

Wardrobes were also touched by the winds of reform. The *fez*, the headgear of the officialdom, and turbans were banned. Hats and caps, personally shown around by Mustafa Kemal, found a surprising acceptance.

The westernization of women was not merely cosmetic; granting of political rights beat a path for faster progress towards emancipation. They were also encouraged to compete with men in every profession while the civil code adopted from Switzerland ensured their equality before the law.

Evolving from *Umma* to nationhood made obligatory the adoption of surnames in 1934, setting off a race for sometimes colorful patriotic family names. Kemal himself did not have to search for one. His surname was given to him by the Grand National Assembly, which fittingly called him, *Atatürk*, or Father of Turks.

Building the economy: The jubilation at the abolishment of capitulations with the Lausanne Treaty had hidden from view such setbacks as the refused relief from the debt burden and the restriction on Ankara's powers to set tariffs. But leaders of the new state were not discouraged. Expectedly, the Kemalist cadre reached for what they perceived as the key to the supremacy of western civilization: capitalism. Private banks were set up with state funds to back private enterprise and a vast array of incentives were put at the disposal of businessmen.

The 1929 crisis, however, came as a turning point. The great crash had a disastrous effect on Turkey's crop exports and discredited capitalism in the eyes of the ruling military-bureaucratic elite to whom the apparent immunity of the planned Soviet economy from the global catastrophe seemed to be the key. The state took upon itself the burden of development and the

State Economic Enterprises (SEEs) were put at the forefront of the industrialization drive. Self-sufficiency and import-substitution, to minimize the effects of the crisis, were the order of the day. The first Five-Year Development Plan (1934 to 1939) was drafted with Soviet influence and helped a rapid buildup of the country's industries.

Changing of the guard: While concentrating on the development of the economy, leaders of the Republic were casting increasingly worrisome glances at the gathering clouds of war in Europe. The death of Atatürk against such a background came as a major blow to the nation. On November 10, 1938, the great leader, bedridden for

months, died of cirrhosis of the liver at 57. The next day, his lifelong friend and comrade-in-arms, Ismet Inönü, was sworn in as the Republic's second president.

Inönü devoted his energies to keeping Turkey out of the general conflagration which erupted the following year. This required not only a skilled tightrope act between the warring sides – and a certain departure from treaty obligations at times – but an iron hand in the country which the "national chief" employed through the RPP bureaucracy. The country, amazingly (or maybe shamefully) remained neutral until the closing weeks, when Inönü declared

Left, Nationalist Congress at Erzurum with Mustafa Kemal in the centre. **Right**, Atatürk teaching the nation.

proforma war on the moribund Nazi state.

The honeymoon of the 1920s and early 30s between Turkey and Russia, its traditional enemy, had long since given way to mutual hostility after Ankara's repeated crackdowns on domestic communists. The worst fears came to near materialization at the end of the World War II when Moscow demanded control of the Turkish straits and asserted territorial claims in the east. Turkey stood fast and the Soviets withdrew their demands after the United States and Britain firmly backed Ankara with the battleship *U.S.S. Missouri* dispatched to Istanbul as a convincing symbol.

Democracy: Despite the attachment of political adversaries for a while, the leaders of the republic shut them up, leaving the RPP to monopolize power for 27 years and train militants for the future.

Then there was the impressive recovery of Italy and Germany from the turmoil of the post-World War years. Italy and Nazi Germany were western, modern and European, and openly admired for the "national discipline" enforced by a patriarchal party which permitted rapid progress.

The outcome of World War II inevitably reflected on the Turkish conception of democracy. In 1945, a group of rebels, headed by Adnan Menderes, an active politician and cotton grower, and Celal Bayar, a banker

Kemal Atatürk to legality and a mandate from the people, the development of democracy after the proclamation of the Republic could not match the speed of westernization in other respects. To make the regime conform more to the western democracies, Kemal Atatürk allowed the formation of opposition parties in 1924 and 1930, headed by trusted friends loyal to the cause. In both cases, the tolerated opposition attacks on the government and the thundering of the opposition press encouraged the reactionary fundamentalists to raise their heads and call for a complete return to Islam. So, after putting up with vociferous and a collaborator of Atatürk, were allowed to form the Democrat Party. This was partly because Turkey was anxious to be accepted as a fully fledged member of the new world order and to receive US assistance under the Truman Doctrine.

The RPP was ready to adapt to a multi-party system, but not necessarily to a different role. It won the 1946 election only through heavy rigging. The Democrat Party (DP), meanwhile, kept attracting an odd combination of supporters. These included feudal landowners and the traditionally conservative rural masses for whom the new party provided a chance to avenge the bullying RPP *apparatchik*. But it also recruited the emerging middle class in towns which could not forgive the RPP's switch to etatism. Together, they swept the DP to power in 1950 with an overwhelming majority in the Republic's first free elections. Bayar was elected President and he appointed Menderes as his Prime Minister.

Erratic progress: The Democrat Party's taking office and the flow of US economic and military assistance gave a new, if markedly pro-American impetus to Turkey's progress towards fuller integration with the west. In 1950 a brigade of Turkish troops was sent to South Korea where it displayed outstanding valor.

In 1952, Turkey became a member of the North Atlantic Treaty Organization (NATO) together with Greece, which had become a cordial friend shortly after the Independence War. In return, Turkey granted base facilities to the United States. Besides the electronic surveillance bases and an air base, these included bases for Jupiter missiles which were dismantled as part of the package deal which ended the Cuban crisis. The downing of a U-2 spy plane in Russia after taking off from Turkey embarrassed Ankara, but the Turkish government proudly stood by its western friends during the Cold War years, siding with its allies without hesitation even when military action against fellow Islamic countries was undertaken.

At home, the abandonment of etatism and new incentives to free enterprise led to an early expansion. The supply of tractors to the farmers boosted the production and exports. But the liberalization of imports eventually led to a deterioration of the balance of payments, causing repeated devaluations of the national currency and mounting of the foreign debt. As his popularity suffered, Menderes became increasingly repressive, censoring the press, jailing political opponents and manipulating elections. Finally, when he moved to silence the opposition through more drastic measures, a popularly supported military coup deposed him in May 27, 1960. A year later a military tribunal sentenced him to death. He was hanged with two of his ministers.

Left, opposition leader Celal Bayar at a rally in the 1940's. **Right**, Ismet Inönü, credited with allowing the opposition to contest elections.

Strangely, the coup leadership tends to be regarded as progressives by many Turkish historians. General Cemal Gürsel and his cadre first had the constituent assembly draft a new and more liberal constitution which was then adopted by a national referendum. Soon Marxist literature inundated bookstores and university libraries, and students – whose demonstrations had sparked the coup a few years earlier – steadily became radicalized. The country's first socialist party was allowed to form, and eventually gained representation in the national parliament. Followers of the banned DP, meanwhile, flocked to the newly formed Justice Party, the name of which immedi-

ately conjured up images of the "martyred" Menderes. The party, founded by an exgeneral, was soon taken over by a young, American-trained engineer by the name of Süleyman Demirel, who would figure prominently in Turkish politics until 1991.

Unlike most military coups where the soldiers remain reluctant to pass over power to the civilians, the coup leaders of 1960 called for elections in 1961. No one party was able to achieve a majority, and a coalition government was formed – a mixture of old line Kemalists, conservatives and nationalists led by the aging leader of the RPP, Ismet Inönü. In 1965, the coalition fell apart and the Justice Party headed by Demirel swept into power. Demirel repeated his victory in 1969 to continue his policies of rapid growth and development.

But the price of growth was inflation and a parallel deterioration of the balance of payments. Strikes and increasing tension between extremist leftist and rightist groups led to another coup in 1971. This time, however, the generals cracked down not only on the traditional conservatives but on the radical left as well, with thousands of militants jailed.

Inönü, the very personification of the old Kemalist school, was seen as being too accommodating to the military, and, when the generals once again restored parliament in 1972, the young Bülent Ecevit managed to unseat Inönü and give the RPP a new social-democratic direction. In 1973, Ecevit and the reshaped RPP formed a new government along with the aid of the Islamic fundamentalist National Salvation Party – the so-called "historic compromise" which once again allowed the Muslim factor back on the political stage of the nation.

Cyprus: Ecevit reinforced his popularity in 1974 when he ordered Turkish troops into Northern Cyprus to prevent its union with Greece after a right-wing coup sponsored by the colonels regime in Athens. The action, which has been branded as an "invasion" by most of the world, is regarded in Turkey as a legitimate intervention in accordance with agreements signed between Ankara, Athens and London meant to insure the independence of Cyprus. In 1983, the Turkish community in the northern half of the island voted for independence as the Turkish Republic of Northern Cyprus, but the state remains unrecognized by all countries with the exception of Turkey.

Descent into chaos: The Ecevit government fell in 1975 when the Prime Minister attempted to capitalize on his surge in popularity and called for early elections. In vain. The National Front coalition led by Demirel was once more able to take control with its major partner being the National Action Party of Alpaslan Türkeş, whose fiery brand of nationalism many thought too close to the tactics of the national socialists of Hitler's Germany.

The freewheeling, table-banging and fist-fighting of parliament soon spilled into the streets and, inexorably, Turkey headed for near civil war. Left-right feuding, sectarian violence and separatist activities erupted, leaving 5,000 dead in the late1970s. With the social order and national unity breaking down, the generals once again stepped in on September 12, 1980.

This time, however, the generals were determined to make a thorough job of establishing order. The constitution of 1960, blamed in part as being "too loose a shirt", was turned into a strait jacket.

First, all political parties were banned and their leaders detained. Tens of thousands of suspected terrorists were rounded up and tried in military courts, with 25

executed for major crimes and massacres. Coup leader, General Kenan Evren, and the commanders of the armed forces, formed a National Security Council, which assumed totalitarian powers and cared little for domestic or foreign reaction when it tailored a new democracy and political structure for the nation. More so than with the Cyprus action of 1974, the country was isolated and looked upon as a pariah in the west, with ties to such bodies as the European Community being suspended for years.

Return to the democratic fold: Finally, in 1983, the military allowed tightly controlled parliamentary elections. The party least favored by the generals, ANAP, or the Motherland Party of Turgut Özal, was swept into power with a landslide victory, forming the first outright majority in 30 years. Özal, who had served for a time under Demirel and the generals, unrolled a program of economic and social reform which gave a sudden boost to Turkey's growth and helped break its political isolation.

For the first time, Turks started looking outside the country for business opportunities and allowed foreign goods on the local market to compete with products made by the aging and inefficient state monopolies. The removing of political bans on the former leaders in 1987, plus a hasty face-lift with

respect to human rights and jail conditions in the country, soon showed results and Turkey was accepted back into the Council of Europe. Reelected in the 1987 elections without military supervision, Özal tabled the country's application for full membership in the EC.

Turkey's last decade has been marked by the consolidation of democracy and economic liberalism, which go hand in hand. The democratic institutions and traditions have evolved to a point where a relapse to

Left, Bülent Ecevit and Süleyman Demirel. Above, Prime Minister Tansu Çiller.

authoritarianism seems totally impossible. The roots of democracy have been strengthened also by a rapid and forceful development of a vocal civil society. The level of the freedom of the press including a mushrooming of uninhibited private television and radio channels is probably even above that of many European countries. And the issue of human rights, which in the past was mostly a concern of Western public opinion, has become a direct concern of Turkish society.

In industry, the liberal policies initiated by the late President Özal have been maintained. The supporters of an economy managed by the State are finding themselves increasingly isolated, to the point that parties on the left have difficulty in asserting a different identity. These policies have produced sustained growth in recent years despite the severe world recession. Although there are still considerable areas, notably in the East, lagging behind, Turkey has reached a standard of infrastructure and of living comparable to developed Mediterranean countries in particular in the Aegean, Mediterranean and Marmara regions.

The collapse of the Soviet Union and the end of the Cold War has changed the political equation in Europe, the Middle East and Asia in favour of Turkey. It finds itself now the most advanced and politically mature and experienced country among newly independent states, most of which are linked to Turkey by common language and culture.

Turgut Özal died in April 1993. But his legacy is maintained by Süleyman Demirel who succeeded him in the presidency. Nothing perhaps symbolises the new Turkey more than the election as Prime Minister of a professor of economics, Tansu Çiller, a young, elegant and dynamic *woman*. Her quick promotion reflects the willingness of the country to abandon traditionalist politicians and to follow the modernity and political sophistication of younger generations.

There are still serious problems. In the east the PKK Kurdish terrorist organisation is fighting for separatism. The government has not been able to control severe inflation. Turkey faces huge problems in the fields of education, health, social services and environment. But it is a country which has proved its dynamism, its inventiveness, its capacity to adapt to change. It has the self-confidence required to stand up to these challenges.

Dimensions of bronze statues occupying the choicest spot of every single town worth the name – the bigger the better for aspiring governors – do not exactly conform to the national average; nor do the cold blue eyes, glowering down from 5,000 sq-ft (500 sq-meter) canvases adorning the facades of public buildings, bear a resemblance of the Central Asian ancestors he identified for his people.

Yet the idol of what is possibly the longest enduring personality cult in modern history was not merely a Turk by conscious choice but also, as his bestowed surname illustrates, a literal "Father" for the modern nation that he had created.

The Turks have always been accustomed to a succession of father figures over the centuries due to the fact that their adopted religion and increasingly autocratic rulers both demanded filial obedience. But what sets Atatürk aside for true reverence (which somehow survives the rituals of official deification) is his success in reversing the fate of a doomed nation.

He started by changing his own fate. Born the son of a customs official in the now-Greek northern Aegean port of Salonica in 1881 (where the house of his birth is – oddly enough – a national museum). Mustafa had his first violent row with the chief "Mullah" of the district religious school at an early age; an experience which seemingly left him with a lasting hatred for religious fundamentalism. Conversely, he had always been favorably impressed by the tight-fitting uniforms worn by the men of the local military academy, and he secretly enrolled by taking the entrance exams.

At the academy, his prowess in mathematics soon won him the name of Kemal, or "the complete one." It was there that he developed a keen interest for the works of Rousseau, Voltaire and Auguste Comte, as well as visions of becoming the Napoleon of the East.

His clandestine activities soon resulted in a transfer to Damascus as staff captain – far

A shining golden bust of Mustafa Kemal Atatürk – "Father of the Nation".

away from the locus of power. He nevertheless managed to set up a revolutionary society which eventually merged with the pan-Ottoman Union and Progress Party (UPP) headed by the ill-fated triumvirate of Enver, Cemal and Talat. Unlike the leaders of UPP, Mustafa Kemal remained a strict legalist, calling for the separation of the military from politics, and in the process evoked the lasting suspicion of the better known leaders of the time.

In 1911, Mustafa Kemal volunteered for service in Libya, which was then under attack by Italian troops. However, the break-out of the catastrophic Balkan Wars the following year brought him back home where he assisted Enver in the recapture of Edirne, although it was the latter who was given all the credit for the success. Enver would be the man to drag the Ottoman state into the disaster of World War I a few years later, and after its collapse, flee and meet death at the head of a cavalry charge in Central Asia.

When Talat, as well as Cemal, met their end at the hands of Armenian assassins, it was only natural that Mustafa Kemal, the only undefeated general of the savaged Ottoman armies, would take up the leadership of the struggle to save the heartland of the lost empire. Upon the successful conclusion of the fighting, he saw himself as the generator of a new and different nation known as "*Türkiye*," or the Land of the Turks.

Today, half a century after his untimely death on November 10, 1938, at the age of 57, Mustafa Kemal, now Atatürk, remains a source of contradictory wisdom for all: man or woman, rich or poor, right, left, or centrist, all have need of his quotations, whether painstakingly translated out of the old Ottoman script, or made up on the spot to suit the occasion.

But above all, the official memory of cadet number 1238 is jealously guarded by the officer corps committed to the preservation of his heritage. And each year, when his number is called out at the roll call of the graduating class of new cadets, there is but one solemn and uniform response: "He is among us."

"Ne mutlu Türküm diyene!" ("Happy is he who calls himself a Turk!").

The quotation, taken from Atatürk's marathon speech of 1927 elaborating the future values of the Republic, is now etched on walls, monuments and even mountains throughout the country: the hardships and defeats of the past are abolished; the "Sick Man of Europe" is dead – long live the Anatolian youth...! "Turkishness" itself is sufficient to overcome all; there is no time

the help of folkloric researches and the discovery of long forgotten, new ancestors like the Hittites.

Half a century after his death, Atatürk's principles are still – at least, officially – the guidelines of the Turkish Republic. Booming cities, new highways, gigantic dams, a spreading touristic infrastructure have given the country an authentic modern touch. But the vital question remains: have the 55 million inhabitants of this developing country not neglected the "work in progress" of

to waste sterile anguish on the quest for identity when the key to attaining contemporary civilization has been put conveniently in one's hand.

If it is true that the question of a Turkish identity has become more complex in our age of communication, when Atatürk made his historic speech, westernization seemed unquestionably desirable and the return to Turkish roots possible. Moreover, these two goals appeared compatible. Islam was tolerated as a religion, but not as a lifestyle.

The program was not to be an "Islamic-Turkish" synthesis on a human background, but a "Turkish-European" synthesis, with

a search for a national identity because they were satisfied with an identity tailored for 10 million Turks trying to overcome the trauma of military defeat and economic chaos? Perhaps one of the reasons for the lip-service paid indiscriminately by all circles in this country to Atatürk's principles (which are not necessarily actually understood) can be attributed, unhappily, to a certain intellectual sloth that finds it easier to repeat clichés than explore new nuances.

Walking in the streets of Istanbul or Ankara, one sees school children everywhere, and at every corner youngsters, idle or busy, well or poorly dressed. This is a young nation, in more than a demographic sense. Compared with such countries as France, where the idea of nation dates back to the end of the 18th century, and with Germany, or even the United States, the Turkish republic looks like a junior.

But take a look around Turkish cities – walls from the 12th century, palaces and mosques from the 16th and 17th centuries – history expressed in monuments is everywhere. How, then, can it be called a "young nation"?

It is worth emphasizing this duality of the old and the new. But seen from today's perspective, the gap between the late Ottoman Empire (the old) and the Turkish Republic (the new) which succeeded it seems perhaps smaller than it was at the founding of the Republic in 1923. At that time, Turkey began viewing its present in technicolor and the Ottoman past in black and white. Everything "Ottoman" was seen through a distorted, dirty lens and was despised as being somehow unworthy of modern times. Whereas the noun "Turk" in Ottoman times had been a label of derision, all things "Ottoman" at the founding of the Republic were equally reviled as elitist yet backward, sordid yet imbecile. The nation was to be left without a past.

This attitude of "Turkey: ground zero" left the nation with little to go on. Not only did she have to recover from the ruins of war (over 50 percent of the 1914 population were either dead or displaced), but the very foundation stones of a new order – political continuity and cultural heritage – were nearly entirely lacking. Under these circumstances, the new Republic's "nationalistic" founders found it most efficient to deny the past and launch the new nation into the modern world via radical reforms.

The hat replaced the fez. The Latin alphabet supplanted the Arabic script, leaving generations of Turks removed from 500 years of written cultural heritage. Even the language itself was radically revised. An

institute of scholars was set up to "expunge" Arabic and Persian words.

However strange (and possibly unreasonable) many of these reforms by diktat might have seemed, they took a strong hold among the masses, and, with the exception of several pockets of entrenched resistance, the birth of the nation was completed within a remarkably short period of time. Turks were no longer Muslims first, after which followed by being members of a transnational agglomeration called "the Empire,"

but Turks first with the other elements of religion and race falling in behind.

Today more than three million Turks work and live abroad (1.5 million in Germany). Millions of tourists (7 million in 1992) invade Turkey's remotest corners. In addition, Turks travel more and more, see foreign films, watch more television (12 Turkish channels, plus international satellite and cable TV), and the press tells glamorous tales about life in those faraway places. In short, today's average Turk has a much wider range of comparison possibilities than a few decades ago. Turks in major cities now also listen to the latest western

Preceding pages, Atatürk's Mausoleum. **Left**, a group of surveyors in eastern Anatolia. **Right**, two boys after a circumcision ceremony.

music from many private radios, a medium which was under state monopoly until 1993.

From an economic angle, the Turk observes the revolting inequality among nations. On the psycho-sociological level he either tries to adopt or imitate this lifestyle. Some, especially those living in a foreign and frequently hostile environment, reach back into their own history, legends and religion in order to find or to create a national identity, capable of competing with, or compensating for, the material advantages of western *Weltanschauung*.

Yet, despite more international exposure, Turks still have to face certain hard facts: for example, a Turk traveling abroad rarely

underdevelopment acted as a stimulus to bring about social and political progress.

At this point, Turkey's geographic location should be mentioned. The Turk, coming from Central Asia, is in one respect near-Easterner, but in another respect, Balkan. He is partly Mediterranean, meaning that he is placed in a web of relationships spanning the Orient and Occident, to Italy or Spain and partly, via the Black Sea, to the Slavic or Caucasian worlds. In other words, the elaboration of a serious theory of Turkishness in the spirit of typical western philosophy would bring Turkey nearer to Europe even if Turks finally discover or establish that their worlds are too different.

feels welcome when he sees how immigration officers at various frontiers react at the sight of a Turkish passport. Nor do the images of Atatürk or Mehmet the Conqueror on Turkish banknotes exactly impress foreign bank clerks. But instead of the rather paranoiac accusations directed against Europe of "reviving the spirit of the Crusades," it would be more pragmatic to be aware of one's differences as compared with the other nations in order to discover one's similarities with them. The awareness of Turkey's shortcomings will help the country to overcome them, just as the awareness of the nation's condition with regard to

Now, before one can jump to the conclusion that the simple recognition of the diversity of the Turkish population signifies a total understanding of its identity, two supplementary aspects of this question have to be examined. The first, the Turkish intellectual's role, must be dealt with. The second aspect is more general, more philosophical and exists in the important difference between the western intellectual and his Turkish counterpart.

Most western intellectuals have left the quest for national identity behind them (even Spenglerian ideas about the decline of the Occident are nowadays out of fashion).

They don't consider themselves anymore as "mentors" of the nation. By contrast the Turkish intellectual – especially the "progressive intellectual" – sees it as his obligation as well as his privilege to guide the nation, which, in his patronizing ways, he "prepares" for democracy.

In reality the Turkish masses display more common sense and political foresight than the so-called intellectual elite. *They* are the real believers and defenders of democracy. Identifying themselves with one of the existing political parties, they try to answer many abstract questions with their concrete votes at ballotings.

This insight allows us to assert with only the slightest touch of oversimplification, that compared with the masses' indirect quest for identity, the intellectual circles suffer from a sort of crisis which stems not only from conflicting western thoughts and ideological currents in their minds, a certain nostalgia for the glorious past (including, partially, the Islamic heritage), but from a severed bond with the masses – the only true depository of Turkishness.

The issue to be dealt with at this point is the isomorphism between the mystery of the self in the individual and the certainly more complex problem of identity in a nation. And in Turkey's case, her self-image cannot be considered separately from her image abroad. Without a clear idea of "what she wants to be", Turkey cannot possibly project a plausible image of herself. On the other hand, the Turkey-image of foreigners has more than a little influence on Turkish self-seeking.

It is obvious that the national debate about the country's promotional efforts, dominating both mass media and public opinion in the country, is interdependent on the perpetual Turkish exasperation at not being impartially represented in western fiction, articles and films – *Midnight Express* being one example.

The Turks feel unhappy about their inadequate self-reflection and even more unhappy about their biased image in the eyes of the foreigners. More interesting than the origin of this feeling of bitterness is the

Turkish reaction to it: either clumsy, aggressive reactions or an excess of unhealthy self-criticism. Both egocentric attitudes don't help Turkey's image abroad.

Nevertheless, there is yet hope, as the majority of the Turks have come to recognize the "absence of malice" in the sheer ignorance of the West in matters concerning Turkey.

With the western world willing to learn more about the "Turkishness" and the Turks, for their part, becoming less suspicious, the "Turkey image" has a good chance of amelioration. But the second aspect of the problem still stands: is one able to propose a definition of the Turkish identity?

To do so, perhaps, the best approach would be to simply restore the worn-out cliché of "Turkey, a bridge between Orient and Occident," but with a twist: instead of the bridge itself, why not consider the Turkish identity as the quintessence of the heavy, two-way traffic on it?

Another advantage of this substitution of a dynamic image for a static one is that it incites us to see the phenomenon of "Turkishness" as a metaphor rather than a dogma: clarity and identity, it would seem, are almost contradictory terms and, even after the crisis of identity is over, the quest will inevitably go on and on.

Left, Two chefs with a statue of Artemis made of butter. **Right**, an easy answer to consumer purchasing priorities.

The call to prayer is one of the most evocative sounds visitors to Turkey will hear. Drifting from the minarets of mosques in cities, towns and villages, it is the eerie music of the Muslim world.

Although modern Turkey is a secular republic, many Turks are devout Muslims who carry out the five duties or pillars of Islam. They declare the *Shahadah*, or the Muslim creed of faith, ("There is no God but Allah and Muhammed is his Prophet") they pray five times a day toward Mecca and fast from dawn to dusk during the month of Ramadan, as well as give alms to the poor and make the pilgrimage to the Islamic holy lands in Saudi Arabia, if financially able.

Islam in the Ottoman Empire: Islam played a crucial role in the Ottoman empire, maintaining solidarity among its diverse Muslim elements and providing the ethical and legal structure by which its subjects lived. The Ottoman state was ruled by the sultan, who became "caliph" or leader of the entire Islamic world following the Turkish conquest of Egypt in the 16th century.

Under the Ottomans, Islamic learned men known as the *Ulema* were in charge of organizing and spreading the Muslim faith. They maintained religious conformity by enforcing the *Shariah* or Islamic holy law. They taught religious sciences, operated mosques and schools and controlled the courts. Islamic education was provided at *mektep* or elementary mosque-schools, and *medrese* or higher institutes of theology.

The Turks' major contribution to Islam was Sufism, based on mystical forms of worship. Each Sufi *tarikat* or brotherhood sought to find the path for the mystical union of man with God.

Pre-Islamic shamanistic practices, such as dancing, music and the use of fire influenced the rituals of the brotherhoods, producing great outbursts of ecstasy among its members at mystic ceremonies or *ayin*. Orthodox Muslims abhorred such rites claiming they were acts of heresy.

In Ottoman times, the Sufi sects operated *tekkes* or lodges, which resembled Christian monastic orders. Each brotherhood was led by a *sheikh*, or a religious guide. The apprentices of each lodge were known as *murit*, and were attached to a full fledged dervish.

Members were required to live in piety and poverty, abstaining from material wealth, living off *zekât* or alms, in their quest to attain salvation. The *türbe* or tomb of the founder, who was regarded as a saint or *evliya*, was the main center for worship in the brotherhood.

Two important Sufi brotherhoods that came

into existence in early Turkish history and which are still popular today are the Mevlevi and Bektaşi orders.

The Mevlevis: The Mevlevi order of whirling dervishes is a mystic group whose members are followers of Mevlana Jelaleddin Rumi (1207–73), a great Turkish poet. The brotherhood is based in Konya, central Turkey, where its founder is buried.

The Mevlevi order holds a festival every year in December to commemorate their founder, and it is a major tourist attraction. During their religious ceremony, the whirl-

An elder Muslim devotee reads the Holy Quran.

ing dervishes wear flowing white robes and conical hats and twirl to the steady beat of drums and strains of mystical music, enacting the death and ultimate union of Mevlana with Allah.

The Mevlevis found followers among urban intellectuals and members of the ruling classes as opposed to the rural peasantry who preferred membership in more nomadic and popular brotherhoods.

The Bektaşis: Members of this order were followers of Hacı Bektaş Veli (1209–71), a Muslim mystic. The order is based in Hacıbektaş, a town in Kırşehir province, central Turkey, where the founder is buried. Since the *tarikat* saw Ali as the rightful successor to Muhammad as caliph, the movement strongly appealed to Turkey's Shiites or Alevis, who regard Hacı Bektaş Veli as one of their great leaders.

The Bektaşis absorbed many non-Muslim rituals, including baptism. Its dervishes were responsible, principally, for converting the Christian peasantry of Anatolia and the Balkans to the Islamic faith. The brotherhood was long affiliated with the Janissary Corps, the elite Ottoman army unit whose members were Christian converts.

Philosophy and science: Turkish Orthodox Islamic scholars accepted the views of Al-Ghazali, a Persian scholar, as a rule. Al-Ghazali, who lived in the 11th century, rejected the idea that scientific knowledge violated Islamic doctrine.

As a result, many Turks achieved fame in the fields of science – notably astronomy, mathematics and medicine.

Kadizade Musa Pasha, a Turk in the 15th-century, founded an observatory in Samarkand and wrote commentaries on Euclid. Ibni-Sina of Bukhara (AD 980–1037), a medical scholar, explained the contagiousness of tuberculosis and described 670 drugs in his medical study, *Al-Kanun*, which was translated into Latin. Al Farabi, a Turk from Tranoxiana, blended Aristotelian, Platonic and Sufi thought in his writings.

Islamic scholars used mathematics and astronomy to fix the *Qibla*, the prayer niche of mosques, toward Mecca. The words "al-gebra" and "cipher," which originate from Arabic, show the Islamic influence in the field of mathematics.

Fetters of religion: Islam soon became an instrument of reaction in the Ottoman empire. As the empire declined, the *ulema* became open to widespread corruption and closed to change and progress. At the same time, the country's clergy completely isolated themselves from all intellectual and cultural changes.

Scientific and technological advances became corrupt, alien ideas to the Muslim clergy. A good illustration of this intellectual stagnation came in 1580 when Sultan Murad III shut down an observatory in Istanbul because, in the words of the *Seyülislam*, the astronomers were "insolent enough to try to pry open the secrets of the universe" – secrets known only to Allah.

While Europe underwent the Reformation and made gigantic strides in the sciences and industry, the Ottoman empire wallowed in ignorance, guided by a rigid clergy who clung to medieval Islamic ideas.

Modern Turkey: When Kemal Atatürk came into power, he changed all that. He abolished the sultanate and the caliphate and replaced the *Shariah* with civil, trade and criminal codes, adopted from Switzerland, France and Italy.

In the modern Turkish republic, religious schools, for example, are carefully controlled by the Ministry of Education. Religious leaders, such as *imams*, are paid civil servants – a measure instituted to curb their influence.

In recent years, there has been a revival in Islam as many Turks have shown interest in learning of their religious past. Quran courses, religious high schools and higher institutes of Islamic learning are flourishing.

Islamic cassette tapes, books and magazines, each expressing views of the different brotherhoods, are proliferating in Turkey today.

One of the most popular cassettes is a series of Islamic spirituals sung by Yusuf Islam, formerly known as pop music star Cat Stevens, who converted to the Muslim faith and changed his name.

How many wives do Turkish men have? One. Are there still harems? Yes, in the Topkapı and Dolmabahçe museums. Do Turkish women still wear veils? Well, some do, but more as a statement of political conservatism than anything else.

There is hardly any other topic where the psychological distance between nations is more pronounced than the status of women. And with Turkish women, the gap of understanding is often profound. Since the 19th century, European art, literature and popular culture have depicted Eastern women as docile, submissive creatures, clad in an all-enveloping black sheet when they are not dancing before their master in exotic, transparent silks.

Although such perceptions were at one time based on some – however tenuous – reality, the cliché has often remained. Modern visitors are fairly shocked when they find Turkish women sitting in a bar enjoying a cocktail after a hard day's work at a bank or some construction business. At the same time, many modern Turkish ladies are equally appalled when they visit their rural sisters, slaving in the kitchen after a day's labor in the family field while their husbands return to yet another game of cards or backgammon at the local teahouse.

The harem: Following their acceptance of Islam about a thousand years ago, the Turks also began institutionalizing the conservative traditions associated with that religion, including the seclusion of women. Accordingly, the area of the house where the men entertained their guests was called the *Selamlık*, while that part of the house reserved for the women was called the *harem*, or "forbidden sanctuary."

Today, enough is known about life in the harem to render the more commonly held fantasies associated with this restricted realm inaccurate or laughable. Hardly a licentious brothel or a "house of ill repute" belonging to the husband and stocked with his favorite concubines, the harem was essentially the

domain of the first wife. Indeed, the Muslim husband required her permission before taking another woman, whom he would have to support in the same style as the first: a gift to one required the same gift to all others; the same held true for his husbandly duties. Needless to say, most men could not afford to practice polygamy, neither financially nor psychologically.

More to the point, the harem was more like a home, school and power base for women, a place where they were trained in arts and

crafts, music, household management and religion. Slave girls who were bought to be trained as servants, nannies or entertainers or just ladies-in-waiting for the wives of an extended family were to be set free at the end of 7 years, for such was Islamic Law. Even the famed Topkapı Harem had to be subject to the same strict protocol.

A potential paramour was chosen not by the sultan himself in most instances, but by the Mother Sultan, who carefully trained the concubine before finally presenting her to the ruler. Strange though it may seem, there are even instances of concubines having rejected a sultan.

Left, some Turkish women enjoy a life of luxury; while **right**, others have to work in the fields to provide for their families.

In many ways, the harem can be considered the real seat of power during the Ottoman period, for it was here that royal marriages were arranged, the future crown princes selected and – in some instances – probably murdered.

Süleyman the Magnificent's second wife Roxalana excelled in the politics of the harem, marrying off her daughter Mihrimah to a certain Rüstem Pasha, who then became Grand Vizier. Family ties established, Rüstem Pasha and his new mother-in-law next conspired to have Mustafa, Süleyman's heir apparent by his first wife Gülbahar, strangled to death by the infamous "silk bow."

We have vivid descriptions of elite Otto-

Following the declaration of the Republic in 1923, one of the most significant elements in the social revolution planned and advocated by Kemal Atatürk was the emancipation of Turkish women, based on the principle that the new Turkey was to be a secular state.

On February 17, 1926, a new code of civil law was adopted which drastically altered the traditional family structure. Polygamy was abolished along with religious marriages, and divorce and child custody became the prerogative of both women and men. A minimum age for marriage was fixed. Perhaps most importantly, the equality of inheritance was accepted as well as the equality of testi-

man women who enjoyed wealth, power and property, often seeming to rival that of the sultan himself in such literature as Lady Mary Montagu's *Letters*.

Winds of change: It took the major social upheavals of World War I and the subsequent Turkish War of Independence to radically change the status of women in Turkey. Suddenly, many urban and village women were found working in munitions factories. At the same time, wives and daughters of the elite classes such as the writer, Professor Halide Edip Adivar, became outspoken supporters of Atatürk's fight for independence, and joined his forces in Anatolia.

mony before a court of law: previously under Islamic law, the testimony of two women was equal to that of one man.

Female suffrage was granted at the municipal level in 1930, and nationwide in 1934. In theory, at least, Turkish women were far ahead of many of their western sisters, and strangely, it was a man – Kemal Atatürk – who was giving them their rights by decree.

Theory and practice: But theory is one thing, and practice another. Even at the elite level, the traditional Islamic ethic concerning female submission to male authority continues to pervade much of modern Turkish society.

However, recent changes to Turkish Civil Code which once enshrined the rights of men now allow married women to keep their maiden name, to work without the permission of their husbands, and to be the legal head of the household. Interestingly, the husband of the lady Prime Minister Özer Çiller has in fact adopted his wife's name.

On the village level the reforms of 50 years ago have not completely rooted out religious marriages and even the practice of taking a second wife, called a *kuma*. A campaign was initiated in 1987 by Mrs. Semra Özal, wife of the then prime minister, to end these practices once and for all. Mrs. Özal and her Women's Association toured the country-

themselves "feminists" and have their own magazine by the same name; for the first time in living memory, thousands of these women marched on Mother's Day in 1987 to protest the continued practice of wife beating.

The other group marches as well, but to the tune of an entirely different drummer: that of Islamic fundamentalism. Called the "rain-coat brigade" due to their penchant for head scarfs and loosely fitting overcoats (which they wear in midsummer heat), the reactionary women are often university students who want to advertise their defiance of nearly all of Atatürk's reforms, claiming that the respect afforded women in Islam is the only bill of rights they need. Doctrinaire secular-

side and performed mass civil marriages, thus legitimizing thousands of children as well as legalizing the wife's right to inheritance. Turkish television, meanwhile, broadcasts periodic "consciousness raising" programmes urging women to refuse to become second wives.

On the urban level, two trends are currently discernible, which can be neatly summed up as progressive and reactionary. The former group is largely made up of professional women, many of whom now openly call

Left, equality means he rides and you walk.
Above, modern Turkish ladies slimming down.

ists perceive the rain-coat brigades as the thin edge of a Khomeini-type of religious fundamentalism that protects itself under the call for "human rights" while preparing to strip all others of theirs if and when they come to power.

Today, Turkish women are bank directors, doctors, lawyers, judges, journalists, pilots, diplomats, members of parliament and police officers. At the same time, while young men are introduced to applied sex in legalized brothels chastity remains a must for young women.

The harem may be history, but there's still a long way to go.

CARPETS AND TRADITIONAL TEXTILES

An unforgettable part of anyone's journey to Turkey is to be pulled in off the street by a multi-lingual carpet dealer, and to have scores of carpets unrolled before you as you sip Turkish coffee or tea from a tulip-shaped glass and listen to the merchant regale you with the origin, meaning and age of each piece.

The Turks claim for themselves the distinction of being the originators of the knotted pile carpet. Certainly, they are the heirs to a long and illustrious tradition of textiles dating back to their origins as nomadic tribesmen in Central Asia, where the earliest known carpets were found. Following their flocks of sheep and goats westward, the Turks who settled in Anatolia also discovered there a century old weaving tradition. It is thought, for example, that wall paintings at the Hittite site of Çatal Höyük (c. 6,500–5,300 BC) show *kilims*, or flat weave floor coverings. At Gordion, many loom weights in the form of pebbles have been found as well as mosaic pavements whose artistry bears a remarkable similarity to textile designs. There is speculation, too, that Turkish weaving designs are related to those of the Navajo in the United States.

Historical carpets: The earliest carpets the visitor to Turkey will see are those on display in the Museum of Turkish and Islamic Arts in Istanbul, and in the Konya Museum. These are the crudely but powerfully drawn Seljuk carpets dating from the 13th century, discovered in the Seljuk capital Konya and the nearby town of Beyşehir at the beginning of this century. Indeed, the famous Italian traveler, Marco Polo, passing through Anatolia at the time, commented on the beauty of the carpets and silks woven in Turkey. Also displayed in Istanbul museums are examples from the entire range of styles and designs in Turkish weaving up to the end of the 19th century, ranging from the familiar geometric designs to the wild floral and arabesque patterns of several Ottoman court carpets which were woven at

imperial workshops in Istanbul and Bursa. The heirs to this tradition today are the finely woven silk and wool carpets of Hereke, where the court established a factory in 1891.

In keeping with the tradition of Ottoman court carpets, today's Hereke rugs are also woven from specially designed cartoons, which are quite eclectic in their source of design. Today, girls you see working at the factory are able to knot an astonishing 30 knots per minute.

A large number of the older rugs on display at the museums of Istanbul were woven in western Turkey in the Uşak region; the town of Kula is still an important center of production, although Kula carpets today bear little resemblance to their forebears, mostly being woven in pastel colors in Caucasian designs for the foreign market. By contrast, the old Turkish rugs have an individual palette, including a rich purple, brilliant yellow and striking green, in addition to the more familiar hues of red and blue.

The Bergama and Yağcıbedir rugs woven today are related to these old pieces,

Left, a "kilim," or Turkish flat weave. **Right**, weavers from Hakkâri.

with their geometric designs together with the usual red and blue.

Henry VIII's 400 Turkish carpets: From the 14th century onwards Turkish rugs were exported to Europe, probably in quite large numbers; many can be found in European churches and seen in European paintings, which are important source of information about Turkish carpets from the 14th to 17th centuries. King Henry VIII of England was an avid purchaser and posed for Holbein on a Turkish rug. He was only too happy to seize the large carpet collection of his favorite, Cardinal Wolsey, when the latter fell from favor. Although the contemporary inventories note that about half of his 800

Folk tradition: A folk tradition of weaving existed side by side with the refined production of the court and city workshops. Until this century most households had looms to produce carpets and floor coverings as well as all sorts of bags, shawls and other items of clothing. Thread for these domestic looms was handspun on spindles or on spinning wheels in the Black Sea region from locally produced wool, goat hair, cotton or linen. Dyes obtained from various plants indigenous to Anatolia gave a rich variety of colors. Madder root, one of the best known of these, produces shades from a brickish red to orange and even to pinks and deep purple. It was a lucrative export crop as one

carpets were Turkish, like many a subsequent collector, he did not look after his rugs, and they rotted away on the damp flagstones of Hampton Court Palace. Not one of his rugs has come down to this day.

The survival of many early Turkish carpets is thanks to the custom of presenting carpets to mosques as pious gifts, where they were preserved for centuries. It is worth keeping an eye on the rugs in a mosque during a visit. Though many have been removed by avaricious collectors or taken for storage or display in safer places, mosque floors can still be a display case of a district's traditional weaving.

of the only reliable red dyes until the synthesis of chemical dyes in the 1860s. Other important dyes were indigo for blue, saffron for yellow and walnut – also an export crop – for black and brown. Most likely the average household had neither the capacity nor the skill to dye self-sufficient quantities of wool, and each district had its own specialist dyer. In some rural areas itinerant dyers fulfilled the community's needs.

It is the *kilims* and carpets woven from vegetable dyed wool in traditional designs which are the most prized by collectors today. Vegetable dyed colors have a luminous yet harmoniously varied brilliance which the harsh monotony of chemical colors cannot match. The first aniline dyes tended to run and fade badly, but today's chrome dyes are more reliable and somewhat more attractive. The limited range of very bright colors from natural dyes also served to curb the Turkish villager's appetite for garish colors, an appetite which had indulged itself to the full on the exciting range of chemical pinks and oranges.

There are several attempts to revive the dying art of carpet weaving and in particular to bring back the use of vegetable dyes. The University of Marmara's project, known as the DOBAG Projesi, aimed at reintroducing vegetable dyes in the area around Art in Istanbul.

Pedigree: Designs, colors, quality of wool and style of weave help in attributing textiles to their place of origin, although the first of these – design itself – is perhaps the least reliable indicator. Intermarriage, resettlement, instructions from dealers and the different influences to which the weavers themselves are exposed mean that designs change before the colors or style of weaving do. A weaver's fancy may be caught which she incorporates into her weaving, or she may be told to weave a popular Caucasian pattern by the trader to whom she sells her work. Turkish families who were resettled in the Cihanbeyli region north of Konya, for

Balıkesir in western Turkey, is perhaps the best known and successful of these. Unlike many other similar projects, the DOBAG Projesi has not established workshops and handed out ready dyed wool and patterns in some underdeveloped corner of the country, but has instead taught the women to use vegetable dyes to weave and to utilize the traditional designs of the area near their own homes. The DOBAG Projesi is featured in a display in the ethnographic section of the Museum of Turkish and Islamic Art in Istanbul.

Left, little fingers at the loom. **Above**, the resulting masterpiece.

example, wove rugs identical to those woven by their fellow Turks near Malatya, hundreds of miles east. Designs in Turkish rugs are similar to those in Central Asian, Afghan, Persian or Caucasian rugs. Kars rugs, for example, closely resemble Caucasian rugs, although this is not surprising given that city's location on the Russian frontier. Less explicable are the designs of western Anatolia in and around Çanakkale in such places as Ezine and Koza, which also bear a striking similarity to Caucasian carpets in design and are woven with the same thick, shaggy pile. Milas rugs, by contrast, are the latest development of a long tradition stretching back to nomadic rugs mentioned in the 14th century by the Persian geographer Hamdullah Qazvini. The carnation motif so often seen in Milas rugs is particularly Turkish, and one of the flowers favored by the Ottoman court.

The nomads of the Taurus mountains weave the lustrous Döşemealtı rugs, while their settled cousins in the Yahyalı region have been weaving their own version of Ladik carpets since the 14th century. Ladik rugs themselves, however, have changed completely to become a finely knotted floral product competing with Hereke carpets.

Undoubtedly many designs and colors originally had significance, but this is no encountered when the Turks and their Mongol brethren were busy battering away at the Great Wall.

By now nobody can hope to disentangle the various influences at play through centuries of change, but one can continue to speculate. Although dealers in the Grand Covered Bazaar and elsewhere can spin a good yarn, their interpretation should be regarded as a sales pitch and nothing more. The majority of the carpets and *kilims* on sale in the bazaars of Turkey are commissioned with the weavers of, say, Kars producing Milas rugs from pictures provided by the carpet merchants whose choice of pictures is determined by what they believe

longer known to the weaver, who does, however, attach meanings connected with her own daily life. Each of the Turcoman tribes who migrated to Anatolia had a *damga* or tribal mark, often a bird or beast, and indeed early carpets do show abstract animals or birds and very stylized survivors of these forms can be detected in some of today's designs. Another common motif is the *elibelinde* or "hands on hips" design seen on many *kilims* which has a striking resemblance to the ancient Hittite statuettes of the fertility goddess, fat figure with her arms akimbo. Still other designs may be linked with symbolic Chinese characters, to be favored by Germans or Italians.

The one possible exception to this confusion are the *kilims* produced in the eastern provinces of Hakkâri and Van, which were not much valued until about 20 years ago, and thus escaped the direct influences of the marketplace much longer than pile rugs. Today, they are prized for the vigor and boldness of their abstract designs, and the harmony and brilliance of their composition have led to their being compared with contemporary abstract art. Sadly, but inevitably, with the rise in popularity, there has been a concomitant rise in production, and fall in quality.

Shopping in the bazaar: Buyer beware! What your hear is not necessarily what you get from the rug shops in the Grand Bazaar, and what you receive in the mail is not always what you bought from that friendly merchant who invited you to stay with him and his family during your next trip to Turkey. Obviously, some dealers are better than others, but all share one common trait: their job is to sell carpets at the highest possible price. Signs posted in the windows and on the walls notwithstanding, all of them will bargain. Also to be remembered is that due to Turkey's strict law on the export of antiquities, any carpet or *kilim* you purchase must be cleared by a museum

and scarves are still made, and many areas have a special style of headcovering for their women. In Bayburt and Erzurum the women venture out of the house wrapped in handwoven shawls called *thram* of various shades of undyed brown finely spun wool ornamented with blue cotton embroidery. Along the eastern Black Sea coast, women sport pink and red striped cotton shawls and aprons known as *kesan* after the town in Thrace where they are manufactured. In the Aegean, girls weave silk and cotton shirts for their husbands-to-be, and embroider dresses and trousers for themselves. The ancient, almost undoubtedly Turkish, craft of feltmaking survives in the manufacture

as exportable, with a letter to prove it. Logic thus suggests that the vast majority of carpets on sale in shops and bazaars throughout the land are likely not to be of the ancient vintage many dealers claim, as it would be not only illegal to sell them, but also illegal for a tourist to bring them out of the country.

Shawls, scarves and socks: Several branches of textiles have been less affected by commercialization. Traditional shawls

Left, not all are collector's items. **Above**, myriad styles and shapes and colors, but only one is just right.

of thick felt shepherd's capes for use in bitter Anatolian winters. Much of the felt is produced in the bazaar area of Urfa in the southeast region.

Knitting is a popular craft in both towns and villages. Sivas is especially famous for its traditionally patterned socks and gloves. Ankara, the hometown of the mohair goat, and once the center of a thriving mohair cloth industry, specializes in lacily patterned, undyed mohair socks and gloves. Knitting has a large and specialized Turkish vocabulary, indicating that it has been a traditional craft amongst the Turks since time immemorial.

What do the Ottoman Janissary bands and the Mardi Gras marching bands of New Orleans have in common? Some students of musical history say everything: cymbals, clarinets, big bass drums; in short, a healthy taste for volume.

In the Ottoman empire, military bands were an essential element of the shock-troop tactics of the Janissary corps. During the battles, the *mehter* would create a tremendous din with mounted timpani, horns, and bagpipes, adding to the blast of blunderbuss and cannon as the Ottomans marched through the Balkans into Central Europe. Retreating, they left many of their instruments behind, and these eventually found their way into the orchestrations of such composers as Mozart, Haydn, Beethoven, and even John Phillip Sousa.

Ottoman music: In addition to the traditional war music a rich patrimony with cultural novelties developed under the Ottomans. This included classical music, a synthesis of Asian music, which by the 19th century had reached a level of eclecticism and subtlety rarely found elsewhere. Among the Ottoman sovereigns there were fine composers like Mahmud I (1730–54) and Selim III (1789–1807).

All the women of the harem played the *ud* (lute) and sang in groups, while the more talented among them were taught the *kanun* (lateral zither). Musicians who played for women were women themselves, dressed in men's attire.

A particular aspect of Turkish music was the almost total absence of written notation. An Ottoman Armenian, Hamparsum Limonjuian (1768–1839) created a system of notation, but the accepted value system of the times was memorization. Unhappily, interpretations differed, and some original compositions were forgotten and many pieces lost forever.

Instruments: The *kanun*, which is a favorite instrument among the Arabs, was introduced to the people of Turkey in the 18th century and was mostly favored by the women of nobility. It is a flat, trapezoidal zither with 72 strings producing 24 notes, in three octaves of minor thirds.

The *keman* is no other than the European violin, which was imported to Turkey, but which is tuned D-A-D-G.

The *tambur*, a Turkish instrument par excellence, is a long-necked lute with eight double strings tuned D-D-C-A and covers two octaves. When the *tambur* is played with a bow its timbre is similar to the ancient Turkish instrument *rebap*.

The Arab *ud* (lute) is the ancestor of all western lutes and guitars. It has a pear-shaped body, a keyboard without frets and its neck is at a characteristic angle of 60 degrees. It usually has 11 or 12 strings, tuned two-by-two on C-G-D-A-E-D.

Kemençe refers to a small violin with a pear-shaped body. Its three strings, D-G-D, when played by the fingernails, emit a delicate and strident sound.

The *ney* is a wooden, oblong flute which is common to the Persians, Arabs and Turks. It has 10 fingerholes and in Turkey, this flute can be found in 14 tonalities. According to the position of the head and the force of breath, it is possible to play an extension of three octaves. It was (and still is) the primary instrument of Turkish mystical orders, such as the Whirling Dervishes, who say the sound of the *ney* is akin to God's voice.

Folk Music: The art of the *aşık* (traveling minstrel) first appeared in Anatolia in the 15th century. Like the medieval French troubadour, the *aşık* traveled from village to village, playing the *bağlama* (or *saz*, a long-necked instrument with three pairs of strings) and his songs were about political and social satire. The *aşık* can still be heard in such places as Erzurum and Kars as well as in the occasional festival in Konya.

Western-style Turkish classical music: With the formation of the Turkish Republic, there appeared a school for music instructors in 1924 and the State Conservatory in 1936. Then in 1946, the State Opera and Theater were founded by refugees from Hitler's Germany such as Hindemith.

A number of composers made outstanding contributions in the form of western classical music, but with Turkish folk themes and rhythm. Among them were Ulvi Cemal Erkin (1906–72), composer of five symphonies, one symphonietta, a concert for klavier and violin, a symphony concertante, and the *Köçekçe* – a truly Turkish rhapsody. Ahmet Adnan Saygun (born 1907) is famous for his adaptations of Turkish folk music for choirs, the most popular of his compositions being the *Yunus Emre Oratorio*.

Contemporary popular music: Popular music reflects the plurality of contemporary Turkish society. While the social milieu has changed because of domestic migration and population explosion, so has popular cul-

than her music) sings kitsch songs while Sezen Aksu sings more original Turkish pop tunes à la Barbara Streisand. More western and youngish in their style and arguably more talented are the popular group Mazhar/ Fuat/Özkan, and the not so popular but equally original Bülent Ortaçgil, the songwriter/singer/guitar player.

Arabesque: When you get in a cab, the chances are you won't hear cassettes playing any of the types of music mentioned above. The shantytown culture, especially in large

Saz player and young girls sing folk songs.

ture. Hence contemporary singers, musicians and composers represent different schools.

Representatives of the old school who made a transition from classical Turkish music are the ever popular Zeki Müren and Emel Sayın. Another artist of this school is Bülent Ersoy, who braved a sex-change operation but was barred from public appearance from 1980–86 because the state insisted that she was still a man by birth. Miss Ersoy and doctors contend otherwise.

Superstar Ajda Pekkan (who gets more media attention for her cosmetic surgery

cities, has embraced a new and peculiar brand of music – the Arabesque. The star of this style is Ibrahim Tatlises, a former construction worker from Urfa.

Orhan Gencebay (the pioneer of this style), Küçük Emrah and Ferdi Tayfur are other popular stars of Arabesque. On a more sophisticated level are Zulfi Livaneli and Timur Selçuk who stood out as representatives of protest music but are pro-establishment now.

Livaneli collaborates with the Greek musician Nikos Theodorakis, putting the politicians of their respective countries to shame by calling for love, peace and solidarity between the two Aegean coasts.

For 500 years, the Ottoman empire ruled much of the medieval world and at the Topkapı Palace in Istanbul, great chefs created a sumptuous cuisine which came to rival the epicurean foods of ancient Rome.

Perhaps due to the infinite variety of fish, fowl, meat, fruits and vegetables produced in Turkey or to the numerous cultures that took roots in ancient Anatolia – archaeologists have recently deciphered a Sumerian tablet that turned out to be a cook-book of sorts, with nearly all the items and spices

are surprised at the epicurean paradise they find throughout the country; few leave without having radically transformed their opinion, and most immediately set about finding the nearest Turkish restaurant back home.

Over the centuries the Turkish palate has become a refined one. So it isn't surprising that in Istanbul today, people choose their drinking water as others would select their wine. One never simply orders peaches but specifies what type of peach. With fish, one specifies the age of the fish when caught:

listed familiar to Turks today – contemporary Turkish food is amazingly varied, and has left its mark on all who have come into contact with it.

Today, from the Balkans to North Africa, virtually all the nations share a taste for the savory *kebap*, *pilav*, egg-plant specialities and the tangy white cheese known as *feta* which had their origins in the kitchens of the Topkapı Palace or in the province of Bolu, where young men seeking their fortunes started by peeling potatoes in one of the dozens of exclusive gourmet schools set up by imperial decree. It is thus more than a little strange that many visitors to Turkey

çinakop is a generation younger than *lüfer*, *torik* a year older than *palamut*.

This critical palate has lead to the development of a very subtle and varied array of dishes. Along with this delicate palate, sensitivity is extended to include the environment in which food is eaten. Fish should be eaten at a table set alongside the water; *kebap* and other meat dishes preferably enjoyed overlooking a rural scene. In fact, the origin of the open-air café was in Ottoman Turkey and the idea was brought back to Europe by the Austrian ambassador to the Ottoman court who had enjoyed the open-air cafés along the shores of the Bosphorus.

The *kebap*: The dishes which are the most Turkish have their origins in the foods prepared by the Turks living on the high Central Asian plateau – the *kebap* often very different from the standard *şişkebabı* most Americans and Europeans know. *Kebap* is a small piece of meat, and it is only when it is skewered on a metal *şiş* or skewer and grilled that it becomes a *şişkebabı*.

Kebap is a word that has figured prominently in Turkish cuisine for more than 10 centuries and its meaning has developed to many villages. Other wonderful *kebap* dishes often related to their region of origin are *Adana kebabı*, ground lamb seasoned with red pepper and oregano, wrapped around a skewer and grilled or Bursa and *Iskender kebabı*, with luscious slices of meat from a *döner kebabı* placed over *pide* bread and smothered in yogurt, tomato sauce and hot butter. *Çöp kebabı* meaning "scrap" *kebap* made from tiny pieces of leftover lamb is often accompanied by a hot tomato sauce or chopped onions and parsley.

include meats that have been boiled, baked and stewed. Meat is usually cooked with vegetables; as with the *şişkebabı,* pieces of green pepper, tomato and onion add flavor to the morsels of meat, or the *güveç* dishes where meat is cooked in a casserole with fresh vegetables. Lamb is the meat par excellence in Turkey and is used to make various types of *dolma,* stuffed vegetable dishes, or for the classic Konya dish of *tandır kebabı,* where a whole lamb is baked in a brick oven, still built in the ground in

Left, the döner kebabı – a basic. **Above**, şişkebabı at a typical lokanta.

One delicious dish that requires cubed beef or lamb and a delicious puree of eggplant, has an interesting story – from which the dish acquired its name – behind it: *Hünkârbeğendi* or "Her Majesty Was Pleased." When Empress Eugenie, the wife of Napoleon (the third) , was in Istanbul as guest of sultan she fell in love with this eggplant puree, a specialty of the Topkapı Palace. She asked if her own cook might be taught how to prepare the dish. The sultan obliged, but the next day the French chef begged to be excused from this impossible task: "I took my book and my scales to the Turkish chef," he said, "and he threw them out. 'An Imperial chef', he told me 'cooks with his feelings, his eyes, and his nose.'" The Empress returned to France without acquiring the recipe, but to this day it has been known as *Hünkârbeğendi*.

Dolma: The Turkish courts of Isfahan and Khorsan introduced the very delicious and popular dish known as *dolma* made of any of the following: squash, eggplant, peppers, grape leaves, cabbage leaves, tomatoes, mussels and artichokes, which are filled either with a meat mixture or a mixture of rice, pinenuts, currants, herbs and spices. They are then cooked in olive oil and lemon and served hot if prepared with the meat, and usually served cold if prepared with a

Tartarböregi and *su böregi* stuffed with meat and spices make substantial main meals and are to be found in many restaurants and at special stores in Turkey.

Eating establishments: In the cities and larger villages, every street seems to offer someplace to eat and one could certainly never starve anywhere in Turkey. The produce and the prices are usually quite unbelievable: melons cost about 50 cents a kilo; mountains of tomatoes, peppers, eggplants are all incredibly cheap in their season. Street sellers abound, their calls, along with the call to prayer, are some of the nostalgic memories one will bring home after a visit to Turkey.

rice mixture. They are often accompanied by yogurt, which it must be said is so special that it tastes almost like a cross between cream and yogurt.

Another classic Turkish dish which a visitor is sure to come across is *börek* made from layers of wafer thin, flaky pastry known in Turkey as *yufka*. These savory pastries may be stuffed with cheese, herbs, spinach, fish or meat, and are served either as an appetizer or as a main dish. *Sigaraböregi,* the pastry rolled into a cigar-shaped form and stuffed with parsley, *feta* cheese and egg, is the most frequently served and makes a delicious snack with afternoon tea.

Although some precaution is needed when buying meat and fish from street sellers, most of the delicacies offered are unlikely to upset travelers' tummy. Highly recommended are the *simit*, twists of sesame seed bread, the fresh nuts – almonds on ice, walnuts and hazelnuts, the roasted chestnuts – and for the adventurous, *kokoreç* or grilled intestine with spices!

For serious eating, however, one has to consider several aspects of dining out when choosing a spot. A meal out can be as inexpensive as it is pleasurable or it can be a luxurious affair, fit for a sultan at prices comparable to dining in New York or London. Restaurants vary from the most elegant of dining clubs to the very simplest of *salonu* or eating halls. The former are sometimes overrated and the latter often underrated. The *lokanta* (restaurants) or *gazino* (clubs) have, probably, that special atmosphere most visitors enjoy for an evening out. The former are usually spacious and attractively decorated, often specializing either in meat or fish.

Some of the more elegant serve both but when one is dining out with Turks, one is often asked which one would prefer to eat, fish or meat, so that the best location for one or the other might be chosen. For upmarket dining, head for the hotels, where unlike

display. This is particularly convenient for foreigners as written descriptions of the dishes often don't do them justice or are not well translated. On top of this, dishes will often vary from evening to evening according to the catch of the day or the fresh produce in season. Be forewarned, it is wise to go easy on these appetizers as main dishes may be even better and deserve abdominal space.

Selections in the fish restaurants are likely to include *tarama* or creamed red caviar; mussels stuffed with rice, pinenuts, spices; fried calamary and shrimp; *balık köftesi* (hot fish-cakes); shrimp *güveç* (a casserole of shrimp, hot peppers, tomatoes and

many parts of Europe, some of the finest restaurants are found.

Many of these restaurants really specialize in resurrecting old Ottoman menus and provide exquisite settings for an evening out. They do, however, tend to be more expensive than the *kebap* houses and local fish restaurants.

A typical meal out: A typical meal out in Turkey will usually start with a vast array of assorted *meze* (hors d'oeuvres) being brought to the table or selected from a

Left, "forest kebabı" – a basic. **Above**, a typical Turkish pastry.

cheese); *çiroz* salads; (cured mackerel salad with fresh dill and vinegar). Other hors d'oeuvres that are a must include *humus*, pureed chickpea salad, and *cevizli tavuk* – Circassian chicken. Düzce, a small town between Ankara and Istanbul, may claim credit for this last dish of cooked, boned chicken, smothered in a sauce made from walnuts, bread crumbs, garlic, red pepper, oil and lemon. Cold honeydew melon and fresh white cheese is a favorite among all Turks, along with plates of *çöban salatası*, or shepherds' salad, a combination of finely chopped fresh cucumbers, onions, tomatoes and peppers.

Drinks: The delicious *meze* are traditionally enjoyed with the national drink *rakı* or "lion's milk," as it is often called. This anisette-tasting liquor is drunk with water added to it, hence it changes from a clear liquid to a milky-white and does, in fact, go extremely well with hor d'oeuvres and fish. This drink was developed because of the literal injunction of the Quran against wines; today, however, wines also grace the table in secular, republican Turkey.

Turkey was the cradle of the sultana raisin from which delectable Aegean wines are produced. The hills surrounding the coastal areas have vineyards turning out grapes. Wine making has been popular in

dishes in the Mediterranean. The locals, after lifetimes of eating fresh fish, can often tell you where and when the fish was caught after one mouthful. Hence, any good restaurant will not be caught serving day-old fish, and often one selects seafood from display tanks where your meal is still very much alive.

Some of the most delicious dishes include *kılıç* or swordfish skewered with peppers and tomatoes, or simply grilled *lüfer*, bluefish, or *kalkan*, turbot served with lemon wedges. Another favorite is *buğlama,* an exotic type of fishstew which can be made from any of the larger catch of the day. Giant shrimp (*karides*) and clawless Medi-

this part of the world since the neolithic period when man first began organised agricultural communities. Some well-known, easily-found choices might include: *Villa Doluca* – a delightfully light, dry white wine with a pleasant fruity taste; *Kavaklıdere, Çankaya* – a light white; *Doluca Riesling* – smooth with a hint of sweetness, white; *Dikmen* – a very decent table wine made from Central Anatolian grapes, robust and dry; and *Kulüp Özel* Reserve, something special, a light red with a fine bouquet.

Fish: A country blessed with fruitful waters, Turkey offers some of the tastiest fish

terranean lobster, are also available in season, though pricey even then. If one is visiting the Black Sea, one is sure to be offered fresh anchovies (*hamsi*) either delicately fried in butter or made into one of the other 80 *hamsi* dishes of the area.

Pilav and vegetables: If your main course is a meat dish, be it one the *kebap* or grilled meat specialties, it'll probably come accompanied by rice. Turkish *pilav* or rice has to be some of the best in the world; either simply cooked with butter and meat broth or richly seasoned with pinenuts, currants, herbs and liver, it is delicious by itself.

The next course of cold vegetable is

cooked in olive oil. The *zeytinyağlı* dishes are made from the seasonal vegetable and are delicious eaten as a main dish with plenty of wonderful Turkish bread.

Turkish delights and more: Most people with even a mildly adventurous palate have heard of or tried *baklava* or *kadayıf*. They are the favorite throughout the Middle East, but are essentially of Turkish origin. These two flaky, pastry types of dessert dominate menus although there are an infinite variety of others.

Desserts with such exotic names as "Lady's navel" (*kadın göbeği*), consisting of delicately lemon-flavored cakes soaked in syrup; "belle lips" (*dilber dudağı*) or fried

able. Another type of dessert that should definitely be sampled is the *muhallebi*, or milk pudding, which is served cold and deliciously dusted with pistachio nuts or chocolate. A lot of the *kebap* houses specialize in these milk pudding; particularly good is the rich rice pudding which is cooked slowly and thereafter served cold.

Fruits: Turkey is a fruit paradise. Izmir's figs, melons, and sultana grapes have been coveted since the days of antiquity. Cherries have their origin in ancient Cerasus, modern day Giresun. Romans took the fruit kernels for their peach orchards from the foot of Mount Olympus in Bursa. Restaurants love to prepare fresh fruits for the

dough sweetened with syrup; and *künefe* or shredded wheat-type strands of pastry with a mild cheese inside, served fresh off the griddle with hot syrup. They are also the delicious, richer desserts. If you prefer lighter delicacies, especially after a large meal, stewed quince topped with walnuts or cream, or "Noah's pudding" (*aşure*). The latter is made from numerous types of dried fruits and pulses.

Stuffed, fresh apricots and pumpkin dessert, are other fruit based creations avail-

Left, "Pide," or Turkish pizza. **Above**, a fish restaurant with accompanying "meze".

table and arrange them often with candles under glasses holding up elaborate "sculptures" of fruit.

Coffee: To finish your meal, a taste of Turkish coffee and one of their wonderful desserts is a must. Coffee is an important drink in Turkish society as indicated by the following proverb: "A cup of coffee commits one to 40 years of friendship." It is served either plain, medium sweet or very sweet in demi-tasse cups and goes very well with your choice of desserts.

If you dine with Turkish friends, one of them looks at your fortune by examining the remains of your coffee cup.

After having managed to pack the history of the ancient world – from the Hittites to the Romans, Parthians, Byzantine Greeks as well as that of the Ottoman and Republican Turkey into less than 100 pages, the volume you now hold will attempt to make some sort of reasonable itinerary out of modern Turkey.

The first chapter starts with Istanbul, once known as Constantinople and the capital of the 1,000-year Byzantine empire before becoming the Imperial city of the Ottoman Turks for 500 years. Rounding up the chapter are subsections on the previous Ottoman capitals of Bursa and Edirne.

The Aegean region is divided into northern and southern sectors, with Izmir smack in the middle, just as the Mediterannean section is divided into eastern and western halves, with Antalya as the point of departure. So far, so good.

The vast, complex area of the Turkish east presents an organizational problem for any book; the editor has elected to divide the east into northern and southern halves, starting from the southern

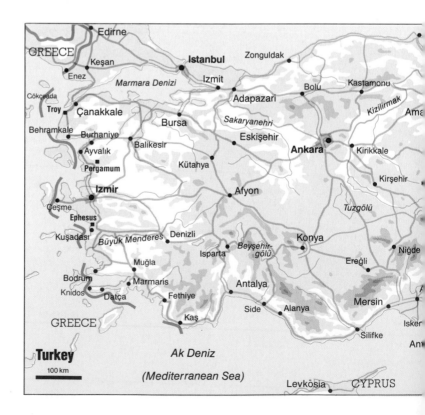

sector with Antakya and its environs. From Antakya, we plunge east to the Euphrates River and the astonishing monuments atop Mount Nemrut, following the mighty river north to Elazığ and Lake Van. From Van, we swing south and west to Diyarbakır, completing the loop at Urfa, the hometown of the prophet Abraham.

Central Anatolia comes next, with excursions designed from the capital of Ankara to Hittite and Phyrgian sites as well as the "fairy chimneys" of Cappadocia and the Whirling Dervishes at Konya.

The last leg of the exhausting journey leads east again, via Sivas and Erzurum to Mount Ararat and Ani, the ancient capital of the Armenians, and beyond, to the special world of Artvin, where old Georgian churches still dominate obscure, exquistely beautiful, alpine valleys. Finally, we arrive at the Black Sea and move ever westward, ending the journey at Zilve, where Caesar uttered his famous lines: "I camc. I saw. I conquered."

So, on to Istanbul, the city that strides two continents, the bridge between east and west

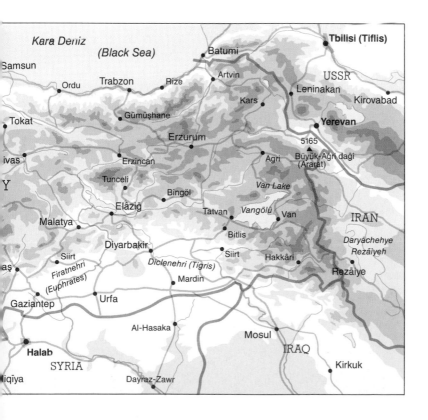

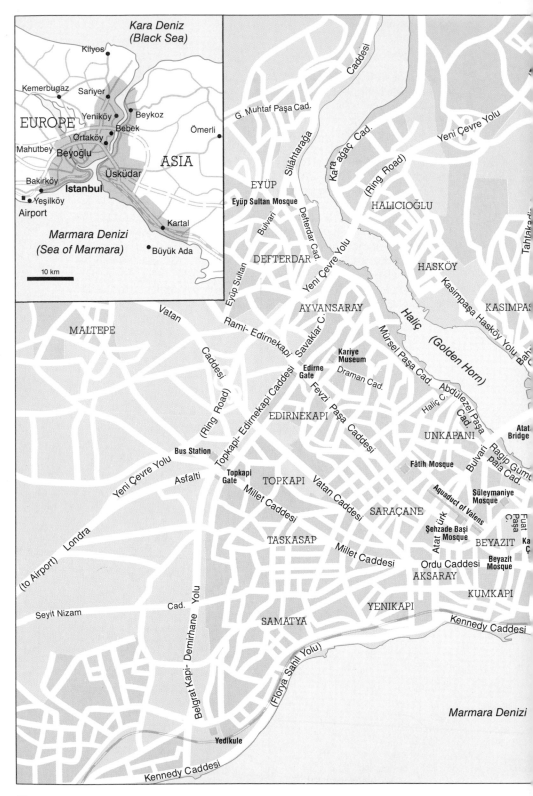

Kara Deniz (Black Sea)

Kilyos

Kemerbugaz · Sariyer

EUROPE · Yeniköy · Beykoz

Ortaköy · Bebek

Mahutbey · Beyoğlu

Üsküdar · ASIA

Ömerli

Bakirköy · İstanbul

Yeşilköy

Airport

Marmara Denizi (Sea of Marmara)

Kartal

Büyük Ada

10 km

Caddesi

Kara ağaç Cad.

G. Muhtaf Paşa Cad.

Silâhtarağa

Yeni Çevre Yolu (Ring Road)

Tahtakad

EYÜP

Eyüp Sultan Mosque

HALICIOĞLU

HASKÖY

KASIMPAŞA Hasköy Yolu

KASIMPAŞ

Bulvari

Defterdar Cad.

DEFTERDAR

Yeni Çevre Yolu

Eyüp Sultan

Haliç (Golden Horn)

Mürsel Paşa Cad.

Abdülezel Paşa Cad.

Haliç C. Cad.

Vatan

MALTEPE

Rami- Edirnekapi

Savaklar C.

AYVANSARAY

Kariye Museum

Draman Cad.

Fevzi Paşa Caddesi

UNKAPANI

Atat Bridge

Caddesi

(Ring Road)

Topkapi- Edirnekapi Caddesi

Edirne Gate

EDIRNEKAPI

Fâtih Mosque

Ragip Gümü Paşa Cad.

Bus Station

Topkapi Gate

TOPKAPI

Vatan Caddesi

SARAÇANE

Aquaduct of Valens

Süleymaniye Mosque

Yeni Çevre Yolu

Asfalti

Millet Caddesi

TASKASAP

Millet Caddesi

Şehzade Başi Mosque

Atatürk Bulvari

Fuat Paşa C.

BEYAZIT

Ka Ç

Londra

(to Airport)

Ordu Caddesi

Beyazit Mosque

AKSARAY

KUMKAPI

Seyit Nizam

Cad.

YENIKAPI

Kennedy Caddesi

Belgrat Kapi- Demirhane Yolu

SAMATYA

(Florya Sahil Yolu)

Marmara Denizi

Yedikule

Kennedy Caddesi

98

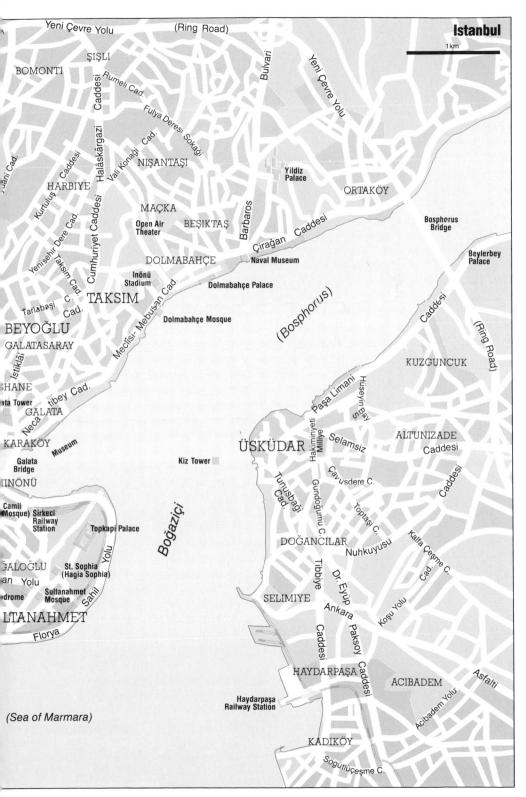

Istanbul

1 km

Yeni Çevre Yolu   (Ring Road)

ŞIŞLI

BOMONTI

Bulvari

Yeni Çevre Yolu

Caddesi

Rumeli Cad.

Fulya Deresi Sokaği

Vali Konaği Cad.

Halaskârgazi

NİŞANTAŞI

Yildiz
Palace

ORTAKÖY

HARBIYE

Kurtuluş

Caddesi

Yenisehir Dere Cad.

Cumhuriyet Caddesi

MAÇKA

Open Air
Theater

BEŞIKTAŞ

Barbaros

Çiragan   Caddesi

Bosphorus
Bridge

Beylerbey
Palace

Taksim Cad.

DOLMABAHÇE

Naval Museum

C.

Tarlabaşi   Cad.

TAKSIM

İnönü
Stadium

Meclisi- Mebusan Cad.

Dolmabahçe Palace

Caddesi

(Ring Road)

BEYOĞLU

Istiklâl

Dolmabahçe Mosque

(Bosphorus)

KUZGUNCUK

GALATASARAY

HANE

itibey Cad.

ta Tower

Neca

GALATA

Paşa Limani

Hüseyin Bay

Hakimiyeti
Milliye

Selamsiz

ALTUNIZADE

Caddesi

Caddesi

KARAKÖY

Museum

Kiz Tower

ÜSKÜDAR

Galata
Bridge

İNÖNÜ

Tunusbaği
Cad.

Çavusdere C.

Gundogumu C.

Toptaşi C.

Kalfa Çeşme C.

Boğaziçi

Camii
Mosque)

Sirkeci
Railway
Station

Topkapi Palace

Yolu

DOĞANCILAR

Nuhkuyusu

ĞALOĞLU

an Yolu

St. Sophia
(Hagia Sophia)

Tibbiye

Dr. Eyüp

Koşu Yolu

drome

Sultanahmet
Mosque

Sahil

SELIMIYE

Ankara Paksoy

LTANAHMET

Florya

HAYDARPAŞA

Caddesi

ACIBADEM

Asfalti

(Sea of Marmara)

Haydarpaşa
Railway Station

Acibadem Yolu

KADIKÖY

Sögütlüçeşme C.

ISTANBUL

The story has it that the city was first established by the Megaran leader, Byzas, in the 7th century BC. Having consulted the oracle of Delphi concerning the foundation of his new colony, he was instructed to settle across from the "land of the blind ones." Encountering a community living at Chalcedon on the Asian shore, Byzas concluded that the earlier colonists had, indeed, been deprived of their sight when they overlooked the superb location across the mouth of the Bosphorus in Europe, and the colony of Byzantium was born.

Remarkably, Byzas was the only one during the ensuing centuries who saw the strategic value of the European shores of the Bosphorus, and, with the exception of the occasional raid by marauding tribes and Persians on the move against ancient Greece, the settlement was left in peace until captured by Septimus Severus in AD 196; Byzantium was then absorbed into the Holy Roman empire.

Even at the time of Constantine the Great, who was in search of an ideal location for the establishment of his New Rome, Byzantium, the settlement atop Seraglio Point, was the second choice. Constantine initially chose the alleged tomb of Ajax on the field of ancient Troy on the Dardanelles for his new city, and had even started reconstruction of the city walls there before he reconsidered, marched on Byzantium to oust its residents, and turned their rustic community into the biggest construction site the world had seen.

Officially founded on November 26, AD 326, Constantine filled his new city with the treasures of the ancient world, resulting in a bizarre and startling mixture of the classical pagan age and the recent Christian era. Never in the west had a city of such magnitude existed, and the contemporaries of that day wrote of the city in one hushed and amazed voice upon their admittance to Constantinople. The city's name itself conjured up images of wealth beyond the dreams of the petty kings and princes of medieval Europe, whose capital cities ranked as villages in comparison with Constantinople, which recorded a population of nearly one million in the 9th century. The main streets of the city were not only paved, but covered, and decorated with columns and fountains. The products of the state monopolies and the exotic goods traded in the capital made the city, in the words of one writer, the "biggest luxury shopping center in the world."

Precious little remains of the city today, save the broken remnants of the great walls and the occasional sacred structure, such as the St Sophia museum, to evoke the memory of the Byzantine city. One theory has it that the closest replica of old Constantinople might be found in the period architecture of Venice, which, emerging as a city of refugees from the Italian mainland, first became Byzantium's lesser partner in trade, then its emulator in sacred and secular architecture, and finally its enemy, allied with the Crusaders to sack the city in 1203. The four golden horses atop the portal of St Mark's

in Venice, removed from the great hippodrome in today's Sultan Ahmet Square, were but a part of that city's war booty from Constantinople, and give a hint of what the older and grander city must once have looked like in its days of power and glory.

Byzantine relics: Aside from the walls, the most salient remains of old Constantinople today are intermixed (and often identical) with the primary Muslim monuments and places of interest in the city. Most are in the vicinity of the **Hippodrome** adjacent to **Sultanahmet Park.** The Hippodrome itself was initially constructed by the Roman Emperor Septimus Severus, but it was Constantine the Great who established the arena – with a crowd capacity of over 100,000 people – as the secular center of his city.

It was here that Justinian's mate, Theodora, first appeared on the stage of history (or so Gibbon informs us) as a dancing girl in a circus troop to catch the eye of her illustrious benefactor and eventual partner. The Hippodrome was also the site of the notorious *Nika* or "victory" riots between the Green and Blue religious factions. Some 30,000 died in five days of urban warfare; St Sophia was destroyed for the second time; and Justinian was nearly driven from his throne.

There are three monuments left in the Hippodrome worth noting: the **obelisk** of **Pharaoh Thutmose**, brought from Karnak in Egypt by Constantine the Great during his general plunder of the portable monuments of the ancient world; the **Serpentine column**, formed by three intertwined snakes, which originally stood at the Temple of Apollo at Delphi; and the **column** of **Constantine VII**, erected in AD 940, but of obscure origin.

The original bronze plates covering the column were carried off to Venice following the Latin sack of the city in 1203. Perhaps the most curious of the three remaining monuments is the Serpentine column, which represents Constantine's eclectic (and not necessarily Christian) decorative tastes for

The Sultan Ahmet or "Blue Mosque" according to an European artist.

his new city; one is obliged to reflect on what the priests and vestal virgins of the various shrines of late antiquity must have thought when the movers (say, 10,000 slaves) arrived to strip them of their ancient relics.

For those with time and imagination, the remains of the **Bucoleon Palace** is several blocks south of the Hippodrome. First built by Constantine, and the very essence of lost Byzantium, it was here that the fabled golden tree with mechanical singing birds once stood. The palace now forms part of the old sea walls facing the Sea of Marmara. Partially destroyed during the riots, and completely sacked during the Latin occupation of the city, only traces of the palace walls, with marble framed windows, remain to remind one of the ostentatious splendor of Byzantium.

St Sophia: The main Byzantine edifice still in the city is the **Hagia Sophia** or **St Sophia** church, now a museum. Dedicated in AD 536 during the reign of Justinian, the church was the architectural wonder of its time, although it was the third such edifice on the site: the first church built on the orders of Constantine's son, Constantinus, burnt in AD 404, while the second structure, built by Theodosius in AD 415, was torched during the *Nika* riots of 532.

The present structure is essentially the creation of Anthenius of Tralles and his assistant, Isidorus of Miletus, who labored for nearly six years before the church could be consecrated on December 26, 537. It was reconsecrated in AD 563 after repairs following an earthquake which ruined the symmetry of the dome. It now measures 101 ft (31 meters) from east to west and 104 ft (32 meters) from north to south, and stands 183 ft (56 meters). Special, thin marble panels absorbed and reflected the light of thousands of candles and lamps, which illuminated the entire building so well that it was used as a lighthouse by ships at sea. The myriad of candles, possibly, accounted for the first great fire that destroyed the original edifice as well as much of the city.

Tradition maintains that the roped-off area, where the emperor's throne

sat, was the center of the world. On the main floor is the "sweating column" where Justinian was said to have cured a migraine by resting his head against the stone, which led to the belief that each of the pillars in the church could cure a specific disease if rubbed against. Centuries of visitors touching the spot has resulted in a deep dent, now framed in brass and called the "holy hole."

When Justinian built the St Sophia, he filled it with decorative mosaics. Later emperors added figural ones, but these were destroyed by the iconoclasts between AD 729 and 843. The mosaics in the church today all postdate that period, and were preserved after the Muslim conquest of the city, thanks to the simple expedient of whitewashing them over; The mosaics were rediscovered only during renovations in the 1930s when Atatürk converted it into a national museum for posterity.

Most of the mosaics on the main floor are dingy and ill lit – you need a pair of strong binoculars with which to see them. More accessible are those on the eastern

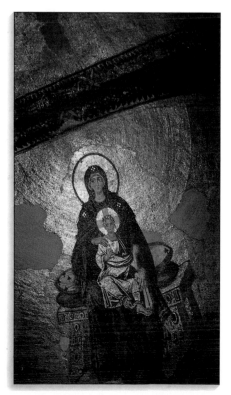

Byzantine mosaic of the Virgin and Child.

wall of the south gallery, showing Christ, John the Baptist and the Virgin Mary. One particular mosaic that should not be missed is located in last bay of the same gallery depicting the Empress Zoe and her husband, Constantine IX Monomachus. The latter's head was superimposed over that of Zoe's first husband, Romanus, the stable boy who seduced the 50-year-old spinster before trying to shuttle her off to a nunnery.

He failed and his face – and his life – were removed from association with the throne forever. The last significant mosaic in the structure is the Donor mosaic, showing Constantine and Justinian giving the city of Istanbul and the St Sophia to the Virgin and Child. It is found over the exit door, and thus easy to miss unless one turns around.

The Basilica Cistern: Diagonally across from the St Sophia and just north of the beginning of the Divan Yolu (or Imperial Way) is the recently renovated **Basilica Cistern**, a wonderfully eerie underground chamber of 336 columns built by Justinian in AD 532 for storing the imperial water supply. It was subsequently used as a dumping ground for all manner of wastes, including corpses. For those who have visited the cistern before the renovation, a surprise is in store: immaculately clean, with sturdy walkways throughout, and replete with tasteful piped-in music and a subtle light-show, the cistern has a magic all its own and is well worth a visit. (Alfred Hitchcock once planned to film part of a whodunit in the old cistern).

The Topkapı Palace: Sources suggest that upon the Turkish conquest of Constantinople and the disappearance of the Second Rome, the Ottoman Sultan Mehmet the Conqueror fancied himself the head of a new world order inspired by Islam, but the heir to all the lands and loyalties of both Constantinople and the older Rome on the Tiber. Indeed, much of Ottoman history is the largely successful expansion of the Ottoman state to the traditional frontiers of Rome in the western Mediterranean (with the exception of Italy, France and Spain), with even greater gains in the north and east against the Rome's and Byzantium's traditional enemy, Persia.

Located right behind the St Sophia, is the **Topkapı Palace**, which was the nerve-center of this far-flung empire. It was the venue of both the sublime, as well as the sordid events of the 500-year Ottoman history, until the construction of Dolmabahçe Palace up the Bosphorus during the mid-19th century.

Built by Mehmet on Istanbul's first hill, overlooking the confluence of the Bosphorus, the Golden Horn and the Sea of Marmara, the sprawling, eclectic compound reflects no one particular architectural stamp. It was elaborated on by every new sultan according to need, while four major fires did little to preserve whatever architectural unity might have existed.

The only original buildings left from the time of Mehmet, are the **Raht Hazinesi**, or Treasury building (his original palace), the inner and outer walls and the *Çinili Köşk* or Tiled Pavilion, which now serves as the **Museum of Turkish Porcelains**.

The Topkapı Palace consists essen-

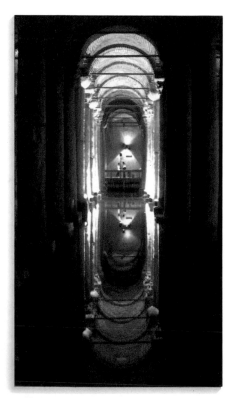

The Yerebatan ("Basilica") Cistern.

tially of three distinct areas, namely the **Outer Palace** (or *Birun*), the **Inner Palace**, (or *Enderun*) and the **Harem**, which are further broken down into various *avlu* or courtyards connected by gates. Over 50,000 people lived and worked on the palace grounds, making it a veritable city within a city, replete with dorms for various craftsmen, gardeners and guards, all with their own distinctive color-coded garb for easy identification: the Topkapı was a very colorful place during its heyday.

In addition to discreet neighboring mosques and baths, the Topkapı even had its own zoo, where lions, elephants, bears and other gifts from foreign rulers were kept. Considerably reduced from its original size (the palace used to extend down to the Sea of Marmara, including today's Sirkeci railway station and the neighboring Gülhane Park), the grounds are still substantial, and the visitor should give one full day to really explore the Topkapı. For those with more than a casual interest, repeated visits are advised.

The "Fruit Room" of the Topkapı Harem.

A rococo marble fountain built in 1728, celebrating the Silver Jubilee of Sultan Ahmet III, sits to the right of the main entrance to the palace, known as the **Bab-ı-Hümayün**, or **Imperial Gate.** Erected by Mehmet in 1478, it leads to the First Courtyard where the Janissaries, the Praetorian Guards of the Ottomans, were once headquartered and where buses now park. To the left upon entering is the **St Eirene Church**, the oldest Byzantine church in Istanbul. Never converted to a mosque, the church was used as an armory, and is open to visitors only when used as a venue for concerts associated with the annual Istanbul Festival.

The second gate, known as the **Bab-ü-Selam** or **Gate of Salutations** is the entrance proper to the Topkapı. Built in a quasi-European style by Süleyman the Magnificent as a result of his Balkan and Central European campaigns. Only the sultan was allowed to ride through, with all others obliged to dismount. Perhaps as a reminder that all should bow the knee, the sultan had a fountain

outside adjacent to the gate used for cleaning the blood from the executioner's axe; the **Executioner's fountain**.

The Harem: Possibly the most exciting part of the Topkapı complex is the *Harem,* or Forbidden Place, where the mother, wives, odalisques and children of the sultans lead their lives, sequestered from the rest of the world. The only men allowed into the *Harem* were the various princes, black eunuchs (color-coded for easier identification) and, during emergencies, the so-called *Zülfülü Baltacılar* or "Firemen with Lovelocks", who were obliged to wear coats with exaggerated collars in order to screen their prying eyes from the women within.

But the *Harem* was hardly the image of a den of unfettered sex and iniquity conjured up by many. The *Valide Sultan* or mother of the sultan, was the effective queen of the domain, followed by the legal wives of the sultan (according to Islamic law they could be no more than four) who had borne him children – next in the pecking order, followed by supervisors, nannies and favorites, as well as servants.

Sex with the sultan was hardly a spontaneous affair, and each new woman would be bathed and prepared before her encounter with the royal personage, the date and time duly recorded. If she became with child, that, too, was recorded, and if the birth resulted in a boy, she acquired the elevated status of *Haseki Sultan.* Submission to the whims of the sultan was not a foregone conclusion, however, and there are instances of *odalıks* (concubines) who refused the sultan's favors and lived to tell the tale.

Several sultans, most notably Osman II, were not fond of women. Osman acquired the habit of putting spikes on his shoes so that when he was obliged to walk through the *Harem*, the grating noise of steel on tile would inform the women to clear out of the way.

Although only 30 of the over 300 rooms in the *Harem* are open to visitors on guided tours, one gets a real sense of the cloistered affects of life within the confines of the building. One of the most peculiar rooms in the complex is the **Veliaht Dairesi** or so-called **Gilded Cage**, where the heir apparent was obliged to live out his life of utter indulgence in preparation to taking ultimate power. Formerly, the young princes were sent out to the provinces with loyal governors to acquire some sense of statesmanship, but in the later days of the empire, this practice was abandoned, leading to spineless leaders inclined only to the internal jealousies and intrigues of the *Harem.*

The Enderun: The entrance to the Inner Palace proper is through the **Bab-üs Saadet** or **Gate of Felicity**, through which only the sultan and his personal aids were allowed to pass without special permission. It is here that the annual production (in mixed Turkish and German) of Mozart's *Abduction from the Seraglio* is staged during the international Istanbul Festival in June-July, and it is difficult to think of a more fitting location. Passing through the Gate of Felicity, one first encounters the **Arz Odası** or **Petition Room**, where the grand vizier studied cases both bold and

The **Kaşıkçı** or "spoon maker's" diamond of Eric Ambler's *The Light of Day* and the film Topkapı based on it.

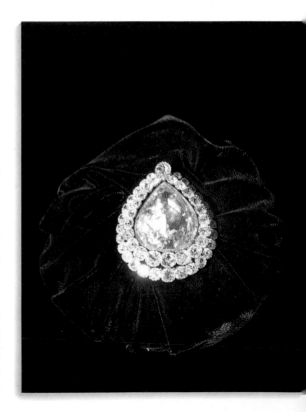

106

banal before passing his recommendations on to the sultan for approval or disapproval.

To the right is the **Treasury**, originally Mehmet the Conqueror's residence, but now the display case for the plethora of gifts received by the sultan from foreign emissaries, as well as objects of art produced by inhouse craftsmen known as the *Ehl-i Hiref*, or People of the Fine Arts. On the left side of the courtyard are the rooms which now house the **Holy Relics** or the various objects allegedly belonging to the Prophet Muhammad and his early companions, ranging from swords to clippings of the Prophet's beard.

Of particular veneration for Muslims is the *Hırka-ı Saadet* or Holy Mantel, which was the center of a grave ceremony following the fast of Ramadan during high Ottoman times. Perhaps the most dubious (if venerated) object in the collection is a letter written on leather, addressed to the Coptic ruler of Egypt, and signed by the Prophet – despite the fact that Muslim tradition maintains he could neither read nor write. The buildings at the back of the courtyard house the portrait and miniature collections of the Topkapı, the latter, especially, are a major source of documentation about the lives of the Ottoman princes in their prime years.

The Fourth Courtyard, entered via narrow walkways from the third, seems to be nearly residential, and consists primarily of several pavilions with exquisite views over the Bosphorus and Golden Horn. The most dramatic of these is the **Baghdad Pavilion**, built to celebrate the Ottoman conquest of that city. Note, too, the **Sünnet Odası** or Circumcision Room, built by Sultan Ibrahim in 1640, possibly in honor of his own wild libido; after years of apparent sterility, the sultan finally found his form and spent his last years in what appears to be a constant orgy, usually performed in front of mirrors.

The tiles in the circumcision room are a riot of disorder, some younger than the building itself, others contemporary or older. Scholars suggest that the hodgepodge effect is the result of the collapse of the empire: short of treasury funds to repair crumbling edifices (especially after the move to the Dolmabahçe), tiles from other buildings were seized and simply slapped in place of those needing repair without regard for form. Today, the bastard tiles are being replaced by newly fired ones in keeping with the original designs.

The **Mecidiye Pavilion**, facing the Bosphorus and the Sea of Marmara is now used as a restaurant specializing in Turkish foods; it is a good place to take a breather, although usually crowded.

The last part of the Topkapı complex is, in fact, outside the inner walls themselves, and consists of three museums downhill from the middle gate. The **Museum of the Ancient Orient** (essentially, a poor man's copy of the much better museum in Ankara dedicated to the same subject); the **Archaeology Museum**; and the **Çinili Kösk** or **Tile Pavilion**. The Archaeology Museum houses an excellent collection of Greco-Roman and Near Eastern antiquities, as well as fine Trojan jewelry. It also has

The Harem according to Bartlett.

an atmospheric tea garden. The Tile Pavilion boasts exquisite examples of Turkish tile-work.

Islamic Istanbul: If the workings of state bureaucracy were stamped in the Topkapı (and later, the Dolmabahçe), Islam, the state religion, found its expression outside the walls of the palace in the dozens of grand mosques whose needle-like minarets spike the city's skyline, making it one of the most distinguished vistas in the world. The prolific number of mosques in the city make an exhaustive account of all of them quite impossible. The traveler would be best referred to a guide devoted specifically to mosques or, alternatively, join a tour that provides interesting details such as the colourful history of the institution and information about the architecture. But the following brief listing should whet the appetite for more.

The most distinctive mosque in old Istanbul is that of **Sultan Ahmet I** or the **Blue Mosque**, due to its exquisite Iznik tiles on the interior walls. Facing the St Sophia across the Sultanahmet Square (with which it shares the limelight in the simple but tasteful Sound and Light Show on summer evenings), it was built between 1609 and 1616 by the architect Mehmet Ağa. A student of the great architect Sinan, the Ağa possibly built the mosque as a means of showing the world that he had outdone both his master, as well as the architects of the St Sophia, which the mosque resembles in many ways.

Whether he succeeded is open to debate, but the mosque, with its 260 windows, six minarets and associated religious school, hospital, caravansary and soup kitchen (the *külliye* or "complete social center" in the Islamic sense) is impressive indeed. Unhappily, the young Sultan Ahmet was able to enjoy his creation for only one year before his death at age 27. Today, the **Museum of Turkish Carpets and Kilims** is behind the mosque, as well as the **Mosaic Museum** in a lower row of commercial shops, whose rents still go towards the upkeep of the mosque.

The Hippodrome with the Sultan Ahmet ("Blue Mosque") in the background.

108

An interesting side trip at this point is the **Ibrahim Paşa Palace** across the Hippodrome from the Blue Mosque. Although today the Museum of Turkish and Islamic Arts, in its time the palace was the finest residential building in Istanbul, inhabited by Ibrahim Pasha, the Grand Vizier under Süleyman. The sultan's wife, Roxelana, persuaded her husband that the Vizier was getting too big for his turban, and after being invited to spend the night at the Topkapı, he was murdered in his sleep and all his possessions seized – a not uncommon fate for Grand Viziers.

The Bazaar: The Divan Yolu, once the avenue of state, down which viziers and pashas trod, is now lined with small and cheap hotels and restaurants, the most famous of which is the **Pudding Shop**, a favorite hangout for old hippies, young travelers and undercover narcotics policemen. Several blocks west, the Divan Yolu changes its name to **Yeniçeri Caddesi** (the Avenue of the Janissaries) which leads into the heart of historical Istanbul.

Lined by lesser (but often beautiful) mosques and tombs tucked in between shops and low budget hotels, the avenue finally ends at **Beyazıt Square,** and the entrance to the **Kapalı Çarşı** or **Grand Covered Bazaar**. The former commercial hub of Istanbul, the Bazaar is today a favorite tourist attraction where all manner of carpets, trinkets and clothes can be purchased for wildly different prices, depending on the mood of the shopkeeper or one's own ability to haggle a $10 item down from an initial bid of 10 times that amount.

Today, many shops have signs announcing fixed prices, but don't take them seriously. A good rule-of-thumb is to half the initial asking price, and then walk away when the merchant feigns being insulted. Without fail, he will rush after you the very moment you set foot outside his shop.

Just west of the Covered Market (lining both sides of the street, which is now called **Ordu Caddesi** or Army Avenue) are the various elements comprising the **Beyazıdiye,** or **Beyazıt Complex,** which

The Grand Covered Bazaar: Images of the past and present.

among other things serves as the primary campus of **Istanbul University**. Students of architectural history note that the construction of the **Beyazıt Mosque** marks the beginnings of the classical age of Ottoman sacral buildings. Clearly inspired by the St Sophia, the domed mosques of the Ottomans soon covered the Islamic world replacing the traditional open courtyard structures favored by the Arabs.

The spire in the centre of Istanbul University is known as **Beyazıt Tower**. Originally constructed of wood and used as a fire tower, it burned in one of the periodic infernos which have plagued the city since earliest times, and was replaced with the present structure in 1828. Before the recent advent of helicopter rides in Istanbul, the tower was perhaps the best observatory to get a bird's eye view of the city, although the 150 wooden stairs to reach the top are a bit rickety.

Five minutes walk north of the Beyazıt Complex, lies the **Süleymaniye**, or **Mosque Complex of Süleyman the Magnificent**, the largest and, perhaps, most impressive design of that extraordinary and tireless architect, Sinan. Construction of the mosques began in 1550, and it was not completed until 1557, nine years before Süleyman's death at the age of 72.

The interior of the mosque is almost square, measuring 190 by 186 ft (58 by 57 meters), the diameter of the dome is 186 ft (57 meters), and its height 154 ft (47 meters). Much less ornate than most of the other imperial mosques, the structure invites one to find a corner to recline and meditate; far away enough from the main bus tour axis, the mosque is never crowded with tourists.

The tombs of Süleyman and his wife, Roxelana, are found in the back garden, through a forest of ornate tombstones. Süleyman's tomb is octagonal and covered with Iznik tiles, while his wife's is smaller and of a peculiar shape: a cylindrical base recessed from the octagonal corners of the building, also adorned by tiles, as well as a rather wordy inscription forming a frieze around the top of the building.

Nearby, and next to the **Aquaduct of Valens** built by the Byzantine Emperor, Valens, is the **Şehzadebaşı**, or **Princes' Mosque**, dedicated to two of Süleyman's sons who died before their time. Designed by Sinan, the noteworthy feature of this mosque is the lack of columns, with the dome resting only on the walls.

"The Süleymaniye is glorious, Sultan Ahmet is beautiful, but it is the Eyüp Mosque which is holy". So the saying goes, and, indeed, after Mecca, Medina and Jerusalem, the **Eyüp Mosque** on the upper reaches of the Golden Horn vies with Mecca, Damascus and Kerbala as the fourth most important place of pilgrimage in the Islamic world. The mosque was originally built in the 15th century under Mehmet the Conqueror on the spot where Eyüb Al-Ansari, an elderly companion of the Prophet Muhammad, fell during the first Arab seige of Constantinople in AD 688. The mosque was reconstructed in the early 19th Century. It is usually crowded with the pious.

The **Golden Horn** itself has been "reconstructed" as of late; previously, the inland body of water was the private lake of the sultans and a favorite place to picnic. With the city's population explosion during the 1950s, coupled with ineffective zoning laws, the once pristine waters became Turkey's Lake Erie, in which no living thing could survive. From 1984, however, the Municipality of Istanbul made cleaning up the area a matter of honor, and officials sent bulldozers to clear it; it is now becoming a pleasant place to spend an afternoon.

Although not an Islamic site *per se*, a visit to the vicinity of Eyüp, the Golden Horn and the city walls of Theodosius should also include a stop at the **Kariye Museum** just inside the Edirne Gate. Originally called the St Savior in Chora (or in the country), the church boasts some of the finest Byzantine mosaics in Istanbul, and indeed the world, depicting dozens of Biblical scenes ranging from the genealogy of Christ to the annunciation of Mary.

The area around the Kariye walls is one of the more pleasant of Istanbul's traditional neighborhoods, if slightly

A view of the Golden Horn from Eyüp.

disfigured by cinderblock apartments dwarfing the older houses. Recently, the Turkish Automobile Association and its infatigable director, Çelik Gülersoy, the man responsible for such projects as the Green House Hotel and Soğukçeşme Street row houses near the St Sophia, have renovated several houses as an inspiration to other home owners to spruce up the area; the fortunate visitor to the Kariye might find Gülersoy at the tea shop facing the church on a Saturday afternoon.

The modern town: Istanbul, happily, is more than just a city of mosques, *medrese* and assorted edifices of another age. Indeed, the modern city – at last count, 11 million and growing daily – with its traffic problems, pollution and eyesore slums, threatens to overwhelm the areas of historic interest. Despite the fact that the city was dethroned as Turkey's capital in 1923, when Ankara was declared the center of political authority in the country, Istanbul has remained the commercial and cultural hub of the nation, where nearly all businesses maintain their head offices, and where all new trends in art, literature, music and film begin.

An immediate comparison is to be made with New York and Washington in this sense, replete with the rivalry felt between residents of the competitive cities. But unlike New Yorkers, an Istanbulite can only sneer at the boring, if functional, new capital – an attitude best summed up by the line regarding the best thing about Ankara: the road returning to Istanbul.

At risk of offending those Istanbulites who chose to live in the newer districts out toward the airport, it can be maintained that modern Istanbul consists of those business areas and associated residential neighborhoods on the northern shore of the Golden Horn, and especially the districts of Taksim, Harbiye, Cihangir and Nişantaşı.

This was not always so. The area of **Karaköy**, (immediately across the Galata Bridge from the New Mosque dating to the 17th century and the Egyptian Bazaar), and **Pera** (the former area

A street in Pera.

of Genoese settlement during the Byzantine period and the neighborhood preferred by Istanbul's non-Muslim minorities and resident foreigners until the last 20 years), were once high-rent residential areas, but then became little more than slums supported by spare parts shops, with only the occasional hint of former wealth. In recent years, though, the areas have been slowly recovering their dignity with reanimating efforts such as the restoration of the old Crimean Church, now called Christ Church.

Still, there is no question that the neighborhood has turned seedy. Perhaps the most shocking example of this deterioration is the two legal **red light districts** here. One is down a muddy alley pinched between Kemeraltı and Necatibey streets – the two main thoroughfares leading from the bridge toward the upper Bosphorus.

The second, more extensive area, is up Yüksek Kaldırım street – the cobblestone alley leading past a 19th-century synagogue toward the Galata Tower. You will know the street for the density of sellers of shirts, socks, shoes and watches and the near total absence of women. The whorehouse area itself is only for those determined to see a little bit of Dante's "Inferno" here on earth. Frisked by a policeman at the entrance to the area, one plunges through the gauntlet of a thousand elbows belonging to gawking men of all walks of life shoving their way to the front of one of the 40-odd shops lining the narrow passageway downhill.

Forget about the concepts of traditional Turkish hospitality and courtesy here, and just try to stay on your feet. The ladies themselves range from "nice-girl-next-door" types to hideous old hags with dyed hair and bellies as large as their busts. Although allegedly controlled by health officials every second day, many of the girls go through a dozen customers a night, and in this day of herpes and AIDS (this is a favorite call for multinational sailors) only those deranged for want of sex should brave the hygienic hazards of the place. Price for the truly hardup starts at around $5 and goes upward, depending on services offered; expect to spend less than five minutes with the lady of your choice.

Elegant district: An alternative way of getting uphill (and thus by-passing both the whorehouses district and the Galata Tower) is to take the **Tünel**, the oldest and shortest subway in the world, with exactly two station stops: one at the bottom of the hill, and the other at the top, at the head of Istiklâl Caddesi and the area known as **Beyoğlu**. The area is now pedestrianised with only old trams running on Istiklal street. Beyoğlu is fast regaining its former glory as the city's most elegant district: stylish new cafés and bars are being opened every other month, streets and buildings are being cleaned and revamped.

Beyoğlu figures large in the 19th-century and early 20th-century history of the city, for it was here that the western powers built their embassies (most are now used as consulates, nearly ridiculous in the case of Sweden or Holland, who must staff their 30-room mansions with two or three functionaries), and gave a decidedly western stamp

Painting a new face for the city.

to an essentially eastern neighborhood. This is the stomping ground of the characters who appear in Eric Ambler's novels about the city, and indeed, many still seem to exist, despite the fact that the area, as a whole, has been depopulated of its original Levantine/White Russian/minority/foreigner mix. Beyoğlu today is mainly an entertainment, shopping and cultural area. It has more cinemas than any other part of the town, many shops including the two most stylish fashion houses, Vakko and Beymen, nightclubs, theaters, and art galleries including Yapi Kredi Bank's exhibition halls and its small private museum in Galatasaray.

Casino à la Turca: Everyone should go to a Turkish club at least once; if you walk around Beyoğlu at night it will be difficult not to, as the doormen tend to be rather aggressive and have been known to literally drag the unwary inside in the dim hope of getting a tip. Drink prices depend on the club; ask before ordering, and be fully aware that any little extra will also be charged.

Almost every club – except the **Maksim's** on Taksim Square and other upmarket establishments with bonafide artists – is stocked with whiskey dollies, whose job it is to get you to buy them round after round of drinks at ridiculous prices on the vague but never fulfilled promise of action later. Unless one is prepared for arguing with the swarm of waiters and bouncers who attend the girls, the best idea is to kindly, but firmly, let them know that neither the first nor the last round is on you.

Somewhere between Maksim's and the down-the-stairs-to-the-smoke-filled-basement variety of clubs, there are several fairly clean casinos that provide an honest show, usually with foreign dancers working for room and board as well as the inevitable (and, sometimes very entertaining) belly dancer. The majority of these casinos, it is sad to note, tend to be pretty low-class, with bored musicians and far too much vibrato on the PA system to cover some poor girl's vocal faults.

Today, there are scores, perhaps hun-

Left, a belly dancer; and **right**, "nightclub row" in Beyoğlu.

114

dreds of clubs in the Beyoğlu and Taksim area, including the **Taxim Night Park**, extremely popular with the jet-set for its disco and transvestite shows as well as its avant-garde decor.

The famous, century-old hotel of Agatha Christie, the **Pera Palas**, is one of the landmarks of Beyoğlu. In fact, it boasts one of the most atmospheric bars and charming dining rooms in all of Turkey, with 19th-century furniture cluttering the halls and lobbies.

If discreet charms and good taste are to be found at the Pera Palas, the other extreme, and a must for all travelers to Istanbul is the famed **Çiçek Paşajı**, or **Flower Passage**, consisting of a series of bistros with imaginative foods served al fresco all summer. In addition to the standard *meze* of white cheese, eggplant and deepfried mussels, one can also acquire such delicacies as goat's eye, whole lamb's head and lymph glands stuffed with spices, all washed down with beer or *rakı* – the aniseed-like national drink – while being serenaded by the wailing strains of wandering mu-

sicians or peripatetic magicians guaranteed to make at least five silly mistakes per show. Old-timers will tell you that the place has never been the same since the top floor collapsed a decade ago, but it makes a great, boisterous evening.

Taksim: Istiklâl Caddesi terminates at **Taksim Square**, the Piccadilly Circus of Istanbul. Dominated by the large and unoriginal **Atatürk Cultural Center**, the venue for most dance, theater and music concerts in the city, the area is also famous for its alternative cultural spots. Although tame by most standards, the **Twenty** and **Fourteen** are the city's primary gay bars.

Just down the street is the **Taksim Sanat Evi**, which offers a good view of the Marmara Sea and the Maiden's Tower in an artistic ambience, and just off to the left of Cihangir Caddesi is the **Istanbul Sinema Derneği** or Istanbul Cinema Association bar-restaurant, known as Arif's or Çiçek. Again, it is an arty sort of bar where journalists, actors and Istanbul yuppies meet.

Farther down Cihangir Avenue, and

Istiklâl Caddesi leading to Taksim.

left after the German Hospital is the **Bilsak Association** housed in a building entirely devoted to lectures, recitals, meetings and, inevitably, late night drinking in the club bar. Again, it is frequented primarily by the Turkish equivalent of the German "Greens". Bilsak also has a sea-side branch in Findikli near the Fine Arts Academy.

In addition to the private bars and clubs in Taksim Square, there are also those within the larger hotels such as the Marmara, Sheraton and Hilton chains. As one might imagine, these are pleasant – often with spectacular views – nevertheless quite expensive and utterly devoid of any local atmosphere.

Readers familiar with Graham Greene, Eric Ambler and other writers who wrote novels set in Istanbul, will shed a private tear to learn that the **Park Hotel**, the former spy center of the city during World War II and the gathering place for the Istanbul intellectual elite within recent memory, is no more: bankrupted, it was sold to a large trading family who almost completed building a tall, bulky and ugly hotel in its place before being stopped by the Municipality. The Municipality is known for its habit of pulling down buildings on the grounds that they are illegal or that they "spoil the skyline of the city" only after the buildings are nearly completed!

The Dolmabahçe Palace: At the bottom of Inönü Caddesi leading down from Taksim to the Bosphorus is the 19th-century **Dolmabahçe Palace** in all its outlandish glory. It was built by Sultan Abdülmecid to compete with his European rivals.

Tons of gold were wasted on it, resulting in the bankruptcy of the state. Abdülmecid died shortly after its completion; his successor and brother, Abdülaziz, was apparently so disgusted with the building that he went and built his own palace, the Beylerbey, across the Bosphorus, ignoring the fact that there was no money left in the till.

True, there are some interesting carpets and objects d'art to be found in the Dolmabahçe, but the general impression it conveys is one of complete irre- **The Dolmabahçe Palace.**

sponsibility with state funds and overwhelming bad taste; one might ungenerously suggest that the last sultan, Mehmet VI, decided to abandon his throne not so much because of the threat of the nationalists under Atatürk, but due to the daunting prospect of having to live out the rest of his days in the gaudy labyrinth of the Dolmabahçe.

Strangely, perhaps, Atatürk himself set up his residence in the Harem section of the palace, and it was here that he died on November 10, 1938, the simple clock in the room noting the exact time, and a crimson Turkish flag over his bed.

The rest of the Taksim area is of little interest to the casual traveler, save for travel-related services: up and down **Cumhuriyet Caddesi** are the myriad travel agencies, restaurants and airline ticketing offices associated with "downtowns" everywhere. Farther down the street, is **Nişantaşı**, the most fashionable residential area in the city proper, and a place where eyes, tired of conservative women dressed in bags and shawls, can study Turkish fashion –

both male and female – at its most ostentatious; the fur and jewel bedraped women of the area even affect a singsong lilt to their Turkish just to impress one another with their cultural level.

The area teems with fashionable bar-restaurants, such as **Ziya's**, **Şamdan** and the **Bronz**, where one can order continental dishes such as steak, roast beef and artichoke hearts. For more of the same, the suburbs of **Levent**, **Etiler** and **Bebek** also offer a quasi-European air for those in need of jazz clubs, Korean restaurants and huge discos, which have become such a craze among the upper crust that mom, dad, Uncle Mehmet and Aunt Ayşe often come along for the ride, dressed in three-piece suits with ascot or tight, leather dresses and ermine stoles, keen on making the scene to the tune of $15 a Scotch. So much for Byzantine mosaics, grand mosques and the traditional garb of those who frequent teahouses around Sultanahmet Square.

A Bosphorus cruise: Better, then, to return to the **Galata Bridge**, cross to the

Left, the
Ortaköy
Mosque; and
right,
Rumlihisarı
on the
Bosphorus.

Sirkeci side, and pick up one of the regular Bosphorus ferries for a cruise up the waterway to see the city as it was meant to be seen. Depending on which ferry you take (the "touristic" boat runs a more defined route, but with the same stops as most others), one first passes out of the mouth of the Golden Horn, with Topkapı and Seraglio Point to your right, and the Dolmabahçe to your left, with the first stop being at **Beşiktaş,** the site of the **Naval Museum**. Unfortunately, the ferry only pauses for a matter of minutes at any given stop save the last, and so once one alights, it is a matter of buying a new ticket and waiting for the next boat.

Next along the waterfront is the **Çirağan Palace**, built, like the Dolmabahçe on the European side, by Abdülaziz. Burnt to a shell in the 1920s, it is now restored into the luxury **Çirağan Hotel Kempinski** complex. Behind it, on the slopes leading uphill, is the **Yıldız Park**, which was an area once overgrown with weeds and trash, but now lovingly restored by Çelik Gülersoy and

his Touring Association and a favorite place for lovers, joggers and those seeking a moment of peace and quiet away from the city, offering such elegant cafes as **Makta Köşkü** and **Çadir Köşkü**.

Just beneath the first Bosphorus Bridge, the once modest village **Ortaköy** has recently been turned into a colorful pedestrian quarter with galleries, gift shops and ambitious bars and restaurants. Around the jetty square an artisans' market takes place on Sundays. The ferry jags across the Bosphorus to such quaint and quiet suburbs as **Kanlıca** on the Asian side (famous for its yogurt); **Arnavutköy** (Albanian Village) on the European side; and **Anadoluhisarı** (Anatolian Castle) on the Asian side once more before gliding past the latter's counterpart, the **Rumelihisarı** (Thracian Castle) on the European side again. The two castles may look quaint and innocuous enough today, but working in tandem, they were used with great effect to choke off all aid to beleaguered Constantinople during the final siege of the city in 1453.

Geopolitical strategists will be reminded why the Russians – be they Czarist or Soviet – have always regarded the Turkish straits as the lock to their backdoor, a fact driven home by the sheer volume of Soviet shipping through the Bosphorus and the Dardanelles everyday.

As the ferry boat passes under the second Bosphorus bridge, the tumult of the city fades away to be replaced by the sounds of tiny fishing boats hauling in the day's catch. An occasional Romanian or Soviet oil tanker sails by, underlining the importance of the Turkish Straits for the Black Sea nations.

You can disembark at Yeniköy, Sarıyer, Beykoz or any of the quaint villages along the upper Bosphorus to dine at one of the dozens of fish restaurants. Try some *lüfer,* or bluefish, or red mullet, and also order an assortment of *meze* dishes, including fried mussels, roka salad, white cheese and tomatoes. Take a sip of *rakı* and contemplate Istanbul, the city of 1001 nights, and organize your next move into the vast hinterland that is modern Turkey.

Left, winter on the Bosphorus. **Right**, the Bosphorus Bridge, linking Europe and Asia.

GREEN BURSA

"Green Bursa" as the Turks lovingly call their old capital is a jewel of a city, nestled against the verdant foothills of Uludağ, the Mount Olympus of the ancients. According to Pliny the Younger, who was appointed governor of Bursa by the Roman Emperor Trajan, a city was first founded on the site by the Bythynian King Prusias in 550 BC at the instigation of the great Carthaginian general Hannibal.

It was Prusias who gave his name to the city "Proussa." Later the city was held by the Romans and became a prosperous spa. Under the Byzantines the district of Çekirge was further embellished with baths and palaces. Still, Bursa remained a sleepy Byzantine resort town overshadowed by the more important neighboring town of Nicaea (now modern Iznik).

Bursa's days of glory began with its capture in 1326 by Orhan, son of Osman, the eponymous founder of the Ottoman state. The 13th-century Arab traveler Ibn Battuta wrote of Orhan Gazi that he was "the greatest of the Turkmen kings, and the richest in wealth, lands and military forces, possessing nearly 100 fortresses which he is continually visiting for inspection and putting to rights."

Until the capture of Bursa, the Ottomans had been little more than a frontier Turkish tribe, alternating between tending their flocks and raiding their sedentary neighbors. Bursa was their first capital in the true sense of the word, and remained so until 1416. The early Ottoman rulers lavished money and care on the town, which is considered by many to be Turkey's preeminently "Turkish" town.

The present day form of the city was laid out in those years, and the main districts, setting aside the modern urban sprawl, are still clustered around the mosques and religious foundations built by the first six Ottoman sultans. Bursa still glows with the civic pride which must have been felt by its first Turkish citizens in the 14th century as they stepped past the newly built mosques and monuments.

The industrial prosperity of the city, the fifth largest in Turkey (due to, perhaps, the large numbers of Turks from the former Balkan provinces of the Empire, evincing the typical immigrant qualities of thrift and industry), has dictated a certain unsightly swelling of warehouse, factory and highway, and there is too much traffic. Nonetheless, for the visitor, the older quarters of the town present an unrivaled display of early Ottoman architecture, including some buildings which must be counted among the loveliest in all Turkey.

Mineral baths: Most of Bursa's best hotels are located in the hot spring suburb of **Çekirge** on the hill above the town's popular recreation park (Kültür Park), which has a large selection of excellent restaurants serving traditional Turkish food. Bursa's best hotel is the **Çelik Palas**, a grand, art nouveau building with a beautiful marble pool, traditional Turkish bath and sauna. Most of the hotels also have their own hot

Left, the Koza Han in Bursa. Right, studying the Quran.

mineral baths, with marble basins at which to wash. The mineral waters gush out of the mountainside at temperatures ranging from 37 to 75 degrees Celsius, and are rich in iron, sulfur and other minerals. The **Yeni Kaplıca**, built in 1552 by Rüstem Pasha, and the **Eski Kaplıca**, erected by Justinian in the 6th century, are just two of Bursa's many historic spas.

In addition to the Kültür Park restaurants, there are several fish restaurants tucked away behind a fishmonger's on the main road in Altıparmak, almost in the center of the city. These fish restaurants have something of the lively, *meyhane* (tavern) atmosphere of some Istanbul restaurants. Nor is a visit to Bursa complete without a taste of one of the city's gastronomic specialities, *Iskender kebabı,* consisting slices of meat roasted on a vertical revolving spit laid on flat bread and drenched in tomato sauce, yogurt and melted butter. The dish was first created by Iskender Bey, whose sons still manage a restaurant midtown, where however much the western palate might crave a beer to wash down the meal, the only thirst quenchers that are available are the traditional *ayran* (a yogurt drink), grape juice and Coca Cola.

Early Ottoman architecture: The Turkish Historical Monuments Commission lists over 125 mosques in the city of Bursa alone. Of these, unquestionably the most important, interesting and beautiful are the foundations of the first six Ottoman sultans.

A good place to start the tour of Bursa is in the heart of the old city – the market quarter founded by Orhan Gazi in the 14th century – which is still the commercial center of town. Work was in progress on it from 1340, and successive sultans added to it to provide income for their foundations or to facilitate the thriving trade which provided wealth for the state.

Plunge into this shopping area, crowded with Bursa shoppers inspecting local wares laid out along the narrow **The Grand** alleys and passages lined with small **Mosque in** shops and dealers. You will see the **Bursa**.

traditional goods for which Bursa is famous, including towels, knives and silk, as well as a selection of antiques aimed at visitors.

The heart of the bazaar area is the **Bedesten**, an impregnable building for the store and sale of valuable goods, with massive doors in each of its walls, which are still locked every night. It was built by Sultan Beyazıt I on the site of the earlier building by Orhan Gazi. Today it houses shop after shop of goldsmiths. Part of the revenue of the Bedestan went to Orhan Gazi's nearby mosque foundation, while the majority went to support Beyazıt's own foundation of the Ulu Cami. This is a typical example of the interchange between commerce and good works and piety under the Ottomans.

Amid the narrow, bustling streets is a group of stone *hans* with shops and storehouses built around courtyards with trees and fountains. Of these, Orhan built the much restored **Emir Han**, the earliest example of an Ottoman *han*, built in accordance with the requirements of

inner city commerce: a courtyard, a pool and trees surrounded by rooms which could be used as shops, storage area or dwellings. One of the grandest of the Hans is the **Koza Han**, on the same two storied plan around a courtyard. In the center of the courtyard is a tiny octagonal mosque, built over a fountain. Not far from the Koza Han is the **Orhaniye Mosque** built in 1339 by Sultan Orhan. Despite its rather massive and impressive five-bay porch adorned with Byzantine columns and the charming ornamentation in the brickwork above the porch, the mosque seems rather simple and unassuming today by contrast with the bustle of the commercial district.

Perhaps this is appropriate for the mosque of Orhan Gazi, who died a simple fighting man, not so very distant from his sheep tending ancestors, though he was the brother-in-law of a Byzantine emperor, the friend and ally of the Genoese, and near master of Thrace. The mosque is an early example of the so-called *eyvan* plan, with a central

The Tomb of Orhan Gazi.

domed hall (which in Orhan's time was probably open to the elements with a fountain beneath to catch rainfall.)

The central hall is surrounded on three sides by domed chambers, with the *mihrap* in the domed chamber facing the entrance. The *eyvan* plan of a central covered hall surrounded by rooms was developed by the Ottomans from the plan of Seljuk Medrese in Central Anatolia, and the mosques of Central Asia and Iran. It is thought that the rooms off the central hall were used as Dervish quarters.

To the west of the market, next to Cumhuriyet Caddesi, rises the massive bulk of **Ulu Cami**, the **Grand Mosque**, built by Beyazit I in 1399–1400 with the booty from his victory at Nicopolis in Macedonia in 1396. Beyazıt is said to have vowed before the battle that he would build 20 mosques if victorious, and then to have hit on the rather shabby compromise of building a single mosque with 20 domes instead.

The mosque remains the religious and social center of conservative Bursa and dominates the surrounding area like a great fortress. The walls of rough-hewn blocks of warm yellow stone are pierced at intervals by windows. On three sides, doors surrounded by carved marble portals are set into the walls. One of these is said to have been added by Tamerlane. The effect of size and space is continued within. Five rows of four domed units, supported by huge pillars decorated with calligraphic renditions of holy names divide up the interior space.

Beneath the central dome, somewhat higher than the others, is a marble pool and fountain. The earliest Ottoman mosques, in Bilecik and Iznik, are small single-room interiors, covered by one dome, with the main architectural interest in the means of transition from the square wall to the circular dome. Beyazıt's Ulu Cami is a development of that simple plan, being 20 of these units, set side by side, thus achieving grandeur and monumentality by sheer size alone. It is not a graceful building, but it is impressive.

The interior of the Grand Mosque.

The Green Mosque: Leaving the market area, continue along the main road until you reach the traffic junction known locally as Heykel because of the statue of Atatürk there, and follow the yellow visitor signs to the **Yeşil Cami**, or Green Mosque, an exquisite complex built in 1419 by Çelebi Sultan Mehmet. One is immediately struck by the Green Mosque's refinement and luxurious fittings. The outside is almost all marble, wth delicate carving and a band of turquoise tile decoration around the windows. Within, the eye is immediately drawn to the richness of the tile decoration with its marvelous intricacy of design and color. Circles, stars and geometric motifs in turquoise, green, white and blue succeed and supplant each other in an endlessly changing composition which in its harmony and complexity can be none other than a representation of the Divine Heavens.

In such Islamic design, rigorous for all its lush use of color, the eye cannot summarize the pattern and repose as in western art; the design is boggling.

The interior of the Green Tomb.

By the gorgeously decorated *mihrap* a neat little inscription in Persian records that the tiles are the work of the master craftsmen of Tabriz, a thousand miles to the east in Iran. We know nothing of how or why the master craftsmen came to Bursa, but their magnificent works here have outlasted the tiles of their native city. The Green Mosque, like the Orhaniye, is an *eyvan*-type mosque, with a fountain in the middle of the central hall and raised prayer halls on all four sides. To the right and left of the central hall, doors open to rooms with elaborate stucco shelving and fireplaces. The function of these rooms is made a little clearer by the tile inscription in Persian over the doors, lauding Çelebi Sultan Mehmet and wishing woe upon such of his enemies as should care to threaten him. This secular message seemingly implies a secular purpose for the rooms. Were they used for royal audiences or for planning battle strategy? We cannot know. Immediately to the right and left of the entrance, narrow stairs lead to the richly decorated apartments of the sul-

tan, overlooking the prayer hall. Ask the mosque attendants for permission to ascend, bearing in mind that their policy is to discourage large groups from going upstairs. Patience – and even a little pleading – may be necessary, but for the student of Islamic tile decorations, it is worthwhile.

Next to Green Mosque is the **Yesil Türbe**, or Green Tomb of Çelebi Sultan Mehmet, perhaps the loveliest building in all Bursa. Its gloriously tiled exterior is a reminder that many other buildings in Bursa originally had radiantly colored tiled domes which were destroyed in earthquakes or lost in restorations. Walk slowly around the tomb to enjoy the extraordinary turquoise of the plain tiles and the richness of the patterned tiled lunettes over the seven windows. Within, each wall is decorated with plain turquoise tiles on which is set an elaborate lozenge of patterned tiles.

The exception is the wall facing Mecca, on which a richly decorated tiled *mihrap* is placed. In the center of the tomb is the extraordinarily elaborate, almost frivolous tomb of Çelebi Sultan Mehmet himself. Was it the difficult years fighting for the throne after the ignominious death of his father Beyazıt the Thunderbolt that made him crave this luxury? Or was it simply the availability of good craftsmen and the wealth of the Ottoman state that brought into being this candy box of a tomb? To the side of the sultan's are the tombs of his five daughters in a lovely variety of blues and designs, making one wonder if choosing tomb patterns was a popular pastime at court.

The Green Mosque affords a glorious view over the city and plain of Bursa. Ahead on a rocky outcrop one sees the complex of Beyazıt I; slightly to the right, set among the cypresses of a large graveyard is the mosque of Emir Sultan, an 18th-century rebuilding of a mosque which was built originally in the 15th century in honor of the mystic and holy man Emir Sultan.

The Beyazıt Mosque: The complex of Beyazıt I is reached by descending sharply from the Green Mosque and

The Green Tomb of Mehmet I.

walking through a quiet neighborhood of small houses, asking directions until one climbs a steepish slope to the outcrop on which the complex was built. The Beyazıt Mosque, built in 1390–95, is a bold, impressive building, which makes clear the architectural heritage which produced the Green Mosque, although the former building does not have the delicacy and the lavish decoration of the latter.

Nearby is Beyazıt's tomb. His body was brought back to Bursa by his son Süleyman Çelebi after his unhappy death at Aksaray, a prisoner of the Central Asian conqueror Tamerlane. Reviled by subsequent sultans for his defeat, Beyazıt lies in an unpretentious tomb, where even in death his humiliation continued, as when Murat IV visited Bursa with the express purpose of kicking the tomb.

The Hüdavendigâr Mosque: The mosque built by Beyazıt's father Murat I Hüdavendigâr in 1366–85, is located in Çekirge, on the left of the main road. Across the road is the tomb of the war-

The Muradiye Complex.

rior sultan in a lovingly tended garden. The mosque's square exterior recalls an Italian building, with its mellow brick arches and patterns. Some historians have suggested that it was constructed by a Genoese architect, but there is no concrete evidence for this.

Within, the interior is a pleasant rendition of the *eyvan*-style mosque, but with a major difference: the second floor is a conventional *medrese*, with cells around an imaginary courtyard, which is in reality the central dome of the mosque. Scholars have had a field day speculating on the reason for this unique arrangement. Some suggest that the rooms below were for dervishes, while the *medrese* above was for "conventional" Islam, and that its position above represents some sort of victory over the heterodoxy of mysticism. Today, alas, only the bottom floor is open to visitors, representing a victory of bureaucracy over curiosity.

The Muradiye Complex: Descend from Çekirge, and turn to the right at a signpost to the Muradiye Mosque complex,

built in 1425–26. Set in a garden of earthly delights, this mosque is a blessed haven of peace and tranquility. Above the portico, brick patterns highlighted in blue tiling represent heavenly spheres and stars. Thunderbolts in blue glazed tiles are set into the marble on the right of the entrance. This mosque is also built on the *eyvan* plan, but with a more unified interior space than hitherto. Around the *mihrap* are bold plain blue and white tiles.

In the lovely garden are twelve tombs of various styles. Murat II's own tomb is here, the simplicity of the catafalque covered in bare earth and open to the elements in astonishing contrast to the luxury of the Green Tomb where his father Çelebi Sultan Mehmet is buried. Like all the early Ottoman sultans, Murat was a renowned fighter on the battle-field, the scourge of Europe, yet he was also attracted to the life of the mystic and contemplative. Eschewing pomp and circumstance, he chose to be buried here under the rain and stars.

Deeper in the garden, past flower beds or roses and lilies edged with box hedges is the tomb of Cem Sultan, one of the most tragic figures of Ottoman history. Cem was the favorite son of Mehmet II, and, upon his death, there was a race between his two sons to reach Istanbul. Beyazid II was first and declared himself sultan. The two brothers fought briefly, and Cem then fled abroad, only to be used as a pawn in the tawdry intrigues of international politics. He was eventually murdered in exile, poisoned by the Borgia Pope Alexander in Rome. A poet and man of culture, Cem's ascension to the throne might have considerably changed the course of Ottoman history. His verse bitterly evokes the pain of separation from his homeland. Now he rests within the tomb built for his nephew, a building of great beauty and peace, lined with gilded octagonal blue tiles.

Nearby, Süleyman the Magnificent's unlucky son, Şehzade Mustafa, strangled in his father's tent with a bow string amid court intrigues, lies in a tomb lined with Iznik tiles covered with hyacinths, **Uludağ national forest and ski resort.**

tulips and blossoms. These tombs are sometimes locked, but the custodians are glad to open them up for occasional interested visitors.

The Muradiye is situated in a pleasant old quarter. Across the square from the mosque is a 17th-century Ottoman house, restored and open to the public. One may go on foot up the steep hill from the Muradiye to the citadel. Here are buried Osman and Orhan Gazi. Dating from the 19th century, their present tombs were built after their former burial place, a Byzantine monastery, collapsed in an earthquake.

Uludağ: On a visit to Bursa, take the opportunity to go up Uludağ National Park, a richly forested mountain area, which also boasts Turkey's premier ski resort, a favorite hangout for the pretentious and wealthy. Scores of over-expensive hotels have mushroomed at the bottom of the limited slopes, making what would normally constitute intermediate slopes into obstacle courses that require expert control. Serious skiers should look elsewhere for their sport,

such as Kayseri or Palandöken/Erzurum. Off season, however, the National Forest area is worth a day trip at the very least, especially for those interested in natural history or just good fresh air. In spring and summer, there are mountain brooks, wild flowers and opportunities for long walks up to the tarns on the summit, above the ski resort and its hotels, some of which remain open for the quiet summer season.

A cable car departs several times daily from the center of the town, but note that the service may be cancelled without notice depending on the weather. By road, the ascent is about an hour. Within the National Park, *Kendin Pisir/Kendin Ye* ("Grill Your Own") meat restaurants abound, particularly in the Sarıalan picnic area.

Nicaea: Fifty miles (80 km) from Bursa and easily reached by car or bus from either Bursa or Yalova is **Iznik**, the former Byzantine town of Nicaea. Now little more than a shabby lakeside village, Iznik boasts a glorious past, and has the buildings and ruins to prove it. Iznik is worth a visit for its attractive lakeside situation alone, which provides pleasant walking and fishing. There are several restaurants and simple hotels by the lake. The Roman Byzantine walls and four gates stand almost intact and the ruins of the Byzantine Basilica of Saint Sophia are now the museum.

In addition to being the site of two ecumenical councils, Nicaea also served as the Byzantine capital following the sack and occupation of Constantinople by the Crusaders in the 13th century. During its hundred years as capital, the city flourished, with substantial additions to its fortifications and sacral buildings. The Ottomans captured Nicaea in 1331, renaming it Iznik. Both the early sultans and their chief men of counsel built mosques and other charitable institutions here. Following the conquest of Constantinople, Iznik became the center of the ceramics industry when Selim the Grim sent 500 Persian potters and their families from Tabriz to settle in the town. The extraordinary tiles which adorn the great Ottoman mosques of the classical period were all produced in here in court controlled kilns, which numbered a total of some 375 in 1575.

One of the more interesting Islamic monuments in Iznik is the Haci Özbek Mosque which, built in 1332, owns the distinction of being the earliest dated Ottoman mosque. The **Yeşil Cami**, or Green Mosque, built in 1378–92 during the reign of Murat I by Hayrettin Çandarlı is an interesting example of an early Ottoman mosque with a Seljuk-looking minaret. Near the Yeşil Cami is the archaeological museum housed in the *imaret*, or soup kitchen, of Nilufer Hatun, wife of Orhan Gazi. She was a beautiful and distinguished Greek lady whom Orhan Gazi left in charge of affairs of state during the time he was in the field. One remarkable exhibit to be seen in the museum is an anonymous Ottoman lady's tombstone inscribed with the pious wish for plenty of dancing boys in heaven.

Yalova: On the shores of the Gulf of Izmit is the town of Yalova, a historic spa-town, now popular with middle-class Turks as a seaside resort as it is not only accessible from Bursa by road, but also connected to Istanbul by daily ferry service. The excellent **Turban Hotel** at the spa, some 8 miles (12 km) inland, is on the site of hot springs which have been frequented since Roman times. A few ruins and antiquities attest to this lengthy past.

Mudanya: On the coast of the Marmara Sea near Bursa is the small town of Mudanya, also a popular seaside spot for locals. Mudanya is where the Turkish nationalists negotiated an armistice in 1922 with Britain, Italy and France, thus narrowly avoiding a fresh war with the Allies who were in occupation of substantial parts of Turkey, including Istanbul and Thrace. There is a beautiful, unspoiled coastline beyond Mudanya with olive groves on the hills and small fishing ports. A number of the mosques were formerly Byzantine churches, including that at Zeytinbağı. There are no hotels in these small places, but there are many fine spots at which to pitch camp.

The walls of Nicea (Iznik).

THE STORY OF SILK

It was the Chinese who first realized that the small white worms which infested the leaves of the mulberry trees spin themselves a cocoon whose gossamer threads can be used by man to produce fabric of a filmy lightness but of remarkable strength. For some 4,000 years the Chinese jealously guarded their secret and monopolized the market in the west for their silken goods.

In the 6th century, however, two Russian monks succeeded in stealing a quantity of the precious silkworm eggs, smuggled their treasure out of China in a hollow bamboo staff, and brought the "golden eggs" to the Byzantine Empire. During the latter part of Justinian's reign, the cultivation of silk became a state industry which the Ottoman Turks inherited when they became the new lords of Asia Minor.

The Turks encouraged the development of both the local manufacture of silk as well as the traditional international silk trade from the far east to the west. Under the Ottomans, much raw silk was imported from Iran to be woven in the court workshops of Bursa, but the constant wars between the Turkish and Persian states hampered this trade with the result that more raw silk was produced within the empire.

Silk brocade and velvet weaving were of a very high order indeed during the halcyon days of the Ottomans, attested to by the 2,500 items on display in the wardrobe collection of the Topkapı Palace Museum in Istanbul, including caftans. Indeed, when Sultan Selim I took Tebriz in northwestern Iran in 1514, part of his booty were 91 Bursa-made garments, the Safavid rulers of Persia apparently preferring Ottoman silks to their own.

By the 19th century, after long years of slow decline, the weaving industry fell on hard times, with Turkey becoming a mere supplier of raw silk.

Fortunately, state intervention led to the re-establishment of silk cultivation and the opening of modern factories, and today, Bursa is the center of the modern Turkish silk industry, with 300 companies involved with the manufacture of silk for the domestic market. Seventy percent of the silk produced is used in the weaving of silk carpets, the best known of which is the *Hereke* type.

A good time to visit Bursa is in July, when an annual silk cocoon fair is held

in the Koza Han, an historical structure in the middle of the old town, where villagers from around Bursa who have nurtured the silkworms for the past 6 weeks bring in sacks of white cocoons to sell.

Merchants now say that they are unable to buy enough silk, while villagers seem increasingly reluctant to raise silkworms which they regard as a chancy and troublesome business compared with the growing of sure-profit crops. How much longer the trade will last is a matter of conjecture, but further automation seems inevitable.

A moth breaks out of its cocoon.

EDIRNE

Due to its position at the junction of the great rivers, Maritsa and Tunca, **Edirne** has been a settlement since prehistoric times. It fell under the sway of the Romans in the 2nd century BC, and a visit by the Emperor Hadrian led to its being named Adrianopolis, in 123–124 AD. Initially a Roman fort, Adrianopolis became a provincial capital too, and its importance was enhanced when Constantinople became capital of the Eastern Roman Empire. Over the years, Adrianopolis was often threatened by invading barbarians on the edge of the empire. First the Goths, and then the Bulgars and Crusaders upset the calm of the provincial city. At last in 1361 the last set of intruders, the Ottoman Turks, captured the town, which surrendered during the flood season of the year.

Edirne, as Adrianople became known, was the capital from 1416 until 1453 and knew days of peace and security for some 500 years. The Ottoman Court retired to Edirne for long hunting holidays to escape the suffocating heat of Istanbul, and used to break their journeys in Edirne during the course of campaigns in Europe.

But with the decline of the Ottoman empire in the 19th century and advent of the nationalist movements for independence, Edirne's secure tranquility was over. Edirne was occupied four times, by the Russians in 1829 and 1878, by the Bulgarians in 1913 and by the Greeks in 1920. The town was recaptured by Enver Pasha to tremendous popular acclaim in 1913, while the Greeks were in occupation for a full 2 years until 1922, when they were dislodged by the terms of the armistice at Mudanya.

Not only was Edirne the scene of occupation, hardship and privation within living memory, but it was also an entrepot for thousands of refugees from all over the former European provinces of the empire. Not surprisingly, the town's population fluctuated tremendously during these troubled times, and has still not returned to its former strength.

Today, however, Edirne is probably visited mostly because of its proximity to the Greek and Bulgarian frontiers. Many overland travelers pass through Edirne and consequently the town has a somewhat cosmopolitan air which contrasts oddly with its other function as a sleepy market town.

Edirne, however, is a veritable museum of Ottoman architecture, but her great monuments stand rather forlornly and have an unkempt air. Work is only just beginning on their restoration, by contrast with the beautifully kept buildings of Bursa, which Edirne succeeded as the Ottoman capital in 1416.

It is not only Edirne's historic monuments that are a bit down at heel. Edirne possesses no excellent hotel; one has to make do with the **Sultan Hotel**, whose pleasant gardens belie the dank and musty rooms. For a time it was possible to stay in the 16th-century **Rüstem Paşa Caravansary**, beautifully, if plainly, restored as a hotel. It seems the project

Left, the Selimiye Mosque Complex in Edirne. **Right**, Gypsy lad and painted wagon.

was not a success, and the hotel was briefly a brothel before closing down all together. It is quite shut up these days and one may not even peer into the spacious courtyards.

Edirne does have several pleasant restaurants. In town there is the **Çatı Lokantası** and the restaurant of the Sultan Hotel. Just out of town on the Karagas Road by the Tunca River is a recreational area, with tea and beer gardens, and the **Lalezar** and **Villa Restaurants**, with lovely river views, serving rather dry river fish as well as the usual restaurant fare.

Principle monuments: The first great Ottoman building in Edirne is the **Eski Cami**, located in the heart of the town on the E5 motorway. Built between 1403 and 1415, the mosque is modeled on the earlier Ulu Cami of Bursa, being a rectangular building divided into nine-domed units. Opposite Eski Cami is the **Bedesten**, built in 1418, for the storage and sale of the most valuable items of commerce, its revenues in trust for the upkeep of Eski Cami.

The 17th century Turkish traveler, Evliya Çelebi, waxed lyrical on the precious stones he saw here, "worth several Egyptian treasuries" and noted that there were 60 night watchmen to guard the treasures. What better indication can there be of Edirne's decline into provincial obscurity than the disappointing array of goods on sale in the Bedestan today? Nearby stands the great caravansary built by Sinan for the Grand Vizier Rüstem Pasha, now closed up.

Farther along the E5 road, one sees the entrance to the covered market built by Sinan in 1569 for another Grand Vizier, Semiz Ali Pasha. On the other side of the main road, behind tea gardens, is the Üç Şerefeli Camii, the mosque of the Three Balconied Minarets. Built between 1438 and 1447 in the time of Sultan Murat II, this mosque represents a complete stylistic innovation in early Ottoman architecture. For the first time a massive central dome was placed over a rectangular floor plan, marking the first step towards that obsession in Ottoman architecture with

The Rüstem Paşa Caravansary.

the centralization of interior space beneath a crowning dome. Not surprisingly, the architect had some difficulty with the realization of his dramatic conception, as evidenced by the excessively massive pillars supporting the dome and the awkwardly wedge-shaped areas filled by turret-like little domes at the sides. Although this is an experimental building, the interior breathes strength and reassurance. The exterior has beautiful decorative details in the pleasant local red sandstone.

The pretty courtyard with its arcades of pillars is the first such courtyard to be built by the Ottomans, and the three minarets, each decorated in a different pattern, were the tallest in Edirne till the Selimiye Mosque was built. Each of the balconies is approached by separate staircases within the same minaret, a miracle of engineering. Marvelous views of Edirne and the surrounding countryside are to be had from the minarets. You must ask permission to ascend, and be warned that minaret climbing is pretty **The Hospital** arduous exercise.
of Beyazıt II.

The Selimiye: It is not difficult to find the **Selimiye Mosque**, which towers over Edirne on its hill. This masterpiece, considered by many to be the highest attainment of Ottoman architecture, was built between 1569 and 1574 by the Ottoman master architect Sinan for Sultan Selim II. Sinan himself considered the Selimiye to be his greatest work. He was 84 when he oversaw the construction of this supreme example of Ottoman architecture.

The mosque is approached through a small *arasta* or shopping arcade, selling holy souvenirs, which was added alongside the mosque by Sultan Murad III. From the outside, the Selimiye has a delicacy and intimacy not found in the other great imperial Ottoman mosques of Istanbul. The soft red Edirne sandstone has been used extensively and effectively in decorative details, particularly in the courtyard over the arches of the arcades.

Within, one is awed by the extraordinary sense of absolute space and light conveyed by the great floating dome

supported by eight stately pillars marching in an orderly circle. One does not at first realize that the mosque is built on a rectangular plan, and that indeed this is the ultimate development of the plan used by the architect of the Üç Serefeli about 120 years earlier.

The rectangular plan is cunningly masked by an arrangement whereby the lower floor of the side galleries is open to the outside, and the upper floor open to the inside, thus altering the dimensions of the internal space. Around the *mihrap* and in the sultan's gallery to the left of the *mihrap* are exquisite Iznik tiles. The stained glass and marble work of the mosque are outstanding examples of their crafts. Behind the mosque, at the edge of the complex, the *medrese* is now in use as a museum, whilst in a modern building behind and below the complex is Edirne's other museum.

Other monuments: Follow the road which leads down out of the center of town behind the Selimiye and past the museum. A small mosque built on a hillock will appear in the near distance.

This is the **Muradiye Mosque** built by Sultan Murat II in 1434. Though barely out of the town, this little mosque, said to have been built initially as a Mevlevi convent, has the peaceful air of a country church. You will probably have to send specially for the *imam* or wait for prayer time to have the mosque unlocked, but the interior is well worth seeing.

Built on a simple T-plan in accordance with the *eyvan* style of mosque so common in early Ottoman architecture, the mosque is distinguished for the beautiful tiles of the *mihrap* and surrounding area. The *mihrap* has much in common with that in the Green Mosque in Bursa, and the hexagonal plain turquoise tiles interspersed with chinoiserie-style blue and white tiles are close to some of the tiles in Bursa's Green Tomb. Notice too the wall decoration on the central arch dividing the two domes for it is a rare example of original 15th century work.

Back in the center of town by the Üç Serefeli Camii, take the side road past the **Bath of Sokollu Mehmet Pasha** (built in the 16th century by Sinan). In the small streets behind the bath stands the remaining tower of the **Castle of Edirne**, which was built on the foundations of the Roman fort here. The castle was allowed to collapse when Edirne was a prosperous Ottoman town, secure within the bosom of the empire. Today the one surviving tower is used as a fire station. Just after the Sokollu Bath it should be possible to board a minibus to **Yeni Imaret**.

The minibus will take you over bridges and dykes out into the countryside, where you will suddenly find laid out before your eyes the gleaming white complex built in 1484 to 1485 by Sultan Beyazıt II. This complex, which consists of mosque, hospital, medical school, soup kitchen, pharmacy, bath, kitchens and storage rooms, was once one of the greatest charitable foundations of the Islamic world. For a time the buildings were empty and decaying, but happily the newly founded **Thrace University** is now using several of them for art courses and they are cared for and busy

Sharpening knives.

once more. The single unit of a domed mosque is pleasant enough were it not for the over enthusiastic Italian restoration which left the interior covered in horribly unsuitable murals.

Perhaps the most interesting part of the complex is the hospital, which is to the right when facing the complex. Of this the most remarkable section is the asylum, with a hexagonal treatment room in cool white stone, with domed alcoves for the patients who were treated by the sound of water, music (provided by musicians in another alcove) and flowers, according to Evliya Çelebi. One feels that the lovely treatment room and peaceful country setting of the complex would be enough to cure any madness. It was here that Lady Mary Wortley Montagu took the revolutionary step of having her children inoculated against smallpox.

If one walks back to the town from the Beyazıt complex, one may enjoy the riverside walks and observe the complicated dyke system erected to protect the town from floods. Note too the remark-

able engineering of the many Ottoman bridges around Edirne over the deep flowing Maritsa and Tunca rivers. It is as well to be circumspect around the rivers, where there are a number of military posts and photography may be forbidden. Edirne is still a sensitive border region.

Many today know Edirne better as the town where greased wrestling is held annually than as the former capital and showcase of Ottoman architecture. Perhaps then it is not surprising that the great open field by the river where the wrestling is held has usurped the nearby site of the former palace of the Ottoman, called **Sarayiçi**.

Little is left now, save a ruined arch or two and Sarayiçi is really not worth a visit unless you like the littered and deserted air of a fairground out of season. What was left of the palace was damaged during the Russian occupation in 1829, and destroyed before the Russian occupation of 1874 when the governor ordered the arsenal located there to be fired.

The fertile fields of Thrace.

Along the width and breadth of the nation, bulls are pitted against bulls, camels against camels, dogs against dogs and roosters against roosters, with all contests falling under the general rubric *Güres*, or wrestling.

But "wrestling" is not confined to animals and, with the possible exception of soccer, easily the most popular sport in the country is to pit two human beings against each other, either the internationally accepted Greco-Roman or Free-style forms, or – what really brings the crowd to their feet – the Turkish version of the ancient gymnasium tradition of swabbing oneself with oil and then trying to get a hand-hold on one's equally slippery opponent and flip him before he flips you.

Such *"Yağlı Güres,"* or grease wrestling contests, are held throughout the country during the summer months in various localities, but the most prestigious of them all is held on the hallowed field of Kırkpınar outside Edirne during the second week of July.

Legend has it that in 1360, 40 champions from all over the empire were invited to wrestle for the greater glory of God and Sultan. They greased themselves down, checked the bindings on their leather breaches, squared off and began to wrestle. At the end of the first hour the field had been halved; after another 2 hours the contestants had been reduced to a dozen, then six, and finally two. On and on they struggled, oblivious to the fact that the crowd had long departed and that night had fallen.

At dawn the next day, the curious who returned to witness the continuation of the spectacle were met with a grisly sight: there stood the two champions, still on their feet, but locked in a motionless death-embrace. When their bodies were lifted from the blistered field, 40 springs miraculously gushed forth from the earth, instantly turning the dusty field into a lush, green meadow. Thus the name, Kırkpınar, or "The Forty Springs."

The tradition lives on: With the exception of periods of war or occupation by foreign forces, the Kırkpınar tradition has continued until today unchanged but for the number of would-be champions and the size of the crowd. The average turn-out of wrestlers in all classes (gauged on height and not on weight) is around 1,000 every year, who show up at Kırkpınar for fame and glory and cash prizes.

Swabbing each other down with watered-down olive oil (the pure product is not only expensive, but would literally fry the skins of the contestants during the broiling midsummer sun), the wrestlers then parade around the field to the whine of fifes and the thunder of drums played by local gypsies.

First come the young boys – some only 5 years old, slithering around the field of long grass to the delight of the crowd. The contests then move to "Mid-height," "Full-height" and "Complete-height" – the championship or *Pehlivan* class that is the equivalent of a heavyweight boxer.

As might be expected, betting in the stands is brisk, and a listless match will be scorned with minute-long booings.

"Oh *Pehlivan*!!" shouts a former champion through a bullhorn. "Let the holds be legal, and may Allah guide him of truest heart to victory! Let the rites begin!"

The 40 *Pehlivan* class contestants, shining in the midday sun, move out unto the sacred field in a line, slapping their leather breaches as they literally skip through the oil and sweat-soaked grass before pairing off. No quarter will be given, nor points by the colorfully dressed referees, whose only job is to monitor illegal holds (there are few) and to announce the winner after one wrestler has forced the other's shoulders to the ground or one or the other collapses from exhaustion. An ordinary match will last about half an hour or more; some have lasted – in keeping with tradition – up to three hours. And after a victory, the gladiators pair off again, and then again, until only one is left standing.

Quickly, a 40-year-old favorite from Izmir with 20 years experience faces off against a much leaner, muscular upstart from Ankara who cuffs the old man illegally around the ears before trying to sneak a foot around his opponent's right leg. Suddenly, the older man takes a step into the other's arms, hoists him off his feet and flips him in a fall that brings the crowd to its feet.

Over there, a local hero from Çanakkale drags his opponent around and around on the slippery grass, working his slithery hand down into his rival's breeches until he finds his hold, yanking the dazed and crazed man to his feet before forcing him down to his back and rising to claim victory. Alas! The judge has not blown his whistle, and the limp form on the grass manages to pull

winning film *Pehlivan* starring Tarik Akan, who portrayed a penniless youth from a village in Thrace torn between becoming a "guest worker" in Libya or borrowing money from family and friends to train to be a *Pehlivan*.

For those who have a chance to see the film, Akan did not use a double for the actual wrestling sequences, which were filmed live on location with the actor grunting and sweating beneath his coat of oil under the midday sun.

himself to his feet, grasp the victor behind the back and turn defeat into stunning victory.

In recent years, the Prime Minister has taken to visiting the stadium on the final day of the three-day spectacular to crown the new champion, the most recent of whom, oddly enough, was a university graduate majoring in sports. The majority of the wrestlers, however, tend to be farm boys with dreams of instant riches, depicted with heart-wrenching accuracy by the award-

Grease wrestlers battle for honors and big money at Kırkpınar.

A circus of gypsies: Possibly as colorful as the events inside the Kırkpınar arena are the events going on outside at the time of the wrestling championships, when caravan after caravan of gypsies descend on Edirne to set up a week-long carnival and fair, replete with ferris wheels and merry-go-rounds as well as Bingo, Throw-The-Hoop-And-Win-A-Pack-Of-Marlboro games, wild animal cages, and dancing bear attractions. It is one of the few places in Turkey to meet with such concentrated numbers of this much maligned but little understood society, so the chance should not be missed.

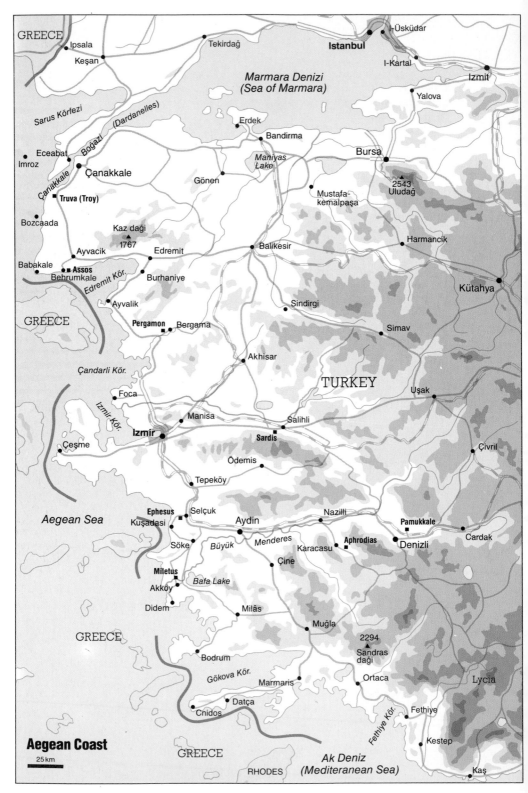

GREECE
Ipsala
Keşan
Tekirdağ
Istanbul
I-Üsküdar
I-Kartal
Izmit

Marmara Denizi
(Sea of Marmara)

Yalova

Sarus Körfezi
Boğazi (Dardanelles)

Erdek
Bandirma

Eceabat
Imroz
Çanakkale

Maniyas
Lake

Bursa

Gönen

Mustafa-
kemalpaşa

2543
Uludağ

Truva (Troy)

Bozcaada

Kaz daği
1767

Edremit
Balikesir

Harmancik

Ayvacik

Babakale
Assos
Behrumkale
Edremit Kör.
Burhaniye

Kütahya

Ayvalik

Sindirgi

GREECE
Pergamon
Bergama

Simav

Çandarli Kör.

Akhisar

TURKEY
Uşak

Foca

Izmir Kör.

Manisa
Salihli

Izmir

Çeşme
Sardis

Çivril

Ödemis

Tepeköy

Aegean Sea

Ephesus
Kuşadasi
Selçuk
Aydin
Nazilli
Pamukkale
Cardak

Söke
Büyük
Menderes
Karacasu
Aphrodias
Denizli

Miletus
Bafa Lake
Çine

Akköy
Didem
Milâs

Muğla

2294
Sandras
daği

GREECE

Bodrum

Gökova Kör.
Marmaris
Ortaca

Lycia

Datça

Cnidos
Fethiye Kör.
Fethiye

Aegean Coast
25 km

Kestep

GREECE

RHODES

Ak Deniz
(Mediteranean Sea)

Kaş

142

THE AEGEAN COAST

The northern Aegean coast is the beginning of Asia Minor. Over the course of time, this long peninsula forming the western-most part of Turkey (and indeed, of Asia itself) has been the site of some of the most famous military battles in history, ranging from the siege of Troy to the Gallipoli campaign of World War I. But where once the great armies of antiquity clashed, now only a gentle wind blowing off the azure-hued Aegean caresses the ancient monuments and ruins of the past to remind newcomers of what came before. Even the seasoned international traveler, however, will be struck by the unparalleled geographical variety and historically significant locations found in the area.

The three major tourist destinations of Gallipoli, Troy and Pergamun, together with myriad mountain villages and seaside beach resorts, pine forests and Turkey's most fertile agricultural region conspire magically to make the northern Aegean area one of the most rewarding and relaxing places to visit in all Turkey. Conveniently located along highway E-24, these sites are easily accessible from Istanbul or Izmir by car or any of Turkey's modern, inexpensive and excellent bus transport services.

Çanakkale: Only requiring a few hours by car or bus from Istanbul and situated on the Dardanelles Straits, **Çanakkale** became an active trading and transit point from Asia to Europe after Sultan Ahmet II built a fortress here in 1452.

It was also here that the Persian King Xerxes built his bridge of boats across the narrowest point of the Dardanelles to land 100,000 troops on Thrace as part of his planned conquest of Europe, only to end with an emphatic defeat at the Bay of Salamis. Ever since, Çanakkale has remained a crucial geographical choke-point controlling the crossing between Europe and Asia, as well as access to the Sea of Marmara region and the Black Sea beyond.

Although it has not reclaimed its international atmosphere of the 19th century, when it played host to scores of consulates and customs houses, Çanakkale has made decisive efforts to improve its image and has begun to show impressive results. The deteriorating dock area has begun to be refurbished and a new marble fountain has been constructed.

The local restaurants still specialize in serving the freshly caught seafood from the surrounding local waters and the small outdoor cafés are ideal places for a cup of tea while you savor the bustling activity of the port and its never ending parade of transport ships, fishing boats and *caïques* (small light traditional Turkish boats).

To get a bird's eye view of the entire area, walk or drive to the small promontory near the entrance to a Turkish military installation at the north end of town. From there you can enjoy a spectacular vista including the protrusion of Çanakkale into the narrows, the old Ottoman fortress, the docks which provide regular ferryboat service to Eceabat

Preceding pages, Medusa at Didyma. Left, map of the Aegean Coast. Right, the Trojan Horse.

directly across the straits and a broad panorama of the Aegean at the mouth of the Dardanelles.

Also visible from there and almost everywhere else is the giant white figure of a soldier against a hill on the European side pointing up the straits and reminding everyone of the Gallipoli Campaign (*Gelibolu* in modern Turkish) and the military battles fought on the beaches and hills of the surrounding area. Under him there is a stern inscription taken from a poem by Necmettin Onan entitled *Stop O Passerby* written in large letters warning the visitor:

> *"This earth you thus tread unawares is where an age sank. Bow and listen. This quiet mound is where the heart of a nation throbs."*

The **Çanakkale Archaeology Museum** located at the other end of town contains a small treasure trove of varied antiquities featuring artifacts, sculpture and ceramics from Troy which some people say would be best displayed at the original site. In addition, the museum also has a collection of exhibits displaying typical examples of costumes and styles of the periods worn by inhabitants of various ages along with an exclusive display of Atatürk's military clothing: his shirt, trousers and accessories – all strangely immediate, given the proximity of Gallipoli where the founder of modern Turkey established his reputation as a man of courage and daring.

Gallipoli (Gelibolu): "Damn the Dardanelles! They will be our grave!" said Admiral Fisher in his April 5, 1915 letter to Winston Churchill. Those words came to haunt the Naval Forces of the Allies in their efforts to force passage through the Dardanelles and capture Istanbul in order to force Turkey out of the war.

After nine months of fierce and heroic fighting on all sides, especially in the months of April and May, the number of dead and wounded was staggering. In total, each side employed nearly a half million men and, ironically, suffered nearly the same number of casualties: 500,000, making it one

Kilitbahir Castle on the Dardanelles.

of the bloodiest campaigns of the Great War of alternating bayonet charges against enemy trenches which were defended by machine guns.

According to most accounts, General Liman von Sanders, the German commander of the Ottoman armies, could not have guessed what forces he had set in motion both for the fate of that battle and for the future of Turkey when he appointed his junior officer Mustafa Kemal. Using a compass and small map, Kemal forged up a hill to discover the importance of the Conkbayır mountain range, from which he could observe the activities of the entire Allied fleet below.

It was during one of the many desperate struggles that followed that Kemal gave his exhausted and nearly panicked troops the now historic command: "I am not ordering you to attack, I am ordering you to die." They did so, winning the day.

All visitors are advised to visit the military museum with stops at the **Lone Pine Cemetery** and **Anzac Cove** where Australian and New Zealand troops lie, a moving testimony to the waste of humanity that is war.

The new **Turkish Memorial** at Anzac Cove unveiled in 1985 by the Turkish Government on Anzac Day, April 25, bears a powerful and eloquent message of reconciliation written by Atatürk to the mothers of those slain Allied soldiers who lie side by side with Turkish soldiers:

"There is no difference between the Johnnies and the Mehmets to us,
Where they lie side by side here in this country of ours,
You, the mothers who sent their sons from far away countries wipe away your tears;
Your sons are now lying in our bosom and are in peace after having lost their lives on this land,
They have become our sons as well."

And, finally, every year on April 25, the remaining Anzac veterans who fought and spilled their blood on the beaches and hills of Gallipoli return to this historic scene to be reunited with their Turkish brothers in arms to embrace in eternal friendship and to trade untold stories and remember comrades who have fallen here.

Gökçeada: Formerly known by its Greek name **Imbros**, the Turkish island of Gökçeada is accessible from Çanakkale by a pleasant daily ferryboat ride and lies slightly northwest of the entrance to the Dardanelles Straits. The island, which served as the headquarters of the Allies during the Gallipoli campaign, was ceded along with the neighboring island of **Tenedos** (Bozcaada) to Turkey by the treaty of Lausanne in 1923 to insure Turkish control over the Straits. Today it has a mixed population of native Greeks and migrant Turks.

Deep sea anglers can make arrangements to fish for sea bass and tuna in the clear, deep blue waters of the surrounding Aegean Sea. Visitors to the island are advised to contact security officials in Çanakkale as the island lies in a military zone and permission is usually required.

Troy: More than just a reference point in Greek antiquity but an idea to fire the

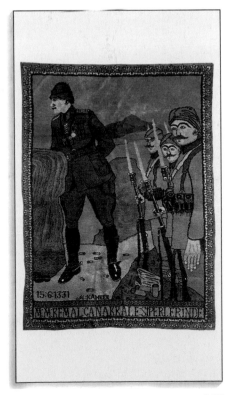

Rug representation of Atatürk during the Battle of Gallipoli.

imagination, the name **Troy** triggers a series of exalted characters and places that evoke the mystery, adventure and heroes of the events leading to the great destruction of the nearly mythical city.

In the earliest surviving account of the Trojan War, the *Iliad*, the blind poet Homer (or the group of scribes and poets who wrote in his name) chronicled the exploits of figures the likes of Agamemnon, Clytemnestra, Helen, Paris and Odysseus and the fate of the fabled city, marking the beginning of western literature as we know it. Did these events actually take place, was there really a siege of Troy? The debate over the accuracies of Homer's city continues to this day.

Whether one regards Homer as an early minstrel who made his living touring the Greek countryside and city-states singing songs and reciting poems or as the bearer of history's most profound myths, the adventures of these legendary figures have become an integral part of the world's heritage, and their fates and the forces they set in motion have served as the bedrock of scholarship and object lessons to generations.

Schliemann's fantastic discovery: In Mecklenburg, Germany, in the 1820s a young boy first read about Troy. The fabled city and its heroes made an indelible impression on the imagination of the lad. So inspired, Heinrich Schliemann made a vow to locate this distant city if it existed at all. As the story goes, Schliemann was initially fired by the Greek legends and stories of the Trojan War recited to him in his childhood by his pastor father or a drunken miller. Later as an adult, the energetic and clever Schliemann made several fortunes both in Russia and the goldfields of California but could never give up his dream of finding the real city of Troy as described by Homer.

Eventually, Schliemann requested a friend in Greece to send him pictures of beautiful young Greek girls who might help him reach his goal. Choosing the innocent, raven-haired beauty, Sophia, who could recite Homer, he set out to

Theater at Troy.

meet her and ask her father for her hand in marriage. Then off they went to discover Troy in 1872, using the *Iliad* itself as their guide.

For over four months Schliemann led his team of more than 150 workers in the world's first major archaeological dig (or rape, as some suggest). And while the world laughed at the mad German squandering his fortune on the legend of Troy, Schliemann and his team dug on until he discovered, first a necklace, then a treasure of golden cups, daggers, lance heads, silver vases and two extraordinary golden headbands worn by royalty: Troy, Homer's mythical city, was as real as London or New York.

Ongoing controversy: Schliemann's fabulous find was by no means the end of the story and subsequent investigations have revealed that there are at least nine Troys represented in the archaeological trenches at Hissarlık.

Studied by well known archaeologists from around the world, there still exists today no unity of opinion on the remains of the nine levels of Troy nor even the authenticity of the jewels found by Schliemann.

Professor Blegen, the leader of the Cincinnati expedition in 1932–38, maintained that Troy VIIa was the city of Priam, destroyed in about 1260 BC, at about the same time as Mycenean age. The late George Bean, a lecturer in Classics for 25 years at Istanbul University, maintains there is not the slightest evidence from the excavations at Hissarlık to connect the destruction of Troy with a Greek invasion. Bean claims the paltry remains of Troy VIIa bear little resemblance to Priam's splendid city, as described by Homer, and that the civilization depicted in the poems is a mixture of the Mycenean and that of the poet's own time.

Finally, it was the poet's own imagination, not a respect for historical fact, which created the Homeric world of poems. It has been left to the Turkish archaeologists to disagree with everyone and claim that it is a sub-level of Troy VI which is Priam's city. The debate goes on.

Ottoman bridge leading to Assos.

Another point of controversy is the Trojan Horse itself, or at least the modern replica of it supplied by the Turks. Garish at first glance, the huge wooden structure nonetheless can grow on the visitor – a visual reminder of the stunned reaction of the defenders of the city when they realized that they had been duped and were indeed doomed. Just as in the original, the modern reconstruction of the Trojan Horse can be entered from underneath by a set of stairs that lead to its eyes, where you can look out over the plains of Troy and see with modern eyes what Homer could only envision.

Recently, the horse that once symbolized military cleverness has been converted by a younger generation of Turks from a war memorial into a symbol of peace. Each summer in August, Turkish school children release a white pigeon from the Trojan Horse and shout in unison "Peace, Peace, Peace."

Assos: Behramkale, the ancient sight of Assos, is strategically located on the Bay of Edremit 60 miles (100 km) south of Çanakkale along highway E-24. To get there you must first pass through Ezine and then take a right at the picturesque village of **Ayvacık**, being careful to follow the road signs along the narrow and winding mountainous road for 12 miles (20 km).

During this seemingly short trip, you will be able to observe closely many traditional aspects of Turkish village life. The roadway is strewn with shepherds guiding their wayward flocks, donkeys carrying heavy loads, busy farmers working their fields and everywhere the ruggedly beautiful and constantly changing landscape.

Finally, the road emerges on to a low flat valley and you drive across a splendid 14th-century Ottoman bridge. Rising majestically in the distance is the outline of the acropolis of ancient **Assos**, with the citadel at the top and the village of **Behramkale** clinging to its steep hillsides.

After parking your car near the bottom of the hill you may want to stop for some refreshment and a rest before the **Lesbos in the mist.**

walk up. Then you take a 10-minute walk that winds its way through the ancient village past typical houses, several small shops and a way of life that hasn't changed significantly in centuries. Near the top you reach a mosque converted from a church with a cross and Greek inscription above the door reflecting the time when Assos was part of the Byzantine Empire.

The citadel itself is built on an outcropping of solid granite, with stone walls that stand up to the height of 46 ft (14 meters) and which are nearly 2 miles (3 km) long.

Temple of Athena: Within the walls of the citadel are the remnants of the Temple of Athena, built around 530 BC, and cleared by a team of scholars from the American Archaeological Institute in 1881–83. Destroyed as an unwanted reminder of the recent pagan past by the Byzantines, all that actually remains here are a few Doric columns and the platform of the acropolis itself. Athena, the daughter of Zeus, was known both as a goddess of war and handicrafts; according to mythology, it was Athena who taught local women the craft of weaving, and Behramkale and the surrounding area are still famous for fine rugs and carpets.

What comes before you next is in itself a pictorial commentary, and no description can effectively convey what is only to be experienced. From atop the citadel you walk among the remaining Doric columns and stand on the platform of the Temple of Athena looking out over the Aegean. From here you may take in the breathtaking panorama, spreading out before you nearly to the horizon of the Gulf of Edremit, the isle of Lesbos and the deep blue Aegean Sea beyond.

In ancient times, the eunuch Hermeia, called the Tyrant of Atarneus, ruled the Troad, the area around Troy and Lesbos. He had been a student of Plato's at the Academy of Athens and had sought the master's advice in developing this territory into the ideal city-state described by Plato in his famous political work, *The Republic*.

Aristotle, Plato's most famous stu-

dent, was invited to Assos and spent over three years living and working there. He married the niece of Hermeia, founded a school of philosophy and conducted his early exploratory work in zoology, biology and botany. A peaceful stroll among the remaining columns still invokes the inspiring atmosphere in which the great rhetorician and thinker lived and worked.

Behramkale: Down a near vertical drop of 750 ft (240 meters) below the Temple of Athena, lies a ribbon of seashore that is home to the small fishing village of Behramkale, consisting of 300 houses and three small hotels perched on a minuscule quay facing the nearby Greek island of Lesbos, with children and young ducklings playing together in the village streets. The hotels were converted from abandoned chestnut storage depots, and serve the many tourists to the ancient village.

At the beautifully renovated **Hotel Behram** with 20 well-appointed rooms facing the breakwater, the congenial owner (and publisher), Öcal Elmacıoğlu

Emerging from the surf.

had accepted the challenge of a friend several years ago to start a pension here in what he calls true paradise. Today, referring to his new cook from Bursa, he reminds visitors that at the top (Temple of Athena) their spirits were filled and at the bottom their stomachs were filled as he offers them a taste of delicious *avcıböreği* (the recipe includes meat and cornmeal and is imported from Bursa) and a menu that includes frog legs and shrimp seemingly available at any time. To wash it all down, he produces a bottle of a pretty good homemade white wine with a modish label of a female windsurfer sailing on turquoise waves framed by a facade of Doric columns.

Tourists (some of whom come to bathe here in the nude) have begun to discover the pebbled beaches at the nearby Kadirga Bay, and Behramkale has, as a result, become an oasis for some of Istanbul's artists, actors, academics and other trendies who find this nearly sequestered port irresistible and inevitably stay longer than they planned and

almost always come back in the years afterwards.

Turkey offers even the most jaded traveler many unexpected discoveries and rewards, both large and small. One of these is **Babakale**, which can be reached by a short 45-minute drive back from Behramkale along an unmarked road that comes up along a jagged coastline. It seems to run out at Babakale, a drowsy traditional village at the westernmost point of Asia Minor. Here the children rush out from under the shade of the giant Sinan tree in the village square to greet you with happy smiles and a warm welcome.

A few miles north of Babakale up the rugged coast is the perfect place for those who crave complete secrecy and anonymity. Perched on a small mantle of rock above a perfect half-moon beach is a place with two very small hotels, a handful of private houses and the most dramatic sunsets in the northern Aegean.

From Behramkale you return to the small town of **Ayvacık** in order to pick up on route E-24 and continue southeast along the coast. If you are there in late April, you must make it a point to visit the *panayır* held each year in Ayvacık. The *panayır* is derived from a primitive Greek festival and is a most unusual and exciting week-long celebration of food, dance and music which brings together all the people of the area. Ayvacık is also a center for weaving DOBAG carpets, with guaranteed natural dyes – a rarity in the Turkish carpet trade.

Ayvalık: Turning south, the E-24 passes through the typically touristy small beach resort of **Ören**, where in the summer there is a ferryboat service across the gulf to **Akçay**. The highway then moves inland and through the ever-present olive orchards before arriving at **Ayvalık,** a large resort town by the sea with a picturebook perfect fisherman's harbor that looks out on a glistening bay and beyond to some two dozen deep-green islands which are scattered about like thrown dice.

Inexplicably neglected in most guides, Ayvalık is indeed a special find: it boasts not only some of Turkey's most extensive beaches, but also some of the best **Fruit in all seasons.**

seafood dining in the country. The traveler will long remember sitting on the quay while the lavender sunset slowly envelopes and transforms the distant isle of Lesbos (Midilli) into a thing of mystery.

A sleepy "Greek" town: Old Ayvalık is a sleepy town of handsome wooden houses lining meandering lanes, more reminiscent of a town in Greece than in Turkey; indeed, it was nearly entirely Greek until the massive population exchange of 1923, when Muslim Turks from Crete were uprooted from their homes and given the houses of the departing Greeks in exchange. Many of Ayvalık's well-to-do families are said to have come into their riches without much effort as a result of this exchange of neighborhoods. The departing Greeks, with the conviction that they would one day return, mortared their gold and jewelry into the walls or hid their treasures under floor boards, only to have them discovered by the new residents of the exchange.

Local lore also has it that the reason for the narrow back alleys was to assist smugglers trying to escape from the authorities. Alas, many of the older houses are falling steadily and surely into dilapidation due to family inheritance quarrels and the inability of the owners to raise enough cash for repairs or renovations. This is especially sad when one reflects on the use such old houses have been put to as pensions in neighboring Greece or even in other parts of Turkey.

Sarmısaklı: For beach lovers, nearby Sarmısaklı 5 miles (8 km) to the south has it all, with miles of the finest white-grained sandy beaches in all of Turkey, wind surfing activities and daily group excursions by yacht. There is also a fairly lively promenade by night, lined with scores of hotels, cafés, discos, bars and restaurants. The hotels range from pensions to low, moderate and high-priced establishments along the beach to more interesting old-style mansions converted to motels that dot the southern shore of Ayvalık Bay.

A good choice for an up-market hotel

Harbor at Ayvalık.

is the **Murat Reis**, a discreetly located hotel tucked away on its own baylet in Küçükköy with a small private beach, windsurfing and scuba diving. Although it presumes to offer special services, the hotel is slightly overrated: it does not take credit cards (despite information to the contrary on the hotel registration cards), and the innocent traveler should beware of an occasional eerie sound that may awaken you in the middle of the night. Not to worry, the plumbing has begun to sing.

A few miles beyond the hotel and perched on the highest point of land in the Ayvalık area is **Şeytan Sofrasi** (the Devil's Table), which affords a spectacular view of Ayvalık Bay and the nearby pine-covered islets that seem to meander gently off toward distant Midilli (Lesbos).

The pride and joy of Ayvalık is its beautiful and luscious tasting olives grown on huge plantations in the surrounding area. The Komili family controls and owns the largest olive oil and soap producing factories in Turkey, and now exports olive oil to the United States, the Soviet Union, Libya and even to Italy. Recently, however, Ayvalık's reputation as the olive capital of Turkey has become tarnished as a serious problem has developed as a result of its chief agricultural crop. The olive oil factories, despite public protests, still pump black water waste (with a higher nitrogen content than sewage) from their ancient olive oil presses into the town's streets, and this waste eventually pollutes the beaches.

Across the bay on **Alibey Island**, (sometimes called **Cunda**), a walking tour will reveal beautiful bays, places to swim, some interesting ruins of ancient walls and an occasional eccentricity. Its natural charms have managed to attract notables such as Ptolomeo, Plinius and the German geographer Phillipson, among others, to live and work here. You may wonder at the sight of an odd looking house sitting on the side of a hill. The colorful owner of the Çağaloglu Hamam in Istanbul, Faris Çağdaş, has built himself an eccentric fairy-tale **Goats in the olive grove.**

mansion that has attracted the curiosity of tourists who now stop by here to get a free tour.

Nearby, the ancient village of Cunda has survived the Hellenistic, Roman and Byzantine periods and continues to thrive with an active little harbor lined with good seafood restaurants. The architecture of the town itself reflects the Greek style and there is a beautiful old Greek Orthodox church – however, in deplorable condition – that is well worth a visit. It contains vandalized religious frescoes of Matthew, Luke, John and an old portrait of Father Nikolai being released from a dolphin's mouth and deposited on the shore after 40 days of hiding.

While you are walking along next to the quay-side tea houses some night, listen carefully and you may still hear Greek being spoken by members of the old Greek community paying a visit to their former hometown.

Bergama: After leaving Ayvalık, the E-24 leads you south through ancient Aeolia, veering inland past boundless and verdant fields, where farmers use modern tractors to prepare the soil for the new planting season. Along the road you pass traditionally designed and colorful horse-drawn wagons bringing the workers (usually women) back, from the fields. Periodically, gypsy camps appear under a cluster of trees with their wagons pulled together for shelter from which the children can be seen fetching water from local streams.

In the villages, towns and cities along the way a recurring phenomenon, that of a building boom, contrasts directly with these bucolic scenes. Housing construction sites have popped up in every available space.

As you make the approach to **Bergama** (population 56,000) up through the valley of the Bakır Çayı, the ancient Caicus River, you notice two odd-looking hills or mounds just outside the city, built overnight, as the story goes, by local inhabitants to protect Bergama from invasion. Happily, foreigners are no longer feared, and Bergama – both old and new – is an important and interesting destination for

Bergama ("Yağçıbedir") carpet.

all, whether their interests are in rugs or in ruins.

Asude and Berksoy are decent 3-star hotels, and a good time to visit may coincide with the colorful annual Bergama Festival, which takes place in early June for 5 days highlighting the handcrafts, food and folk dancing of Bergama and the surrounding area.

Pergamun: Towering 1,000 ft above the city, the ruins at **Pergamun** command an extraordinary view in nearly all directions. One can understand how Pergamun dominated the entire region and cast its shadow over the realm. This great Hellenistic City, a center of culture, commerce and medicine, once rivaled the other centers of Mediterranean Hellenism such as Ephesus, Alexandria and Antioch.

The ruins date back to the Attalids, the powerful kings of Pergamun who ruled during the zenith of its glorious history, the third and second centuries BC, when Pergamun was a place for artists and scientists. It was at Pergamun that parchment was invented after the

Egyptians cut off the supply of papyrus.

As F.E. Peters says in his authoritative book, "*The Harvest of Hellenism*," Pergamun was not merely the hub of a thriving west-Anatolian economic complex; it was an intellectual center that possessed a famous grammatical and medical school. It came into particular prominence with Galen (AD 129–199), who studied medicine and philosophy in his native Pergamun and became known as the greatest physician and medical authority of ancient times. His work, which began with practicing medicine in a gladiator's clinic, refocused interest on the medical school at Pergamun and greatly influenced medical developments in both the East and West.

The Aesclepion: The ruins of the Aesclepion in the western section of the lower city, is a good place to start one's tour. Initially dedicated to Aesclepios, the God of Medicine, this was not your average medical clinic but the first complete health spa in history. The process must have gone something like this: an average tired and overwrought Greek or Roman businessman, politician or military leader arrived at the Aesclepion to be greeted by attendants. He was then led down the Sacred Way, the colonnaded *Via Tecta* (a bazaar of merchants and advisers) before choosing from a variety of services or sensuous experiences to relieve himself of the burdens of the day.

The prospective patient could seek out psycho-therapy treatment (where dreams were analyzed 2,000 years before Freud), the library for good books, a dip in the sacred healing springs and finally, the Roman style theater for an exciting production of a new play by Sophocles and some socializing with friends. The process could take as little as a few hours, but one usually spent a couple of days relaxing and recuperating from the strains of stressful Greco-Roman life.

Driving back through Bergama itself, a stop is recommended at the small but interesting **Pergamun Archaeological Museum**, which is located on mainstreet

The Basilica St John at Bergama.

and was one of the earliest museums to collect artifacts from Pergamun and the surrounding area.

Next, as you approach the Bergama Çayı you come upon an imposing structure straddling the river, the **Kızıl Avlu** or the **Red Court**. Dating from the 2nd or 3rd century, the original function has never been made clear although it probably served as a temple for various Egyptian deities. Later, it was converted into a basilica by the Byzantines and dedicated to either St John or St Paul. Just across the river and in the fascinating old **Turkish Quarter** is the **Grand Mosque (Ulu Cami)** which was commissioned by Sultan Beyazıt I in 1398–99.

The old Turkish Quarter is a great spot for lunch with its intriguing narrow streets, restaurants and shops overloaded with items Bergama is particularly known for goatskins, fresh white cheeses, fruits, tulips, honey, yogurt, pistachios and the world famous Bergama carpets. These strikingly exquisite deep red and blue patterned carpets hang in front of shops all over town, like the elegant laundry of a sultan.

A few words are in order about Bergama's most famous export. The carpet industry has changed quite a bit and become more problematic. There is a great deal of competition around, but Bergama carpets are still made the old-fashioned way: by hand and of lush, high quality.

Contrary to the quaint stories told by the fancy carpet merchants of Istanbul, it's not just eight to 16-year old girls whose supple fingers are capable of the delicate weaving process. Women of all ages can be seen practicing this ancient art. It is true, however, that marriage and better opportunities in newer vocations are luring away more and more of the young girls who traditionally have made them, but the carpet business continues to flourish.

The Acropolis: Now you are ready for the main attraction, the fabled **Acropolis at Pergamun**. From the old Turkish Quarter, you cross the Bergama Çayı, turn left and follow the road up a steep

Foundations of the Temple of Zeus; the rest is in Berlin.

hill, past the lower Agora and the sanctuary of Demeter until you reach the car park of the Acropolis.

Passing through the royal gate, you have entered one of the great centers of Hellenism. The first thing you become aware of is the tall, yellow construction crane which immediately puts you on notice that most of the impressive monuments are in various stages of restoration, if foreign support continues. Even though you have the natural impulse to wander around this massive sight on your own, it's probably best to follow the posted signs which provide helpful information to guide you along.

Some background is necessary to put the evolution, history and the contribution of Pergamun into perspective. The wise Attalid kings of Pergamun, rather than opposing the invading Seleucids of Antioch, joined forces with them and literally made a deal to use large gifts from their treasury which they presented to nearby Greek cities on the coast to form alliances and, once again, prevail over the entire region. They were re-

sponsible for constructing the beautiful palaces, temples and other buildings making Pergamun the rival of Athens or Alexandria. Then a very unusual event occurred in 133 BC, King Attalus II saw that his erratic nephew, Attalus III, had allowed the city to deteriorate to such an extent that, upon his death, he willed his entire kingdom to the Romans who gladly accepted it and transformed it into the capital of the Roman Empire in Asia Minor.

After entering the royal gate, to the left is the **Temple of Zeus**, of which nothing but the foundation remains. The altar itself was removed to the Pergamun Museum in East Berlin in the 19th century and where it was rebuilt in all its former glory.

Your walk continues past the **Temple of Athena Polias Nikephoros**, the oldest temple in Pergamun built in the Doric style at the end of the 4th century and was dedicated to the city-goddess Athena "who brings victory."

Especially impressive, at least in one's imagination, are the ruins of the famed library of Pergamun once filled with over 200,000 volumes written on parchment and collected by King Attalus I, making it one of the most famous libraries of the times; it was later presented to Cleopatra by Antony as a wedding gift in Alexandria and perished with the rest of the huge Alexandrian collection in early Christian times.

Nearby is the massive **Temple of Trajan** (restoration fully underway), dedicated to the deified Roman Emperor Trajan I and completed during the reign of Hadrian II, from which you have an excellent view of the geographical formation of the valley below that reveals how the sea once came all the way up to the base of the Acropolis.

Finally, retracing your steps you come to the **Grand Theater**, a most impressive structure of 80 rows divided into three tiers allowing seating of nearly 10,000. Standing at the top and gazing down at a most precipitous angle on to the stage with its long terrace, orchestra and royal box, it is difficult not to conjure up fleeting images of a Greek chorus and the beginnings of modern drama: **The colors of the harvest.**

unforgettable characters like Medea, who slaughtered her children after being scorned by Jason; the unfaithful Clytemnestra who slew her husband, King Agamemnon; and, of course, Oedipus tearing out his eyes after learning he had slept with his mother.

After these flights of fantasy, give the vaunted acoustics of the theater a test by having a friend stand on stage and speak to you. In our electronic age, with Broadway's best theaters using microphones to amplify actors speaking and singing voices, you will be surprised how well this beautifully designed theater still works.

Of all these important ruins, however, the **Gymnasium** is most interesting for it was here in the ephebeia that the young minds of Pergamun were shaped and guided. The institute of the *ephebeia* was initially conceived of as a two-year paramilitary course of study in the late Periclean age. Although originally aimed at forming "sound bodies and sound minds" through military skills, it eventually evolved into something far broader and ambitious than mere drill and tactics. Indeed, the "curriculum" of most schools and colleges we study at today are based on this early idea as expanded on by Aristotle and the ancients. Beyond the *ephebeia*, essentially a civic institution, lay the world of higher education. For the more serious and professionally inclined, there could be a career at one of the four major philosophical schools at Athens, or perhaps, even the medical school at Pergamun, an early and very busy university town.

As you leave Pergamun take special notice of the enclosure walls of the ancient city which show clear evidence of former restorations made during the Ottoman period when rocks, stones and bricks held together by mortar were used instead of the mortarless tight fit of granite slabs.

Foça and Dikili: After Bergama, a leisurely visit to one of several nearby seaside towns is in order. A short distance directly west is **Dikili**, a small seacoast port where an enjoyable, breezy

The remains of the Great Theater at Bergama.

walk along the Kordon Promenade offers the visitor several fresh seafood restaurants, a number of modest hotels, and an occasional view of ocean liners temporarily anchored in the bay, where a refreshing sea breeze invites you to linger on.

For those with less time, take the main highway from Bergama, which continues south, passing through rich valleys and periodically alongside the beautiful coastline. A series of ancient Aeolian cities can be visited along the way if time allows, but their ruins consist mainly of a few walls and fragments of columns.

To reach them, make a right at the turnoff for **Candarlı**, a modest village occupying a small peninsula jutting into the bay and with a 13th century Genoese fortress in excellent condition that sits in the middle of a quiet neighborhood. Getting back on the E-24 highway, you should continue around Çandarlı Bay (Çandarlı Körfezi) staying close to the coast until you reach **Aliağa**, another Aeolian city at the southern end of an inlet which is connected to the bay.

Unfortunately, Aliağa's chief claim to fame now seems to be its petrochemical complex which has been pouring waste into the beautiful blue waters of the nearby bay.

For more pleasant consideration, **Eski Foça** and **Yeni Foça** are two delightful and picturesque seaside villages of some historical significance. A few miles beyond Aliağa is the turnoff to the right climbing through the hills until the winding road emerges along the coast, revealing a series of dramatic vistas and passing the beautiful Club Med location and finally ending in Yeni (new) Foça on the northeast coast of the peninsula.

Most guide books, if they mention Foça at all, refer to Eski Foça, the site of ancient Phocaea on the southwest end of the peninsula and remind readers of the quote attributed to the ever dependable Herodotus, who said in Book One of his *Histories*, "The Phocaeans were the pioneer navigators of the Greeks, and it was they who showed their countrymen the way to the Adriatic, Tyrrhenia and the Spanish peninsula as far as Tartessus." In order to achieve these naval feats, the Phocaeans had to solve the problem of shallow waters and heavily loaded boats by designing a new flat-bottomed vessel. The Phocaeans were the founders of many colonies in the Sea of Marmara, Black Sea and the Mediterranean, including the city of Marseilles.

Manisa: Returning to the main highway near the village of Buruncuk, turn right until Menemen where you turn left and head due east towards Manisa. This is a pleasant drive through dry but verdant low valleys rich in a variety of agricultural products corn, wheat, sunflowers, grape vineyards and tobacco. The land continues to flatten out and becomes part of the great plain of Gediz. Gradually, outlined sharply against the horizon are the Boz Dağı Mountains and Mount Sypilus, from which the ancient city of **Magnesia ad Sypilum** was named.

Spread out below it is the modern and unexpectedly interesting city of **Manisa**,

The tear-stained rock of Niobe outside Manisa.

whose history boasts an imposing list of conquerors from the earliest Hittite cave dwelling civilizations through the Greeks, Persians, Seleucids, and Egyptians. There are also splendid examples of Seljuk and Ottoman architecture to be seen. Manisa's impressive variety of religious buildings include the **Muradiye Camii**, built in the 16th century by the great Turkish architect, Sinan. The *medrese* next door to the mosque now houses the Archaeological Museum and is also worth a visit.

Manisa, however, boasts not only of its ancient past but also of its contemporary heroes, however eccentric: recently, a special statue of Tarzani, the celebrated citizen of Manisa, has been erected in a small park next to the Muradiye Camii. Every day, as the story goes, dressed only in loincloth, he ran to the top of a nearby mountain and planted forests of pine trees all day long and then ran back down to pray and meditate on the teachings of Mevlana, the founder of the mystical whirling dervish sect.

A good time to visit Manisa is in April when the weather is cool and the annual Mesir Bayramı, the Spiced Candy Festival, is in full swing. Some say the *mesir*, made of 41 different spices, has special healing properties; others tend to associate the tradition with the ambrosia and nectar of the Olympic gods; some experts say the candy has aphrodisiac qualities.

Sipildağı National Park: Near Manisa, in Sipildağı National Park, are several sites more interesting in description than in the actual visit. One is the famed **Crying Rock of Niobe**, allegedly the petrified remains of proud Niobe, the arrogant daughter of Tantulus (from whom we get the word tantalize). Her 14 beautiful children were slain by the goddess Leto to teach Niobe humility after which the unfortunate Niobe begged Zeus to change her into stone, in order to end her pain. Alas, the bereaved mother continued to weep, day and night, the very stone wet from her tears. Unhappily, the tale is more evocative than the site itself, which appears to be nothing more than weather-worn rock.

Circumcision atop a camel in Manisa.

IZMIR

Resting peacefully with the languid grace of an experienced and seductive woman, Izmir (ancient Smyrna) occupies a stunningly beautiful location: a perfectly formed half-moon bay on Turkey's sunny Aegean coastline. The country's second largest port and third largest city, Izmir also doubles up as one of the country's major industrial and commercial centers, which is underlined by the important International Trade Fair held each September and the recent opening of the Adnan Menderes International Airport.

For international travelers, Izmir has been traditionally used as a starting or ending point for excursions to the more imposing and well-known archaeological sites and ruins that lie to the south (Ephesus) and the north (Pergamum).

But things had not always been so rosy for Izmir. History shows that Izmir experienced centuries of successive rulers, occupying armies and jealous conquerors – all lured to her by ideal geographic location and mild climate.

Bayraklı: During the prehistoric period, the tiny, initial settlement of Bayraklı (near Smyrna) grew in size and importance until it began to undergo a nearly unprecedented series of destructive conquests (even for Asia Minor). The Ionians finally managed to take over the Smyrna region in the 9th century and turned it into a prosperous settlement.

Much later, the long shadow of Alexander the Great in 4 BC was cast over the area when he ordered a new citadel built atop Mount Pagus. Afterwards came the Romans, who ushered in an era of prosperity, and, in their customary manner, added grand edifices and other structures, of which only a few traces remain.

Those salad days, which extended through the rise of Christianity and Byzantium, were brought to an abrupt halt when an Arab armada swept into Smyrna bay and sacked the town on their way to the conquest of Constantinople and the defeat of the Byzantine empire, dreams which were to end in frustrated defeat in AD 678.

At the beginning of the 11th century, the Seljuk Turks had their way with the city, only to be ousted by the Crusaders, whose fleet sailed triumphantly into Smyrna's harbor placing the city in the hands of the Knights of Rhodes. It was next sacked by Tamerlane.

Smyrna burns: During the desperate evacuation of Greek troops from Anatolia in 1922, a mysterious fire suddenly began to burn one evening deep in a Turkish quarter of the city. First, from shore and then, from a unique position aboard the British warship, Iron Duke, the British correspondent, G. Ward Price, wrote dramatic eye-witness accounts of the spreading blaze. "Without exaggeration" he wrote, "tonight's holocaust is one of the biggest fires in the world's history."

Pandemonium broke loose and thousands of crazed people gathered on the quay waiting to be rescued by the British boats. Untold numbers of others

perished in the inferno. Who started the blaze? And why? Price left the big questions unanswered.

One of the consequences of these traumatic events was the great population exchange of Asia Minor in 1923, when the entire remaining Greek population was sent to Greece in exchange for the ethnic Turks who resided in Greece and the Greek islands. Izmir's population today, aside from a few Levantine families, barely reflects its rich Greek past.

Izmir today: Once the equal of the fabled city of Troy and a rival to Pergamun as a center of education and medicine, Izmir continues to attract throngs of Turks from throughout Anatolia and the east searching for work to support their families. As the city grows and develops, she must brace herself to overcome the all-too-familiar problems of the modern era – too rapid expansion and sprawling urbanization. Still there is plenty to see and do.

Kadife Kale: The imposing fortress of Kadife Kale on Mount Pagus rises up majestically behind the city and offers an unparalleled view of the harbor and the city below. The best way to get there is by foot. There's no need for a map: just pick any street headed towards the castle and start walking. The path will inevitably take you through a fascinating variety of Izmir's commercial districts and neighborhoods, rich and poor, until you reach the citadel.

The grounds of the castle contain a wonderful mixture of people and activities: picnicking local folks, well-dressed citizens out for a stroll, as well as young romantics smiling deeply into each others' eyes over glasses of Turkish tea in one of the gently shaded outdoor restaurants.

Just inside the main gate, climb up the steps leading to the top of the wall overlooking the city. Walking slowly along this parapet, every few steps reveals another unique view of the city in a different perspective, from Çeşme in the southern horizon toward Karşıyaka across the bay and also to Manisa and the mountains to the northeast.

The promenade at Izmir.

The Agora: After leaving through the main gate, follow the road down to the left, past the main group of tourist restaurants, and turn right at the first set of descending steps built into the street. Just ask anyone for the direction to the **Agora** and you will be guided down the narrow streets and walkways strewn with friendly people, playing children and lots of cats. Several poorer neighborhoods later, you will emerge at the Agora, a relatively small clearing surrounded by a fence and containing a variety of colonnades around a central esplanade built during the reign of Marcus Aurelius in the 2nd century. Well-preserved statues of Poseidon, Artemis and Demeter from the Roman era can be found in the northwest corner of the Agora.

After the exciting Agora, turn right until you reach the first main street, Gaziosmanpaşa Caddesi. Walk south and take any street to the right into the **Covered Bazaar**. Although it cannot be compared to the one in Istanbul, it does offer a wide variety of bargains, especially in leather, clothing, jewelry and copper wares.

Konak: Pushing through the crowded, narrow and winding streets of the Covered Bazaar, you pass the university and finally emerge on the waterfront at **Konak Square**, with its distinctive clocktower and statue dedicated to the first Turkish citizen who gave his life to stop the Greek invasion of Izmir in 1920. Now a pedestrian area, Konak is a combination of a park and a ferry boat landing for commuters to **Karşıyaka** directly across the bay (a worthwhile trip for the fresh seafood restaurants and the brilliant evening view of Izmir), and home of the Public Library.

Bordering it to the left, going south on Mithatpaşa Caddesi, is Izmir's new **Atatürk Cultural Center**, the **State Theater** and **Conservatory**. The latest attraction in the city is the 86-year-old **Asansör** (elevator) that used to lift the locals from one neighborhood to another between Mithat Paşa and Halil Rifat Paşa streets. The Asansör tower together with the surrounding streets

A typical scene at the Izmir Bazaar.

have now been turned into an arty district with a gourmet restaurant atop the tower which offers an amazing view of the Izmir Gulf. Going to the right past the new city hall, you begin a pleasant walk along the quickly developing waterfront: a series of seafood restaurants (several on boats) serving Izmir's favorite fish, *tarança* and *çipura*, and a few slightly cheap nightclubs featuring belly dancers. Next is Izmir's main square, **Cumhuriyet Meydanı**, with its statue of Atatürk mounted on a horse occupying the centerspace, surrounded by a number of good hotels including the **Efes Hotel**, Izmir's finest, with a commanding view of the bay.

The Kültür Park: The road on which the Efes Hotel entrance faces, the Şehit Nevresbey Bulvarı, runs directly to the main entrance gate of the **Kültür Park**, Izmir's largest recreational area containing many outdoor and indoor activities and is the home of the well-reputed **Archaeological Museum**. Here, you can find Greek and Roman antiquities excavated from many sites including the ancient site of Bayraklı. The Kültür Park is also home of the Izmir International Trade Fair, where each year at the end of August, the newest industrial products exhibited by foreign manufacturers from around the world attract thousands of visitors. The park also recently saw the advent of the annual Izmir International Arts Festival, presenting stellar international performers like Ray Charles.

Kordon Promenade: Just after sunset, take a walk along the palm tree-lined **Kordon** to watch an unusual sight: hundreds, perhaps even thousands of Izmir's good citizens come out each night to promenade along the splendid bay from Cumhuriyet Meydanı to the Atatürk Museum. Take a seat on the quay and feel the *imbat*, the famous gently cooling breeze of Izmir, and enjoy this justly famous city and its softly seductive Mediterranean caress.

Çeşme: One hour or 50 miles (80 km) directly west of Izmir, on the tip of the peninsula, is the stunningly beautiful and very popular fishing village of

The Altın Yunus Resort complex at Çeşme.

Çeşme, which was originally sought for its healing thermal baths at nearby Ilıca. The new entrance road leads around town, down to the newly refurbished waterfront and ends near the small but helpful tourist office near the old Genoese castle. This is where the international Çeşme Song Festival is held every year in late August (it featured Peter Gabriel and Sinead O'Connor in 1993). From Çeşme, there are regular ferryboat services to the Greek islands of Chios, Samos and Cos and to Ancona (Italy).

Oddly, the fare is nearly three times as high going as coming. Then, to check into a small hotel, like the **Ertan** on the quay, and settle in to enjoy the special experience that is Çeşme; the slow pace, freshly caught seafood that is delicious, and local folks who are genuinely warm and go out of their way to help the traveler. For upmarket travelers an international class resort, **Altın Yunus** (The Golden Dolphins), offers a year-round marina to park your yacht, a swimming pool, tennis courts, horse-back-riding, sailing, scuba diving and a private beach.

SARDIS

Sardis has been occupied for over 5,000 years and has always been known as an important, ancient city. It was the capital of the Lydian empire which had the curious custom of eagerly condoning the prostitution of young girls in order to earn their dowries. Archaeology shows Sardis' development from pre-historic lakeside community to a major Roman city and Byzantine bishopric.

The Pactolus stream which flows next to the unpaved road south of the main highway that leads to the Temple of Artemis, was said to have been affected by Midas's "golden touch" when he bathed in its headwaters. The expression "rich as Croesus" is applied to someone who flaunts his riches, as Croesus, the last of the Lydian kings did. According to Herodotus, he gave away at least 10 tons of gold and funded

A leisurely ride gives an insight into the present and the past.

the building and decoration of the lavish Temple of Artemis at Ephesus.

An early method for the collecting of gold dust was to lay sheepskins in a shallow part of the stream to catch the particles. The legend of the Golden Fleece was supposed to have developed in this way from a gold-bearing branch of the Phasis River.

The Lydians claimed to have invented all of the pastimes that were common to them and the Greeks, including dice and knucklebones. A more significant invention attributed to King Alyattes, the father of Croesus, was the invention of coins. They were made at first of "electrum" an alloy of gold and silver usually without inscriptions, bearing only the lion's head, the royal emblem of Sardis. Croesus later introduced coins of pure gold and silver.

The most spectacular structure of the Sardis excavations is the **Artemis Temple**. Its massive scale – about 150 by 320 ft (45 by 99 meters) while the Parthenon is about 100 by 320 ft (30 by 70 meters) – rivals the three great Ionian

temples at Ephesus, Samos and Didyma. The construction was begun sometime before 200 BC, over 100 years after the conquest of Alexander the Great.

The temple is in the Ionic order with eight columns at the short end and 20 on the sides. The Ionic capitals are among the most beautiful in existence. The altar sits at the west end of the temple, a peculiar feature which may be explained as a natural way to avoid making it look into the slope of the hill, as it would if it were facing eastward.

Boz Dağı, the ancient Mt Tmolus, looms above the broad plain of the Gediz River, the ancient Hermus. Rising triumphantly over the plain behind the city is the 100-foot (300-meter) pointed peak of the acropolis. The acropolis was considered an impregnable fortress, until it was captured when the Persians felled the empire of Croesus around 547 BC.

The ascent to the acropolis takes about 45 minutes and requires sturdy walking shoes, but the fantastic panoramic view of the area you get from the peak makes it worthwhile. On the far side of the plain is the Lydian royal cemetery whose numerous eerie burial mounds give it the name *Bin Tepe* or "Thousand mounds." Just beyond Bin Tepe lies Marmara Gölü, the Gygaean lake, by which shores there were settlements in the 3rd century BC.

These memorable, natural landmarks played a part in the folklore of Latin and Greek literature. In the *Illiad*, Homer sang of the Gygaean lake: "snowy" Tmolus and "eddying" Hermus. In Ovid's *Metamorphoses*, a personified Tmolus judged the musical competition between Apollo and Pan. Some sources, including Euripides *Bacchae*, say the mountain was the birthplace of Dionysos and Zeus.

To the north of highway E23 is a fascinating complex of buildings that should not be missed. The **Marble Court** is a grandiose entrance way to the Roman gymnasium, constructed in the 2nd century and reconstructed over a 10-year period. The entrance to the court has columns decorated with heads of gods and satyrs, including the memo-

The many-breasted Artemis.

rable "Laughing Faun," a mastery of masonry workmanship, whose mischievous smile and features can be traced back to Greek origins.

The remains of the largest ancient **synagogue** ever found are in a large hall on one side of the gymnasium. The rich floor mosaics and elaborate geometric wall designs are made of small pieces of marble. A majestic marble table with eagles on the legs was set up at the altar end and a wallshrine preserved at the other, apparently in defiance of Judaism's ban on human and animal representation in temples.

Directly to the south of the bath-gymnasium complex, lies the **House of Bronzes** which owes its name to the varied bronze vessels and utensils found within, such as a chandelier with six lights and an embers' shovel decorated with a cross and two dolphins.

The only lodging in this area is the **Alkent Motel and Restaurant**, 8 miles (13 km) from the site in the direction of Ankara, just outside the town of Salihli. It is probably best to stay in **Izmir** and

drive to the site in a rented car or taxi. Day tours are occasionally offered by various tour agencies and guides in Izmir and a public bus leaves every two hours from the Yeni Garaj bus station in Izmir.

Kuşadası, which means "bird island" is set in a superb gulf and is known for its sparkling water, broad sandy beaches and large marina with a capacity for 600 boats. A little more than a decade ago, sleepy Kuşadası was considered a stopover on the way to Ephesus; now dozens of concrete hotels and holiday villages line its shores and chic seafood restaurants and discos cater to tourists.

Even so, Kuşadası has retained a certain earthiness to it and inexpensive meals and pensions can still be found inland. The many carpet and leather shops do a brisk trade with passengers from the numerous cruise ships that dock for the day, allowing enough time for a trip to Ephesus and a shopping expedition. At night, the tempo is more relaxed and the number of Turkish visitors, especially summer residents from Izmir, matches the foreign guests.

The reconstructed ruins of Sardis.

The tiny **Güvercin Adası** (Dove Island) is connected to the mainland by a causeway. Its romantic setting includes a well-maintained flower garden which surrounds the restored 14th- or 15th-century fortress housing a restaurant and disco frequented by lovers or those hoping to find one by the evening's end. In the 16th century, the vaulted fortress was the retreat of the infamous Barbarossa brothers, Greek converts to Islam and ruthless pirates who terrorized the entire Mediterranean area.

Beaches close to town tend to get quite crowded during summer. If you prefer more serenity, head for **Dilek Peninsula National Park**, known locally as Milli (National) Park. About 17 miles (28 km) from Kuşadası. Try to avoid weekends, though, when it's overcrowded.

Its untouched rocky mass of woods, canyons, valleys and caves, is worth a visit. Luxuriant forests include the common plane trees, laurels, red and black pines, plus several types of lime trees, chestnuts and oaks that are found only in northern Anatolia. Seals and turtles are government-protected and live and breed along the coastline. Numerous species of reptiles, birds and mammals proliferate in the mountainous terrain.

Hikers are warned to be cautious on steep cliffsides – especially those on Mt Mycale, modern **Samsundağı**, 4,000 ft (1,200 meters) which plunge into the strait facing Samos. They would also do well to avoid isolated paths, unless they wish to have an encounter with bears or the nearly extinct Anatolian cheetah.

Remains of an assembly building, dating to the 8th century BC Ionian Confederation, are on Atomatik Hill. Day trips can also be made from Kuşadası to Ephesus, Priene, Miletus and Didyma. Some package tours combine a visit to all four into one day but these are not advisable since Ephesus is huge and requires a good part of one day to take in the sights.

An alternative to a combined visit is to ask for a guide at one of the tourist agencies and hire a taxi which can take you to Ephesus, the museum of Selçuk, **Kuşadası, the island of the birds.**

the Church of the Seven Sleepers and the House of the Blessed Virgin. Guides also congregate outside the site of Ephesus but some have more interest in getting you into their cousin's tourist shop adjacent to the site than they are in giving you a historical background.

EPHESUS

Unmatched by any archaeological site anywhere in terms of sheer magnitude, Ephesus appeals to every visitor, from the serious archaeology scholar delighted by the visual evidence of long pondered facts and figures, to the casual visitor titilated by ribald hints of brothel complexes. To fully appreciate it in the warmer months, visit it in early morning or late in the afternoon; middays are unbearably hot and shady areas are hard to find.

Information on the origin of the founders of Ephesus is inconclusive. Strabon and Pausanias agree that Ephesus was founded by the Amazons but the majority of the city's population were the Carians and Lelegians. The Carians considered themselves the oldest inhabitants of Anatolia and Halicarnassus was their major city, according to Herodotus.

Athenaeus relates the colorful legend of 10 BC, of the original settlement: it seems the founders could not decide on a location for a site, so they consulted an Apollonian oracle which gave them the cryptic instructions to establish the city at the spot indicated by a fish and a boar.

Androklos, the son of Kodros, the King of Athens, and his friends wanted to fry some fish while contemplating this. A fish jumped out of the frying pan, scattering live coals and setting a bush on fire; this spread to a thicket in which a boar was hiding. The boar rushed out and was killed by Androklos, thus fulfilling the conditions given by the oracle and the new city was founded at the northern foot of Mt Pion.

By the 6th century BC, Ephesus had prospered, which is, perhaps, why it was the first chosen to be attacked by King Croesus of Lydia in 560 BC. The Ephesians naively stretched a rope from the temple of Artemis to the city and retreated behind it, believing the goddess would protect them. The Lydian army entered the city, but contrary to what was expected, Croesus treated the captives as friends.

The **Archaic Temple of Artemis** (564–546 BC) was still under construction at that time. To please the Ephesians and the goddess, Croesus presented column capitals with reliefs, one of which had his name inscribed on it. These relics are on display in the British Museum.

In 356 BC – tradition states on the night of Alexander the Great's birth – the temple was set on fire by a lunatic named Herostatus who wanted to be remembered in posterity, a goal he apparently achieved. The Ephesians at once began work on an even finer structure which was in progress when Alexander the Great arrived in 334 BC. He was so impressed by their industriousness that he offered to pay for all expenses if he could be permitted to make the dedicatory inscription in his name. The offer was politely refused, on the grounds that one god should not make a dedication to another.

The **Great Temple**, completed later by the Ephesians, ranked as one of the Seven Wonders of the World. Yet it had completely sunk below ground level when J.T. Wood, a British engineer, working for the British Museum began searching for it in 1863.

The crucial clue to its location was provided by an inscription found in the theater which indicated it lay in the direction of the **Sacred Way**, which it does: about ½ mile (nearly 1 km) from the excavation, just north of the Kuşadası road. A lone Ionian column that rests among the reeds on a few foundation blocks rising above the ground, but often submerged in the marsh, is a pitiful reminder of what was once a glorious stone structure.

The worship of the mother goddess, called Cybele, was firmly established in prehistoric Anatolia and in neighboring lands; she was known as Isis in Egypt, Vesta in Rome and Latin Arab territories. The oldest statues of Artemis were made of clay from Çatal Höyük (dated to 7,000 BC) and to emphasize the quality of fertility, have exaggerated hips, genital organs and breasts. The oldest statue of Artemis from Ephesus is thought to be of the *ksoanic* type, meaning carved out of solid wood.

The three staggered rows of nodes on the chest of the statues of Artemis were originally thought to be an overabundance of breasts. In fact, the name for this type of statue is Artemis *polymastros* or "many-breasted." A later interpretation identified them as eggs, also a symbol of fertility.

The structure of the worship of Artemis has been compared to that of the bee hive, with the drones serving the Queen bee.

Ephesus entered a golden age during the Roman era, when Augustus declared Ephesus the capital of the province of Asia instead of Pergamun. An inscription from Ephesus at this time calls itself "the first and greatest metropolis of Asia" and indeed it was. As the per-manent residence of the governor of Rome, it had a population of a quarter-million, and was the trade and banking center of Asia; the only threat to its prosperity being the constant silting up of the harbor by the Cayster River. Despite many inspired or misguided attempts over the years to deepen the channel or divert the course of the river, Ephesus now lies 3 miles (5 km) from the sea.

During its heyday in the 1st century, Ephesus allowed religious freedom for its inhabitants, which included those who followed the Jewish, Anatolian, Roman or Egyptian faith, as well as the first traces of Christianity. St John was in Ephesus then with the Virgin Mary who had been entrusted to his care by Christ. St Paul came to Ephesus in AD 53, and gained enough followers to es-tablish the **Church of Ephesus**.

A backlash against the new religion was spurred by secular rather than sa-cred interests. The jeweler Demetrius and the others who had a lucrative busi-ness selling silver statues of Artemis

Colonaded street in downtown Ephesus.

were incensed by Paul's proselytizing, and arranged a rally of thousands in the theater shouting, "Great is Artemis Ephesia!" St Paul, whose friends Gaios and Aristarhos were dragged into the theater, wanted to face the crowd but was refrained from doing so, departing shortly thereafter for Macedonia. Strangely, however, the new religion spread quickly in Ephesus and eventually supplanted the worship of Artemis.

The Ruins: The surviving ruins of Ephesus belong almost completely to the Roman imperial period. An outstanding exception is the Circuit Wall built by Lysimachus, a fine example of a Hellenistic fortification. It has disappeared on the lower ground but still stands along the crest of **Bülbül Dağı**, (Nightingale Mountain) to the south of the city, where those energetic enough to climb up will find the wall well-preserved and incorporating gates and towers of high quality workmanship.

The road leading from the Kuşadası highway to the ruins brings one to the **gymnasium of Vedius**, constructed in the 2nd century as a gift to the city by a wealthy citizen. In typical Roman fashion, the building combines both the gymnasium and the baths which had hot, cold as well as tepid water and rich mosaics and statuary.

The horseshoe-shaped **Stadium** was built during the Hellenistic period but restored to its present condition during Nero's reign (AD 54–68). The stadium was an important focal point for the Ephesians from the Early Ages when various sports events such as boxing and wrestling were held there. Camel wrestling matches are still held here during winter. During the 3rd and 4th centuries, gladiators were pitted against wild animals before huge crowds. A number of Christians met their deaths in this same fashion, which may help to explain why the stadium was destroyed by vengeful fanatics when Christianity became the official religion.

The **Church of the Virgin Mary** lies across the road and to the south. Built in the 2nd century as a museum, it was converted to a basilica in the 4th cen-

The Library at Ephesus.

tury. It holds a place of honor in Christian history for it is the first church that was dedicated to the Virgin Mary.

Beyond the parking lot are the remains of the **Harbor Gymnasium** built during the reign of Hadrian, entered through an elliptical courtyard which is paved with mosaics and surrounded by columns. On the side of the door opening onto the atrium is a decorated pool (used for physical exercises), paved with colored marble and surrounded by rooms used by students for various services.

The **Harbor Bath** is one of the largest structures in Ephesus, built during the 2nd century. A large elliptical pool measuring 100 ft (30 metres) in length is located in the center of the frigidarium. A row of 36-ft (11-meter) high columns made of pink and grey granite support the vaulted brick roof. All that remains of the harbor is a small lake in a swampy area, reached by passing through a splendid gate at the end of Harbor Street.

Harbor Street or Arcadiana, named after Arcadius, who remodeled it in AD 395–408, stretches between the harbor and the theater. About 1,600 ft (500 meters) long and 36 ft (11 meters) wide, both sides of the streets were covered with porticos paved with mosaics, and behind these, the stores. One of the excavations unearthed an inscription that was a startling revelation. It indicated the city was lit during the Early Ages, at a time when only Rome and Antioch shared this distinction.

The **Theater**, at the opposite end of the Arcadiana from the harbor, is still an impressive structure, large enough to hold 24,000 people and used for the Ephesus Festival, held in spring. It was constructed during the reign of Lysimachos and carved into the slopes of Mt Pion. From the top seats, there is a splendid view of the entire city. The acoustics of the theater are excellent, further enhanced in ancient times by placing clay or bronze sounding vessels at various points.

Below the theater is the **Library of Celsus**, an edifice so grandiose that it is easy to imagine it as part of a movie-set left behind after the shooting of a Ro-

The Pope at the Virgin Mary Shrine.

man spectacular. It was actually built in AD 114–117 by Tiberius Julius Aquila for his father Tiberius Julius Celsus, whose sarcophagus is in a tomb under the library.

The **Mazeus-Mithridates Gate**, located between the Celsus Library and the Agora, was built by two freed slaves of Emperor Augustus. Its three passages within greatly resemble a Roman victory arch and it is topped by a richly decorated frieze.

A road with steps passing the **Agora** leads to the **Temple of Serapis**, which had eight massive columns with Corinthian capitals that individually weighed 57 tons, although there are indications that the structure was never completed. According to an unearthed inscription, the red baroque temple was dedicated to the Egyptian god Serapis, sometime in the 2nd century. Serapis stood for life after death, whereas in the Roman faith, the spirits languished eternally in Hades.

At the library, the street turns and becomes the **Curetes Street** which

stretches to the **Heracles Gate**. At the beginning of the street on the left stand the **Baths of Scholasticia** built in the 1st century and reconstructed in the 4th century by the lady whose headless statue can be seen in the entrance hall. The three-storeyed building was very popular during the Roman empire, when both the poor and the rich would make use of the complex of heated rooms and pools – free-of-charge – although only the rich could afford to linger for hours, discussing politics and local gossip while being massaged by their servants.

Adjoining the baths of Scholasticia is a peristyle house known as the **Brothel** from an inscription most appropriately found in the lavatory. The upper storey has been destroyed and only traces of frescoes, which once covered spacious groundfloor walls, remain. A vivid mosaic in the dining room portrays the four seasons while a delightfully simple mosaic on the floor of an adjacent pool depicts three women, a servant, a mouse eating crumbs and a cat, evoking the flavor of ancient, quotidian life. A clay

The Theater at Ephesus.

Priapus, with the obligatory oversized phallus, was found in the well and now decorates the **Ephesus Museum**.

One of the most memorable sights in Ephesus is the fascinating **Temple of Hadrian** on Curetes Street. Built by AD 138, the four Corinthian columns support an arch with a bust of Tyche, the goddess of the city, in the center.

The plastercast on the site of the original frieze, which is now in the Ephesus Museum, has four sections which depict gods and goddesses, including Artemis Ephesia, along with Emperor Theodosius and his family. This is remarkable when one considers Theodosius's position as an opponent of paganism; the pagan goddess Artemis must have still had a strong grasp on the imagination of the Ephesians, even at this late date.

Selçuk: The Ephesus Museum in nearby Selçuk has an exceptional collection, all tastefully displayed and labeled. Mosaics and frescoes from the houses at Ephesus, statues, coins and relics all create a vivid impression of the rich decoration of the ancient city. The most famous include the bronze statuette of Eros on a dolphin, the two marble statues of Artemis polymastros, a fresco of the philosopher, Socrates, with a Greek inscription and a marble statue of Priapus, balancing a tray of fruit on his pride and joy.

The **Basilica of St John** is located at the southern foot of the hill dominated by the Selçuk fortress. St John is said to have lived the last years of his life here and after his death, a shrine was located over his grave. Emperor Justinian erected a monumental structure here in the 6th century, which was covered by a central dome and several smaller domes to form a cross.

The burial chamber of St John is at the end of the central nave, raised by two steps and covered with marble reproductions of the original mosaics. This area is being restored. Marble and brick pillars which supported the dome are extant; the blue-veined marble columns between them bear the monograms of Emperor Justinian and his wife, **An early advertisment to the local house of iniquity.**

Theodora. The chapel, temporarily covered by a wooden roof, has frescoes showing St John, Jesus and a saint. The baptisterium was constructed in the 5th century, before the church was built. At the foot of the hill are the ruins of the Isa Bey Mosque.

The **House of the Virgin Mary** (or *Meryem Ana*, in Turkish), is 5 miles (8 km) southeast of Selçuk. Tradition states that Mary came with St John to Ephesus between AD 37 and 48 and died there.

The house, worth a visit if only for the refreshing wooded paths and mountain streams, has been converted to a chapel. The icons are reputed to have curative powers attested to by the crutches and braces left in the corner by healed pilgrims. Greek Orthodox worshippers have come for centuries to the chapel on August 15, to celebrate the *Panagyri* of the Assumption of Mary, which includes a liturgy known as *Panaghia*. The chapel is recognized by the Vatican as a shrine and in 1967, Pope Paul VI honored it with a visit. The House of Meryem Ana, also a popular Saint among

the Muslim Turks, is frequently visited by local residents.

PRIENE

Priene is reached by a short drive from Kuşadası through some of the most beautiful scenery of Turkey. The road winds through silver-tinged olive groves, fields of cotton, bursting with the delicate rosebud blooms or fluffy white balls, pine-covered hills past peaceful hamlets surrounded by pink oleanders.

Priene has the most spectacular location of any of the ancient Ionian cities, resting on a slab of hillside rising above the Maeander Valley with the pine-clad spur of Mt Mycale presiding majestically above the ruins. Priene was once an active port on the coast; unfortunately, the siltings of the Maeander have landlocked it.

The advancing coastline made a new site necessary in the 4th century BC. The new Priene was laid out in the strict geometric gridiron devised by the city

Modern gladiators in the ancient stadium.

planner Hippodamos of Miletus.

One of the first structures seen after entering the site through the northwest gate, is the interesting **Theater**. It is small and horseshoe-shaped in the classical Hellenistic style and at the center is an altar which was used for sacrifical offerings to Dionysus.

Immediately below the theater are the foundations of a Byzantine church. Nearby is the Agora, the central market of the ancient city. The most important monument of Priene is the **Temple of Athena**, designed by the architect, Pytheos, who also planned the **Mausoleum of Halicarnassus**. An inscription identifying Alexander the Great as the donor of the temple was once on its wall but is now in the British Museum.

Miletus: The present ruins of **Miletus** date from the second foundation after the original city was destroyed by the Persians in 494 BC. Although Ephesus enjoys more present-day fame, Miletus was the most important city of the Ionian league; it was the principle port (on the same Gulf of Latmus as Priene), and its favorable position and spirit of enterprise made it not only the wealthiest emporium of its time but also the intellectual center.

Herodotus relates that the site was inhabited by Cretans and Carians when Neilus, the son of Codrus arrived. The intruders slaughtered all the men and married their wives, since they had no women of their own. This did not lend itself to domestic tranquility since the women bound themselves by oath never to sit at a table with their new husbands or to call them by their name.

Miletus, undoubtedly, has the finest existing **Roman period theater** built around AD 100 and seating 24,000 people, which sits on a hillside facing the parking lot. On some of the front rows of seats are a number of inscriptions, (such as "place of the Jews also called the God-fearing,") which reserved for those individuals or groups whose names they bear.

Most of the buildings of the city to the east are badly ruined. The precinct of Apollo Delphinius was the principle

The Theater at Miletus.

sanctuary at Miletus with ancient origins brought from Athens by the Ionians. The pinkish Hellenistic building was reconstructed in Roman times and was the source for nearly 200 inscriptions which aided in recording city history.

The *bouleuterion* or **Council Chamber** built between 175 and 164 BC is among the oldest buildings surviving in Miletus and has remains of an altar dedicated to the Roman imperial cult. Opposite the council building stood a *nymphaeum*, an ornate three-storeyed building with reliefs of nymphs, fed by an aqueduct which distributed water to the city but now lies in complete ruins.

The best-preserved building in this area is the **Baths of Faustina**, which dates from around AD 150 when it was built as a gymnasium. The exercise field was to the west of the bath's long entrance hall. A number of small rooms which were used for lectures and discussions are off the main hall. The baths, dedicated to Empress Faustina, the extravagant wife of Marcus Aurelius, were modeled on the Roman *thermae*, the forerunner of the Turkish *hamam*.

The beautiful **Mosque of Ilyas Bey** was built in 1404 by a member of the Menteş dynasty, the Turcomens who ruled this part of Anatolia before the Ottomans claimed it. Ilyas Bey built the mosque to celebrate his return, after being held a hostage in Tamerlane's court. The minaret has collapsed but the handsome design, the delicate grillwork on the massive doors and the carving on the sacred niche make it a masterpiece. The **Hellenistic Stadium**, which could hold 15,000 spectators, has two monumental gates. The best time to visit Miletus is in spring when flowers blanket the site.

Didyma: The most impressive single monument on the west coast of Ionia is the **Temple of Apollo** at Didyma. The early phase in the history of Didyma came to an end when the Persians sacked the city and destroyed its temple and oracle. Didyma remained silent until Alexander the Great arrived and the fountain of prophecy, which had dried up, gushed to life. The oracle announced that Alexander was the son of Zeus.

In the picture at Didyma.

Take some time to sit in one of the small cafés and contemplate the site, especially just before sunset, when the marble of the immense columns takes on softened shades and the riveting **Head of Medusa**, with her furrowed brow and tight ringlets carved on a stone relief, looks most sympathetic.

Lake Bafa: Altınkum (Golden Sand) Beach is at the tip of Didyma's peninsula and has a number of hotels. If you want to take refuge away from the trendier coastal areas, head for **Lake Bafa** (Bafa Gölü), once part of the sea but cut off by the silting Maeander, its clear, blue water is now fresh. You'll have to forsake luxury accommodations but a stay at **Turgut Camping and Motel**, set in an olive and pine grove on the shores of Bafa, is idyllic and within easy reach of the ruins of Didyma, Miletus, Priene and Ephesus.

Across the lake is **Heraklea ad Latmos**, one of the most romantic and compelling ancient sites to be seen in Anatolia. It can be approached by land on a new road off the main Bafa-Mylas

highway, or (preferably) go by boat.

Although situated on the Ionian coast, the city belongs in character to Caria. The serrated crest of **Mount Latmos**, some 4,500 ft (1,300 meters) high, gives it its name of **Bes Parmak** (Five Fingers). A bastion of this wild and formidable mountain curves down to the village of Kapıkırı and the walls of Heraklea run up this ridge. These classical walls are the outstanding feature of the site, the gates, towers, parapets and roofs – lending a fairytale atmosphere to the entire setting. An excursion to the remote hermitages of Mt Latmos is only recommended with a guide, for as writer Freya Stark says, one might be "curiously uncertain as to where the confines of reality end or begin."

Aphrodisias: Named after the goddess Aphrodite, whose cult-like status became synonymous with the celebration of sensual love and exquisite femininity the ancient city of Aphrodisias became renowned throughout Asia Minor as a center of medicine and philosophy but above all, of sculpture and the arts.

Buried by a series of earthquakes during late antiquity and abandoned by the survivors after attacks by the Arabs, the once splendid city was largely forgotten by the world until excavations by the late Professor Kenan Erim of New York University, with financial support from the National Geographic started in the early 1960s, revealed a nonpareil cache of sculpture carved from the nearby white marble quarries; these appear to have been the motherlode of much of the statuary of the Roman age. Signatures on statues found at the extensive site corresponding with others found throughout the Roman world, from Spain to the Danube, point to a distinctive and influential school of sculpture based in Aphrodisias.

The well-preserved **Theater** had its orchestra and stage converted into an arena for fights between gladiators and wild animals in the 2nd century. The **Stadium**, which could hold 30,000 spectators, is one of the finest Greco-Roman structures in the world and was once the setting for all kinds of athletic, drama,

The Cotton Castle of Pamukkale.

musical and sculpting competitions.

Pamukkale: Pamukkale, or the "Cotton Castle," is a shimmering white cascade, formed by limestone-laden hot springs, which have formed stalactites, potholes and magical fairy-tables. The water is reputed to be beneficial to the eyes and skin and to alleviate the ills of rheumatism, asthma and dermatitis. Wading in the little pools on the plateau is possible or you can take a plunge in the pool of the **Hotel Pamukkale** which is right on the site of the **Sacred Pool**. It's exhilirating to paddle through what feels like heated Schweppes' water while gazing at the ancient fragments of columns below the water's surface.

As much fun as the baths are, don't neglect to visit the splendid **Hierapolis**. The ruins spread over a mile from the city founded by Eumenes II of Pergamun and bequeathed by Attalus II to Rome. It was leveled by an earthquake in AD 17 but was rapidly rebuilt and enjoyed prosperity in the 2nd and 3rd centuries.

Milâs: Milâs, less than an hour's drive from Bodrum, is a delightful town.

Tuesday is Market Day and the **Milâs Market** is something special. Milâs is famous for its fine fabrics, coarse goats-hair rugs and shoulderbags, as well as for the distinctively colored geometric-patterned carpets.

Milâs also has some fine examples of Ottoman architecture often with intriguingly ornate chimneys and three interesting mosques including the **Ulu Cami** built during the Menteşe empire in 1370. Look for the double-axe on the facade and the Greek inscription on the right side.

Just adjacent to the Ulu Cami is a well-displayed museum with many of the finds from Iassus. The striking **Gümüşkesen** is a mini-replica of the Halicarnussus Mausoleum.

Some 7 or 8 miles (12 or 13 km) from Milâs towards Bafa, is the magnificent Corinthian **Temple of Zeus**, one of the six best-preserved in Asia Minor. Its 16 graceful columns, which sit on a base in an uninhabited field, are easily viewed from Highway 525, but I suggest you stop to admire it anyway.

Aphrodisias: images in marble from the past.

BODRUM

Bodrum or ancient Halicarnassus is situated on a peninsula facing the island of Kos, and is the hometown of Herodutus, known to some as the "Father of History" but to others as the "Father of Lies" because of his fanciful travel accounts. Another label for him might be the "Father of Quotations," due to the plethora of pithy observations of areas frequented by recent travel writers.

Bodrum itself is a good starting point for a journey along the Carian coast which offers a panorama of mythology and history, and spectacular scenery outlined by sandy beaches, rocky coves and inlets resembling small fjords. In ancient times, Halicarnassus was included in the Dorian Confederacy but was dropped from the league after breaking religious traditions during an assembly and also because of its growing alliance with the Ionians of Caria.

Not long ago a pretty fishing village known for its spongedivers, Bodrum is today the yachting center of Turkey and continues its ancient tradition of shipbuilding specializing in wooden-hulled yachts known as *goulettes*. Its striking, whitewashed, cubistic-style houses, draped with cascades of bougainvillea, show a Venetian influence.

Comtemporary Bodrum is primarily devoted to the hedonistic pleasures of boating, bronzing and boozing, giving it the real name of "Bedroom." Its tourist season gets longer each year as its reputation as "party town" spreads among boaters and landlubbers alike.

Yet history buffs will not be totally disappointed: the towers and battlements of the Crusader castle of Saint Peter – the **Petronium**, (from which the name Bodrum is derived), dominates the town as a major survivor of its past. Standing on a promontory by the harbor which is bathed in surrealistic silver and gold floodlights at night, the castle was built by the Knights of St John who plundered the remains of the nearby Mausoleum. Its column bases can be seen in the castle walls and other fragments are embedded

in its dwellings and other structures.

The **Mausoleum** (from which the word for a funereal monument is derived) was one of the Seven Wonders of the World, and for those who take melancholy pleasure in the ravages of time, a walk to the site is recommended. Consecrated to the memory of the ambitious Mausolus, who ruled Halicarnassus and was awarded the Persian title of *satrap*, it was built by his widow after his death. She drank a macabre cocktail of wine mixed with his ashes daily until her death two years later. Her mother, Artemesia I, had joined forces with Xerxes against Athens, and under her command her ships utterly destroyed the Rhodian fleet. This victory caused the great king to say he wished all of his admirals were women.

Bodrum, traditionally, has tolerated – indeed, encouraged – eccentricity. Its fame as a bohemian artistic center began years ago in 1923, during the infancy of the Turkish Republic when Cevat Şakır Kabaağaçli the "Halicarnassus Fisherman" was exiled to Bo-

drum. He wrote a number of fascinating books and stories about Bodrum that attracted other writers and artists to the restful locale.

Other colorful residents contributed to its fame, especially flamboyant Zeki Müren, the semi-retired, raven-haired singer who has a house in Bodrum. You can catch a glimpse of his Liberace-like face framed by dark glasses in the evening as he peeks out from behind his ubiquitous bouquet of roses at his usual table in front of his favorite bar.

The **Hadigari Bar**, the early evening social hub of the "in set," has taken on the function of the village tea house. Conversation centers around the latest financial coups in booming Bodrum – in which fortunes have been made in record time – and local gossip, with the relating of real or imagined sexual intrigues being of greatest interest.

The Halicarnassus Fisherman wrote, "When the moon comes up, the universe turns into a fairytale." Bodrum's nocturnal setting is magical; nightlife is invigorating and often continues until dawn. Cocktails at the **Veli Bar** can be followed by dinner at harborside restaurants. The **Meyhaneler Sokak** (Street of the Taverns), a pedestrian lane off the main shopping street, leads to a row of bars and restaurants in picturesque stone houses. Tables sprawl across the lane and a convivial bohemian atmosphere prevails. Several piano bars and bistros in the same area cater to visitors who crave subdued entertainment.

Farther on **Cumhuriyet Caddesi** is the disco of the Halikarnas Motel. Located on a prominent slope at the end of the seaside, this Bodrum phenomenon is well-known. A recent facelifting has given its immense space a Hellenistic motif. Monumental pillars of a temple topped with torches are bordered by gushing fountains that are lit by garish strobe lights and dramatically sliced by laser beams.

Down the way from Cumhuriyet Caddesi is **Mavi Bar** (The Blue House), a delighful little bastion of intellectual conversation and occasional traditional folk music. The casual **Jazz Café**, a

White-washed streets and flowered balconies.

dancing bar on Paşatarlası street, just behind the Halikarnos Disco, is another favorite late-night hangout of boaters and foreigners alike. In recent years several gourmet restaurants opened in Bodrum. Popular are the Şamdan Hotel's restaurant in Yalikavak, Ece in Gölköy serving deliciously creative Turkish dishes, Alarga and Mey in Türkbükü, and Kocadon and Sapa in Bodrum. Bodrum's success is such that it now has a small airfield with flights from Istanbul, and a new international airport is planned at Güllük nearby.

Environs: Many visitors opt to stay in one of the villages on the peninsula, now easily accessible since a paved highway was constructed recently. **Gümbet** is about 1½ miles (2 km) from Bodrum and its long sandy beach is dotted with motels and pensions. Gümbet means water cistern, referring to the many domed raincatchers in the vicinity. It has a large windsurfing school and offers diving courses. A small caïque runs from the popular beach to the town of Bodrum. **Bitez**, a bay a few miles

west of Gümbet, also has a windsurfing school and wooden piers from which to swim. It is backed by thick tangerine orchards. **Karafaki Restaurant** on the waterfront, run by a gentle bearded hulk named Osman, has some of the most imaginative *meze*, served on a large terrace or in his cozy bar in which clients lounge on rattan mats.

Ortakent, just off the main highway west of Bodrum, has a number of restaurants and motels on a sandy stretch of beach. The village is worth a visit to see its unique towerhouses. The oldest is the **Mustafa Paşa** house, built in 1601, and given a stately appearence by its rampart-size walls and its peaked roof formed by cannon embrasures.

Turgutreis is a large town named after a 16th-century admiral who died during the siege of Malta. The waterfront is lined with restaurants, hotels and boutiques. Its beach is very popular, but if you prefer more isolation, head for one of the quiet areas off the road to Akyarlar. A long sandy beach near the lighthouse usually attracts few swim-

The castle of the Knights of St John.

mers. **Akyarlar** itself is an ideal place to sample typical Turkish village life. Its small sandy beach sits in a well-sheltered harbor and the small restaurants offer temptingly fresh fish.

Gümüşlük is more popular for its secluded setting rather than for its beach. Because it has been designated an archeological site, no drastic alterations are allowed to the landscape. The bay is divided by **Rabbit Island**, the home of a family of rabbits raised by a villager. If you walk on a small sand and rock strait, you can reach the island from which you can get a good view of the seafront and the open sea. Gümüşlük is the site of ancient Myndos, and a fortification wall, ancient tower and submerged seawalls are on the harbor and on the beaches facing west.

Yalıkavak is one of the few sponge-fishing villages left and in warmer months the majority of the male population is off on the boats. One of the seaside windmills that still functions is over 300-years-old. The hills around Yalıkavak are ideal for picnics and walks, especially in the spring when they are covered with an incredible variety of wild flowers.

Türkbükü and **Gölköy** are in a large bay northwest of Bodrum. These lovely villages cater to families and independent travelers who want to spend quiet contemplative days absorbing the fantastic natural beauty, and evenings in quaint seaside eateries. Basic motels and pensions compensate their lack of amenities with unbounding hospitality.

Torba is a short ride northeast of Bodrum. It has a casino, a huge holiday village and a number of upscale restaurants near its ample beach.

All of these villages can be reached by *dolmuş* from the main bus station or by taxi. Bodrum itself has a few sandy pockets on Cumhuriyet Caddesi and some rocks next to the castle but the water is not always the cleanest.

Bardakçı is a nice, sandy beach that is only a short boat ride from the town. Its tiny beach is, unfortunately, packed in summer and covered with refuse.

Karaada: Day trips by boat can be

Fishing boat or luxury cruise...

made from Bodrum to surrounding beaches and islands; the most popular of these is **Karaada**, or Black Island, about a ½-hour by launch across Bodrum's bay. The island was to have been developed into a massive tourist complex, but the project seems to have been put on the back burner. There are restaurants at the tiny port, with a rather seedy hotel run by an Ankara lawyer who decided to abandon the rat race.

North of the dock is a mud-cave frequented by far too many tourists to be hygenic; about 600 ft (180 meters) south is a beautiful pool carved into the shallows by a huge meteorite; a cliff above allows for easy diving, and one should have no fear of hitting anything.

Blue cruising: Apart from its other charms, Bodrum also serves as one of the major centers for the growing trade in *Mavi Yolculuk,* or Blue Cruises into neighboring Gökova bay and other inlets around the Datça peninsula. Several agencies cater to the yachting crowd, and boats are available at various rates.

Those who do want to make this spe-

cial excursion should avoid the common mistake of underestimating the amount of alcohol needed to sustain them throughout a long day and night; bring twice the amount you think you will need. Also, don't expect to dine on fresh fish every night as Gökova has been largely fished-out. Buy extra food and pack it away in the ship's hold.

The cruises into Gökova usually include an overnight at **English Bay**, where several German cruisers were sunk during World War II, the village of **Türkevler** and **Cleopatra island**, allegedly a favorite resort of Mark Antony and his Egyptian bride. Legend has it that the fine grained sand – found nowhere else along the Turkish coast – was imported from Egypt to make the Queen of the Nile feel more at home.

Don't feel shy about telling your captain to linger a little longer at a place you like, or to pull up anchor and sail on if he docks with his other captain friends in an overcrowded cove. You are paying for the journey, and you should be able to call the shots.

Sunbathing on the deck; and a good day's catch.

UNDERWATER ARCHAEOLOGY

The striking castle of St Peter, which crowns the harbor of Bodrum, was built in the early 1400s by the Knights of St John, who were also responsible for building the fortification on the nearby Greek island of Kos, and in Smyrna. The inner castle, which houses the Bodrum Museum of Underwater Archeology, is reached after passing through seven gates embellished with coats of arms and inscriptions. At the top of a long stone staircase on the upper level is the office of T. Oguz Alpözen, the museum's Director.

The museum, recognized as one of the finest of its kind in the world, opened in 1960 with a collection of artefacts from the Cape Gelidonya wreck, the first excavation of Dr George Bass. These finds and those from a number of other sites, are carefully labelled and exhibited in the fascinating museum. The displays include finds from the Şeytan Deresi wreck in Gökova Bay; the Musgebi land excavation in a necropolis which has yielded the richest Mycenaean collection outside Greece; and the "Glass Wreck" found in Serçe Harbor, 24 miles from Marmaris. The delicate, multicolored glass fragments – painstakingly reconstructed by specially trained workers into exquisite cups, bottles and plates, many with designs in relief – comprise one of the most memorable exhibits. Another exhibit that whets one's appetite for more information is a small-scale replica of an underwater excavation team at work. The latest attraction is the hall of the Carian Princess Ada. Her tomb was discovered a few years ago containing her remains from c360 BC, complete with her jewelry and gold appliqued clothing. A team of British specialists reconstructed the skull and facial features, re-creating the princess from her well-preserved remains.

The only present underwater excavation in Turkey is at Ulu Burun, a barren cape near the small town of Kaş on the southern coast. The excavation, which is carried out in summer, is under the auspices of the Institute of Nautical Archaeology (INA), a private institution founded in 1973 by George Bass, affiliated with Texas A&M University.

The institute uses the castle as its headquarters in Bodrum, where a permanent staff of archaeological cataloguer-conservators, supplemented by Texas A&M graduate students in the summer, work on the finds from the wrecks. When massive remains such as ship hulls are found, reconstruction can require fulltime work for several years.

George Bass, the founder of INA, is a familiar name to students of archaeology and readers of the National Geographic. He received the first of 16 National Geographic grants 25 years ago when he caused an archaeological sensation by directing the excavation of a 12th-century BC shipwreck – the oldest found at that time – at Cape Gelidonya, near Finike, on the southwest coast of Turkey. Bass pioneered a new field of archaeology by being the first to systematically explore the seabed, which in his opinion is "the most abundant source of undisturbed historical sites." Until that time it had been exploited mainly by treasure hunters and casual adventurers.

Don Frey, the President of INA, became enthralled with underwater exploration while a Physics Professor at Robert College in Istanbul. He pursued this interest in his spare time until he succumbed to the lure of the sea, resigned his teaching position and headed down to Bodrum. Frey, who is in charge of INA's archaeological surveys, has long realized the importance of following leads given – through "good relations and a few *rakis*" – by the local spongedivers.

The discovery of the oldest wreck ever found – the Ulu Burun wreck, dating back to 14 BC in the late Bronze Age – was a matter of following one such fortuitous lead. Frey's interest was immediately alerted when spongediver Mehmet Çakır reported seeing "metal biscuits with ears" on a dive near Ulu Burun in 1982.

The next summer, a team of INA divers examined the site and confirmed that these "biscuits" were metal ingots similar to those depicted in the tombs at Thebes in 1350 BC. In the summer of 1984, fulltime excavations began at the site, which was only 210 ft (63 meters) from the shore. This proximity may have been the overcaution of the early navigators. However, the vessel was driven onto rocks at the base of the cape as it attempted to round the peninsula.

Archaeologists estimated that the ship was about 65 ft (20 meters) in length and possibly carried a single square sail. Its keel was of fir. It sank without capsizing and settled in such a way that some of the cargo remained in place until discovered by Bass. On land, the stratification of objects may be uncertain, or objects may be found in reused tombs.

Although all INA staff members participate in the diving , the excavation is proceeding slowly because of the great depth of the wreck which necessitates short dives. In deep diving, the body absorbs a more than normal amount of nitrogen, causing a slight dulling of the reactions and a feeling of being "tipsy." Bass comments, "It's as if you had just tossed down three martinis."

Another impediment to the swift retrieval of cargo is the layer of concretion that eventually covered the site like a rock-hard piecrust, making it necessary for many artefacts to be chiseled out by hand. Occasionally, the mere sifting of the sand will reveal an object that has been hidden for 34 centuries.

Jewelry, such as a gold pendant bearing a star surrounded by waves and identified by Bass as Canaanite, have been found in this fashion. Another gold pendant with the figure of a woman with high headdress and a wide dress under which both feet are pointing to the side, has been identified as Egyptian.

A seal with Egyptian hieroglyphics, the earliest glass ingots, dated tin ingots, hippopotamus teeth, elephant-tusk ivory, pithoi, bronze weapons and ceramic pottery and lamps have all been found at the wreck. Among the most striking finds are a scarab encased in gold and a golden goblet. Yet the object that proved invaluable in dating the wreck was a humble Mycenaean calyx.

The cargo is from the Canaanite, Cypriot and Mycenaean-Greek cultures, but some objects may be Egyptian. Faced with this puzzling diversity, Bass speculates that the boat may have been a multinational ship.

However, more important to him than determining the nationality of the boat is investigating other evidence it has provided. For instance, the boat used the Greco-Roman technique of building the shell first and fitting the frame to it, while modern shipbuilders make the frame first. This is significant because it proves that the first method of building is older than previously realized.

Bass admits his attitude has changed since he began the project. Then he was hoping to find evidence to support his theories about the Bronze Age trade in the Mediterranean. Now he concedes "I am not out to prove any particular point; I only want to find out about the past. I'm going to let this little shipwreck take us on a voyage of its own."

Out from the depths.

TURQUOISE COAST

The Turks call their share of the Mediterranean the *Akdeniz*, or "White Sea." Those familiar with its translucent waters and spectacular vistas punctuated with coves, castles and cities of the ancient world prefer to call it the Turquoise Coast, and a very special place it is indeed.

Long neglected by all but the most intrepid travelers due to its relative inaccessibility, the area is now rapidly developing as a major sun and sea paradise, to the point where old-timers who knew the coast 10 years ago now reflect nostalgically on the past, when the only accommodations provided were primarily family pensions or tents and transportation was best effected by four wheel drive vehicles along the winding coastal highways or on the tortuous mountain roads.

Those days are now long gone, with the area being serviced by three international airports (at Dalaman, Antalya and Adana) and new construction altering the once deserted beaches every year. Former fishing villages such as Kemer have become boomtowns, while sites of archaeological note such as Side now have discos in and around the columns and walls of the solemn temples of late antiquity.

Still, while encouraging the long overdue development, the government has vowed that the Turkish Mediterranean will not become "another Spain," and that all new construction must not adversely affect the natural beauty of the area. According to most visitors, the coast is being ruined.

For the purist who seeks nothing so much as that untouched Arcadia, the Turquoise Coast still has much to offer, while for the more traditional beach seeker, the new development of this very special corner of the Mediterranean is an invitation to visit again and again and again.

Pamphylia region: The area known by the ancients as Pamphylia is a land bent

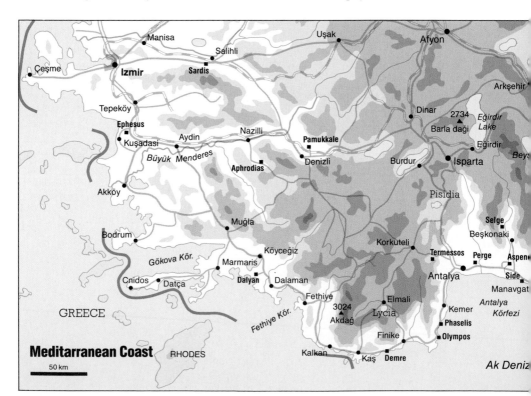

and broken by tectonic upheavals stretching from Alanya in the east, Olympus in the west, and north from the Mediterranean to the Taurus Mountains. Forty settlements flourished in the fertile plain, a region abundant with heather and laurel, olives and pine. Its cedar was coveted timber for the fleets of the ancient world.

Of Pamphylia's prehistory little is known. Finds from the **Karain Caves** 16 miles (27 km) north of Antalya, however, go back to the paleolithic or Old Stone Age, and yielded tools, axes and other crude implements, most of which lie in Antalya's museum. Other findings were the skull of a Neanderthal child, and bones of an ancient elephant, hippopotamus and bear.

Trojan refugees: Most historians agree that the fall of Troy around 1,184 BC brought about the real settlement of the area. The word *Pamphylia* means "land of all tribes" in ancient Greek, presumably referring to the motley survivors of Homer's doomed city.

But the Trojan refugees – or their descendants – were unable to find the peace they were looking for, and Pamphylia was regularly subjugated by the host of world conquerors that passed along the great East-West axis of antiquity: Croesus of Lydia held the area for a while, followed by the Persian Kings of Kings, Xerxes, and ultimately, Alexander the Great. The subsequent history of Pamphylia reflected the see-saw fortunes of the rest of the Mediterranean during late antiquity: held by the Seleucids of Antioch, it was next conquered by the Ptolemites of Egypt, only to be recaptured by the Seleucids once again.

Finally, following the defeat of Antioch at the hands of the inchoate Republic of Rome at Magnesia in 190 BC, the province was ceded to King Attalus II of Pergamun, who had aided the Romans against his Hellenic kinsmen. Fifty years later, Attalus III bequeathed all his land holdings – including Pergamun – to the Romans, who then proceeded to give the coast its distinctive stamp.

Preceding pages, a beach on the Mediterranean Coast. **Below**, map of Southwest Turkey.

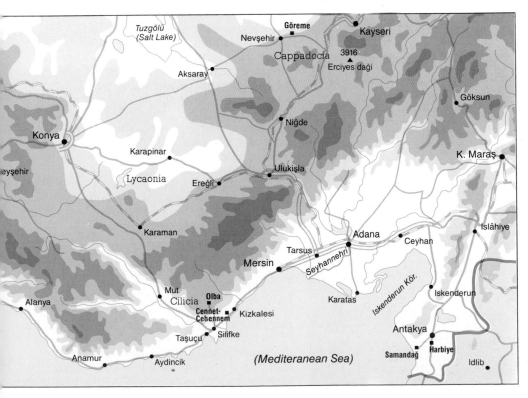

However, the right of inheritance could not enforce acquiescence, and the coast of Asia Minor soon became notorious for its pirates; Mark Antony the Elder was sent out to subdue them, but failed, leaving the task to Pompey, the hero of the Spanish wars. Along with the heads of the slaver-pirates, however, Pompey also brought back a new religion to Rome: Mithraism, an Iranian cult that celebrated male bonding and other masculine virtues through masses in chapels replete with fathers, baptism and a sacred meal, quickly spread through the ranks. Mithra was even adopted as the official protector of the Roman empire in AD 307, in a last ditch stand by Diocletian and Galerius to stem the tide of Christian influence in the empire.

St Paul: Indeed, the continued attachment of the local population to the cult of Mithra was the most formidable obstacle faced by Paul and Barnabus during their peripatetic wanderings around the Levant, a fact duly noted in the Acts of the Apostles.

At Lystra, the proselytizers were hard pressed to convince the local population that they were not the incarnations of a pair of pagan dieties, and it was not until the new religion began to assimilate various popular aspects of the cult religions (such as confessions, incense and the Eucharist) that Christianity found general acceptance.

Assimilation into the Christian fold did not, however, mean eternal peace for the region: Muslim Arab incursions started in the 7th century and led to the gradual depopulation of the coast. Later, the Crusaders used Antalya as well as much of the coast as a staging ground for their military pilgrimages to the Holy Land, and the ruins of many crusader-period fortifications still dot the coast, giving witness to the often bitter struggle between the Europeans and the Seljuk Turks who had begun their migrations westward from Central Asia around the first millennium.

The strangest bit of war-related history, however, belongs to the beginning of our own century, when irredentist Italy claimed the entire southern coast of Asia Minor as well as numerous offshore islands by dint of a "birthright" established during the period of Roman hegemony 2,000 years before. Not surprisingly, the new Republic of Turkey thought its own claims to the area were somewhat stronger, and the Italians were obliged to withdraw.

Today, it might be noted, the most numerous "invaders" are the droves of German tourists, who have set up little communities throughout the region, most notably in Kaş, Side and Alanya.

Antalya: The hub of Turkey's 700-mile-long Mediterranean coast is **Antalya** (ancient Atteleai), a small city of some 260,000 souls whose population swells to at least twice that for most of the 300-day-long summer season. The city could hardly ask for much more in the way of natural assets: its stunning harbor, rustic old town and long, languid climate have made it a favorite port of call for many a European yachtsman. Those who prefer terra firma are pretty well done by too, for **An old** town planning has been carried out with **pirate's town.**

taste and intelligence. The careful restoration of the harbor earned the city the "Golden Apple Award" from the World Federation of Travel Writers and Journalists in 1984.

Acres of parkland skirt the clifftops arching east and west of the harbor, giving tricky but rewarding access to swimming off the rocks below, a bird's eye view of the port activities, and some charming walkways. Behind loom the Taurus Mountains, and eastwards rise a dramatic expanse of cliffs with waterfalls tumbling down to the sea. If Antalya wears a smug smile of complacence, she can well afford to do so, for this is perhaps Turkey's most beautiful city, with surroundings to match. It is perfect for tourists – small enough to allow everything central to be seen in a few days, and charming enough to make you stay longer.

Antalya's harbor now shelters vessels both sleek and seedy in a setting that could hold its own on the Riviera. The recently restored quayside is lined with outdoor seafood restaurants and cafés along with the inevitable souvenir shops. Fishermen, their regular marina teahouse of old having been razed to make way for the tourist trade, continue to mend their nets, pretending not to notice the change. Others hawk their sea charters to the passing foreigners. Daily boat tours, including lunch on deck, cost about $12 per person, with longer sea trips for charters. Most crew speak rudimentary German or English.

On the clifftops above stand the old city walls and ramparts built by the Greeks and restored by the Romans and Seljuks, while just to the east of the harbor rises **Hıdırlık Tower**, once a Roman lighthouse. The lower section is believed to have been a tomb, as the somber design suggests. All three flights of stone steps lead up to sprawling outdoor teahouses with fine panoramas. The **Mermerli Café** (take the eastern most steps) serves samovars of tea which can be taken with a *nargile* or water pipe, a favored form of relaxation for Turkish men, but not recommended for the hygiene-conscious traveler. Both the east-

The restored harbor at Antalya.

ern and central flights of stairs lead to the charming **Old Quarter** of the town, still in the process of being restored. Most renovated buildings seem to sell carpets.

Minarets, mosques and monuments: At the top of the old town and near the main commercial street of the new city is the **Fluted Minaret**, the symbol of Antalya and the oldest Seljuk monument in the city. Its 13th century construction dates from the reign of Sultan Keykubat, who acquired most of the southern coast for the Seljuks. Exquisite turquoise tiles are set into the minaret itself, while the pool in front is of marble.

The **Alaaddin Mosque**, also 13th century, lies just to the west, and is thought to have once been a Byzantine church, although no traces of such architecture can be seen. Also nearby is the simple and elegant octagonal "*türbe*," or tomb, made of fine white masonry, built in 1377 in the tradition of central Asian Turks. The big white-washed building to the side, once a dervish convent dating from the 14th century, now serves as the **Gallery of the Fine Arts**.

From this vantage point you may notice a decapitated minaret across to the east at the other end of **Karaalioğlu Park**. This is the unfortunate **Yivli Minare** (Truncated Minaret) struck by lightning before the introduction of lightning conductors. Originally a 6th century church dedicated to the Virgin Mary, its construction was made up of 2nd- and 3rd-century spoils.

Arab attacks in the 7th century led to its destruction, although it was subsequently rebuilt in the 9th and 14th centuries. Today, the structure makes its hybrid past visible to all visitors who brave the broken stones, shards and thorny bushes protecting it (and not a very good job of protection at that: the building, alas, also serves as a toilet *al fresco*).

In **Atatürk Caddesi** stands **Hadrian's Gate**, a stately triple arched structure of white marble, built in honor of the Emperor's visit in AD 130. Step down through the gate and you will find yourself back in the old city. Atatürk Caddesi itself leads down to Karaalioğlu Park, atop the cliffs to the east of the harbor.

A wander down this street will take you past the colorfully dressed vendors of Maraş ice cream, originating in the Central Anatolian town of Kahraman-maraş. The ice cream is extremely elastic, and often sold by the meter. Don't be surprised when the vendor sends your cone swinging through the air on a light chain, which lands with the clash of a gong, without smudging your shirt pocket.

A noisy bazaar lies in the center of town, where you can find everything from plastic buckets and *çorap*, or hand-woven socks, which are long, colorful and thick as boots. Leather sandals seem to be a more reasonable purchase, given the year-long warm weather on the coast.

Recommended restaurants: As one would expect, the harbor restaurants specialize in seafood. In addition to such standards as seabass, red mullet and swordfish, one can sample the Turkish version of bouillabaisse, the "*tarança şiş.*" This is not skewered fish, as the name would suggest, but rather a fish stew using grouper, grida, or seabass as its base.

The **Kral Sofrası** restaurant just off the main square serves a recommended version. Another restaurant, pinned high into the western wall of the old harbor is the **Hisar Restaurant**, whose proprietor of 13 years, Emel Surel, refuses to serve fish she believes are out of season, providing trout and other freshwater fish from the Lake Region north of Antalya instead. High above the madding crowd of boatswains, yachtsmen and families with baby carriages promenading on the harbor floor, the Hisar possesses a uniquely calm and possibly even aristocratic atmosphere. One can only hope that the rumors suggesting that the government intends to revoke the lease in order to turn the restaurant into something a bit more trendy are unfounded.

Back atop the walls, near the corner of Atatürk and Cumhuriyet Caddesi, is an alley of outdoor restaurants serving a variety of Turkish dishes, including *tandir*, or oven-baked lamb served with flat *pide* bread. Served by weight, a 150-gram portion should satisfy a sightseer's hunger. Those with more fortitude may care for the *kelle*, or roasted head of sheep. The meat can be cut from the bones before being served. A particularly charming and out of the way eating establishment lies back in Karaalioğlu Park, almost hidden on the water's edge. This is the **Adalar Restaurant** where the tables are perched on craggy rocks jutting out of the sea. Swimming between courses is not frowned upon. Antalya's other good restaurants are **Club 29** commanding a view of the marina, the **Marina Hotel's** restaurant in the old town, and **Develi**.

In addition, there are any number of *Kendin Pişir-Kendin Ye* (Cook It and Eat It Yourself) restaurants on the high-road out to Lara Beach east of town. A revolving restaurant constructed on a bluff to the west of Antalya, alas, has never been opened because the architect (or the backers) neglected to put in a decent road, and the municipality refuses to build a cable car shuttle saying it is "elitist".

As of this writing, the hotel-restaurant complex has been offered for rent at an incredibly low rate, but with the caveat that the proprietor must build an access road to international specifications before entertaining guests. Although steep and a bit bumpy, the road is still useable by car and worth the climb for the breathtaking view of the city and the entire bay from the top.

The colorful jars lining the windows of the pickle seller (*turşucu*) is proof of the ingenuity of Turkish cuisine. Not confined to the usual "peck of pickled peppers", Turkish pickles embrace a wide range of varieties. They are sold by the piece so sampling is conveniently simple. Jams and jellies find favor in Antalya too, with the enormous variety of local fruits lending themselves happily to the confection. A speciality is rose jam from the produce of the gardens of Isparta to thc north.

The Museum: Take time to visit the archaeological museum, which houses

Windsurfing near Kemer.

the finds from the surrounding terrain. The **Hall of the Emperors and Classical Art** displays statues of the Greek gods, the Emperors Hadrian and Septimus Serverus and their empresses. Other exhibits include part of a stunning mosaic collection from Xanthos depicting the infant Achilles being dangled by his mother into the River Stix, the extraordinary finds from Karain Caves which date back to the Old Stone Age, as well as a comprehensive ethnographical collection. The bits of dust and bone said to be the remains of St Nicholas from his tomb in Demre, are third generation: his grave had already been robbed twice during the Crusades, making the claim that the display holds the remains of Santa Claus about as believable as the claim that the Topkapı Museum really does have 64 strands of the Prophet Muhammad's beard.

Beaches: Past the museum to the west stretches the pebbly **Konyaaltı Beach**, unfortunately marred by row after row of unsightly identical holiday huts and crowded tent sites; the municipality has long stated that it intends to demolish these local bungalows to make way for touristic hotels once investors are found. Indeed, the 5-star **Falez** is already there.

Lara to the east is a better bet, being more upmarket and offering some excellent swimming. Accommodations here ranges from family-run pensions to the new 5-star **Sera Hotel**, replete with a helicopter landing pad, rental cars, tennis courts, windsurfing facilities and a host of other aquatic sports activities. As with Konyaaltı, Lara is spotted for hotel development.

For those with a taste for festivals, the city also hosts the annual Golden Orange Film and Arts festival the first week of October, as well as the *Akdeniz-Akdeniz* ("Mediterranean, Oh! Mediterranean") International Song Contest held in September, when fancy Turkish artists strut their stuff along with a handful of international luminaries.

In addition to its intrinsic charms, Antalya is the starting point for excursions to such echoes from the ancient

Roman sarcophagus at Antalya museum.

world as the cities of Perge, Aspendos, Phaselis and Termessos, as well as other sites farther afield such as Kaş and Xanthos to the west and Side and Alanya to the east.

Perge: The ruins of **Perge**, although not on the scale of Ephesus or Pergamun, are still vast. To reach them take the left turnoff at **Aksu**, east of Antalya. A visit to Perge is best made after a stroll through Antalya's museum, where the truly magnificent finds from this ancient city are displayed. A 2nd-century sarcophagus of Hercules, on which his 12 labors are depicted, a statue of the benefactress Planca Magna, and most of the colossal statues of both gods and emperors are just some of the exhibits.

The city proved an easy conquest for Alexander the Great, largely due to the fact that the city had no defensive walls. Perge later flourished under the Seleucid kings when the city was fortified for the first time; the towers remain standing at almost their original height today.

Most of today's Perge, however, belongs to the period of Pax Romana – the theater, **stadium**, **baths** and **colonnaded street**. The stadium is one of the best preserved of the ancient world. Of its 30 outward facing chambers, 20 were used as shops; several wall inscriptions reveal the names of their proprietors as well as their trade.

One name that crops up frequently on statue bases is that of a woman, **Plancia Magna**. Priestess of Artemis, goddess of the moon, her legacy contributed approximately 20 statues to the city. Her tomb, or what remains of it, lies just outside one of the city gates.

Sillyum: Perge's most eastern gate leads to **Sillyum**. Its ruins are not as well preserved as those of Perge, with part of the theater carried away by landslides. To reach the site, take the dirt road which branches off the Antalya/Alanya highway at **Eskiyörük**, about 18 miles (30 km) outside of Antalya. Although Silliyum was important during the Hellenistic era, it gradually declined, and with the advent of the Seljuks the name changed to **Yanköy Hisarı**, now nestling at the foot of the hill.

The ruins of Perge.

Aspendos: Some 25 miles (45 km) east of Antalya and 3 miles (5 km) off the main road lies **Aspendos**, graced with a theater that rivals any single edifice on the Turkish coast. Built in the 2nd century and seating 15,000, the structure is nearly entire except for part of the upper cornice. Its architect was Xenon, a local lad, whose secret formula for creating such perfect acoustics has not yet been discovered – a coin dropped from the orchestra pit can be heard distinctly from the galleries. The Seljuks used the theater as a caravanserai in the 13th century, and reinforced part of the north wing with a typically Islamic arch; Atatürk suggested that it be used for grease wrestling. For 1,800 years neither earthquakes, the ravages of war, nor time have taken their toll. Behind lie the ruins of the acropolis, agora, nymphaeum, and what may be the best surviving example of a Roman aqueduct. The annals inform us that the river was navigable as far as Aspendos, and the city was used as a naval base, although this seems to be fairly improbable at first blink. The ancient theater hosts concerts in summer.

Selge: Just beyond the turnoff to Aspendos, a tarmac road cuts off the main coastal highway leading toward the town of Beşkonak and beyond, to ancient **Selge**, now called **Zerk**, in the mountains above. As Selge is not included in any organized tours, the only way to get there is by private car, preferably with four wheel drive or at least high clearance.

Today, one needs imagination to recall the old city, as very little remains aside from the theater: the stadium has been turned into a terraced field for one of the farm families living in the hamlet that is the modern Zerk. Get ready for a swarm of begging children whose taste for candy, pencils and coin has been whetted by some no-doubt well meaning tourist; once the children settle down, they – and they alone – might lead you to the few remains of the ancient town: a relief of a centurion turned at an angle beneath a massive pile of cut stones here; a relief of a Roman eagle similarly jammed in a rock slide there.

The view of the valley below, however, is stupendous, and well worth the effort required to get to Selge, which seems to be a community that has always been suspicious of the outside world: in the summer of 1987, the Turkish electrical monopoly was erecting poles to bring electricity to the village, but discovered that the holes they drilled by day were being refilled by the villagers at night on the logic that electricity might mean refrigerators, but it also means paying the state for the juice. Be prepared to drink your after-ruins Coca-Cola warm.

The national park leading up to Selge is cut by the headwaters of **Köprü Çay** (Bridge Brook), babbling white and rapid down through the astoundingly beautiful canyon. Fishing for brown trout is performed at one's own risk, although this poacher was casting wet fly alongside an Antalya policeman whose metal lures seemed to be more effective.

The American rainbow trout available at the riverside rest at **Beşkonak**, it should be noted, are pellet-fed creatures

The Amphitheater at Aspendos.

raised in tanks outside of Antalya, and have never taken an honest leap in their lives, a fact reflected in the mushy flavor of their flesh.

In addition to poaching trout, one can legally – if expensively – clamber over crag and rock in the mountains flanking Zerk or in those around Termessos northwest of Antalya with rifle in hand for wild goat. The enthusiast should apply well beforehand to the Forestry Ministry through the nearest Turkish Ministry of Tourism office or consulate for permission. To the north of Antalya, by taking a right turn on the westbound road to Kemer and climbing through thick-wooded scenery for some 25 miles (40 km), you will reach the skiing resort of **Saklikent** (the Hidden City). In March, you can ski here in the morning and swim in the afternoon in Antalya!

Termessos: The ancients knew a good beach when they saw one, but they also had a taste for inland vistas, and the plateau behind Antalya (which is known as Roman Pisidia) is as studded with the remains of the ruins of the old cities as are the shores of the Mediterranean.

One of the most remarkable of these inland sites is Termessos, high in the mountains above Antalya to the northwest, on a vast acropolis with yet higher peaks around it and with a distant view of the coastline. To locate it, take the main road north in the direction of **Burdur**, then left towards **Korkuteli** and another left at the yellow sign leading to Termessos.

The defenses of this Pisidian city so daunted Alexander the Great when he came conquering in 333 BC that he passed Termessos. It is easy to understand why: the steep, winding road and the remains of the stout defending walls are enough to show the motorist a little of what the Greek adventurer would have faced. Another theory has it that Alexander did not think the town deserved his time.

The road leads to a car park from where the major ruins are a stiff 45 minutes walk further up, with a fascinating series of sarcophagi to be explored on the other side of the valley. The vast, cut stones of the walls and the magnificent theater lie in a jumble as if tossed around like a giant's plaything – the great earthquake of AD 527 destroyed most of the towns on the coastal plain, and left all in a state of ruins. Other remains include an agora, a gymnasium, an odeon and five vast water cisterns carved into the rock.

The origin of the city is uncertain but the founders, who called themselves the **Solymians** are identified with the Pisidians who occupied the lake district further north. The Lake Area makes an interesting 2 or 3-day excursion from Antalya, from the southern Aegean area, or even from Ankara. The traveler beginning from the capital is urged to take the country route via Polatli and Aksehir.

Buçak: Some 65 miles (105 km) north of Antalya, and a little to the right of the main road, the town of **Buçak** is the stopping-off point for the ruins of **Cremna**. The town itself has a couple of simple hotels but little of interest. A signposted side road to the left off the highway at Buçak, however, leads to **Incirhan Caravanserai**. Such caravan-

Tumbled masonry of the theater at Termessos.

serais are typical of the medieval motels that dot the ancient trade routes. This one is in reasonable repair, if spoiled by a build-up of wind-blown soil up one outer wall, and has elegant stonework around the entrance.

Cremna: Cremna is located about 8 miles (13 km) from Buçak but is poorly equipped for visitors. The road east from the town towards Kocaaliler winds attractively along a pine-clad valley, but to reach Cremna take a left after 3 miles (5 km) at a point which is signposted *"Tatbikat sahası"* (maneuver area). The site is 5 miles (8 km) further on near a settlement called **Çamlık**. To find the ruins, take the upper of two ways that proceed beyond the settlement, walking a short distance through the scrub when the track becomes difficult.

Cremna, once thought to be a minor Pisidian town, has gained in importance through recent archaeological work. In particular it has yielded a full picture of how the Romans conducted a siege. After a long campaign, ending in AD 278, the forces of emperor Probus suc-

ceeded in retaking the town from a brigand named Lydius. An inscription tells how Lydius drove out of the city all those too old or too young to be of use. The Romans, however, drove them back, whereupon Lydius hurled them into the ravines around the city. He even dug a tunnel under the walls to allow residents to steal food, which worked until an informer told the Romans.

Lydius' downfall came when one of his commanders defected after a severe dressing-down and pointed out to the Romans the gap in the wall from which he liked to watch the battle. A marksman took aim and mortally wounded him, whereupon the rebellion collapsed.

A massive earthwork used by the Romans to reach the height of the Cremna walls is still visible today since the soil is a reddish color compared to the gray-brown of that around it. The remains are late-Hellenistic and Roman but many of the buildings have been badly damaged by earthquakes and general decay. The best preserved is an arched structure which formed part of the baths. Its walls stand to their full height and house some fine inscribed statue bases. Archaeologists have also recently found evidence of the complex hydraulic system of aqueducts and animal-driven wheels which brought water to Cremna from a lower altitude.

Sagalassos: Some 20 miles (30 km) further on, a right turn signposted Isparta-Aglasun is the stopping-off place for the ruins of **Sagalassos**, the second city of Pisidia after Antioch (see below) and much more interesting for the casual traveler. Set high in the mountains, its theater is virtually intact while other relics include the foundations of a basilica, of a royal palace and a series of rock tombs. A fine bust said to be of Alexander the Great graces the hillside near the theater.

Isparta was founded by Greeks from Sparta and was still an important Greek town until the deportations of the 1920s. A few ruined Greek churches can still be found in the back streets.

A winding drive of an hour or so brings the traveler to the town of **Eğirdir** at the southern tip of the most attractive

Poppies in bloom near Isparta.

of several lakes in the area. The hotel of the same name which overlooks the shore can be recommended. Two tiny islands are joined to the town by a causeway and the furthest, **Yeşilada**, has several pensions and an old Greek church worth exploring. The ruins of an old **Seljuk fort** stand in the town near the 15th-century **Ulu Cami**, or Great Mosque, and a *medrese*, or religious school which now serves as a small shopping arcade.

The drive up the eastern side of the lake is the more attractive and leads to Yalvaç, the ancient Antioch-in-Pisidia, much visited by Christian pilgrims because of its associations with St Paul. As recorded in the New Testament (Acts: Chapter 13) it was here that Paul made his first recorded sermon. This was so successful that the Gentiles pleaded with him to speak again the following Saturday and the synagogue was packed. The Jews, out of envy, drove Paul from the city. Some church authorities believe that he revisited the site twice.

The town was founded between 301 and 280 BC on the site of a Phyrgian settlement by Seleucus Nicator, and was for a long time the principal town of Pisidia. Today little is visible on the hillside site except the foundations of an arched entranceway (*propylaea*) and the remains of a Byzantine church and of a basilica. Across the valley stand arches of an aqueduct, as well as a temple to the Phyrgian moon god-man on the hill.

A representation of how the University of Michigan archaeologists who worked here in the 1920s imagined the propylaea hangs is in the entrance of the small local museum (closed Tuesdays), which also houses relics from the site and a small ethnographical collection. It vies with Antalya for the neatest, prettiest garden of any museum in Turkey.

The traveler may wish to go on from here on the country road via Senirkent to Keçiborlu, past numerous fruit orchards, and on to Burdur, which houses the local museum. A few miles south of Burdur and signposted left off the main road are the **Insuyu Caves**, among the most extensive in Turkey.

LYCIA

The Lycians, a people believed to be of Cretan origin, were an independent-minded race prepared to fight for their freedom. They settled and defended the wide peninsula between present-day Fethiye and Antalya from around 1,400 BC. They had their own unique language, still to be seen on inscriptions though as yet not fully understood, and a unique style of tomb design which for the visitor, perhaps, would be the most memorable feature.

Lycia fell under Persian rule when General Harpagus conquered western Anatolia about 540 BC, though by all accounts the hegemony was not onerous. Herodotus' reports state that the general advanced on the plain of Xanthos, the leading city of Lycia, and the people, though greatly outnumbered, went out to meet him in battle. They were forced back behind their walls and besieged. Rather than submit they collected their women, children and slaves, enclosed them in the citadel and burned the place to the ground. "Then, having sworn to do or die, they marched out to meet the enemy and were killed to a man," he says.

The Hellenistic period began when Alexander the Great arrived about 333 BC and the cities of Lycia surrendered one by one. After his death, during the reign of general Ptolemy, King of Egypt, the Lycian language died out to be replaced by Greek, seen more widely than Lycian in inscriptions in the area.

In 197 BC the land was taken from the Ptolemies by Antiochus III of Syria. Most of Lycia was given to Rhodes by the Romans in 189 BC after they defeated Antiochus at the battle of Magnesia, but it was an unhappy relationship and the Senate declared its cities free in 167 BC. Later in the 2nd century BC the Lycian league gradually acquired economic as well as political prominence.

In 42 BC, two years after the murder of Julius Caesar, Brutus besieged Xanthos but again the people fought to the death and he gained control of a city that had been razed. The historian Appian relates in great detail how the Xanthians dug a ditch around their city, perched high on a rock in a bend on the river of the same name, to keep out the invaders. Brutus, however, managed to have this filled in and a dramatic battle ensued with siege engines, ladders and many of the attackers falling to their deaths down the precipice by the river.

When plotters Brutus and Cassius were defeated at Philippi later that year by Mark Antony and Octavius, Lycia came among Antony's spoils and he gave the territory its freedom, leaving it the only part of Asia Minor at that time not under Roman domination. The emperor Vespasian, however, who ruled from AD 69–79, brought the joint province of Lycia and Pamphylia under Roman control.

Kemer: The visitor to Antalya in search of somewhere to swim may head east, to the sands of Lara beach, or west along a coastline backed with the shade of a long line of pine trees towards **Kemer** 30 miles (45 km) away. It is reached

from the former highway which is now a holiday strip just behind the coast with campsites, pensions and hotels.

At Kemer itself, among the peasant houses on the north side of the main road, is an area used for camel-wrestling, a winter sport. Kemer is well-developed as a tourist center and has many modern holiday villages including **Club Méditerranée** and **Club Robinson** but little charm. The traffic-free area around the modern harbor, with associated boatyard, is, however, a pleasant place for a stroll. Anyone making a decision to stay here should be prepared for the feeling of life on a construction site. It has been one for the past 10 years and shows every sign of remaining one for the next 10 years, particularly along the road from Antalya to Kemer. Every year in May, Kemer hosts the Eastern Mediterranean Yacht Rally.

Phaselis: The site of ancient **Phaselis** some 8 miles (13 km) beyond Kemer is one of the most charming in Lycia and offers the visitor several beautiful sandy beaches as well as the chance to wander among ruins of the Roman and Byzantine periods. These, scattered among the undergrowth and the trees, have seen little excavation. A theater in poor repair stands beside a monumental street dotted with inscribed column-bases. Three agoras, side by side, and a building believed to have been a bath stand at the other side.

Some distance away are to be found the remains of an aqueduct. The pine tree-lined bays that once served as the city's three ports are today used by those seeking to swim in the clear Mediterranean waters or sunbathe. One might wish for less seaborne garbage on the shoreline, however.

Olympos: Some 30 miles (50 km) from Phaselis, near the village of **Çavuşköy**, burns a natural fire believed to be the origin of the Greek myth of the Chimera, the fire-breathing monster with a lion's head, a goat's body and a serpent's tail that was finally destroyed by Bellerophan. The phenomenon apparently results from the issuing of methane gas from the earth, but it is hardly

Dalyan – the tombs of the kings.

worth the trouble of looking for it.

The people of nearby Olympos, inhabited from Hellenistic times, constructed a sanctuary here. Olympos itself offers the visitor the shattered remains of a monumental gateway, an acropolis, a river port and a small theater which is nearly overgrown with vegetation. The area also has one of the longest large-pebble beaches in Turkey.

Finike: Finike, the ancient Phoenicus, is famous throughout Turkey as one of the country's orange-growing capitals. Oranges litter its long, pretty beaches, making swimming there difficult for travelers visiting Finike. The town is cheerful and clean and has sandy beaches but little else to offer the traveler save the recollection that this was the site of the "Battle of the Masts" in AD 655, the first major naval victory of the Muslim Arabs over the Byzantines. The Arabs managed to overcome the enemy's "Greek fire" and turned the fight into one of hand-to-hand battle conflict by tying each of their ships to one of the Greeks'. The Arab chronicler Al-Tabari

describes how the water became thick with blood.

Up in the hills, 5 miles (8 km) away, stand the ruins of **Limyra**, with the most extensive necropolis in Lycia and from where there is an astounding view of the coast. The tombs, such as that of King Pericles of Lycia, date back to the 4th century BC. They also include a mausoleum to Gaius Caesar, grandson of Augustus, who was destined to be emperor but died here of battle wounds before he could wear the purple robe.

Demre: Some of the finest examples of Lycian funerary architecture are to be found at **Myra**, near the expanding present-day town of **Demre**, some 15 miles (27 km) west from Finike. The site, about a mile from the town, includes a vast Roman theater in good repair and built against a cliff face that also houses two impressive sets of Lycian rock tombs. The best time to make a visit is as early as possible in the day to catch the sunlight.

Many of the tombs have log cabin features carved into the rock, presum-

Pebble beach.

ably reflecting the domestic architecture of the period. A few accessible ones have inscriptions in the Lycian language. Carvings above are mostly in poor repair but the overall effect of this jumble of architecture of death is dramatic.

In the theater – at 490 ft (150 meters) in diameter one of the largest in the area – many carvings and inscriptions are visible, and cavernous tunnels and access ways to the side have been cleared. While much of the seating is intact, the stage building is partly collapsed. A macabre set of three carved masks, presumably from the frieze, lies among the remains in the approach to the theater and will be visible if the staff has cleared the grass and shrubbery away.

Saint Nick: In the center of the town is the **Church of St Nicholas**, best known as the patron saint of children, who was born at Patara around AD 300 and was bishop of Myra, where he died. The miracles he performed in his lifetime and stories that surrounded him have left him identified today in the west with Santa Claus and thus Father Christmas.

The link stems perhaps from two legends: that he cast three bags of gold coins into the home of a merchant who had hit hard times, enabling his daughters to marry, and that he restored to life three boys who had been cut up by a local butcher. The first of these stories is also said to be the origin of the three gold balls that are still used today as the sign of a pawnbroker.

Guides at Demre will point out St Nicholas' reputed tomb in the church, which is of much later date, even though his very existence is the subject of controversy. Muslim Turkey invites journalists, foreign experts and clergymen here every year around St Nicholas' Day, December 6, to take advantage of the legend. His remains have not been here since 1087, when a band of merchants carried them off to Bari in Italy.

Demre has several pensions; one near the town center offers fine home-made jam for breakfast but is severely infested by mosquitoes because of nearby swampland. The visitor is advised to seek accommodation either in Finike to the east or Kaş and Kalkan to the west, not that they are free of the insects. Among smaller hotels and pensions, Kaş has a 4-star Aqua Park Hotel, and Kalkan, a luxurious Club Patara.

Demre itself is several miles inland and the main settlement in a vast plain that, viewed from the hills above, constitutes an ugly sea of plastic-covered tomato-growing greenhouses. This blot on the landscape is one of the most unattractive spots in Lycia. The harbor of Demre, known locally as **Çayağzı**, the ancient **Andriace**, houses a reasonable beachside restaurant and a team of resident boatmen who offer trips to **Kekova Island** or to secluded beaches.

A good road of some 3 miles (5 km) along a marshy river-bed – hence the mosquitoes – leads to the harbor from the ring-route around Demre. The traveler arriving from Kaş should not enter the town but follow the sign for Finike. (The remains of a huge Roman mausoleum stand at the junction.) The route confusingly heads west and the road to Çayağzı splits off right at the point where the main highway turns **Statue of St Nicholas at Demre.**

east. Coming from Finike, the traveler should not enter the town but continue westward on the coast road to this point.

The ruins of ancient Andriace stand on both sides of the road at the approach to the sea, the most impressive building being the granary of Hadrian to the left, similar to the one at Patara and built to serve the wheatfields that predated the tomato plantations.

Kekova: Kekova Island and the town of Kale make an idyllic daytrip for the traveler looking for a combination of sunshine, swimming and fascinating historic ruins. It is the most unspoilt spot on the western Mediterranean coast. Many operators run trips from Kaş but the journey is much shorter from Çayağzı, the harbor of Demre. From here boatmen charge about $20 per boat for a journey of any length. Along the stony coastline the boatman may stop at a cave, or point out the occasional goat or the smoldering pyramids of wood used by peasants to make charcoal – the product may sit in plastic sacks at the water's edge, waiting to be taken away.

Along the edge of the island facing the mainland lie the fascinating half-submerged remains of a sunken city, probably from Byzantine times. Signs warn against skin-diving, and locals say anyone getting off here is likely to be spotted by wardens with binoculars from the mainland and possibly detained. The boatman will allow the passengers on board off for a swim further to the west, where the remains of a Byzantine chapel stand on the beach and where further sunken remains can be explored at ease by the swimmer with mask and snorkel.

A fascinating Lycian necropolis, with chest-type tombs spread out along the coastline, lies at **Tcimiussa**, near the present-day **Ucağız** on the mainland across from Kekova. This can also be reached by track from the main road between Kaş and Demre, where it is signposted. The boat-tripper may be content with a sea-born view and pass to **Kale**, the ancient **Simena**, which sits nearby below the crenellated ramparts of an earlier hilltop Roman castle. The castle houses a small theater, cut into

Bicycle riders outside of Kaş on the Wild Coast.

the rock, for just about 300 people, a sign that this was a minor settlement in Roman times. Down in the harbor the turquoise sea laps at waterside restaurants offering good Turkish menus including locally caught fish. A lone Lycian sarcophagus standing in a few inches of water at the western side lures visitors to pose beside it for photographs, but the spiny sea urchins make this a delicate operation.

Kaş: The town of **Kaş**, some 29 miles (46 km) from Demre, has probably been the fastest rising tourist destination in the area, and has smartened itself up considerably in recent years. It has an alluring harbor, some good restaurants and keen, enterprising landladies ready to offer relatively cheap rooms.

The traveler hoping to get to sleep before 3 a.m., however, may want to find somewhere to stay away from the harbor, where a discotheque plays until the early hours. In addition, many local artisans have made Kaş a center for arts and crafts, notably jewelry and textiles with many original designs.

The town of Antiphellus, on the site of present-day Kaş, began to develop in Hellenistic times and by the Roman period was the leading city of the region. The well-preserved Hellenistic theater, with the Mediterranean as its astounding backdrop, stands less than a mile (2 km) west of the town. Rock-cut and sarcophagus-type Lycian tombs can be seen on the hillside above.

The island of **Kastellorizon** (Turkish: Meis), just out to sea from Kaş, is the easternmost of the Greek islands. Elderly Greek women who have made the day-trip to Kaş may be seen sitting on the benches along the harbor, or shopping. Like Kalkan to the west, Kaş was home to many ethnic Greeks until the 1920s when Turkey and Greece exchanged their minority populations. The Greek past is reflected in the classically-inspired architecture of even small Greek homes that clearly differs from that of the Turks.

Kalkan: The dramatic route westward winds around several small sandy coves, linked to the road above by steps, which

Patara beach and Roman ruins.

make good stopping places. **Kalkan**, much smaller than Kaş, has also become increasingly popular in recent years and has built up its harbor to attract yachting tourists. The mosque that stands out near the harborfront appears to have been converted from a Greek church by little more than the addition of a minaret. The waters around Kalkan are a favorite for spear fishermen and abound in natural freshwater springs that make diving a fascinating experience. The springs provide the opportunity of a freshwater shower where divers surface at the shore; offshore they produce a strange phenomenon that makes the surface much colder than deeper waters.

Patara: Seeing Roman and Hellenistic sites of Asia Minor may sometimes seem like one long blur of agoras and theaters, but **Patara** is something special. The site is 3 miles (5 km) off the main road from a junction some 7 miles (11 km) west of Kalkan. There is a small restaurant at the end of the road. The 11 mile (18 km), sandy beach is the longest and widest in Turkey and, unlike much of the Mediterranean, has a tide, which allows body surfing. It is blisteringly hot in summer, an irony when one thinks that this is the birthplace of St Nicholas, the Santa Claus associated with snowy winters in the northern hemisphere.

An attendant may leap out from beside the triple monumental arch from the 1st century BC to charge admission to this open air museum, whether one intends to view the ruins or merely lay on the beach.

The theater, dating from the 2nd century BC, is intact but has been virtually filled by sands that have drifted in and invaded much of the site. From the top of the theater, there is a fine view of the other remains and of the coastline. The most important of the other buildings in the area, to the northwest, is the granary of Hadrian, a vast building standing to its full height save for its roof.

North of Patara and near the present-day town of Kinik lies **Xanthos**, the leading town of Lycia. Its chequered history is that of the province. The site

Olive trees instead of spectators.

was virtually intact in 1838 when British explorer Sir Charles Fellows arrived here. He was inspired to return four years later in *HMS Beacon*, whose sailors spent two months carting away the monuments in one of the great archaeological rapes of the 19th century. Today, two tombs that tower above the upper seats of the theater, and an inscribed "obelisk" – in fact also a tomb – have become the trademark of the site.

The so-called **Harpy Tomb** takes its name from an interpretation of the reliefs around the top which has been revised. The reliefs – the originals are in the British Museum – depict winged women at first thought to be Harpies, the foul-smelling ugly monsters of Greek mythology. Historians now believe them to be Sirens, carrying away the souls of the dead to the Isle of the Blessed. The other is a regular sarcophagus standing atop a short pillar tomb. Pottery found inside the pillar dates it to the 3rd century BC but a relief on the side, since removed, was of the 6th century and had apparently been reused.

The obelisk stands at the corner of the agora. It is mostly in Lycian but with a few lines of Greek and gives an account of the life and exploits of the local hero whose remains it contained. Elsewhere on the site are the remains of a later agora, a basilica, a monastery and the Byzantine walls. The views from the walls to the west down across the **Esen Çayı** are impressive, and standing here, one can picture the scene as the Xanthians, twice in their history, fought to the last man to retain their independence as their proud city was burned to cinders around them.

Near Xanthos, 3 miles (5 km) from the main road on the coast side is the **Letoon**, one of those lesser sites that are easier to manage and still give an impression of the might of ancient civilizations. Partly submerged by the rising water table, the site features the foundations of three adjacent temples to Leto (said to have been the lover of Zeus) and to her children Apollo and Artemis.

To the north is the Hellenistic stoa and beyond it a well-preserved theater standing at close quarters with the local farmland. An interesting feature of the theater is the series of 16 masks above the entrance to the vaulted passage beneath the upper seats on the south-west.

The main road which winds inland from near Patara reaches the coast again at **Fethiye**, a small, attractive port town that has tidied itself up considerably in recent years, with sidewalk restaurants and several old buildings behind the main street converted to attractive stores. Most of the town, however, is brand-new: it was virtually flattened by an earthquake in 1957; strangely, it left the huge Lycian sarcophagi that stand around untouched save one whose lid moved a few inches.

The damage they have suffered is all human-inflicted. Little else remains of the ancient city save a series of Lycian rock tombs in the cliff behind the town. The largest of these is that of Amyntas, identified from a 4th century BC inscription, but about whom nothing else is known. The town itself has no beaches, and those wanting to swim must either

The Ölüdeniz near Fethiye.

take a short boat trip to one of the many bays or islets in the gulf of Fethiye or travel across the peninsula some 15 miles (25 km) to the Dead Sea (Öludeniz).

The Dead Sea: This idyllic location, featured on the cover of many tourist brochures, has also been developed dramatically but not totally spoilt. Dozens of pensions and campsites, with cabins that can be rented by the day or week, are scattered here behind one of Turkey's most beautiful beaches. To the west is a lagoon, at the foot of a wooded slope, where yachts have now mercifully been banned but where so-called pleasure boats clutter and pollute the outer side of the sandbar. Access to the sandbar is limited by a small admission charge payable at the village end. The back of the lagoon houses a few pensions and a luxury motel, the **Meri**, which is horribly overpriced.

The eerie ghost-town of **Kaya**, which was home to tens of thousands of Greeks until the deportations of the 1920s, makes a fascinating excursion from Fethiye. It is reached most easily off the main road to Öludeniz but a more interesting route, if a little difficult, is that running directly up from Fethiye, starting from the street at the foot of the rock tombs. A hermit, known as Robinson Ahmet, inhabits a beach near Kaya.

Dalaman: From Fethiye the road meanders some 50 miles (80 km) through pine forests before the turnoff for **Dalaman**, an attractive port, and the airport by the same name. Opened in the early 1980s, it was one of the better ideas of Turkey's tourism masters. Daily charter flights from many European location and scheduled services from Istanbul mean easy access to a wide selection of resorts in the southern Aegean and western Mediterranean.

Dalyan itself means fishery, and a complicated system of barriers has been built among the reeds to allow the gray mullet and sea bass that breed in **Köyceğiz Lake** to be caught as they head for the sea.

A road of some 15 miles (25 km) winds up and down past blooming hibiscus along the coast from Dalyan to a

The unshakable tomb in downtown Fethiye.

beautiful, remote location which has recently become famous as the "**turtle beach**." Locals say it has no name. It is one of the few places in the Mediterranean where giant loggerhead turtles come to lay their eggs. Conservationists are opposed to the development of the beach, as hotel buildings would scare off the mother turtles, and disco lights and other activity would confuse the newly hatched young that normally move into the sea at night, drawn by the reflection of the moonlight.

Caunus: Through seven centuries of active life, under the Persians, the Greeks and the Romans, **Caunus** was one of the leading towns of ancient Caria. It was always known as an unhealthy place and whether it was abandoned because of the mosquitoes that plagued it or because of the silting of the harbor is not clear. Most visitors will hire a boat from the Dalyan cooperative (i.e. monopoly) with high charges for the pleasant though unnecessarily long voyage around the reeds to the site across the river. The most striking feature of the ruins today

is a series of rock tombs situated close to Dalyan, which includes the largest one that is uncompleted. It shows clearly the method of construction – starting at the top. The acropolis is impressive, standing on a bend in the river, and the traveler who has taken a one-way trip to the landing stage beyond here can easily return by waiting on the Dalyan side of the hill to flag down any passing craft.

The visitor is unlikely to climb to the city walls but the ruins of a Roman theater, a huge Byzantine basilica and a Roman fountain house with a long inscription are easily accessible.

Muğla: About 30 miles (50 km) north of Marmaris, the pretty town of **Muğla** is unique – along with Safranbolu in the Black Sea region – for having clung to its architectural heritage. Its many old Turkish houses, caravanserais, fountains and mosques have been preserved and are still used by the townsfolk. With a population of some 35,000, Muğla is the administrative capital of the region, under the direction of Lale Ataman, Turkey's first female governor.

Sails set at Marmaris.

The Marmaris Peninsula: Marmaris is reached along a 20-mile (32-km) road off the highway between **Fethiye** and **Muğla** that starts with a mile (2 km) avenue of eucalyptus trees. Sadly they are too close together for modern traffic needs. A new and larger road now serves cars while the old road is left to donkeys and horse-drawn carriages.

The town has a busy, near-perfect natural harbor, and vies with Bodrum as the starting point for cruises along the Turkish coast. While still offering plenty of entertainment, shopping and eating opportunities, and scenery of equal beauty, Marmaris is somehow less frantic than its rival. The Marmaris peninsula as a whole is much less developed than the Bodrum area but still offers plenty of accommodation.

The picturesque village of **Bozburun** with its yachting harbor makes an interesting detour off the main road west of Marmaris toward Datça. There are any number of small hotels in towns and villages, as well as campsites. One of these, Camp Amazon, has been carved into the jungle on the northern side of the peninsula. It is well sign-posted 5 miles (8 km) off the main road halfway between Marmaris and Datça along a track with lovely coastal views.

The site, only recently equipped with electricity and telephone, caters best to the traveler with caravan, motorhome or tent, but also has a few small hotels and pensions. It has a fine restaurant, good bathhouse facilities and a pleasant sandy beach at the end of the nearby cove. Anyone seeking a beach with real isolation must take the forest track a few miles farther on.

Datça and Knidos: A favorite with yachtsmen, **Datça** is a pretty, sleepy town with one modern hotel and several pensions and the attraction of being virtually surrounded by the sea. The ancient city of **Knidos** may be reached by sea from Datça, where a few boatmen offer the facility, or at the end of a 90-minute bone-shaking drive off the main road a short way outside the town.

The site itself is almost permanently windy, as it was in antiquity when it was infamous among sailors. It occupies a fascinatingly beautiful location at the tip of the peninsula. Experts debate whether this was always the location of Knidos, or whether the settlement was moved here from present-day Datça.

Among the most interesting features are a stepped street with some dwelling houses and a theater to the right of the main road as one approaches the village. Other ruined buildings overlook the twin harbors, including the foundation of a small round building known as the temple of Aphrodite, believed to have housed a statue of the goddess by the Greek sculptor Praxiteles (390–330 BC) that was famed throughout the ancient world. That discovery was made by the American Professor Iris Love whose other, more controversial, claim is that a battered head she found in a basement in the British Museum is that of the Aphrodite statue.

Of the two harbors that benefited the ancient city, the larger, southern one now benefits tourists with some four or five restaurants. The daily ferry each way from Bodrum to Datça stops here.

Lagoon at Dalyan.

THE CILICIAN COAST

The road east from Antalya leads through cotton and orange country, but aside from the ancient sites at Perge, Aspendos and possibly Selge, there is ultimately little to delay the traveler until one approaches the peninsula town of **Side**, some 50 miles (70 km) down the road.

Although founded as long ago as the 7th century BC, Side has undergone perhaps its most startling transformation over the past 15 years. Until recently it was a sleepy fishing village; most of today's pension and restaurant owners were yesterday's fishermen who have lost interest in the humble hook and line.

Tourism, in fact, has become big business in Side, and the ruins of the Greek, Roman and Byzantine eras are almost overshadowed tourist oriented setups. Responding to demand and supply, the entire area has seen a recent mushrooming of hotels, holiday villages and hostels, with accompanying restaurants, carpet shops and snack bars. Still, between the discos and cafés stuffed between ancient columns, Side retains its charm, and is unique in Turkey as being a living open-air museum in a spectacular setting.

The incoming road is a maze of twists and turns littered with Byzantine ruins. Suddenly the Roman theater looms into full view, heralding the entrance to the town. Opposite the theater, which accommodated 25,000 people in its time, lie the old Roman baths, now the museum housing finds from local excavations. The headless statues inside are the result of overzealousness on the part of the locals after their conversion to Christianity by St Paul, when they promptly decapitated their former pagan deities. In fact most monuments lying in such profusion in the village are relics of the early Christian era, although the history of the settlement is actually much older.

Alexander the Great's biographer Arrian recorded that when his master captured the city in 333 BC, its people spoke a tongue unknown to the invaders – in fact it remains undeciphered to this day. Rampant piracy flourished, with prisoners sold as slaves in the town Agora to be sent next to the island of Delos, a notorious depot for human wares in antiquity.

Christianity arrived with the ubiquitous St Paul, and Side served as a bishopric in the Byzantine period. It declined in the 7th century under relentless Arab attacks, and was completely abandoned in the 10th century. Earthquakes, too, have taken their toll on the town, and one must wonder what the local inhabitants felt as their world came crashing down on top of them. Sand drifts now cover most of the southeast section of the old city, and it is perhaps here that the stadium has been concealed. Take a walk off the beaten paths, and one has that special sense of being the first to find this ancient wall or shattered cistern, buried in thistles and weeds.

Beaches line either side of the peninsula, so swimming is invited; diving off the rocks and foundation stones of the old harbor is pleasant but frustrating: too many other divers have had the same thought, and few fish remain. For those interested in going further afield, boat trips are available that follow the coast east for an hour and then up the Manavgat River to a small waterfall. For groups of eight or 10 the cost is about $12 each including lunch, or $6 without.

Natural vegetation forms a tropical curtain over the river – a shady haven after the crowds of Side. Be prepared to get out and dig at the mouth of the river, as it sometimes silts up overnight. The falls are nothing spectacular, but it's a pleasant excursion. Farther upriver are the Big Waterfalls (again don't get your hopes up), unapproachable by boat. Take a *dolmuş* from either Side or **Manavgat**, the bustling little town 5 miles (8 km) east on the main route, where the cotton harvest piles up mile after patient mile on trucks, carts and tractors awaiting admittance to the government controlled depot.

Town market day is Monday, when villagers troop in from all over to stock

Sunset on the eastern Mediterranean.

up and to sell their wares. This is a good opportunity to buy local crafts, old coins or the rugs found among the colorful displays of fruits, vegetables and squawking chickens.

Ten miles (17 km) east of Manavgat, take a left turn at the yellow signpost and follow the scenic road to a well preserved Seljuk caravansarai on the banks of the Alara River, constructed in 1231. Above, on a rocky crag, sits **Alara Castle**, with a fortress wall running crazily along the summit.

A long tunnel has been cut through the mountain to the castle, down which donkeys were allegedly herded to fetch water, thus protected from surprise attacks en route. The tunnel has partially collapsed, and a flashlight is necessary for explorers.

Alanya: Seventy miles (110 km) east of Antalya stands the massive fortress dominating the town of **Alanya**. The castle is perched 800 ft (250 meters) above the sea on one of the finest promontories of the Mediterranean, with dizzying views to the sea on three sides, and behind to the orchard covered foothills of the Taurus Mountains. The ancient walls wind 4 miles (6.5 km) toward the summit, crowned by three turrets, forming a jutting wedge which effectively divides the thriving town of Alanya into two. Each side boasts good sandy beaches backed by a host of hotels and pensions, although the eastern part of the town sports a wider selection.

The town is the prosperous center for the outlying orchards which year round produce fruit and vegetables for both domestic and export markets. It is an elegant, broad avenued town, with a fine harbor and a peaceful unhurried air, and is justifiably one of Turkey's most popular resorts. Outdoor seafood restaurants, cafés and tea gardens line the harbor and the beaches. Possibly due to the heavy German influence, Alanya also boasts a profusion of public toilets, a rarity in Turkey.

Although the exact foundation date of Alanya is unknown, it traces back to Hellenistic times, when it was named Coracesium, with the Romans, Byzan- **The show must go on at Side.**

tines, Armenians, Seljuks and Ottomans all taking their turn at power. Pirate chieftain Diototus Tryphon built his fortress on the peak in the 2nd century BC, as a base to store his booty and to sell his slaves. This was the last bastion to fall to the fury of the Roman General Pompey in his crusade to wipe out the pirates in 65 BC. Later Mark Antony presented the land to Cleopatra. She made good use of the fine timber in the area, using it both to rebuild her fleet and for export.

During the decline of the Byzantine empire, the south coast was poorly defended, and various Armenian dynasties took advantage of the weakness. In the 10th century Alanya proved no exception to this change of fortune. When the Seljuks tried to wrest control of the fortress in 1222, they found it to be a formidable target.

Legend has it that Sultan Kaykubat, at his wit's end, gambled on a last desperate bid. He conscripted into his army hundreds of wild goats. Tying a lighted candle to each of their horns, he shep

herded his new recruits ahead of his army up the cliffs. The enemy, upon seeing the obvious strength of the invaders, surrendered at once and were exiled to Konya – but not before Keykubat had wed the daughter of the ousted leader.

Today, the markedly different contributions of the Romans, Byzantines and Seljuks to the fortress are clearly discernible. There is a domed Byzantine church (6th-century) dedicated to St George, a flight of red brick stairs said to have been used by Cleopatra when she descended to the sea to bathe, store rooms, numerous cisterns – the largest of which could hold 120,000 tons of water – a hefty advantage during protracted sieges. Just outside the wall lies the *bedesten* with its vaulted shops, now lying almost in ruins in a very attractive old quarter of stone houses under a tangle of vines and fruit trees.

You may notice Turks throwing pebbles from the summit. Legend says that condemned prisoners were given the same chance – if they managed to throw

a pebble into the sea (no mean feat, for the cliffs jut out prominently), they were set free. If not, they were hurled immediately to their deaths.

Sultan Keykubat substantially extended the fortress, and ordered construction of the red tower on the edge of the sea below, to protect his massive dockyards built into the cliffs nearby. Both are still intact, and the tower is a fine example of the influence the crusading Franks had on the architecture of military structures during their occupation of that corner of the Mediterranean. On the third floor are lancet windows for firing upon the enemy, and for pouring down hot oil once the invaders had begun scaling the walls.

Although the road to the castle is a mere 2 miles (3 km) it's a steep climb. Taxis cost $3 one way; I suggest saving your energy for the walk downhill through carob and fig trees, and scented jasmine, with stunning views of the harbor below. The inevitable tea house sits on the summit, but no food is sold. Take a picnic hamper, as the surrounding area offers fine hillside scrambles.

Just west of the fortress at sea level is the Damlataş Cave, an exquisite grotto with curtains of dripping stalactites and stalagmites dating back 15,000–20,000 years. This is the site of a "magic cure" for respiratory ailments, especially asthma, the success due apparently to the atmosphere. Turks come from all over for this cure, for which a doctor's certificate is required: four hours per day for 21 days. Little knots of scarved women while away the hours as they knit, sew and crochet their way to a clear respiratory system in this warm, damp enclave. The success rate is claimed to be 80 percent, and for those interested, doctors in Alanya will examine you and write the necessary report. The cave is closed to the public from 6–10 a.m. when it is reserved for those taking treatment. People with heart ailments may have breathing difficulties here, for the dense air pressure makes the heart work overtime.

Alanya's coast is lined with grottoes, and boat trips can be arranged to any or **Alanya Beach.**

all – Pirate's Cave, Lovers' Grotto, and one where phosphorescent pebbles shine up from the sea bed; or to the "wishing gate," an enormous natural hole in the rocks. It is said that barren women who go through this gate will gain the ability to conceive.

While foreigners fry on beaches, native Alanyans shake their heads and take to the cooler hills, believing that mountain air is the key to a long life. Their favorite spots are in **Mahmut Seydi Village**, 21 miles (35 km) north, in a grove with fresh spring water and a 13th-century Seljuk mosque; or **Dimçay**, a pretty wooded area. A foreigner would be welcomed at either.

Anamur: For departures east from Alanya, the early morning is best; if you are traveling by bus, book a seat on the right, the better to see the coastline. The afternoon sun on this leg has been known to reduce travelers to quivering jelly and tends to take the joy out of some of Turkey's finest coastal scenery, particularly after **Gazipaşa**.

The road climbs through terraced ba-
nana plantations that step resolutely down the cliffs into the sea, between tiny coves jostling for space, and acres of pine covered mountain with mud-plastered, flat roofed houses clinging absurdly to the hillsides. The views are stupendous, and the journey justifiably famed, the whole being studded with ruins from Hellenistic, Byzantine and Seljuk periods.

Eighty miles (130 km) east of Alanya and 3 miles (5 km) south of the main highway slumber the ruins of **Anemurium**, a great Phoenician trading city in its day, situated on the southernmost tip of Asia Minor. The cemetery is a vast sprawl of domed tombs, and several churches, crumbling houses and an aqueduct can be made out. Village children press fistful of wild flowers onto visitors, as if to make up for what they deem nothing but a boring collection of debris.

Anamur lies several miles inland (shuttle service by minibus) with no particular claim to fame except for a newly discovered cave in the foothills

Harbor and fisherman.

behind the town, which supposedly cures asthma, and its proximity to both Anemurium and the **Anamur Castle**, standing to the east with one foot in the sea. This magnificent castle was built around 1230 on the site of a 3rd-century fortress by the Rupenian dynasty of lesser Armenia, who reigned in this area for 300 years, entrenching themselves in castles throughout the Cilician coast and the slopes of the Taurus. The mosque and two rooms watching out over the sea from the upper battlements were added by the Karamanlis, after which it changed hands many times until the Ottomans seized it in 1469.

Eight miles (12 km) further on broods an anonymous medieval fortress, looking as if it may topple at any moment down the cliff. Another 50 miles (80 km) onwards, **Liman Castle** looms out of the sea from a promontory, while **Tokmar Castle** lies off to the left (yellow signpost) just west of Taşuçu.

Taşuçu and Silifke: Ascending and descending in a series of hairpin turns, the coastal road finally hits the Cilician flats near Taşuçu, one of the two embarkation points (the other is Mersin) for the Turkish Republic of Northern Cyprus, which was founded in 1983 in the wake of the division of the unhappy island in 1974.

Ferryboats leave daily except Sunday with the trip lasting about 6 hours at $10 per head. Taşuçu itself is a peaceful hamlet dominated by a monstrous paper mill; there are several hotels and pensions on the waterfront to the east of town out of factory range.

Six miles (10 km) east of Taşuçu is **Silifke**, a non-prepossessing town made interesting by its old quarters amid ancient ruins. It was the **Göksu River**, on which the town sits, that brought about the abrupt end of the Third Crusade when the Holy Roman Emperor Frederick Barbarossa drowned on his way to Jerusalem in 1190 while bathing some 10 miles (16 km) north of town. Today, the river sees some rafting, especially upstream towards the town of **Mut**, but on the whole remains unknown by the white-water crowd.

The Alanya Castle.

Of the ancient Seleucia and Calycadnum which once stood on this site (one of the nine sister cities founded by Seleucus Nicator in the 3rd century BC when he gained control of Syria on the death of Alexander the Great), precious little remains. The fortress dominating the town is probably from Crusader times, while an enormous Roman cistern, 150 ft (46 meters) long is carved out of the rocks at its foot. The stone bridge over the Göksu has ancient origins, while on the right of Inönü Boulevard leading to the bus terminal stands a single column of the Temple of Zeus, believed to belong to the 2nd or 3rd century.

The **Ulu Mosque** in town is of Seljuk origin, and while no trace of decoration remains, the *mihrap* and the entrance are original.

A recommended first stop is the local tourist bureau, near the bridge. One of Turkey's most enthusiastic, its boundless zeal has ignored its limited resources, even running Turkish language courses for foreigners who generally stay longer than they had anticipated.

For those weary of Turkish tea, Silifke specializes in *kenger kahvesi*, made from prickly acanthus fruit, the leaves of which provide the decoration motif of ancient Corinthian columns, and two herbal teas – *ada* and *dağ* (island and mountain) tea. The latter is made from sage and is recommended for a queasy stomach. This is also the land of strawberries, thick-skinned oranges and yogurt as thick as clotted cream.

Ayatekla, just left of the highway between Silifke and Taşucu, is said to be the burial place of St Thecla, virgin and martyr, and one of St Paul's first converts. She first heard Paul preaching the virtues of chastity in Iconium (Konya), and thereupon renounced her betrothal. On a visit to the apostle in prison to listen further to his words, she too was arrested and sentenced to be burned at the stake as an example to local women. She was tied naked to a pyre in the arena, but a divinely inspired deluge doused the flames. Wild beasts were brought in to devour her, but "there was

about her a cloud, so that neither the beasts did touch her, nor was she seen to be naked," according to Acts of Paul and Thecla, written in the 2nd century by an unknown Asian presbyter. She later set up a nunnery near ancient Seleucia, where her miraculous cures were said to have taken business away from the town doctors. At Ayatekla stands a section of tall defiant wall, part of the 250-ft-long (75-meter) basilica dedicated to this saint, near which lies a cistern and another church, though little remains today.

Olba: Twenty miles (30 km) north of Silifke, tucked high in the Taurus Mountains, the ancient city of **Olba** suns itself in its past glory. The city – known also as Diocaesarea – is a stupendous conglomeration of Hellenistic, Roman and Byzantine remains. The monumental gate with Corinthian capitals stands near the **Temple of Zeus** built in 295 BC, one of the oldest such sanctuaries in Asia Minor. Thirty columns, four still with their capitals, are standing today, while nearby lie six columns of the **Temple of Tyche**, or Fortune, each made of a single piece of granite nearly 20 ft (6 meters) high, brought from Egypt in the 1st century.

The city gate is a massive structure of three richly ornamented arches. At a distance is the ancient cemetery, set in an eerie valley of rock-cut tombs. Hiring a guide is advisable. For those keen on staying a second day here, there is a pension and an eating house of sorts.

Back on the coastal road heading in the direction east is **Yapaklı Eşik**, a tiny cove just east of Susanoğlu, where water of 28 degrees Celsius swirls over a tower current of eight degrees – a surprising swimming experience.

Ten miles (16 km) north of **Susanoğlu** are the remains of a Roman city and the **Mausoleum of Priape** the Fearless Satrap. On this huge monument, in all its erect glory, stands the sculptured yard-long phallus of this god of fertility. Legend says that Priape was the illegitimate son of Zeus and Aphrodite, and that Hera, jealous wife of Zeus, de-

The choice is yours.

formed the child, giving him a phallus equal to his height. He was abandoned out of shame by his mother near the Dardanelles, and was brought by shepherds to Lapsacus (Lapseki).

Twelve miles (20 km) east of Silifke is the bay of **Narlıkuyu**, a pleasant seaside cove lined with seafood restaurants and a hotel along with the remains of a Roman bath with its mosaic of the three graces, or daughters of Zeus. Many say that their well proportioned figures are the most beautiful surviving representation of the graces existing today. For those interested in imbibing wisdom from a well, there is a spring whose water was claimed by the ancients to enhance gray matter.

Heaven and hell: Two miles (3 km) inland lies your chance to glimpse both heaven and hell without leaving the comfort of this earthly domain where two caverns were formed by underground chemical erosion. Heaven ("**Cennet Deresi**"), happily, is larger than Hell, with 452 stairs leading down to a chapel dedicated to the Virgin Mary.

In the bowels of the grotto is an opening known as **Python's Cave**, home of the fearful, scaly, fire-breathing monster. Just north is the gloomy pit of Hell ("**Cehennem**"), happily inaccessible, as both sides are concave.

Three miles (5 km) eastwards on the main road is **Kız Kalesi**, or the Maiden's Castle. Actually, there are a set of twin medieval castles, one on terra firma, while its sister sits on an offshore island. It was a refuge for pirates before it was fortified by the Romans, Byzantines, Armenians, Turkomans, and at last the Ottomans in 1482. Legend, of course, has its own say with the rather tired but charming belief that the sea castle was where King Corycus sequestered his daughter after a dire prediction that she would die from snakebite. Naturally a basket of grapes sent to her by a lover contained a viper.

The town of Kız Kalesi itself is pint-sized, best appreciated in early summer before a new kind of Turkish nomad descends on this part of the coast – this time with orange and blue canvas tents,

Kız Kalesi, or the Maiden's Castle.

two-door refrigerators, stereos and television sets: the well-to-do of Adana have arrived to plant their tents row upon row along the water's edge to get back to nature and stay that way all summer. But there is escape yet: a few miles west is **Akkaya**, which has its own Pamukkale in miniature, with smooth white rocks curved like waves, and excellent swimming. However, camping is prohibited.

On both sides of the highway to Mersin rise crops of Roman and Byzantine ruins, and in valleys one can still see giant Roman aqueducts which once brought water from the Lamus river to the ancient cities.

Mersin and Tarsus: The most delightful thing about the huge port of **Mersin**, center of a region abundant with oranges and lemons, is that there are two ways in which one can get out in a hurry. Boats leave daily for Cyprus, and intercity buses are frequent. For those inclined to archaeology, **Yumuktepe**, a huge mound a mile from the shore has revealed levels of civilizations stepping back into the neolithic age. For those of other inclinations, the city is also known for its relative gaiety. One could possibly make a theory that this is due to the number of sailors who frequent the town, as well as due to the large population of ethnic Arabs.

Sixteen miles (25 km) east lies **Tarsus**, birthplace of St Paul, and a city with a resplendent history reaching back to the 14th century BC. Alas, the ravages of war, inertia and time have destroyed most vestiges of the past, and the ancient city lies 15–20 ft (45–60 meters) below the present Tarsus.

Even the few traces of antiquity left are of dubious origin: **St Paul's Arch**, on the left hand side of the road into town, has nothing to do with the apostle, and was probably named by the Byzantines or the Crusaders, both of whom had a vested interest in liberally labelling biblical names to relics and places of minor pilgrimage throughout the domains of their administration.

In the pre-Christian period, Tarsus' major claim to fame was as the site

The cotton pickin' fields back home.

where Cleopatra seduced Mark Antony following his victory at Philippi, when he sent for the Ptolemite Queen of Egypt to punish her for the aid she gave to Cassius. According to Plutarch, Cleopatra arrived "…sailing up the river Cyndus in a barge with gilded stern, outspread sails of purple, and silver oars moving in time to the sound of flutes, pipes and harps. Dressed like Aphrodite, the goddess of love, Cleopatra lay beneath an awning bespangled with gold, while the boys like painted cupids stood at each side fanning her."

When the engineers of ancient Tarsus envisioned and cut a pass through the northern mountains to the **Cilician Gates**, they created one of the most historic mountain routes of all time, and traders and troopes have poured through the narrow gorge ever since. Xerxes and his 100,000 men and later Alexander the Great passed here; the latter almost lost his life after bathing in the icy waters of the River Cyndus, now called the **Tarsus Suyu**. A fearful and haunted pass, it was named the "Gates of Judas"

by the Crusaders. Tarsus is also the home of a century-old American College for Boys.

A farther 25 miles (40 km) east is **Adana**, the cotton and citrus capital of Turkey, and the economic hub of the vast and fertile Çukurova Plain. A sprawling and prosperous city of nearly a million, it is known as the "biggest village in Turkey," due to the rural atmosphere brought in by the thousands of semi-resident farm workers in the area. It is also known as the birthplace of the famous *Adana kebabı*, and other spicy meats cooked over the coals, with attending spicy *meze* or side dishes, such as garlic and yogurt, onions and yogurt, and red peppers and yogurt. Try **Büyük Onbaşilar Restaurant** on Gazipaşa Bulvar for a good introduction to this distinctive cuisine.

Unfortunately, Adana has little else to offer other than its vast archaeological museum and a Roman bridge built in the 2nd century. There are also two 15th-century buildings – **the Eski Yağ Mosque** with its stunning door, and the **Ulu Cami**, or Grand Mosque.

Adana also has the enormous **Incirlik Air Base**, home for 5,000 US troops and used in the Gulf War. Car repair shops along the road advertise their special services for the G.I.s in such terms as "American spoken here." Another distinctive feature of the city is its unique fleet of 1950s vintage Skoda cars, used as route taxis.

One of the city's most eminent sons is novelist Yaşar Kemal, whose pen drips with the ochres and reds of the surrounding Çukurova Plain. His most popular work, *Ince Mehmet* (Mehmet My Hawk), has been translated into a dozen languages and has made the author a perennial candidate for the Nobel Prize for Literature. The film starring Peter Ustinov has been disowned by the author as a travesty of his work. The leftist filmmaker Yılmaz Güney also used the city and the surrounding villages as the backdrop for his works on social dislocation and poverty; all of Güney's work, however, was banned after his escape from prison and flight to Paris, where he died in 1985.

Taking oranges to the market.

The Cilician plain around Adana might also be known as "The March," as it has been a vital piece of real estate for centuries, and contested by every would-be conqueror of Anatolia ranging from Xerxes to Alexander, the Arabs, the Armenians, the Crusaders and even the Mongols. As one historian of the region puts it, there is scarcely any land in Asia more soaked in blood. Nearly every stubby hill and rise on the valley floor owns a fortress in some degree of dilapidation, and one can imagine how brave hearts skipped a beat when yet another churning cloud of dust was spotted on the horizon, promising yet another enemy horde.

The first castle one encounters on the plain is the **Yılan Kalesi**, or "Snake Castle," still dominating the plain from its perch overlooking a long bend in the Ceyhan River, about 20 miles (30 km) east of Adana. The fortress is in fairly good shape despite the action it must have seen in its day.

The origin of the name is obscure; some writers attribute it to one of the Armenian Kings of Cilicia who made common cause with the Crusaders during the 11th and 12th centuries, while others ascribe it to an apocryphal "King of the Snakes." Calling it the Lizard Castle might have been more appropriate, as this reptile can be seen scurrying over turrets and walls everywhere in the structure. Snakes, on the other hand, are nowhere to be seen.

Kozan Castle: Just beyond Yılan Kalesi, a road turns north, forking after some 20 miles to the left to the farming dorp of Kozan. Seeming to rise perpendicularly from the plain is another castle of obscure origin which has no doubt been occupied and added to by all of the sundry armies that have passed this way.

The structure is approached via an unmarked road in the middle of town, which leads upwards by 45 degree turns through a series of outer walls until one arrives at the castle gate. Unhappily, the entrance doubles as a toilet for shepherds (What are they doing up here?).

The main walls form a sort of saddle linking the twin summits of the long and narrow hill, and are ringed by 44 towers replete with vents for pouring hot oil down on unwelcome visitors. The western summit is topped by the three walls and ceiling of what appear to be the remains of a church; given the height of the castle over the plain, one wonders if the former crusader king had pretensions of talking to the Trinity of a starry night.

Much higher than the Yılan Kalesi, the castle at Kozan is so far above the plain that guards would have to stay asleep for days to miss any approaching enemy; other fortresses can easily be seen in the distance from this panoramic eagle's nest, none of them being more than 31 miles (50 km) from the next.

This begs the question: why so many fortresses? While our contemporaries tend to regard them as edifices of aesthetic interest, one must recall that all were built as garrisons with an eye for defense alone. Will future generations flog donkey and risk heat exhaustion simply to view the remnants of barbed wire and concrete foundation of the officers' mess at Fort Bragg, camera in one hand and a guide book in the other?

Castles, then, are perhaps best viewed as destinations, a place to turn around; often it is the journey there and back which is really the more interesting, as most medieval fortresses ultimately start to resemble one another after the second or third climb of the day. The enthusiast will find dozens of castles in Cilicia, most of which do not appear in any guide book unless, like the Yılan Kalesi, they are within spitting distance of the main road.

The best advice for those who really want to climb every castle in the plain is to choose a mound, any mound, drive as close as the back roads or fields will permit, and then just start hiking up, pretending you are a visiting dignitary of old with plenty of servants to carry your bags, and not a local peon forced into corvée labor, lugging a 500-pound block up the hill for the further glory of God and Country. Each castle, you will find, has an evocative setting.

Stone soldier fights for God and Country.

ARAB BORDER LANDS

Driving east of Adana, one enters the well irrigated **Çukurova Plain**, with vast stretches of the rich alluvial soil being devoted to cotton and other cash crops. Water from the two major rivers feeding the plain – the Ceyhan and Seyhan – is so abundant, in fact, that Turkey has considered selling it via a "Peace Pipeline" that would stretch from Adana to the Muslim Holy Cities in Saudi Arabia via Syria and Jordan.

During planting and harvest time, thousands of migrant farm workers descend on Çukurova, with their rather unhygienic tent cities doting the horizon. (One anecdote about these people concerns a model tent city set up by an affiliate of the AFL-CIO, the US labor organization: the sanitation system failed because the migrants long accustomed to making night soil, had persisted in the use of their traditional sanitary napkins and had filled up the toilets with rocks.) Theirs is a bleak existence of cyclical debt and exploitation, but it is hoped that the new series of dams that will reanimate the Tigris-Euphrate basin in their native provinces further east will allow them to stay at home and farm their own plots of baked earth. Atatürk Dam, the cornerstone of the giant Southeastern Anatolia Project (GAP), started operating in 1992.

Some 20 miles (30 km) east of Adana, one encounters a crossroad; to the right the road leads toward the large Turkish oil terminal and refinery city of **Yumurtalık**; British Petroleum maintains a sizable beach-and-bungalow complex nearby, but the sand is unfortunately tarred by *zift*, or the oily discharge of tankers, making the camp less than ideal.

Karatepe National Park: Taking the left fork and turning inland, the road leads to **Kadirli**, and from there it leads over 12 miles (20 km) of often bad road to the ruins of the neo-Hittite capital of **Karatepe**, which is situated in a pretty national forest along both sides of a

Preceding pages, shepherd tends his flock. Below, map of South East Turkey.

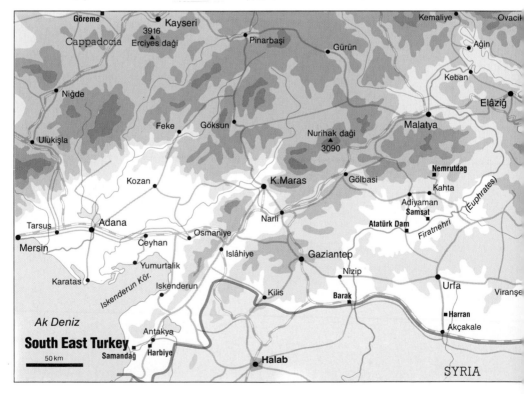

South East Turkey

50 km

Ak Deniz

SYRIA

reservoir on the upper Ceyhan River.

Since the dam was built, one short section of the road actually remains under several inches of water, but is easily passable. One can avoid both the Irish bridge and the rather battered road leading from Kadirli by continuing along the E5 road from Adana to the town of **Osmaniye** before taking the better road to Karatepe from there. Osmaniye itself is best avoided, boasting, as it does, the greatest density of oil tankers anywhere in the world, both on the road or in various stages of repair alongside it.

Karatepe lays its claim to fame as the place where the first Hittite writing was discovered; this consists largely of several massive tablets which are carved with pictographs of ass heads, horses and other creatures and designs. Other reliefs consist of bizarre carvings, such as spear-toting soldiers with hooved feet, as well as several monumental lions, all displayed *in situ* under crudely fashioned tin roofs.

An irritating aspect of one's visit to Karatepe is the refusal of the guards to allow photography. One wonders if this edict was passed by the chief excavator, Mr. Halit Çambel, because the inscriptions contain some highly classified national secret, or simply because his 40 years of excavations have in fact produced so little in the way of concrete results. Whatever the reason for the prohibition, it is not the guards' fault, and they will be as upset as you for having to act like policemen in such a beautiful and historical setting.

The reservoir itself abounds in catfish and carp, and a small, unprepossessing restaurant serves a pleasant lakeside campsite in the national forest. Local villages also produce carpets and flatweave *kilims*, although the old adage of "the stone is heavy in its place" would seem to apply here: the same carpets and *kilims* can be purchased much cheaper from dealers back in Ankara or Istanbul.

Back on the E5 highway at Osmaniye, one has the choice of continuing inland to the seldom visited cities of Kahra-

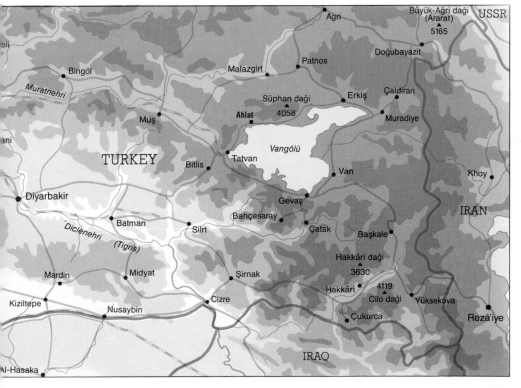

manmaraş and Gaziantep, or proceeding directly to Turkey's southernmost (and most un-Turkish) province of Hatay and the ancient city of Antioch, now called Antakya.

The Hatay: Although most Turks will hotly dispute the fact, there is little question that the province now known as the Hatay is predominantly Arab. The years since the province was ceded to Turkey by the French in 1939 (Syria still includes the province on its maps) have certainly taken their toll in terms of the cultural and linguistic consciousness of the residents of Hatay, but Arabic – even in a somewhat bastardized form – remains the primary language of the home and the street.

In addition to the ethnic Muslim Arabs – most of whom are Alawites, a splinter group of Shi'i Islam whose main religious tenet would seem to be a nearly religious belief in the absurdity of religion – there are also substantial pockets of Arabic speaking Greek Orthodox Christians, Armenians and Roman Catholics as well as a Jewish community of some 150 souls. Indeed, it might not be too great an exaggeration to say that Hatay is the most culturally diverse of all of Turkey's provinces per capita. Coupled with its deep historical roots, the province is a must for any visitor with more than a casual curiosity in foreign parts.

Iskenderun: Turn south at the intersection outside of Osmaniye dominated by the large **Toprakkale Castle.** Built by the Byzantine Emperor Nicophorus II Pocas (AD 963–969), the fortress was used as a base for his successful campaign against the Arabs in Antioch, who had held the venerable old city since the beginning of the Muslim conquests in the 7th century. The road leads past an aqueduct built by the Seleucids as well as several Crusader castles to the port city of **Iskenderun**. The city itself is of little interest, with its most antique building seeming to be a 19th-century Protestant church.

Most of the city was built when Iskenderun served as the administrative center for the mini-state of Alexandretta **Palm-lined boulevard in Iskenderun.**

during the French Mandate, and as a result, Iskenderun owns a pleasant, Levantine feel. There are several good fish restaurants on the promenade serving large shrimps and other seafoods at very reasonable prices, for which alone the city is worth a few hours' visit.

Some 12 miles (20 km) south of Iskenderun and pushed into a hillside is the notorious resort area called **Soğukoluk**, where white slavers kept hundreds of underaged girls captive in a virtual brothel city, catering mainly to Arab customers from Syria and Saudi Arabia. Persistent rumors suggest that the sordid trade might not have been as completely snuffed out as announced, as the area is allegedly honeycombed with underground passageways for the bawds to hide their living wares.

The road leads through several quaint villages and towns before climbing over a high pass and then descending into a wide valley watered by the **Orantes River**. At the end of the valley, pushed against the first outcroppings of the lesser Lebanon mountains, lies Antakya, the former Antioch, which was capital of the Seleucids, and a city that once rivaled the glories of Rome.

Antakya: The rise and fall of Antioch reveals much of the tumultous history of the eastern Mediterranean. The city's original founder was Seleucus Nicator, a lesser general in Alexander the Great's army who, following Alexander's death, established himself as the *satrap* of Babylon with his capital at Seleucia on the Tigris.

During the following internecine wars between rival Macedonian generals, Seleucus traded most of his territory in India for 500 war elephants, which won the day against the forces of Antigonus ("The One Eyed") at the battle of Ipsus in Western Anatolia in 301 BC. The victory established Seleucus as a Mediterranean power, and he quickly moved his capital to Seleucia Pieria (modern Samandag outside Antioch) in 300 BC, but within a month elected to move the seat of government some 25 miles (40 km) inland – and Antioch-on-the-Orontes was born.

Initially conceived of as a *polis*, or city of some 5,300 male citizens – close enough to the ideal number of Hellenic homeowners which Plato advocated – Antioch soon swelled to a population of nearly half a million, becoming the pre-eminent center of Hellenic civilization in the region. The Seleucids lavished attention on their capital, building theaters, baths, gymnasiums, a stadium which hosted a revived Olympic Games, and other public buildings, all connected by colonnaded streets.

But the crowning achievement of their civil works was the famed **Grove of Daphne** where the Seleucids built a massive temple and an oracle complex dedicated to the God Apollo, serviced by very real "nymphs" whose duties also included delighting the self-defied royal family, who claimed descent from Apollo himself.

The complex continued to function down into Christian times, when bones of a bishop were re-interred at Daphne, thus silencing the pagan oracle. When the Byzantine Emperor Julian ("The Apostate") visited the shrine in AD 362, he found but one priest clutching a sacrificial goose instead of the requisite bull. Enraged, Julian had the bones of the bishop removed. The Christians burnt the temple the next day, a signal that even in licentious Antioch, the pagan age was over.

The Seleucids themselves were long gone in any case. Chased out of Asia Minor by the Romans following the battle of Magnesia when the Seleucids' famed war elephants stampeded and thus destroyed their own phalanxes, the rulers of Antioch next became embroiled in the revolt of the Maccabees in Palestine, sparked by the attempt to Hellenize the Jewish population. Followed by a series of destabilizing wars in the east with the Parthians, and then in the west with Egypt, the Seleucids were finally conquered in 83 BC by the Armenian King Tigranes, son in-law of the the redoubtable scourge of Rome, Mithridates the Great. Within 20 years, Roman legions arrived and made Antioch the capital of the newly formed province of Syria.

During the Byzantine period the city was sacked with cyclical regularity by the Persians, until it finally fell to the Muslim Arabs in AD 638. It was reconquered by Byzantium in 969, fell again to the Muslims in 1084, only to be reconquered after a long siege by the Crusaders in 1097, when it became one of the capitals of the four Crusader states in the Middle East. Still Antioch knew no peace, and was constantly ravaged by nature and man: an earthquake in the 5th century killed 250,000 people; when the Mameluke leader Baybars captured the city in 1268, he slaughtered 16,000 soldiers, and hustled the remaining population of 100,000 off to slave markets of Cairo.

Today, the material remains of Antioch's former glory are precious and few, and the traveler must allow his or her imagination to roam over the occasional glimpses of the past that present themselves. The remnants of a wall here; a cave there. If the shattered columns and sarcophagi in the local museum could talk, what tales they could tell

about the great Seleucid Empire that stretched from the Aegean to the Hindu Kush, and from Georgia to Babylon! It is ironic indeed that a lesser member of the family, the petty but megalomaniac King Antiochus I Epiphanes of the buffer state of Commagne on the upper Euphrates, should be known as the quintessential Seleucid ruler due to his outlandish attempts at immortalizing himself in the statuary at Mount Nemrut, without which he would scarcely have even been a footnote in the annals of history.

Daphne (Harbiye): Located some 6 miles south of Antakya on the road to the Syrian city of Lazakia are the remains of the Grove of Daphne, now known locally as **Harbiye**, a favorite place for picnics and recreation. There are a number of unpretentious but pleasant hotels and restaurants in the area, with grilled chicken as the local speciality. Daphne itself is an incredible place, spoiled, unhappily, by the literal free-for-all refreshment concession stands: tables and chairs are set right in the middle of

Bringing home the bread.

babbling streams of water, and plastic bags clutter the bushes. It is difficult to understand why the municipality or Ministry for Tourism does not revoke the licences of offenders, or totally ban all commerce from this very special area. Still, one can gain an insight as to what the place once was by a quick stroll through the park, coupled with several hours in the incredible **Mosaic Museum** in Antakya itself.

The mosaics, fastidiously removed from Roman villas in the Harbiye neighborhood, date mainly from the 2nd and 3rd centuries, and seem to leap off the walls where they have been set. They represent the most extensive and impressive collection of the art form in the Middle East, and possibly, the world: here is a life-size "Oceanus and Thetis," with the creatures of the deep clustered around them; there the "Happy Hunchback," dancing in glee with erect penis; here again the "Drunken Dionysus," swaying toward the next winery with the aid of a small satyr.

The collection is so phenomenal, in fact, that the national department of antiquities is often criticized for not removing the mosaics to Istanbul or Ankara, where they would be more accessible to tourists who don't wish to travel so far.

Peter's Church: Antioch was much more than one of the great cities of Hellenic culture, for it is here that the early followers of Jesus Christ were first called "Christians" by their pagan Roman masters in order to distinguish the new cult from the Jews, who were at the time in a perennial state of revolt in Palestine. It was here, too, that the first non-Jewish members of the splinter group from mainstream Judaism were officially accepted into the early church.

The city was also the base from which Peter, Paul and Barnabas started their proselytizing journeys into the outside world. A grotto several miles east of town is said to have been the cave where St Peter held the first early masses, and still continues to function as a church. The pious will find it moving in its simplicity, whereas the cynic will find in it not much more than another dubious "discovery" made by the Crusaders, who seemed to excel in finding holy sites and relics to suit the needs of the day. Around the same time that the grotto was found, the Crusaders also ran across the "Holy Lance," the spear which was used to pierce Jesus when he was nailed to the cross.

Its discovery was fortuitous, coming at a critical moment during an 11th-century siege of Antioch, and inspired the Norman troops of Raymond of Toulouse to sally forth again and take the day against the attacking Seljuk Turks.

St Simeon: In addition to serving as the seat of the Patriarchate of Asia and as a rival center for early Christian dogma from Constantinople (Antioch was notorious for its heretical scholars opposed to the consensus decisions taken as to the nature of Christ at the Councils of Ephesus and Nicea), the city also stood in the center of a growing number of aescetic monks and other spiritual acrobats who expressed their devotion to God by a complete and utter abnegation of the world.

Tapping out an ancient rhythm.

The most famous of these anchorites was St Simeon the Elder, who devoted his life to sitting atop an increasingly higher pillar, now located right across the Syrian border. Pilgrims used to flock to the saint from across the Christian world to watch him rant and rave and rale against such human frailties as the desire for a good meal and a clean pair of sheets.

Local priests knew a good thing when they saw it, and started marketing the saint's waste to the pious for a fee, with the promise that their contributions worked toward insuring them a place in heaven. "Simonry" was thus launched as a Christian concept.

Following Simeon the Elder's death in 459, a younger Simeon was so inspired by the hermit's way that he, too, embraced the holy life at the age of seven, and climbed his own pillar in 521 to spend the rest of his days in fasting and prayer high above a monastery complex atop **Samandağ**, or Simeon's Mountain. The site is difficult to approach; look for a yellow sign about 12 miles west of Antakya on the way to Samandağ town, and then drive up until you reach a white domed Muslim shrine on the opposite hill. Completely unmarked by this time, you must find a goat path that wanders for about 2 miles (3 km) through wheat fields until you can see a tumble of old buildings atop Samandağ itself.

Here was once a series of monasteries and churches, no doubt filled with visiting pilgrims and meditative monks who thrilled in nothing so much as watching the pious miracle of the young boy sitting atop his pillar in sun, wind and rain. Finally – and perhaps blissfully – an earthquake brought the entire complex into its present state of ruins. It is a strange and fearful place, and well worth one's own meditations on the relative freedom of thought we own in our time.

Samandağ: Back down the mountain road, one turns left to follow the main road to Samandağ, unusually crowded with children, motorcycles and semi-trailer trucks. Drive carefully. The town

The citadel o
Antakya.

itself is a sprawling, disconnected affair with little to offer the visitor other than a fish lunch on the beach and a quick circumambulation of the conical shrine which was built on the place where St Hızır met Moses.

Down the coast towards the Syrian frontier but inaccessible due to security concern looms **Keldağ**, or Bald Mountain, allegedly denuded of trees when its summit was scraped by Noah's Ark during the time of the Great Deluge.

Samandağ claims to be a resort town, and there are several small hotels and pensions, but the beach that looks so delightful from afar is disappointingly filled with plastic bags and other refuse discarded by freighters making their way to the Turkish port of Iskenderun or the Syrian port of Latakia; one wonders why the Turkish authorities do so little in the way of patrolling.

The beach road leads down to the village of **Mağaracık** ("The Little Cave"), built in and around Antioch's port of **Seleucia Pieria**. The area is riddled with the tombs and graves of Roman notables as well as remnants of the harbor walls, best viewed from the foothills of **Musadağ**, or Moses Mountain, which flanks the port; most are ill marked, so it is simply a matter of putting on one's walking shoes and clambering through the ruins.

The most impressive feat of engineering in the area, however, is the huge canal gouged from the living rock during the reign of the Roman Emperor Vespasian in the 1st century in order to divert mountain streams from silting up the port. One particular stretch of the canal is some 90 ft (30 meters) deep, with stairs descending halfway from the top to allow the thousands of mainly Jewish slaves access to their "quarry" below.

All in vain, however: the ancient port is now about a mile from the sea. Again, there are numerous small pensions and guesthouses along the beach, but until the Turkish government does something about the naval waste washing ashore, the area cannot in all honesty be recommended as an ideal Fun-in-the-Sun re-

Poseidon mosaic in Antakya.

Poseidon mosaic in Antakya.

sort, although the potential of being one is great indeed.

Somewhere in the middle of Mağaracık village, a good asphalt road cuts uphill toward the foundations of a Roman temple overlooking the delta, and continues to the villages of Musadağ, or **Moses Mountain**. It is here that the Biblical Moses is said to have learned to eat crow pie prepared by the obscure Muslim Prophet Hızır, or, in the Arabic, Khidhir. Unlike most Old Testament prophets shared by Judaism, Christianity and Islam, Hızır would appear to be exclusively a Muslim saint, although some believe that St Paul was referring to him in Hebrews (6–10) when he spoke of a mysterious being "without descent."

In the Muslim tradition, Moses demanded of God to know whether there was anyone more favored than himself, as he was the only human being known to speak directly with The Maker. God informed Moses that indeed there was, and that Hızır was his name. Moses sought Hızır out, meeting him on the sand outside of Samandağ, and asked permission to follow and learn from him. Hızır agreed on the condition that Moses never questioned his actions. One can guess the rest: Hızır killed a child, built a wall over a pot of gold about to be discovered by an old, poor couple and sank a fishing boat in the harbor. Moses was enraged, and demanded an explanation. Hızır calmly explained that if he had not done so, the end result in each case would have been far worse, making his apparently cruel acts, in fact, "good deeds." Moses was amazed and walked away perplexed. Hızır planted his staff in the ground near a stream to wash his hands, and also went on his way, leaving the staff behind to grow into a massive tree still to be seen (and revered) at **Hızırbeyköy** (Mr. Hızır's Village) a little dorp about six miles above Samandağ.

Will it surprise the reader to know that someone once cut off a piece of the tree for firewood, and that his house burned down as a consequence of his act? **Hızır's Holy Tree** is, in fact, massive and incredibly old; locals claim it is

Left, slave – carved sluice at Samandağ; and right, St Hızır's tomb.

100 ft (35 meters) around, which seems about right, but their claim that it is 300 ft (100 meters) high is clearly wrong; trying to dissuade them from their belief that it is the largest tree in the world is a futile exercise.

Vakıflarköy: Following the road inland from Hızırbeyköy, one encounters the hamlet of **Vakıflarköy**, distinguished as the sole remaining Armenian village in the Hatay or possibly in all of Anatolia.

The story of the Armenians in Eastern Turkey is known in broad strokes: during World War I, a decision was taken to remove all the rebellious Armenians in the eastern provinces of the empire from the war zone with Czarist Russia and move them to "safer" provinces in Mesopotamia. Malnutrition, bandits and security excesses along the forced march killed thousands, and have been styled by Armenian nationalists as the first "genocide" of the 20th century.

Following Turkey's defeat in World War I, the remaining Armenians allegedly made a desperate last stand on Musadağ until evacuated by the French fleet to Lebanon. But the villagers of Vakıflarköy say that their families have been living in the same spot for generations, and that the evacuation of the Armenians aboard French warships from Musadağ did not happen until 1938 – the year that the Hatay was ceded by France to Turkey, and some 20 years after the "desperate last stand" of Armenian annals. Still, out of dozens of villages, the elders of Vakıflarköy were the only ones who took seriously the guarantees of life and property announced by the Turks, and elected to remain behind, and their very presence atop Musadağ would seem to give the lie to the more extreme and radical Armenian propaganda.

The village itself is neat and tidy, and survives primarily through its orange and pomegranate orchards. A stone church still served by a 90-year-old Armenian priest is so immediate in its simplicity that it nearly tempts those fallen from the faith to believe again. It is, all in all, a very unusual piece of real estate, largely forgotten by the world.

Village wedding in the southeast.

KAHRAMANMARAŞ

Take the coastal road started in 1987 north from Samandağ to Iskenderun, and from there pick up the E5 Highway to Dörtyol and Osmaniye and the E24, or return to Antakya and pick up Highway 55 going north via **Kırıkhan** and Ishaliye. A left turn will put you on the E24 to **Gaziantep**; straight ahead is the E99 leading to Central Anatolia and **Kahramanmaraş**.

Formerly known as Maraş, the city acquired the honorific "*Kahraman*" ("heroic") due to the large number of casualties it suffered during the Turkish War of Independence. Historically, an important outpost guarding the second major pass over the Taurus mountains, it was sacked again and again. Perhaps this accounts for the singular dearth of antique buildings in and around the town with the exception of the 15th-century **Ulu Cami**, or Great Mosque, the **Taş Medrese** and the inevitable citadel, within which is the municipal museum with its collection of reliefs dating from the Hittite period.

The most important personality to emerge from Maraş was the Byzantine Emperor Leo the Isaurian, who managed to repel the last great Arab siege of Constantinople in AD 717. It was during his reign that we first hear of the iron chain which closed off the Golden Horn to enemy warships.

Today, aside from the pretty mountain scenery in the region, Kahramanmaraş is known primarily as the source of the best ice cream in Turkey – a gelatinous glob of cold sugar and cream with a peculiar elasticity and longevity; vendors throughout the country are obliged to wear traditional Maraş costumes in accordance with some unwritten law.

The city also owns the dubious distinction of being one of the most conservative cities in the country and having been the scene of Turkey's worst massacre in living memory, when the Sunni Muslim population of the town

Between the mountains and the plains.

went on a rampage, slaughtering scores of "heretical" leftist Alawites from the nearby villages. The tragedy is regarded as one of the key elements that led to the imposition of martial law in the country in 1978, followed by the military coup of September 12, 1980.

Highway 55 to the northwest of town leads to **Kayseri** through a long gorge of black basalt cliffs topped by pines and sliced through by an emerald green river – countryside that demands hiking, climbing and fishing for those who have time. Highway 59 to the southeast leads to Gaziantep through Arcadian scenery of small neat farms and babbling brooks.

Gaziantep: Gaziantep is one of several cities in the Middle East that claims to be the oldest continuously inhabited place in the world; little, however, is left of the city's hoary past, and today it is primarily known as the pistachio capital of the country, as well as the locale where most copper and brass work is done.

Like its sister city Kahramanmaraş, **Antep** (as most continue to call it) enjoys the honorific "*Gazi*," or "Fighter for the Faith" bestowed upon it by Atatürk in recognition for the Alamo-like stand the inhabitants put up against French and Senagalese forces at the end of World War I.

Although it cannot be called a beautiful or truly exotic town, it is strange that Gaziantep remains so neglected by travelers (and Turks) today; most folks just blow by it at 60 miles an hour, passing packs of oil tankers on the right hand side of the road as if to get as far away from the city as quickly as possible. This is a mistake, because Gaziantep does have its own charm, and the area around it enjoys its share of antique sights and vistas.

Squarely in the middle of town is the citadel, open, it would seem, whenever you are on the other side of town: four visits at different times over three days found the draw-bridge bolted shut every time, although the local tourism office made the assurance it was open. There are, however, several pleasant 15th-century mosques and caravansaries in

Eggplant kebap on the spit.

the area where one might idle away an hour or two; even the **archaeological museum** is sparse – aside from a few Hittite reliefs and the standard bits of pottery and old coins, there is very little to delay the visitor in the museum. The garden outside is slightly more promising, with a hodgepodge of statues and reliefs standing unmarked in the weeds.

Of much greater interest, in fact, is the labyrinth of the **old town** just north and downhill of the citadel, consisting of a chaotic tangle of narrow streets, paths and cul-de-sacs; although illegal destruction and construction have taken their toll, there is still enough of the old town left to get a flavor of what life was once like in a traditional Oriental city. Beat-up wooden doors facing neglected streets open on to beautiful courtyard gardens, replete with orange, plum and pomegranate trees and running fountains. The evening, when shadows hide much of the street refuse, is the best time to wander about.

What really makes Gaziantep special, however, is its food; the **Burç** is

perhaps the best restaurant in town, but there are others as well, all clustered around the surprisingly lively main drag, the Istasyon Caddesi. Most of the city's hotels are also located here; none is fancy, but all are adequate. In terms of food, try the dish called *Ali Nazik*, made of diced beef over a yogurt, eggplant and garlic sauce, or *altıezme kıyma*, ("six spices burger") consisting of spicy ground beef on a skewer laid over a plate of sauce with hot peppers on the side. Folks in Antep like their food hot. In addition to the standard *meze* or appetizers, Gaziantep also shares with Antakya the distinction of being one of the few places in the country where real *Humus-b-Tahin* is served in the true Levantine-style with olive oil and some raw onions.

Carchemish (Barak/Kalgamish): One of the most important sites in the Gaziantep area is **Carchemish**, an old Hittite capital until it was conquered by the Assyrian King Sargon II (722–705 BC). A century later it was also the venue of one of the great battles of the ancient world, pitting the Egyptian Pharaoh Neco against Nebuchadnezzar, the Chaldean king of Babylon. After crushing the Egyptians, Nebuchadnezzar rolled into Palestine to defeat the Jewish Kingdom and carry off the survivors to their Babylonian exile.

Two thousand years later, another major engagement was fought in the same area, when the Ottoman Sultan Mahmud sent his forces against his nominal vassal, the Egyptian Khedive Ibrahim. Fortunes reversed this time, with the Egyptian delivering the Asiatic Turks a crushing defeat, and the Ottoman state itself was only saved by European intervention.

Drive 30 miles (45 km) down the E5 east to the town of **Nizip** (ancient Nisibis), and then turn left down an asphalt road lined with pistachio orchards toward **Barak/Carapolous** (Jarabulus). Someone has done a fine job of confusing the issue here, as Carapolous, marked with a big yellow sign designating an historical site, is in fact in Syria, and the tiny Turkish dorp

Nomad tents in the plain.

of Barak holds nothing of interest to the visitor. Fear not. Carchemish remains on the Turkish side of the border (defined by the tracks of the Berlin-to-Baghdad railway), albeit in a minefield overlooking the Euphrates. Get permission from the local commander, whose HQ is some six miles (10 km) outside of Barak (easily recognizable from the flags and barbed wire surrounding it); don't even bother trying to reach the site without stopping there first, as you will only succeed in arousing suspicion and will probably be marched away with a dozen automatic rifles jammed in your back.

With permission, however, Carchemish is well worthwhile, especially for those with enough imagination to envision just what the tattered remains of the once great city looked like. Associated throughout history with the cities and city-states of the Euphrates Valley such as Duru Europus, Hierapolis-Bambyce and Mari downstream in Syria and Samosata upstream, Carchemish sits atop a bluff, dominating the wide expanse of the river. Stepping gingerly through the minefields with your soldier-guide, you can still see the remains of the main city gate leading down to the river and just downstream a bridge defining the border. This must have been the St Louis of its day, and one wonders how many Mesopotamian Huckleberry Finns took this route down from the Anatolian highlands to the Persian Gulf in their day. It would have been a fabulous trip, but for two borders – that between Iraq and Iran – pose a greater obstacle than any rapids or downstream dams ever could.

We have the railway to thank for the paltry ruins that remain: the German box cars that arrived with new ties and tracks did not depart empty; travel notes by such adventurers as Gertrud Bell and T.E. Lawrence (of Arabia fame) as well as photographs taken during the early part of this century show Carchemish to have been a city of columns, altars and temples – the archaeological rape of the site was apparently conducted with all the methodological might the Germans could muster.

A few pieces, however, were apparently neglected by the German scavengers, including a relief depicting elements of the Gilgamesh Epic, now housed in the **Anatolian Civilizations Museum** in Ankara. All that remains *in situ* are a few foundations in the minefield, so remote and unattended that they now mainly serve as a breeding ground for partridges. For the record, Erik von Daniken counts Carchemish among the landing pads for his Chariots of the Gods.

Nizip/Bilkis (Zeugma): For those with a four wheel drive vehicle (or a rented car they don't care about,) the Euphrates Valley north of Nizip claims a number of obscure, I-got-here-first sites dating from the Hellenistic and Roman periods. All these are badly marked at best, so get ready for a certain amount of doubling-back over the gravel road you just came down.

The first of these is **Bilkis**, or Roman **Zeugma**, some 10 miles (16 km) east of Nizip along the old road leading to **Birecik/Urfa**, where the XVI Flavia

Smile, please.

Firma Legion guarded one of the more important fording points of the Euphrates. Again, precious little remains of the crumbled city; a couple of tombs still boast the relief of the master of the house buried there. Most are mere dents in the ground, robbed long ago for whatever coin or bauble they might have held.

The view of the Upper Euphrates from atop the former citadel of Bilkis, however, is worth the circuitous hike upward: below flows the mighty Euphrates, following a long bend, with scores of tiny islands lush with vegetation, as are the banks on either side. Here, indeed, is the Fertile Crescent in miniature, or maybe even the true Garden of Eden. Strange sling-bridges (a basket for one attached to a precariously thin wire) are strung across the stream at points, underscoring the fact that the west bank is primarily ethnically Turkish, whereas on the east bank, the villagers are primarily Kurdish.

Further upstream, and nearly inaccessible except by Landrover, is the Hellenistic site of **Rum Kalesi**, or **The Roman Castle**; your writer will blush and confess that an attempt to reach it by Renault failed, and that he has merely seen pictures and had it described by those fortunate few who have made it there: it seems to hang over the Euphrates, suspended from a cliff, a fabulous destination for those with the time and patience to get there.

Fishing for big cats: A curious lack of interest surrounds the subject of fishing in the Euphrates, which boasts river catfish of such size that until one actually sees a sample for himself, all stories heard about them seem to be outrageous lies. But the wild tales are true, and fishermen regularly pull out giant cats of up to 440 lbs (200 kilos), usually by the net-and-shotgun method. Whether the giant cats go for bait is anyone's guess, but this writer, who used to swim the Euphrates downstream in Syria, is more than a little reluctant to take a dip upstream after finally having seen the whiskered monsters with his own eyes.

Birecik and the Bald Ibis: Some 10 miles east and across the river is the town of **Birecik**, the ancient **Apamaea** which, along with Zeugma on the west bank, was traditionally an important jumping off point for Roman adventures in the East, including Mark Antony's disasterous campaign against the Parthians in 36 BC.

Birecik is also a place for watchers of obscure birds, as it is one of the two places left on earth where the bald ibis nests. A sort of proto-vulture in appearance, the birds are regarded by locals as the harbinger of spring when it arrives in February from its other abode in Morocco, before departing again in midsummer. Long thought to be in danger of extinction (there are only some 30 birds in the world) the ibis is now a protected species, whose numbers have started to grow.

Roman tombs: For those truly in need of adventure and/or obsessed with the Roman sites of the Upper Euphrates, a good tarmac road leads north from Gaziantep through the town of **Yavuzeli** to the village of **Araban**. This would appear to be the end of the line, but it is

The bald ibis, better known as the "Birecik Birds".

not: ask directions of how to get to the **Anıt Mezarı** at **Hasanoğlu**, the last of three farming villages with the peculiar tombs. According to the savants of the local teahouse/grocery/store/hangout, this writer was the first "tourist" to visit the desperately poor village in a decade. The comparison between the contemporary settlement and the ancient site it was built on is so staggering that you may want to weep. Here was the site of an ancient Roman garrison town, with water depots, cisterns and roads, now all hopelessly smashed by the wrath of some god of war or major earthquake; only the tomb itself remains standing, a veritable pearl set in a brooch of rock and mud.

The **Tomb at Eliköy** in the same area is in somewhat better shape, as is the village itself; **Hisarköy**, tottering over a high bank of the Euphrates, owns the best preserved tomb of all, although the village itself is in a sad state of affairs. There are allegedly cliff paintings and reliefs to be enjoyed further down the riverbank for those who dare descend the precipice.

Resist the temptation to try and drive on toward **Adıyaman** and **Nemrut Dagı** from here; the farm roads dissolve into nothing, or end in a bank of wet sand at the Euphrates' edge. There are no signs, and unless one delights in driving around in circles waiting to spot and stop a tractor every 5 miles, it is highly advised to select a more orthodox approach to territories further east. But take a long look before turning back: the low, rolling hills, covered with ripening wheat in the early summer and cut by a myriad of tributaries of the Euphrates, rising in the snowcapped mountains of North East Anatolia and flowing southward to the desert flats of Syria and Iraq, form a subtle but spectacular beauty. The scene could be a setting from the US Midwest.

And right across the river, in a sense, is where Asia really begins: the rich, verdant lands known to the ancients as Mesopotamia – the Land Between The Two Rivers, and the area where civilization as we know it began.

Badlands on the southern border.

WONDERS OF NEMRUT DAĞI

It was, in history, but a tiny buffer state on the Upper Euphrates, pinched between the fleet cavalry of ancient Parthia and the inexorable legions of Rome. The country, Commagene, flourished for the briefest instant during the Roman civil wars which pitted the tyrannicides, Brutus and Cassius, against the fragile coalition of Mark Antony and Octavian, only to be first crushed and then absorbed like so many of the minor principalities of Asia Minor into the Pax Romana and to disappear from history around the beginning of the Christian era.

But unlike most of the other forgotten states of late antiquity, the kingdom of Commagene carved out its place in history from the living rock, and has managed to capture the imagination of the 100,000 visitors who come annually to see the fabulous remains atop **Mount Nemrut** (**Nemrut Dağı**) that Commagene's uniquely self-obsessed ruler, Antiochus I, had built for himself as his final resting place.

The geneaology of the house of Commagene is obscure: apparently a lesser line of the Seleucids of Antioch, who established themselves in the foothills of the upper Euphrates following the rout of Seleucid arms at the battle of Magnesia in 190 BC, they styled themselves as the twin of the Achamenians of old Iran on the male side, and the descendants of Alexander the Great on the other. Indeed, one could even suggest that this mixture of east and west was the finest expression of the cultural synthesis sought by Alexander.

With the increasing decline of Seleucid power and the rise of Rome as the new overlords of Asia Minor during the late Republican era, Commagene seems to be identified with the periodic anti-Roman uprisings along the eastern marches, usually associated with the nacent power of Parthia in Iran. Following the Roman defeat of the Pontic King Mithridates the Great in 63 BC, Antiochus I of Commagene was confirmed in power at the Commagene capital, Samosata, by Pompeii, either as a token of trust for Commagenean support against Mithradites, or – and more likely – as a gesture of *realpolitik* made in order to secure some hold over the distant marches on the Parthian frontier. Whatever the motives of Rome, the arrangement was not effective, as a mere eight years later, the Romans suffered their most humiliating defeat when Crassus and his legions were destroyed at Carrhae in 53 BC – literally on the doorstep of Commagene. When Mark Antony arrived to resecure the frontier, Antiochus was obliged to pay a stiff indemnity for his neglecting to aid his Roman ally (none dared call it treason).

Finally, after maintaining its precarious independence between the Rock of Rome and the Hard Place of Parthia, Commagene was absorbed into the newly established Roman province of Syria during the reign of Nero. It might have disappeared altogether from his-

tory, but for the massive tumulus on Nemrut Dağı built by Antiochus for his own glory and honor, a pile of stones and statuary far outdoing the dreams of any other contemporary self-deifier save, perhaps, those of the pyramid-building Egyptian pharoahs.

The hierothesian: The centerpiece of any tour of Commagene (and possibly of Turkey itself) is a climb to the top of Nemrut Dağı, where the collasi of the gods of antiquity lie scattered at the summit of the 7,000-ft (2,200-meter) mountain; a variety of other ruins including a beautifully preserved Roman bridge and the citadel of Old Kâhta lie scattered along the way, making an excursion up the mountain and back a full day's affair, at the very least.

Nearly all organized trips start well before dawn at Kâhta, a rather unprepossessing town some 60 miles (100 km) away from the top of the mountain, which boasts some 200 beds as well as camping facilities. The **Kommagene Hotel**, run by one Mahmut Arslan, is recommended; a black & white photo-graph at the reception is of interest as it shows one of the statues on the summit actually standing on its base before an earthquake in 1954 finally toppled it to the ground along with the others.

For those wishing to share a minibus with others for a day's excursion, a full day's tour, with driver, costs around $50 for the entire vehicle, or as little as $5 per person, depending on how many squeeze into the old diesel vans which ply the route to Nemrut Dağı and back.

It should be noted that the reason why visitors are encouraged to arrive at the tumulus before sunrise is not because of the over-advertised ravishing beauty of the spectacle of the first red rays of dawn flooding the summit, but because the old diesel vans tend to overheat on the uphill grade during the heat of the day, and the owners like to keep their transport out of the workshop.

The visitor with his or her own transportation is advised to avoid the morning crush (and cold), by waking late, enjoying a leisurely breakfast (ideally in one of the several pensions **Scattered dreams of deities on the terrace.**

248

near the summit), and then ascending the mountain in peace and quiet. The hierothesian of Antiochus I needs no special dawn or dusk lighting effects to impress.

The summit: The summit is approached on foot (or donkey) after a 20-minute climb uphill, surprisingly winding due to the altitude, and made the more difficult by the shattered shale and loose rocks lying around, especially in the twilight hours. The first glimpse of the two terraces flanking the tumulus of Antiochus is indeed astounding, and must be seen to be believed: here, atop the highest peak in the region, with panoramic views in all directions, Antiochus I had his peons drag blocks of cut stone to build twin terraces facing east and west, lined with massive statues of his favorite gods: Apollo, Tyche (or Fortuna, the goddess of fortune), Zeus and Hercules, including himself in their illustrious company between Zeus and Hercules, to whom the king of Commagene traced his descent through Alexander the Great.

The tumulus of Antiochus.

In addition to the four gods and the man-god Antiochus, there are also two fallen statues of an eagle and a lion . All of the heads of the statues – long toppled from their bases – stand taller than an average-sized man.

Of particular note in the line-up of the gods is Apollo, who in the eastern realms of late antiquity was known as Mithra, the god of light and darkness in the cult of Mithraism, and to which Christianity is embarrassingly indebted for many of its sacred rites. Baptism, for example, is more likely a refined version of the Mithraic initiation ceremony of a bath of bull's blood. Mithraism took root among the Roman legions of Pompeii during his sojourns in the east against Mithridates the Great, and was finally declared the official religion of the Roman empire by Diocletian in a last effort to counter the growing appeal of Christianity.

The Leo horoscope: In addition to the statues of the gods, there are also numerous reliefs depicting Antiochus shaking hands with various deities. The

most special of these is the beautifully carved relief of the constellation of Leo on the west terrace, which allegedly contains the horoscope of Antiochus on the coronation of his father, Mithridates, on July 14, 109 BC, and is the subject of much speculation among those of the Erik von Daniken-reincarnation school. A lady, one Laura Crijns, maintians she was there on the night of the coronation, and knows the secret entrance to the tumulus and whatever treasures are thought to lie beneath the tons of fist-sized stone Antiochus had his slave laborers pulverize for the nipple-shaped top of the mountain.

Planning to succeed with intuition where the American archaeologist, Theresa Goell, had failed with dynamite (the tumulus is 50 meters lower than before thanks to her efforts), Miss Crijns had managed to convince the local authorities to give her a chance when her excavation papers were revoked at the last minute, possibly due to religious implications to good Muslims if a zany lady from Holland, who claimed to have attended a coronation ceremony atop the mountain 2,000 years ago, should stumble on Antiochus's tomb, thus "proving" reincarnation to be true.

Eski Kâhta: Down the mountain on the way back to Kâhta and the plains, the first stop on the Nemrut circuit is usually **Eski Kâhta** or **Old Kâhta**, known in antiquity as Arsameia, the summer capital of Commagne.

In addition to the relief of Apollo/Mithridates pointing the way to the sanctuary, there are several inscriptions and statues of Mithridates pressing the flesh with Hercules; of interest here are two tunnels leading to an underground cave clearly used in the Mithraic rites, when novices would enter the underworld to worship the goddess Cybele, fasting and praying for several days before reemerging, enlightened, to the rising sun. Unfortunately, there are no markings or other information for the casual tourist, who is left with the impression that the grotto is just another cave where rustics once made their abode.

Close at hand is the **Yeni Kale** or new citadel, of dubious vintage – its crenellated parapets seem nearly crusader-like; a village attached to the castle provides downmarket beds in several pensions. Farther down the road to Kâhta is the Cendere Bridge over the **Kâhta Çayı** – once known as the Nymphaium river, one of the major tributaries of the Euphrates – a 300-ft (92-meter) long single-span structure built during the period of Septimus Severus with three of four original columns still standing.

Samosata (Samsat): The actual seat of government of the kingdom of Commagene was not atop Nemrut Daği, but at **Samosata**, atop a hill rising next to the Euphrates some 30 miles (50 km) south of Kâhta over farm roads.

Alas, a journey to the site is more rewarding in the going than the arriving, as there is precious little left on the mound save one buttress overlooking the river and the scant remains of several terraces. There will be even less left in future when the reservoir behind the Atatürk Dam project downstream starts to cover the ancient site.

Left, weathering the test of time. **Right**, Hercules and Mithridates.

EUPHRATES REGION

Although the upper Euphrates region is dominated both physically and emotionally by Nemrut Dağı – on a clear day, the strange, man-made nipple of Antiochus's tumulus can be seen from nearly 120 miles (200 km) in all directions – it is by no means the only point of interest for the traveler in this oft-neglected area of Turkey, although admittedly, one often must search for charm in the middle-sized cities and towns in the area.

Malatya, and to a lesser extent, **Adıyaman** – the historic Hisni Mansur – may have been regional centers in history, but today, aside from the odd, old mosque and the remains of a citadel, there is very little to delay the casual traveler. Indeed, Malatya's greatest claim to fame – aside from being a place where Muslims and Christians joined together to (unsuccessfully) defend their town from the Mongol hordes – is that it

is the hometown of Atatürk's chief lieutenant and Turkey's leader, Ismet İnönü. The figure of Turkey's second president overlooks the town square from his bronze horse – one of the few places in Turkey where this honor has been bestowed to none other than Atatürk, the father of the nation.

In terms of cultural events, the most significant regalia is the annual Apricot Festival which is held between July 20–22. For the historically inclined, a visit to the **Malatya Museum** to see its Hittite collection and to the ruins of **Eski Malatya** several miles outside of the new town might prove interesting and provide a distraction, but other than that, the town has nothing much to offer in terms of excitement.

For those still unconvinced and desirous of staying the night, it should be advised that although there are a wealth of third class hotel rooms, they tend to be patronized by fresh recruits of the Turkish army. The boot-campers tend to yearn for the fairer sex, which Malatya provides in the way of several "authen-

The old mosque at Malatya.

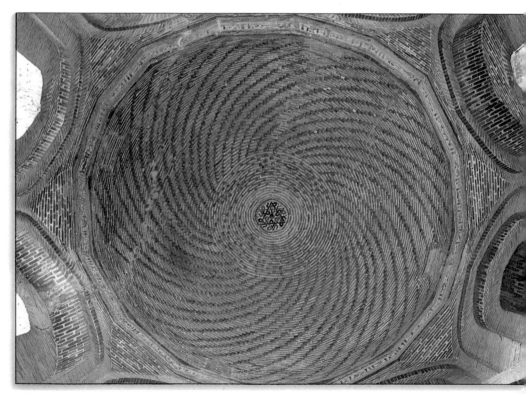

252

tic" nightclubs with belly dancers, wailing singers and whiskey dollies – all ready to regale the adventurous deep into the night.

Elazığ and Harput: A surprising exception to the general trend of dreary, boring construction sites called towns is **Elazığ**, nestled in the hills above the huge reservoir which has been created by the Keban Dam at the confluence of the Euphrates and the Murat rivers as they churn deep and white out of their respective sources in the mountains of the central Anatolian plateau.

A relatively new town, Elazığ was established in the mid-19th century by Sultan Abdulaziz and named after him. The distortion in the original name occurred by design in the early years of the Republic when many of the place names were changed in accordance with the new (and some might say obsessive) nationalism advocated by Atatürk. And like many of the towns and cities of central and eastern Anatolia, Elazığ achieved significance primarily as a military barracks.

But unlike Malatya and cities like Erzurum to the north and Van to the east, Elazığ has surprising charm and is – a most remarkable quality in an eastern Turkish town – clean. It boasts broad avenues, punctuated by traffic lights that actually work, and drivers and pedestrians who obey them. There is also a university which periodically hosts the annual Folk Music Festival in early June, when busloads of students from all over the country descend on the town to strut their cultural stuff. On the university grounds, too, is the local **museum**, with rather rag-tag samples of pots and pans exhumed from the earth, but with a surprisingly good numismatic collection of dating from the dawn of time down through various Arab dynasties to Seljuk and Ottoman times. The **rug and kilim exhibition**, too, qualifies as one of the better collections on display in Turkey – strange in such an out-of-the-way place.

The town has at least two good hotels – which if not the Ritz or Savoy – are eminently respectable with rooftop restaurants serving a variety of local specialities and game in season. Elazığ thus serves as an excellent center to explore not only Harput but the entire east-central region.

Harput: The history of **Harput** is perhaps most appropriately described as a mirror image of the complex, contradictory and often violent history of east-central Anatolia. The citadel was founded by the Urartus some hours after the dawn of time, and conquered successively by every army that passed from east to west or from north to south, including the Hurrites, Mitanis, Hittites, Egyptians, Achaemanids, Macedonians, Parthians, Armenians, Romans, Sassanians, Byzantines, Arabs, Seljuk, Artuk and Akkoyunlu and various other sundry Turks.

Even Baudouin, Crusader King of Jerusalem, spent the month of April, 1193 in Harput, albeit as a captive. The Crusader was so fond of the town, in fact, that heading an army a few months after his release, he reconquered it. The Muslim lords returned his affection by taking him and Harput again in Septem-

ber of the same year. The town and fortress were inevitably sacked by the Mongols in 1244 in their general rape of civilization, but reestablished as a pivotal control point in the east in 1514 when Sultan Yavuz Selim (the Grim) dragged his newly forged cannons east to crush the Safavid Shah Ismael of Iran at Çaldıran.

As might be anticipated, very little remains of most of the erstwhile lords of Harput, save a few coins and the shards of the occasional terracotta bottle. Even more recent history has been largely erased, and there are few remaining traces of the 19th-century town, said to have been one of the most developed in eastern Anatolia, when there were reportedly some 800 shops, a dozen mosques, eight churches and scores of Turkish baths.

Today, the most significant buildings in the town are the **Grand Mosque**, or **Ulu Cami** (with the local equivalent of the Leaning Tower of Pisa for a minaret), the austere tomb of one Arab Baba and the paltry remains of the churches

abandoned by the Armenians during World War I.

Harput was once the center of one of the most important schools established across the Near East by American Board missionaries. The school, which shut down in the early 1920s after the Armenian deportations and the exodus of most of the town's Christians, provided English language education to the Christians that once predominated the city population.

The only contemporary trace of the Christian presence in the Harput/Elazığ area, in fact, is an obscure, walled-off building at the Elazığ edge of town which serves as the local church, and which locals erroneously refer to as the "Armenian church." In fact, a Syriac priest serves the tiny, local Christian community, which includes the odd Armenian doctor, dentist or landowner whose parents apparently went underground during the deportations of World War I. The church, however simple, has peculiar charm, and it is nearly embarrassing for nominal Christians from the West to visit, as voyeurs, a Sunday service attended by local Suriyanis and Armenians, whose entire identity centers so immediately around their faith.

The hot, the cold, the cool: Immediately below the citadel is a mineral springbath, recently rebuilt to accommodate the recent influx of local tourists to Harput. The baths are allegedly an antidote for all manner of maladies, including hepatitis.

Those looking for the other extreme may follow the road east and above Harput through a series of local cemeteries to a peculiar rock formation. Known as the *Buzluk*, or "refrigerator" this rock formation possesses a rather bizarre quality of accumulating ice during summer that melts off in winter.

For a happy medium between boiling mineral springs and frozen caves, there is a local crater lake and resort area known as Hazar Gölü, a long and lovely saline lake 3,900 ft (1,200 meters) above sea level, 18 miles (30 km) south of Elazığ on the Diyarbakır road. Although the area is advertised as a trout-yielding lake by uninformed locals, in fact, it

Hazar Gölü, undiscovered lake.

contains nothing but a species of carp which jump provocatively in the shallows when young, and lurk log-like in the depths when grown. As with so many of the other inland bodies of water in Turkey, one cannot help but wonder why lake-cottage culture has never taken root here.

Keban: Take the road north running by the university, with rich wheatfields to your left and the reservoir flanked by the Munzur Mountains in Tunceli to your right. The area, formerly dependent on snowfall and rain for dryland farming, has become a major source of grains for Turkey due to the massive **Keban Dam** some 25 miles (40 km) north of town. The dam was Turkey's answer to the Aswan and High dams on the Nile in Egypt until the initiation of the even larger and vastly more ambitious Atatürk Dam project downstream near Urfa.

For travelers with a taste for engineering feats, the dam is worth a visit. Those who delight in spectacular cliffs and canyons rivaling all but such sites as

the Grand Canyon itself should move on: the road winds through increasingly beautiful country – at times appearing dangerously close to the precipice above the river, at times miles inland, gouged by lesser rivers and streams which finally pour into the Shatt-al-Arab and the Gulf – thousands of river-miles away through Syria and Iraq.

At the town of **Arabkir**, perched atop a gorge with several sidestreets running precipitously downhill – the traveler is confronted with the choice of taking a rough country road 45 miles (76 km) northwest to **Divriği**, or – as this intrepid guide did – follow the cliffside road along the reservoir to **Kemaliye**, a quaint little town situated on the westbank of the Euphrates at the place where the river starts to fill the valley behind the Keban Dam.

Formerly known by its Armenian name of Egin, the urban architecture of Kemaliye is an abrupt change from that of the surrounding traditional Muslim settlements; fair or unfair as it may seem, it is clear that the Anatolian

The power of the future: Keban Dam.

Christians of the 19th century enjoyed a much higher standard of living than most of the contemporary inhabitants of the area, and that an eye for outward appearance and private ease was a primary concern for them: although having degenerated somewhat, it is nonetheless clear from the gardens, sluices and delicately carved window shutters and balconies that the residents of Egin cared for their environment.

Ilıç or the end of the line: Only the criminally irresponsible or insane have any business proceeding farther up the Euphrates from Kemaliye by car. Distrust all maps of the area, for they have seduced more than one hapless into the deadend town of **Ilıç**, at a bend in the Euphrates some 20 miles (32 km) as the crow flies but well over an hour of mountain passes by land transport from Kemaliye. Ilıç is the closest thing Turkey has to a classic one-horse town, founded solely to service the freight and passenger trains that run through it. There is a teahouse, and a flop-house hotel on top of it.

Locals maintain (against great evidence to the contrary) that a farm road leads from Ilıç to the old Ottoman towns of Divriği, Sivas and points west along the railway tracks. But the traveler is advised to either park his or her car and take the train (there are several each day for the one-hour ride to Divriği) or to double back to Elazığ (or alternatively, to push on northeast over difficult roads to Erzincan) and continue the eastward journey from there. It should be noted, however, that Ilıç (which is arrived at from Erzincan) has begun attracting canoe and raft enthusiasts, who shoot the rapids of the Upper Euphrates here before gliding downstream toward the Keban Dam.

Tunceli: If Elazığ (and the province by the same name) is surprisingly developed due to the Keban Dam project, just across the long reservoir is **Tunceli**, arguably Turkey's least developed and most problematic province. It may also be one of Turkey's most beautiful: consisting of the towering Munzur Mountain range with an average height of

Revealing table cloth covering in a market town.

over 8,000 ft (2,500 meters), the province is the source of many of the small, white-water brooks and streams that eventually merge with either the Euphrates itself or its major tributary, the Murat.

The poverty and underdevelopment of the place coupled with its remoteness have always made the province a security problem for the Turkish state. The jagged mountains that surround the region are honeycombed with caves that have hidden brigands, terrorists and separatist guerillas alike.

The Alevis: In addition to the mainstream Islamic factions like the Sunnis and Shiites (now identified with Iran thanks to the late Imam Khomeini), there exists within the Islamic world a third major group, on whom little information exists, possibly because the members of the sect are so very reluctant to explain their beliefs and practices.

Mis- (and dis-) information abounds about the Alevis (sometimes referred to as Alawites). They seem to have their origins among the great Shia-inspired popular movements of the 12th century, but Anatolian Alevism was crystallized mainly in response to the Messianic revolution led by the Shiite Shah Ismael of Persia in the 16th century. After the decisive victory of the Ottoman Sultan Selim the Grim over the Shah in 1514, Shiites left on the Ottoman side of the newly defined border were subjected to systematic persecution by Sunni zealots. It is not known how many of the followers of the Shah were slaughtered during or after the Persian war under a religious ruling which declared them enemies of the faith, but gradually the local Shiites of the east began to conceal their faith in a variety of ways.

They stopped going to mosques on the rationale that Ali (the son-in-law of the Prophet Muhammad, and the eponymous founder of Alevism) was murdered in a mosque, thus violating the sanctity of the building; and they stopped formal prayers for safety's sake: the ritual and posture being slightly different between Sunnis and Shiites, thus making a Shiite at prayer a possible target for attack.

Through the course of time and alienation from mainstream Shiite practice, peculiar traditions began to surface within the increasingly closed community. A system of traveling holy elders (*dede*) replaced the more traditional Muslim structure of authority. The Quranic ban on wine and alcohol was relaxed, with wine actually used for religious ceremonial functions. The Muslim month of fasting was converted to eight days in the month of Muharrem, with the fast broken by a concoction known as Noah's Soup, consisting of a total of 72 different ingredients for the 72 different species of animals that were brought aboard the Ark.

The Alevis are also known as the "Kızılbas", or "Red Heads", because the followers of Ali wore red headgear to symbolize the head wounds suffered by the Prophet Muhammad in a battle.

In some isolated communities and small towns of central and eastern Turkey, where Alevi and Sunni Muslims live together, there have been tensions between the two communities in the

Whiling the time away.

pre-1980 period that erupted into violent confrontations. Officials said the outbursts of violence were provoked by unspecified foreign circles and their local supporters, claiming that they exploited Turkey's ethnic and religious divisions to keep the nation divided and economically backward.

Some bigoted Sunnis have propagated the most outlandish and scurrilous rumors about the Alevis – fabrications based entirely on their own superstition and ignorance. One of these rumors concerns the alleged holding of secret Alevi orgies, called the "Mum Söndü" ceremonies, in which mass incest is said to take place.

But most Sunni Turks don't share those prejudicial views of the Alevis, and at most know very little of them. As one Turkish diplomat said most Turks don't care whether their neighbors are Sunnis or Alevis. For them, the diplomat said, sectarian differences are unimportant in everyday life and not issues dividing the country.

Nevertheless, the tensions between the Sunni majority and the Alevi minority in eastern Anatolia may be a result of economic class differences, some Turkish scholars argue, with the Alevis being the poorer brethren. In many towns in eastern Turkey, the Sunnis are members of the merchant class, including wholesalers of commodities. The Alevis, on the other hand, are farmers who are forced to sell their produce to the traders at far below market prices.

Because of their lower social standing in the community, the Alevis have generally gravitated toward the support of left-wing political parties, including the now coalition government partner Social Democratic Populist Party, which has done well in Tunceli where Alevis are strong.

Dersim: The most dramatic expression of this deep-rooted dissidence was the Dersim Uprising of 1938, when the local inhabitants revolted against economic underdevelopment and taxes under the leadership of one Seyyid Riza, blowing up bridges and blocking passes

Rocky track in Tunceli.

258

into the alpine valleys, while slaughtering soldiers stationed there.

Reinforcements were shuttled down the newly constructed railway to the east, and the Turkish airforce had its first occasion to dive-bomb strongholds beyond the reach of the ground forces. The general carnage and violence on both sides, as well as the mass forced migration of the survivors to different areas of the country, was such that the entire period has until recently been effectively erased from official history, only to live on in the memories of those who managed to remain behind. It was, in effect, Turkey's Wounded Knee, and only the span of some 50 years has allowed its younger generations to start exploring the roots and consequences of the entire affair.

Tunceli today: Tunceli remains a hard scrabble province, but for those with time, and preferably, a four-wheel drive vehicle with clearance, it is worth exploring, with Elazığ as a natural jump off place.

Perhaps the best way to approach the province is by boat; a ferry station some 10 miles (16 km) north of Elazığ provides transport across the Keban Reservoir, past **Pertek Kalesi**, which once dominated the valley floor of the Murat River from a high knoll, but which now barely keeps itself head above water on an island halfway across the reservoir. For those curious to see what yet another castle might have to offer, small craft service the route to and fro for a nominal fee.

Once on the northbank of the reservoir, one realizes soon enough that one is in a decidedly undeveloped part of Turkey's most underdeveloped region. The road, paved on the Elazığ side, soon disintegrates into a gravel path leading up to the mountain town of **Hozat**.

Spectacular stretches of vistas greet one around every turn of the mountain road, but the driver had best keep his eyes to the track, and leave the viewing to the passengers who are good to have along, just in case your car might get stuck in a mass of mud, ice and roots from a landslide that happened the previous night.

Ovacık: Once over the lesser Munzur mountain range, however, one is greeted by a fabulous sight – **Ovacık**, or "the little valley," which is arguably about as close to Arcadia as any other location on earth. Slivers of water come cascading down from the rocks and cliffs above, rushing together into musically babbling brooks and then streams, all lined by brilliant alpine flowers and backed by dwarf pines. The valley floor itself – flanked by mountains on all sides – is lush with grass, frisky, prancing horses and idly grazing cows; the dairy products of the area, not usually exported beyond 31 miles (50 km) are, nonetheless, famous. And through the middle of this exquisite valley runs the Munzur Çayı or the Munzur Brook – a trout fisherman's paradise. The water literally gushes out of the surrounding mountains and is so cold that one cannot stand to wade in it for more than a few seconds, and even the heartiest trout choose to live some distance downstream.

Strangely and inexplicably, there is also a (rainbow) trout-breeding station just downstream of Ovacık itself, which – like every other similar trout-breeding station in the country – has never released a single fingerling into the river rushing past on the logic that "someone will catch them." Still, for fishermen, campers and mountaineers, the **Ovacık Valley** can be recommended without reservation.

Tunceli town: The clear, white waters of the Munzur Çayi slowly darken as the silt of scores of mountain streams flush into it, creating a frothing brown river as one proceeds down mountain toward the town-city of Tunceli itself. There is, alas, precious little to recommend in the town. There are several cheap hotels and an array of rooftop restaurants, enlivened by the relaxed attitude of the Alevi toward alcohol. It is the place for those keen on seeing the most forbidding part of Turkey. The visitor is advised to stop for tea before moving on, either by way of the Pulumur Pass to Erzincan and Erzurum to the northeast, or – and more reasonably – through Bingöl and Muş eastward to the waters of Lake Van.

LAKE VAN

Turkey's largest inland body of water and one of the world's highest lakes, **Lake Van** stands some 5,500 ft (1,650 meters) above sea level. Flushed with the runoff from innumerable small streams from the surrounding mountains, it has no visible outlet save for evaporation, accounting for the lake's high salinity. Unlike other salt lakes though, Lake Van does contain fish – a sort of smelt, adding color (and not a little odor) to local marketdays.

At the western head of the lake is the town of **Tatvan**, the western station of the Van ferryboat which, in addition to the occasional broken down truck and odd passenger, serves mainly to transport boxcars bound to or from Iran. The existence of the ferry service is fairly mysterious, as the trip takes around 6 hours whereas the road to the south, between Van and Tatvan, is perfectly serviceable and takes a maximum of two hours in a blizzard! The tracks pick up again in the town of Van itself on the eastern shore.

Ahlat: To the north lies Ahlat, a town of no current amenities but clearly with a history behind it, judging by the extensive old cemetery west of the town. This is where scores of apparently wealthy Muslims from the 12th to 14th centuries lie buried beneath ornate, rectangular tombstones, most of which stand taller than an average-sized man. Associated with the cemeteries are some half-dozen *kümbet*, or tombs; several stand near the road, but others are tucked among the walnut groves at the back of the cemetery itself and should not be missed.

Some miles west of Ahlat, a summer road leads up denuded hills toward the lesser **Mount Nemrut**, a triple craterlake which affords a spectacular view for those flying to or from Van itself. Various legends surround the lake, ranging from its creation when the virgin daughter of a local monk jumped into a baking pit to prove her devotion to God, to the story of a strange underground channel which drains it into the Murat river.

Malazgirt: More accessible, if less visually dramatic, is an excursion from Ahlat to **Malazgirt** (Manzikert), approximately 40 miles (50 km) north on the Patnos road. It was here that the Seljuks routed the Byzantine host in 1071 – in what became known as one of the greatest battles of history – thus the opening up of Anatolia to Turkish settlement.

A good road leads east of Ahlat toward the obscure Urartian town of **Adilcevaz**, dominated by a solitary, ancient Urartian castle known locally as *Kefkalesi*. Little is known about the Urartians – largely undiscovered until the 19th century – but some consider them proto-Armenians.

Just north of the lake is Turkey's **Suphan Dağı**, which at 12,000 ft (4,000 meters) is often mistaken for Ararat by the uninformed, but is a favorite of mountain climbers, nonetheless. The next road leads to **Erciş** where several more Urartian remains are scattered around the immediate region.

Afghan refugees: A dirt road leading up into the mountains behind Erciş toward the village of Altınçay ends at one of the most peculiar villages in Turkey, where some 3,000 Afghan refugees belonging to the Kirghiz tribe are settled. Like miniatures of Gengiz Khan, the Kirghiz have a decidedly Chinese look and continue to dress in their colorful national costumes from the Little Pamir Mountains along the Wakkan Corridor, once known as the roof-top of the world.

The clans' leader, Hajji Rahman Qul, led his people out of Afghanistan to Pakistan in 1978, a full year before the official Soviet invasion of that sad country. But dropping from a climate of perennial cold to a hothouse valley in Pakistan, the Kirghiz began to die like flies, and in 1982, Qul finally petitioned the Turkish government to allow them to emigrate to Turkey by dint of the clan's Turkish origins. He also laid out one condition for resettlement: "some place cold." The Kirghiz are now happy in their familiar – if frigid – environment high above Lake Van.

Çaldıran: Some 18 miles (30 km) east of Erciş the road forks, with the town of Muradiye to the left and Van to the

Church on
Akdamar
Island in
Lake Van.

right; just beyond Muradiye lies **Çaldıran**, where Selim the Grim defeated Shah Ismael of Iran.

The road continues north to **Doğubeyazıt** and **Mount Ararat** through weird, volcanic country along the Iranian frontier, a passage which is advised only in summer despite being marked as a reasonable, all-weather road on most maps.

Van: The settlement of **Van**, once called Tushpa, is hoary with old age, reaching back to the days of Gilgamesh and the primordial deluge. Some would have it that Van was the original Garden of Eden.

The capital of the Urartu empire during the reign of Sarduni I (764–735 BC), who built the long castle on the lakeshore (and whose merits are engraved in stone on the south wall of the structure), Van was invested by the Assyrian Tiglath-Pileser III, although the citadel apparently held out until conquered around 590 BC by the Medes. Later, Van became known as one of the principal cities in Armenia before ceding itself to the Byzantines immediately before the battle of Manzikert.

During World War I the old town was leveled by Armenian nationalists who dreamt of an independent Armenia with Czarist Russian support. This was followed by reciprocal destruction of the garden suburb upon the return of the Turkish army.

Both sides – probably with justice – accused the other of killing civilians while destroying buildings in the general chaos of the period. Today, all that remains of the old town is the minaret of the **Grand Mosque**, inhabited by a single stork's nest and two conical tombs as well as a few scattered remains of the town wall.

The citadel itself is strangely impressive, although nearly inaccessible after rain and certainly off-limits in winter. Aside from the **Royal Burial Chamber** on the south side of the summit which has a bit of barbed wire and fence around it, there are no guard rails or obstacles to prevent the visitor from pitching off the side. So be careful.

The Urartian castle at Van.

Those who delight in the sight of foreign-assistance funds gone astray should visit the **trout farm** between the citadel and the lake. Here, scores of mammoth rainbows are used to breed even more trout, but none have ever been released. Unlike other (equally useless) trout stations in the country, this particular one can make a grown fisherman cry: the breeder fish, especially, seem to have developed cancerous growths due to the station's low quality water and pellets thrown indiscriminately at them.

New Van itself is a peculiar city without a real center, and serves mainly as the administrative headquarters for the military and state-security apparatus in the southeastern region – and for good reason. During the Iran-Iraq War, Van was the center for Iranian draft dodgers and refugees who poured in through the mountains from neighboring Iran to be processed in Turkey. Anywhere between 250,000 to 1.5 million Iranians live in Turkey today. Given its location, the town is also a natural smugglers' center, with much of the heroin and opium base from the east moving through the town. One senses that the other smugglers – bellied up to the bars in the town's better hotels (**the Akdamar** and its new rival, the **Urartu**) – are either watching or being watched.

The **market** in the middle of town is colorful and leather goods are cheap: *Van kilims*, or flat weaves are ubiquitous but rather expensive, once again proving the Turkish adage "the stone is heavy in its place." Van and the neighboring province of Hakkâri also specialize in *otlu peynir*, or white cheese with bits of grass and garlic pressed into it. The famous Van cats, each with one blue eye and one green eye, and which allegedly delight in swimming, are unfortunately scarce.

A walk through the local museum, with its collection of Urartian inscriptions and statuary retrieved from the citadel, as well as **Toprak Kalesi**, the ancient residence of the Urartu kings on the mountain at back of Van – makes it a more interesting subject for the visitors.

Akdamar island: An essential part of any visit to Van (indeed, one might maintain, the primary reason) is a boat trip to the 10th-century Armenian church on Akdamar island, some 24 miles (40 km) southwest along the lakeshore just past the town of **Gevaş**.

With the entire edifice of the Byzantine state about to collapse before the onslaught of the Turks, and with only his kingdom standing between the warrior hordes and the soft underbelly of central Anatolia, the Armenian king, Gagil I Artunsi, had the church and its palace complex built as a retreat. It remains in such good condition today, probably, because the famed Turkish horsemen were apparently poor boatbuilders, and the island could have appeared impregnable in its day.

Built in the standard Armenian style of conical dome atop four axes, the chief attraction of the church is the ornate reliefwork on the façade: a veritable zoo of animals and birds ring the roof, door and walls in an orgy of iconography. One senses, immediately, the religious

adies from he field.

tension that must have existed between the Armenian church and the orthodox Muslim clerics, who saw in such sacral sculpture the influence of the devil himself.

Strangely, the Seljuk Turks, as newly converted Muslims, adopted much of the style of decoration from the Armenians for their monumental works at Divriği and Sivas, where even swine adorn the outside of mosque and *medrese* despite the very specific ban on anthropomorphisms in Islam. The interior of the church, unfortunately, has not weathered the winds of time so well, and there is precious little left of the murals and frescoes which once adorned its walls.

Turkish Armenians say there are, in fact, even more impressive churches and monasteries on other islands in Lake Van, but these are largely inaccessible. Indeed, Akdamar itself is reached only by a 3-mile (nearly 5-km) boatride but remains a very special attraction for both foreign and domestic tourists.

So far offshore, away from rug-washing village women, take a dip in the sodium waters of the lake and emerge refreshed and with a strange, silky feeling on your skin.

Hakkâri: In the mountains behind Gevaş lie the towns of **Çatak** and **Bahçesaray**, the former famous for its trout fishing (if somewhat depleted thanks to the use of dynamite), and the latter, as the harbinger of spring. Every year on Turkish television, Bahçesaray makes the news when the roads are finally cleared of snow, usually in May, but often June.

Returning down the Van road from Gevaş, a turnoff leads south to the country's most remote province, **Hakkâri**, which some devoted alpinists describe as the most astounding range of mountains between Switzerland and the Hindu Kush. It is also Turkey's most problematic province, squeezed between Iraqi and Iranian Kurdistan, with considerable separatist sentiments of its own.

Hoşap: Working towards Hakkâri from Van, the first site of interest is the **Hoşap Castle**, built by one Sari Süleyman

The remnants of Old Van.

("Blonde Süleyman") in the 17th century. The extent of the castle area compares a little too favorably with the contemporary dorp of Güzelsu below.

About 30 miles (50 km) farther down the road, now running along the Greater Zap river (a major tributary of the Tigris), is the town of **Başkale**, at 7,500 ft (2,500 meters) which is the highest urban area in Turkey, and formerly a major Nestorian town.

The **Nestorians** (sometimes called Chaldeans) were followers of Nestorius, a 5th-century theologian from Antioch who advocated the idea of two separate, coexistent natures in Christ. The dual-nature doctrine was struck down at the Council of Ephesus of 431 and Nestorius branded a heretic. His followers were reviled as pariahs by mainstream Christianity during Byzantine times and essentially forgotten by the world after the Muslim conquests.

They finally reemerged from their terraced villages in Hakkâri following World War I, when they declared their own ill-defined state in portions of western Iran, southeastern Turkey and northern Iraq. The mini-state was crushed before it was recognized and the Nestorians were obliged to leave their mountain villages for refuge in Iraq, then under British tutelage, to serve as local gendarmes.

Upon the granting of independence to Iraq, however, the Muslim Arabs and Kurds initiated a massacre of their former overlords, forcing the Nestorians to retreat once more to Turkey and to French Syria. In 1933, a League of Nations resolution called for settlement of the entire community to the jungles of the Amazon.

But the government of Brazil evoked a bizarre resolution that restricted all migration to the country, at any given time, to a percentage of the total migration that had taken place hitherto. As few identifiable Nestorians had opted for Brazil during the previous centuries, the number of acceptable emigrants remained minuscule and the bulk was left to its fate, forming a strange footnote to the annals of the League of Nations minutes for the student of history. Today, old Bibles and relics of the church are periodically unearthed in Hakkâri, the only remains of the obscure group of early Christians save the design of the cross still knitted into socks by village women.

Hakkâri town: Formerly known as Merivan, some 30 miles (50 km) south of Başkale, Hakkâri town is best avoided. Half of the population seems to consist of terrified locals condemned to live in hovels along mud streets and the other half consists of those who terrorize officials banned to the province for evil deeds done elsewhere.

In better times, the traveler is advised to push on to **Yüksekova** ("The High Meadow") to use as a base for mountain-climbing in the province. For the truly adventurous, the town of **Çukurca** on the northern Iraqi border awaits; it is a favorite stopoff for hardy journalists interested in an illicit visit to the Barzani-ruled Kurdish forces who have been waging war with the government in Baghdad for the past 30 years.

A fork in the Hakkâri-Çukurca road

stork atop
minaret.

leads west to **Beytüşşebab** ("The Abode of the Boys"), a ramshackle town in the mountains which boasts a one-room/40-bed hotel for itinerants and smugglers, as well as a locally famous hot-spring spa some 20 miles (32 km) in the mountains out of town.

The trip between Hakkari-Çukurca and Beytüşşebab is exquisitely beautiful but very grueling. Less than 60 miles (100 km) on the map, it usually lasts over 8 hours, with the tortuous road leading up and down mountains with turns, it is far better to travel by horse than by car.

The next westward stop is the town of **Uludere**, followed by **Şirnak**, a town in the province of the same name just above the Turco-Iraqi border gate of **Cizre** which consists of scores of tire-repair shops, sleazy hotels and restaurants catering to long distance-truck drivers. The only attraction (if it can be called that) is the generations-long blood feud existing between the two major clans in town. The main street demarcates territory: with the post office on one side and the sanitation department on the other, the respective services of which are off-limits to residents of the other sector. The lights along the horribly clogged road west to **Nusaybin** and **Mardin**, incidentally, are not for drivers but to illuminate the frontier with Syria, in an attempt to limit nocturnal crossings of the border by smugglers and terrorists.

Bitlis: The more reasonable route to and from Van is the highway leading south of the lake through Tatvan and **Bitlis**, the tobacco capital of Turkey. Built along a river gorge that looks much better by night than day, there are several vaguely acceptable hotels. There's one with balconies overlooking the river and the 12th-century **Grand Mosque** – a strange creation which looks more like the monitor with a minaret than a mosque. (The Seljuk overlord of the time apparently could not finance the conical dome, and called off construction before the structure was finished.) A long, winding castle atop the ridge, built by one of Alexander's generals, overlooks the town.

Hoşap Castle in Van Province.

266

Siirt: Some 30 miles (50 km) west of Bitlis is the town of **Baykam**, outside of which is the shrine of an obscure Muslim saint. The curious traveler, interested in the public expression of devotion, is advised to remove shoes and don kerchief (if female) and join the crowds of believers who flock to the tomb to experience vicariously a little Islam without the irritating explanations of a guide.

Some miles west of Baykam the road turns south to the town of **Siirt**, known primarily for the mohair blankets it produces; if there's extra space in the car, the mohair blanket is a good buy. Although not as durable as a carpet or *kilim*, the blankets make excellent floor decoration and are even good (if a bit itchy) on a cold, winter night. An oddity about Siirt is that it is an Arab town in the midst of a province known for its Kurdishness.

Other towns and cities from Van to Gaziantep have a sprinkling of ethnic Arabs, but Siirt has close to 100 percent, albeit, so far and so long removed from mainstream Arab-consciousness that even native speakers have a difficult time with the dialect.

Hotels here are rudimentary, but restaurants are excellent. Don't be surprised to find a few partridges scurrying under your table, seeking takers for a song. Siirt also boasts a 12th-century Grand Mosque which had a *minber* or pulpit so exquisite that it was removed to the Ethnographic Museum in Ankara. The remains of blue tile work are still impressive, if battered by time.

Tillo: A rather bizarre sidetrip from Siirt is the town of Tillo, now called **Aydınlar** (The Enlightened Ones), nearly 5 miles (8 km) into the mountains northeast of the town. This is where the 18th-century astronomer and wiseman, Ibrahim Hakkı, dwelled. His claim to fame rests on his having calculated the earth's exact distance to the moon with a homemade astrolabe and other instruments, all on display in the local museum devoted to him.

As the story goes, Hakkı was born in a village east of Erzurum in the northeast, and then went with his father in search of a teacher. Upon hearing of one Fakir Ullah who dwelled in Tillo, the pair went to visit him, and the rest, as they say, is history. Alas, the local recital of the sage's subsequent growth and intellectual development leaves much to be desired: it would seem that both the seer and his teacher required bitter hunger and the pain of falling into holes to achieve inspiration.

Equally unhappy is the inspiration of some unidentified German team who sought to restore Ibrahim Hakkı's greatest achievements: a hole in a wall set on a ridge which on each 21 March would beam a shaft of light across the town through another chink onto a mirror, which would then illuminate the tomb of his mentor, Fakir Ullah.

Apparently the device functioned like England's Stonehenge until the Germans dabbled with it, and now all the king's horses and all the king's men cannot make the device right again. The entire countryside is dry and arid, devoid of vegetation, but with outcrops of rocks.

Tobacco farmer in Bitlis.

DIYARBAKIR

Locals like to call their city "the Paris of the East," and claim its massive black basalt walls as second only to the Great Wall of China in length, breadth and height. Both erroneous claims should be discounted – the city of Diyarbakır seems given to hyperbole. But no visit to Turkey is complete without a visit to this ancient, walled city on the Tigris.

Known in classical times as Amidiya, the city was annexed by Rome in AD 297, and became an essential part of the line of defense between the Roman and Parthian/Sassanian empires of Persia. It should be noted that in the (unsuccessful) siege of AD 359, the Persian Shapur I was aided by the proto-Turk Chionites, who were making their debut on the Anatolian stage.

Ceded to the Persians after Julian the Apostate's ill-fated campaign down the Euphrates to Ctesiphon in AD 362, Diyarbakır was conquered once again by the Byzantines and held until the walls were breached by the Muslim armies of Khalid Ibn Walid (The Sword of Islam) in AD 639 during the first great expansion of Islam. The city takes its current name from the Arab clan of Baqr, which was granted the town and its hinterland, dubbing it the "abode of the Baqr", or Diyarbakır.

Conquest by the Arab Muslims was not the end of the city's martial history, however, and it was taken again by the Ummayad and Abbasid Arabs, the Marwani Kurds, Seljuks, White Sheep Turcomans and even the Safavid Persians again, before finally falling to the Ottomans with the rest of eastern Anatolia in the course of Sultan Yavuz Selim's campaign against Shah Ismael in 1515. Most of the mosques, *medresses* and houses of interest date from the Ottoman period.

Whoever may have owned Diyarbakır at various times in history, it remains Turkey's preeminently Kurdish city today. Save for the military, civil servants, a few Arabs, fewer Armenians and **The black basalt walls of Diyarbakır.**

an handful of Afghanis (also settled here from refugee camps in Pakistan in 1982), the population of the city is overwhelmingly Kurdish.

There remains a great debate as to who the Kurds actually are. Some say they are descendants of the Medes who ruled the area around lake Van upon the collapse of the Urartian civilization. Others maintain they are the Carduchi encountered by Xenephon on his way back from Persia with his 10,000 mercenaries. Their own local lore brands them as the sons of devils and 40 virgins. Lingual studies would put them in the Persian language realm, rather like Dutch relating to old German. Most of the dialects of Kurdish spoken today in Iran, Iraq, Turkey and Syria are just about mutually unintelligible, although they all borrow heavily from Arabic, Turkish and Persian.

If the ethnic identity of the Kurds is open to question, (and the background to terrorism) so is their number, with Turkish Kurds being variously estimated at about 10 million. Of these, the majority are in some stage of assimilation to mainstream life. Kurds have held (and hold) every position of authority that ethnic Turks do.

Since August 1988, the city has been hosting 15,000 of the 60,000 Kurdish refugees who fled Iraqi poison gas attacks, are camped in a huge tent city just outside the city walls, near the new Dicle University campus. Others are living in houses that were built for victims of an earthquake a decade ago. The refugees are members of the Pesh Merga (forward to death) guerillas which have been fighting for an independent Kurdish state in northern Iraq for more than 40 years. Turkey accepted the refugees on humanitarian grounds.

Mosques, mosques and more mosques: Aside from its distinctive Kurdishness, the most salient characteristic of Diyarbakır is the large number of religious buildings in the town; one might even suggest that in terms of mosques per square kilometer, Diyarbakır comes second only after Istanbul.

The most distinctive of the town's 22 older mosques (not counting the more

intimate *mescit*, or prayer rooms) is the **Ulu Cami**, or **Grand Mosque**, the oldest place of Muslim worship in Anatolia. It is about halfway down Izzet Pasa Caddesi, Diyarbakır's main drag, between the Harput and Mardin Gates on the north-south axis. Originally, the structure was not built as a mosque at all, but as the primary Syriac cathedral named Mar Touma or St Thomas, until Diyarbakır was conquered by the Muslims, after which the church was converted into a mosque.

Similar in design to the, admittedly, much grander Umayyad Mosque in Damascus (a city that Diyarbakır closely resembles), the Ulu Cami is packed with the pious on Friday for prayers – a good time to visit if one is not bashful. The mosque itself is built on the courtyard plan familiar to mosques in Arabia as opposed to the covered and domed mosques of the rest of Turkey. Note the fountain in the middle of the courtyard used for ritual washing before prayers, as well as the wildly different Corinthian columns at the back of the courtyard.

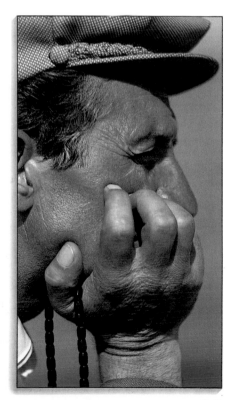

Dwelling on the future.

Up and down Izzet Pasha, one encounters dozens of buildings – either mosques, medreses or caravansarais – that alternating black and white stone blocks – giving the town a decidedly checkerboard look. The first of these structures is the **Peygamber Camii** or **Mosque of the Prophet Muhammad**, so named due to the vocal calisthenics of a 16th-century *muezzin* (the one who calls the faithful to prayer from atop a minaret), whose plaintive invocation of the Prophet's name kept the neighbors awake. It was, in fact, built by Kasap Hajjı Hüseyin ("The Butcher") in 1530. Opposite the mosque, towards the left, is one of the major east-west axis in town, on which the popular **Demir Hotel** is located.

At the end of the street is the entrance to the citadel or **Iç Kale**, and at the entrance of which is another checkerboard mosque, known variously as the **Citadel Mosque**, the Nasiriye Mosque and the Mosque of St Süleyman. It was built in 1155 by Abu al-Qassim Ali in honor of the 24 early Muslim martyrs who first breached the walls during Khalid Ibn Walid's conquest of the city in AD 639, one of whom – Süleyman – was Walid's son. Their tombs are now the place of pilgrimage, especially by local girls who can be seen tying pieces of ribbon on the metal bars of the tombs while whispering a prayer that the young lad of their dreams might take notice of and ask for their hand in nuptial bliss.

The interior of the citadel itself provides a good view of the Tigris (Turkish: *Dicle*) down below. Note, too, the peculiar **Lion's Fountain** at the entrance of the citadel, presumed to date from the late Roman/Byzantine period. There were two lions here within living memory. Whatever happened to the second of the pair is anyone's guess.

One mosque that should not be missed is the **Sheikh Mutahhar Camii**, better known as the **Four-Legged Minaret Mosque**. The mosque itself is of no greater interest than any of the other 16th-century structures in town, but the peculiar minaret, standing in the middle of a crowded thoroughfare, is unique in

Suriyani priest in Mardin.

the Muslim world. Local legend has it that wishes come true to those who pass under it seven times.

An old church: Down a winding and child-clogged street from the Four-Legged Minaret Mosque is an old Armenian church. Ask one of the street urchins for the **Ermeni Kilisesi** and willing, young guides will lead you to a battered door, leading onto an old courtyard, in which stands a rickety church administered by an elderly Armenian from Istanbul who looks after the remains of the old Armenian population of the town. Built to accommodate over 500 people, the church now serves a dozen families, supplemented by the odd Syriac family in from Mardin for Sunday prayers.

The walls: Stretching for some 3 miles (5 km) around the old city, and once possessing 82 defensive towers, the great walls of Diyarbakır were first built during the reign of Constantinus and restored repeatedly, most notably by Emperor Justinian, as well as by the Seljuk prince of Isfahan, Malik Shah. The main entrance to the old town on the north is the **Harput Gate**. Once known as the *Bab al Arman* or Gate of the Armenians, thanks to the road leading to traditional Armenia, the Gate is in good condition, with several inscriptions in Greek and Arabic.

Entering the gate from the new town, a road to the west leads by the walls to the **Urfa Gate**, and beyond that, the **Ulu Beden**, where one has access to the top of the walls through passages which, unhappily, double as public toilets. With courage and a few goat-like leaps, one can continue nearly as far as the **Mardin Gate** to the south, overlooking the vast, festering slum of **Ben-u-Sen** outside the city. The walls, though battered by sundry armies throughout history, are in remarkably good shape in places, replete with inscriptions, geometrical and animal designs.

From the basalt walls of the city, one can view the Tigris River (Dicle in Turkish) meander along a valley east of the city. Some of the the biggest watermelons of the Middle East are grown along the river.

For the adventurous only: Among its other charms, Diyarbakir also boasts one of Turkey's rawest legal whorehouse districts, and a trip from the citadel gate via *phaeton* or horse-drawn carriage has a certain amusement value for those who crave the bizarre and reckless. Just announce the **Genelev** as your destination and a 10-year-old brute will settle you into a fly-infested carriage before mercifully cracking the whip to stir the air inside the claustrophobic cabin. The wooden spokes creak, the ill-oiled axles groan and the team of scrawny geldings squeal as the coach begins to crunch and bounce over streets which have never known repair. The ride can be likened to galloping through the ill-lit, foggy back-streets of London's Soho district in 1840, and should not be missed.

The whorehouse district itself seems nearly sedate and well-kept after the drive through the ghetto. The talent comes in various shapes and sizes, ranging from the fallen darlings to toothless, old hags. All, however, have the dead-

ened look in the eyes of the souls of those who know they have hit the rock-bottom. A visit here costs about $5 and lasts about that long.

For those who prefer to pay more for mere titillation, Diyarbakır also boasts a few nightclubs or **gazino** north of town which can be pretty lively. Again, the uninitiated should be warned that the girls working the bars are paid by the drinks they manage to get a customer to buy them.

Mardin: Standing on a bluff above the Mesopotamian flats about 56 miles (90 km) south of Diyarbakır is the town of **Mardin**, arguably the most Arab town – even more Arab than Antakya or Siirt – in Turkey. The vista afforded from the town's citadel is nearly magical: below, the view stretches across the vastness of the Syrian plain, pancake flat but for the occasional *tell* or artificial hill designating the site of some ancient and forgotten city in the Fertile Crescent.

The political history of the city and province reflects that of its greater neighbor, Diyarbakır, and most of the

monuments share the same style and dates as those in the latter city, with the exception that where Diyarbakır's massive walls were often breached by invaders, the Mardin citadel held militarily and only submitted politically once the raping and plunder of the hinterland had stopped and the new rulers of the land had absorbed a modicum of civilization.

The area east of Mardin, especially **Midyat**, is the center of the 40,000 remaining Suriyanis, or Jacobite Christians who continue to speak a sort of proto-Arabic known to scholars as Syriac, erroneously assumed to be the language of Christ. (This could be because Jesus also spoke in Aramaic, a variant of this ancient tongue native to the village of Ma'loula outside Damascus.) The Suriyanis of Turkey, unhappily, seem to be a community doomed to cultural extinction in the long run, as more and more of their members either migrate to Istanbul and celebrate mass, along with the remnants of the Levantine community there in the Latin or Armenian churches, and it is unclear just how long the monasteries of **Der Zafaran** and **Mar Gabriel** will continue to function as living entities and not as museums.

It is, indeed, strange to run into these distant Christians, so deep into Anatolia, with the girls and boys in close contact and uncloistered, even in the villages. The Suriyanis of Midyat are known throughout Turkey as superb jewellers. Many of the top jewellers of the Covered Bazaar of Istanbul, for example, are Suriyanis from Midyat, and they are better off than their Muslim neighbors.

Adding to the uncertainty of the Suriyanis is the ongoing crisis with their neighbors, the Kurds. Mardin, especially, has been the target of numerous fire-fights and massacres perpetrated by members of the Kurdish Workers' Party, a Marxist-nationalist group, against villages and isolated hamlets. Turkish authorities believe that Syria shields the guerillas, offering them bases on its side of the border to carry out hit-and-run raids against Turkish border settlements.

The checkered plains of south east Turkey as seen from a mosque

URFA

On the plain below Mardin and Midyat runs the long and dangerous E24 highway, connecting Turkey's oil terminals to Iraqi oil fields. There is scarcely any highway in the world so overloaded with exhausted drivers, and one should take care when passing this stretch of the highway. From the town of **Kızıltepe** and **Nusaybin**, the road runs parallel to the heavily patrolled Turco-Syrian frontier.

About 110 miles (180 km) west of Kızıltepe lies the venerably old towns of **Urfa**. According to local tradition allegedly based on the Quran, it is the birthplace of Abraham before his migration to Canaan, now Palestine. Local Muslim legend differs from that of the other great monotheistic faiths by the intervention of one vicious and cruel King Nimrod, who, had Abraham launched from a catapult from the city's citadel to fall into a pile of burning

Urfa – the city of the prophets.

wood. Happily, God intervened and turned the fire to water and the faggots to fish. Today, the visitor to the town can visit the mosque complex surrounding **Abraham's Cave** and the pools of holy carp surrounding it. The cruel ruler's giant slingshot is represented by two Corinthian columns still standing atop the citadel.

The city's history is far more complex than mere legendary myths. Known to the ancient Greeks as Orrhoe or Osrhoe, Seleucus Nicator of Antioch-fame first established the capital of his eastern Hellenistic realm here, populating it with Macedonian veterans who preferred to call it Edessa, after their native province. Urfa remained an important garrison town into Roman times, and was one of the first centers of the early church, but one given over to the monophysite heresy.

It was at Edessa that the great scientific works of late antiquity were translated, with commentaries, into Syriac/Aramaic, from whence they made their way into Arabic after the Muslim con-

quest, only to find their way back to the west following the reconquest of the city by the Byzantines and then the Crusaders. Under Baldwin I it became the first of several Crusader states in the Middle East.

The city was finally sacked by the Zengi dynasty, with all the men put to the sword and all the women sold into slavery during the course of the Muslim "Reconquista" of the Holy Land in 1146. Following the standard Mongul rape of the Middle East, ancient Edessa disappeared from history in the 13th century, reemerging only in the present century. Thanks for its survival as a Turkish town should go to the local population who brilliantly resisted French attempts to include it in greater Syria. Like many of the other towns which offered resistance at the time, Urfa has recently received the honorific "Şanlı" to append to its name.

Today, Urfa is a surprising mix of the old and new, with Arab and Turkish peasants who come from the countryside haggling in the traditional bazaar,

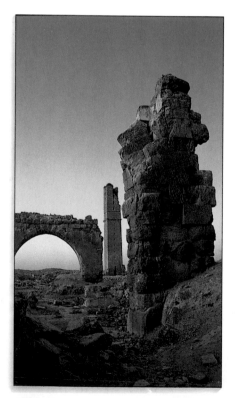

while young technocrats and engineers bustle between offices and shops lining the modern downtown section. A city of some 200,000, Urfa is earmarked to be one of Turkey's largest metropolitan areas now that the nearby Atatürk Dam 50 miles (75 km) north of town came onstream in 1992. Already the city has the single highest growth rate in the country, with many indigent farmers and absentee landlords from the nearby Harran plain returning with the promise of making the city the center of Turkey's new Fertile Crescent. Restaurants are packed with locals and foreigners dining on the famed Urfa kebab and other delights of the area.

The GAP: The center-piece of the Southeast Development Project (or GAP) is the 3,000-million-cubic-ft (84.4-million-cubic-meter) rock- and earth-fill Atatürk Dam, the third largest of its type in the world. Canals leading from the reservoir will irrigate over 350,000 acres (143,000 hectares) of land, turning the area into a three-crop-per-year Garden of Eden. Twelve other dams are now in various stages of construction in the southeast area. Such massive state investment, it is hoped, will be followed by the private sector investments necessary to tie this forgotten part of the country into the national economy at last.

One sour note, however, is sounded by Turkey's downstream neighbor, Syria, which feels it is being compelled into good neighborly behavior with the very real threat of having its own agricultural plans turned into desert with a turn of the tap by the Turks.

Harran: South of Urfa, the landscape once more flattens into the Mesopotamian plain, broken only by the ancient mounds and obscure, mudbrick villages that has become a familiar sight since Mardin. Many of the villages are now being connected to electrical grids, and, with the prospect of greater wealth thanks to irrigation, many locals are investing in such "luxury" objects as refrigerators and televisions. Here lies a part of Turkey experiencing extremely rapid change, especially as it was formerly one of the poorest and least devel-

The university at Harran.

oped of any area in the whole country.

Some 9 miles (15 km) off the main tarmac road leading to Syria, turn left and ask for **Sultantepe**, apparently a major site in ancient Carrhae, where tablets inscribed with the legends of Gilgamesh have been unearthed. Farther down the dirt road are the ruins of **Sumurtar**, a large mound with a labyrinth of passages and underground chambers used by the Sabians – worshippers of the sun, moon and planets. The grottos were clearly used for ceremonial purposes; some seem to have been later converted into subterranean mosques replete with *mirhap* facing the direction of Mecca.

Back toward the main road is the village of **Harran** itself, with its beehive-like dwellings. Here was the site of the Temple of Sin (erroneously called the first university), famous throughout the ancient world for its star readers and savants. It was in Harran where Rebecca drew water for Jacob, from whence Abraham decided to make his move into the land of Canaan. This was also where the Roman Emperor Crassus was defeated by the Parthians, with the Legion standards captured and brought back to Ctesiphon to the undying shame of the Romans; Crassus himself reportedly died by having liquid gold poured down his mouth. Later, the Emperor Julian the Apostate worshipped the moon here on the way to his fateful encounter with Shapur I farther east. Harran was also the last hold out of the Sabians, the pagans who had managed to survive through to the 11th century. Standing atop the ruins of the ancient citadel, one overlooks the scattered bits of rock and material-history stretching back to the dawn of time: the very potsherds crunching underfoot have an immediacy here, the broken vessels having surely been used by some long forgotten ancestor from the land of Ur, an acquaintance of Abraham, or a Roman legionnaire from Gaul, whose memory now swirls with the dust devils across the oblate horizon. The GAP project is expected to turn the Harran Plains into a breadbasket for the Middle East.

Beehive houses on the Harran plain.

ANKARA AND CENTRAL ANATOLIA

Ankara was a small provincial town of only 60,000 people when Atatürk made it the capital of Turkey in 1923. Today, it is a city of just under 3 million people, a thriving metropolis with a lively cultural and social scene.

Actually Ankara was a flourishing trade and administrative center in Roman times. It is said to have been the place where King Midas, of the golden touch, was born. More certain is the fact that around AD 400 Ankara was the summer capital of the Roman emperors who moved their court and entire administration there in order to get away from the sultry summer heat.

A residential rather than a touristic city, Ankara has its own subtle charms, and is a place where you can eat out in style, go to a disco, tour private art galleries, or explore the varied antique shops.

If you want to see the historical sights of Ankara you should begin at **Ulus Square**. The statue of Kemal Atatürk on horseback standing here is part of Turkey's history. Note that the inscription on it is written in Ottoman (Arabic) letters as the statue dates back to before Turkey adopted the Latin alphabet in 1928. Downhill and across the road is the building, now a museum, which housed the first **Grand National Assembly**. It was from here that Kemal Atatürk masterminded his 3-year war against the Greeks and the western powers backing them.

Proceed straight down from the end of the boulevard until Çankırı Caddesi. About 160 ft (50 meters) on the right is the governorate of Ankara, the **Vilayet Binası**, and nearby, a Roman column. Known as **Julian's Column** (c. AD 360), it is one of the few surviving in Anatolia outside Istanbul and evidently impressed the medieval world, for it figures in one or two Arab legends about travelers who came to these parts.

Farther along Çankırı Caddesi, on the left, you will reach the **Roman Baths**.

Preceding pages, scenes from Cappadocia. **Below**, map of Central Turkey.

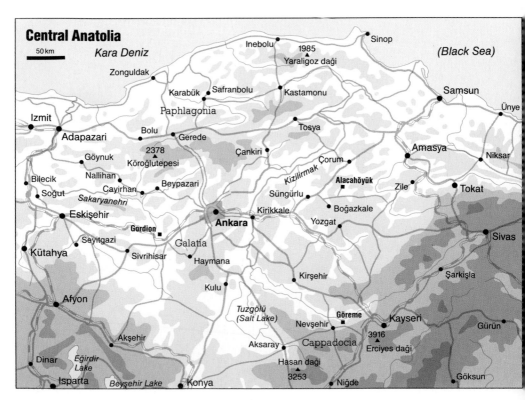

These consist mostly of brick foundations but there are also many pillars, tombstones and other remnants of the Roman city collected here. Notice that the tombstones are often designed in the shape of a door – the so-called "Phrygian doorway." The inscriptions on one or two of them in Armenian are – as the dates show – a sign that they were reused in the 19th century.

A short detour from the Column of Julian will take you to the Hacıbayram Mosque and the Temple of Augustus, the latter ruin being linked to the mosque by a common wall. The **Hacıbayram Mosque** is one of the oldest in the city, dating originally from the 15th century. It is still in use and is one of the main mosques in the city where funerals are conducted.

Look in at the tomb of the "Holy Man," Hacı Bayram himself, who died in 1430. During his lifetime he was head of a dervish order which believed in helping the poor and needy. As can be seen from the stream of visitors to his tomb, he is still not forgotten. Pious visitation of saints' tombs is in theory illegal in modern Turkey, but the practice persists nonetheless.

The **Temple of Augustus** at the back of the mosque was built by the Emperor whose name it bears. Long after his death it was made into a Christian church under the Byzantines. On entering, you will see a Roman inscription in Latin and Greek on the walls. This is the *Deeds of the Emperor Augustus*, a sort of notice which Augustus had posted up about himself towards the end of his reign, and one of the most important sources of our knowledge of Augustus and his times.

A walk up the main road leads to the citadel. On the left side of the main road are the foundations of a small amphitheater discovered during building excavations in 1984, but there is little left of the building.

You will understand why this is so when you get to the walls. The lower ring of walls were restored by the municipality about 20 years ago. They date in their present form from around the

9th century. It doesn't take long to notice that the stones in both sets of walls are made from the ruins of the former classical city.

Between AD 622, when it was taken by the Persians, and AD 838, when it was conquered by the Arabs, Ankara was a city under constant threat from invaders. Its defenders were only a fraction of the classical population of the city, and rather than quarry new stone, they used material from the walls of the classical buildings of Ankara for their defenses.

Until 1915, the open ground between these outer walls and the inner ones was the Armenian quarter of the city. Several thousand Armenians still live in Ankara with occupations as diverse as tailors, contractors, civil servants and university teachers. But most follow traditional crafts such as those of the goldsmith and the jeweler.

The inner walls of the castle are more spectacular: on the west side, they consist of a line of triangular towers, rather like the prow of a ship, jutting out from the wall. Step through the main gate, and a winding path through little streets, where houses have hardly changed in the last hundred years, takes you on the left to the innermost point of the castle where there is an Ottoman tower. Unfortunately, it is kept locked but from outside it you can look at the view to the west and the north stretching out in front of you.

Try finding the railway station on the southwest, beyond the amusement park in the middle distance, where the cemetery of the Roman city was. Ankara in Roman times was quite a large city, and it may have had between 100,000 and 200,000 inhabitants.

The walls, which were built in the mid-7th century, did not always prove effective. In AD 838, the Arabs under the Caliph Mutasim sacked the city and killed or took prisoner its entire population. About 10 years later, the Emperor Michael III restored its walls. Walk through the winding streets down to the south gate of the inner walls and a few yards above the road, and you will see **Young bureaucrats in Kızılay.**

the remains of a large tower which was probably the residence of the Byzantine governor who ruled a large province called Bucellarion. On the right you will see a little mosque, lined picturesquely with classical columns: the **Alaaddin Camii** is one of the earliest Muslim buildings in the city.

Going through the south gate, there is an inscription in Byzantine Greek at the top of the walls which quotes the Psalms: "Rejoice, Oh, Zion." Look carefully and you will see a number of Byzantine crosses above the windows. These were intended to work like charms against the hostile invaders from the south and east. Farther along in the old walls you can see lots of stones with round holes carved in their middle. These are the remains of the "syphon," a kind of ancient water-pump with which the Romans used to bring water into what is now the old city.

The municipality has been restoring the walls, although not entirely successfully, in recent years. Until a year or two ago, there was no plaster in the inner

walls, an engineering triumph for the Dark Ages.

As you emerge from the old town, notice the large merchant houses, with their painted plaster walls and elaborate woodwork. In Ottoman times, the Muslim population lived inside the walls and the non-Muslims, the bulk of the city's merchants, on the edges. These large houses – one or two of them go back to the 18th century – are found all across Turkey in the older cities. Nowadays they are usually divided inside and inhabited by several families.

Walk on to the south gate in the outer walls and you will come to a square in front of the 19th-century Clock Tower. If you turn right, you go down a little slope to the west to the Archaeology Museum. To the left, you go down a street which could be in any small Anatolian town rather than the country's capital. Many of the shops here belong to the wool and goatskin industry, a reminder that "Angora" the old form of the city's name – was a world-famous wool center.

_eft, getting vater at a itadel; and ight, an \nkara cat.

Housed in a former *hamam* or bath house, the **Museum of Old Anatolian Civilizations** is designed to emphasize the pre-classical civilizations of Anatolia, beginning with the Old Stone Age and going on through the Neolithic civilization of Çatal Höyük and the Assyrian traders of Kanes, the pre-Hittite civilizations of Alacahöyük, and finally the Phrygians and the Romans.

Among the most fascinating items on display are the contents of the Great Tumulus at Gordium. These include some very fine Phrygian woodcarvings in astonishingly good condition after 2,700 years. Other things to look out for include Neolithic frescoes from Çatal Höyük, and vast Hittite stone sculptures, as well as the emblems of the Bronze Age reindeer gods found in Alacahöyük.

Return to the square outside the south gate of the walls, walk due east down the road and you stand opposite the **Arslanhane Camii**. This is another of Ankara's Seljuk mosques dating from the 13th century. If it is not prayer time,

it is well worth going inside. Bits of late antique stonework are built into its walls and the brick minaret still retains a few traces of the blue ceramics which once covered it.

The mosque, built upon the foundations of a Roman temple, has an elaborate woodcarved roof, held up by a forest of wooden pillars. At the top of each wooden column is a whitewashed reused classical column, some of which were from the temple which once stood on this spot. To the left, as you face downhill, is a stone doorway with a lion beside it, leading into an old dervish *tekke*. The abundance of Roman stonework indicates that the dervish convent of the Middle Ages was built inside a Roman house of some kind.

Copper Alley: The side streets in this part of town are full of little craftsmen's shops, catering to the needs of an agricultural population coming in from the villages. Turn into Salman Sokak, to the right of the Arslanhane Mosque, and you are in one of Ankara's most famous shopping attractions.

Copper Alley (as Salman Sokak is known among Ankara's diplomats and foreign residents) is what its name suggests. You can find brand-new copper here, old pewter plates and copper jugs (lined with tin if they are to be used), candlesticks, clocks, antiques and curios of various sorts are on display. The best of the shops is probably **Erciyes**, on the left towards the end of the street.

A few years back, ancient coins, and other valuable objects would be stealthily displayed to foreign visitors in some of these shops; recent police crackdown has made this extremely rare. Be warned. Buying ancient objects such as Roman coins or rings is illegal and, if caught, one may be persecuted with a jail sentence. In any case, most of the "ancient objects" on sale in such places are not genuine. A splendid 19th-century plate with Greek, Ottoman or Armenian inscription on it, would be a wiser and cheaper option.

Anıt Kabir: The **Mausoleum of Kemal Atatürk** is something that any traveler to Ankara should visit. Official visitors never miss, as protocol requires that

A forgotten god of the Hittites.

they pay their respects to the founder of modern Turkey. The first thing that a new government does upon taking office in Turkey, is to pay a visit to the mausoleum and write a message in its album.

The Mausoleum is built in a mixture of styles which partially recalls Hittite and ancient Anatolian architecture. Each province of Turkey contributed stone to the mighty hall which contains Atatürk's tomb. His body, however, is not kept in the stone catafalque which visitors see, but buried far below.

On the opposite side of the square is the tomb of Atatürk's deputy and comrade-in-arms, Ismet Inönü, also Turkey's second President. Vehicles used by Atatürk are housed in the square, and a museum contains such personal items and artifacts as Atatürk's clothes, his library, and even some of his visiting cards.

There are several other museums in Ankara. For Turkish handicrafts and costume, one goes to the **Ethno-graphical Museum**, just off Atatürk Boulevard before Ulus. Nearby there is also a **State Art Gallery**, which is chiefly the home of exhibitions. For contemporary Turkish art, you would do better to visit some of the private art galleries in the vicinity of Zafer Çarşısı or in other parts of the town.

A state concert hall close to the rail station stages Presidential Symphony Orchestra concerts every Friday nights and Saturday mornings during winter months. Apart from the state opera and two state theaters, there are a whole host of smaller private theaters, which are generally reckoned to put on better performances than the state-controlled theater. To try one of these, you might look up the **Ankara Sanat Tiyatrosu** just off Izmir Caddesi near the Atatürk Boulevard at Kızılay.

The main shopping areas are around **Kızılay** in the heart of the town and up in **Tunalı Hilmi Caddesi** not far away, just below the new Hilton and Sheraton hotel sites. Tunalı Hilmi Caddesi has a number of shops where you can find gifts – copper, handicrafts, leather goods

Marching on May 19th, Nation Day.

– suitable for taking home. As you move uphill to Çankaya, particularly along Cinnah Caddesi, you can find shops such as **Urart** (also an art gallery) and **Enda** which sell more expensive handicrafts, silver and jewelry.

East of Ankara: Anyone staying in Ankara should seriously think about a visit to the Hittite capital at **Boğazkale**, a drive of 2½ to 3 hours east of the city along the main road leading to Kırıkkale and Çorum. Most people do the return trip in a day, but there is a small hotel in the village at Boğazkale and several other smaller ones in neighboring **Sungurlu** where you may easily spend the night.

It is also possible to approach Boğazköy from the south ascending from Yozgat along a minor road leading through some very wild mountains. At the height of its prosperity, c.1400 BC, the city of Boğazköy – Hattusa, as the Hittites called it – was the capital of a mighty empire which stretched as far south as Cyprus and all the way to the Aegean.

Its majestic setting and the massive size of the former city (about 1½ miles across) are unrivaled. Though the slopes leading to the top of the city are now largely bare, it is not difficult to people them in the minds' eye with the homes, warriors, priests, clerks, saddlers, cobblers and slaves. The sight is made more evocative by the knowledge that not long after 1200 BC, the imperial city was stormed and burned and never recovered its former greatness.

The city is best explored if you have your own car as the distances involved can take a toll on the walker, particularly in the Anatolian summer. The most natural way to begin is from the very topmost ramparts, looking down at the **King's Gate** and the **Lion Gate**. A section of the stonework has been cleared of earth and plants in the last few years, and it is possible to see the rampart, more or less, as it looked in Hittite times.

Notice the curious multiangular stonework of the Hittites. It is called "cyclopaedean" because the Ancient

Pious women visiting their patron saint.

Greeks, living about 500 years later, assumed this type of stonework could only have been the work of a vanished race of giants. Proof of the formidable nature of Hittite architecture is also provided by the **Yerkapı** – a 200-ft (70-meter) tunnel under the walls.

Lower down, on an outcrop of the hill overlooking the valley, is the **Büyükkale** or Citadel. This was where the Hittite kings and emperors had their palace and it is here (in rooms on the south side) that the majority of the 3,350 clay tablets from their archives were found. Thanks to them history can be recorded of a state which was unknown a hundred years ago.

Still lower down, with its foundations clearly preserved, is the **Great Temple**. In its day, the temple may have been the largest building in the world. It was dedicated to the weather god of Hatti and the sun goddess of Arinna. It, too, has proven to be a rich source of cuneiform tablets. Excavations in the area continue with a major discovery which was made in 1986: a gold tablet with details of a treaty written upon it.

The main religious center of the Hittite Kingdom, however, lay slightly over a mile (2 km) northeast of the city, in the rock shrine of **Yazılıkaya**. What the visitor sees today dates largely from the period between 1,275 and 1,220 BC when the shrine was enlarged by two Hittite emperors.

The two main galleries are carved out of the rock itself and on their walls marches a succession of deities wearing long, conical caps. There are 63 deities in all. The Hittites claimed to have a 1,000 gods but could only find room for a fraction of them here.

The names of many of the gods are not Hittite but Hurrian or Hattite, showing how the culture and religion of the Hittite warrior aristocracy had blended in with the beliefs and traditions of the indigenous people they had conquered.

The reliefs make a splendid photograph. To catch the light at its best, however, it is ideal to visit Yazılıkaya well before midday.

Tomb of Mevlana in Konya.

Alacahöyük: About 20 minutes drive further along the road will take you to the third center in the area, **Alacahöyük**. Many of the most famous ancient Anatolian emblems, the deer and the sun disk – which have become symbols of modern Turkey – were discovered here at excavations during the 1930s. Be warned, however, that Alacahöyük is much less picturesque than Boğazköy or Yazılıkaya. It lies in a plain and what one sees, basically, is the ground plan of the Hittite and pre-Hittite buildings. The **Sphinx Gate** is the most impressive thing on the site. Other reliefs found on the walls here are now on display in the Archaeological Museum in Ankara.

South of Ankara: The road down south from Ankara to Konya forks off from the Mersin-Adana road after about 62 miles (100 km). Some of the small settlements along the way date from Roman times, and you will occasionally see a Roman gravestone or the capital from a column.

On the Haymana road, 37 miles (59 km) south of Ankara, near Dereköy village is the Hittite castle of **Gâvurkalesi** where two gods are carved on a stone cliff on the edge of a small fortress, with a central burial chamber. The site makes a rather pleasant afternoon outing from Ankara.

For the most part, however, the journey between Ankara and Konya is swift (it can be done in under 3 hours) but is unexciting.

There are several large lakes in this part of Turkey, the **Hirfanlı Lake**, a reservoir which lies to the east of the Ankara-Aksaray road, while to the west is the vast salt lake known as **Tuz Gölü**, a favorite spot for goose hunters.

Konya was the capital of the Seljuk Empire between 1071 and 1308. Always an important regional center, it was visited by St Paul several times around AD 50. The city has become an industrial center in the last few decades and is now surrounded by bleak concrete suburbs before you get to the Seljuk monuments which lie at its heart.

Of the **Palace of the Seljuk Sultans,** only part of a wall still stands on the **Amasya by night.**

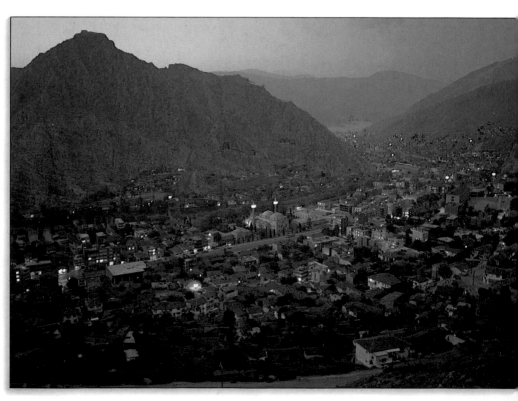

286

mound in the center of the city. This is not a natural mound but a *Höyük* which has been built up by successive settlement over the centuries and has a good vista of the city.

Around the corner on the same mound, is the **Alaaddin Camii**, built in the second half of the 12th century. Unfortunately in recent years it has been closed for restoration. Some of the oldest carpets in the world were discovered earlier this century lining its floors.

The other major Seljuk monument in the town is the **Karatay Medrese** an Islamic school built in 1251. It is now a ceramics and tile museum, housing, among other things, tiles with pictures of Seljuk princesses upon them. Notice how distinctly oriental the Seljuks still looked especially after their first 70 years in Anatolia.

Every visitor to Konya wants to see the **Mevlana Tekkesi**, the home of the whirling dervishes. The *tekke* (or dervish convent) was founded around 1231 by Mevlana Jelaleddin Rumi, an Islamic mystic who was born in Afghanistan and traveled to Konya, at the invitation of the Seljuk Sultan, to write mystical poetry in Persian (the court language of Seljuk Konya). He died in 1273.

The function of the dervishes was essentially to Islamize the native Christian population of Anatolia and bridge the gap between them and their Seljuk rulers. Mevlana preached tolerance, forgiveness and enlightenment, and his poetry, even in a translated version, has an uncanny knack of tugging at the heartstrings.

The dervish convent was shut down in 1925 on the order of Atatürk, but each year in December the Mevlana Festival of the Whirling Dervishes continues, held in a local gymnasium and no longer in the original convent. In their long white robes, the dervishes spin in a kind of ballet, hoping to achieve a mystical union with the deity. However, it is clear from the piety of most of the audience that the *sema* or whirling ceremony has not in any way lost any of its religious significance.

Konya Bazaar.

About 6 miles (10 km) outside Konya is the former Greek village of **Sille**, in which are the remains of the **Church of St Michael** and a spring dated 1732.

The road south from Konya takes you past the turnoff for Çatal Höyük just before Çumra. Most of the major discoveries at Çatal Höyük, a stone-age town going back nearly 8,000 years, are now in the Ankara Archaeological Museum. About 19 miles (30 km) before Karaman, a second turnoff on the left leads to a mountain rising sheer above the plain, on the north side of which is the village of **Madenşehir** and the once majestic Byzantine and Late Roman monastic ruins of **Binbirkilise** ("A Thousand and One Churches"), now sadly pillaged to provide stone for farmers' hovels.

The uplands of Central Anatolia are separated from the southern coast by the magnificent **Taurus Mountains**. After the town of Ulukışla, the road begins to climb, and eventually reaches the famous **Cilician Gates**, a high pass in the mountains. Most travelers today, however, go along an expressway on a lower route, the Adana road, which is very crowded.

If you want to travel from Central Anatolia to the coast in more leisurely fashion, you may prefer the road from Karaman to Silifke. If so, stop to see the 5th-century ruins of a **Monastery of Tarasius** at Alahan in the mountains to the north of Mut.

Southwest of Ankara: This region is much greener and more attractive than the bleak plain around Konya, and eventually gives way to Turkey's "Lake District." Here, farmers grow exotic crops such as roses (for their oil) and poppies (for their opium). Turkish opium is of high medicinal value but since 1975, poppies are only grown on state farms under strict control and smuggling has been largely eliminated. Home of the rose oil industry is **Isparta**, which is also the birthplace of Süleyman Demirel, one of Turkey's most famous prime ministers, and now its president.

West of Isparta lie the towns of Dinar and Çardak, on the way to Denizli and

Lake region near Eğridir, a favorite spot for hunters.

Pamukkale with its famous waterfalls. Driving north, one comes to **Afyon**, one of the best known cities of provincial Turkey because of the crag at the center of the town. Afyon was not a Roman city but the high rock was used as a refuge by the Byzantines in the war against the Arabs and a town subsequently grew up around it. The ascent to the top of Afyon castle is not for the faint-hearted. The town below has a number of good buildings from the last century, and a museum in which classical remains from the surrounding countryside are gathered.

In the town's main street is the **Ikbal Restaurant**, famous in Turkey as a stopping off place for travelers on their way to the south coast. Try some *döner kebabı* there and follow it with *kaymaklı ekmek*, a sweet and thick Anatolian cream cake made by boiling the milk of water buffaloes.

Between Afyon and Eskişehir lie a whole series of villages which must once have been the heart of the Phrygian Kingdom of Midas. **Kümbet**, for in-

stance, has a Phrygian tomb from the Roman period, with lions carved upon it. At **Ayazin**, one finds rock churches not unlike those of Göreme.

Undoubtedly, the most splendid monuments are at **Yazılıkaya**, or Midasşehir, once the Phrygian city of Metropolis. The flat landscape to the north and the east gives way to hills and woods here, and Midasşehir is set on a hill-top in a landscape which might come from an Italian painting of the Renaissance period.

The most striking sight of all is the giant **Midas Monument** (c. 6 BC), on the east side of the hill, with its curious and, as yet, undeciphered inscription in the Phrygian alphabet. On the north side, there are Roman tombs and one or two Hittite reliefs which show that the site has a history stretching back at least a thousand years before Midas. At the summit of the hill is a stone throne, which local folk will tell you, is where King Midas sat with his wives.

About 30 km (19 miles) north of Midasşehir is **Seyitgazi**, where a su-

Spring in Anatolia.

perb Bektaşi *tekke* or convent crowns the hill to the west of the town. In some ways, it is even more spectacular than the headquarters of the Bektaşis located at Hacıbektaş.

Seyitgazi is named after a legendary Arab warrior in the wars between the Arabs and the Byzantines in the 8th century. He is said to have died in the siege of Afyon in AD 740. Legend has it that a Byzantine princess in the citadel fell in love with him, and seeing some soldiers creeping up towards him, dropped a stone to warn him of the danger. Alas, it fell on his head and killed him. His tomb, which is about three times the length of a normal man, can be visited. Beside it is a smaller one which is said to be that of the princess who loved him. The buildings are a mixture of Ottoman, Seljuk and Byzantine architecture, including parts of a former church.

Kütahya to the west is one of the most picturesque towns in Turkey with old streets and a citadel ringed by a curious Byzantine fortress. It is a highly conservative town, where women may still be seen veiled, and wearing colorful Anatolian costumes. Kütahya is the home of the best faience and pottery in Turkey; the craft has been revived in recent years.

A drive south of the town will take you to **Çavdarhisar**, the ancient Aizanoi. Because it lies off the beaten track, this is a seldom visited classical site, but one which is worth the drive. It has a fine temple still standing, with a huge vaulted chamber underneath. In its day, the city claimed to have been the birthplace of the father of the gods, Zeus himself.

West of Ankara: In a famous corruption trial in Ancient Rome, the orator, Cicero – who was defending a sticky-fingered Roman governor of Phrygia, the area west of Ankara – managed to cast ridicule on the prosecution witnesses by describing them as "ignorant Phrygians who had never seen a tree in their whole lives." This rather cruel joke of Cicero's comes to mind as you take the road out of Ankara through Polatlı and due west

Broom maker at his task.

to Eskişehir. It is one of the great roads of history: The Crusaders, Alexander the Great, most of the great armies and generals of the Byzantine and Ottoman empires had traveled on it. But the landscape is mostly one of naked hillsides with hardly a tree in sight.

If you plan to drive along this road, a word of warning. This road links Ankara with some of Turkey's major cities and is usually heavily congested with slow-moving trucks. A journey along it will involve you either in a slow crawl or in some fast maneuvering between lines of trucks. The best time to drive on these roads, strangely, is in daylight when few trucks are on the route.

Driving is not only time-consuming; it can be very dangerous as truck drivers in Turkey do not hesitate to overtake on blind corners going uphill – even if they don't have the acceleration to move quickly. Needless to say, accidents are common.

About an hour out of Ankara is the town of **Polatlı**. It is chiefly notable for having been the furthest point reached by the Greek invaders of Anatolia in 1921. The hightide mark of the Greek invasion is, quite literally, marked in concrete on the hill on the north side of the town.

About 6 miles (10 km) outside Polatlı lies **Gordium** – the home of the Gordian knot which was housed in a temple here and which no one could undo until Alexander the Great, spending the winter of 333 BC here with his army, decided to take the easy way out and cut it.

Gordium was one of the chief cities of the Phrygian kingdom and the home of the fabled King Midas and his father Gordius around 800 BC. It remained a moderately important city into classical times, though it was later eclipsed by Ankara which lies at the center of several trade routes.

The most impressive features of Gordium are the huge tumuli of the Phrygian kings, found 30 years ago. Inside, they discovered a vast variety of objects, but, disappointingly, nothing golden. The discoveries can now be viewed in Ankara's Archaeological

Derinkuyu dolls.

Museum. A special tunnel has been constructed to enable visitors to walk to the center of the mound where they can inspect Midas' burial chamber, built out of huge tree trunks which the centuries have turned to stone.

The actual remains of the king who was buried here are now in the Archaeological Museum in Ankara. Nearby, you can also see the world's earliest mosaic, made out of black and white pebbles, and in the mound which covered the city, the walls of the Phrygian capital.

Gordium, however, is chiefly for the archaeology buff. There are no romantic classical remains here. There are also no trees and little shade which may pose a serious problem if you come in the middle of summer.

Just before the town of Sivrihisar one passes **Nasreddin Hodja**, the birthplace of the "wise fool". Turkey's most famous folk hero, Nasreddin Hodja figures in endless jokes throughout the Middle East. One story goes: "The Hodja brought home a kilo of delicious lamb one day, asked his wife to prepare it for the evening, and set off to the teahouse to spend the rest of the day. Unable to wait, his wife cooked the meat and shared it with her friends. Returning home, the salivating Hodja was told that the cat had eaten the meat. Puzzled, the Hodja grabbed the family's mangy cat and put it on the weighing scales. To his surprise, it weighed exactly one kilo. He barked at his wife, "If this is the meat, then where is the cat?"

Sivrihisar lies about 18 miles (30 km) further down the road which forks at this point, running due west to Eskişehir, and branching south for Afyon, and eventually the south and west coasts.

About 12 miles (19 km) south of Sivrihisar are the Roman ruins of **Pessinos**. This was one of the three great centers of Roman Galatia, and the remains of a Temple of Cybele have been uncovered by excavators over the last few years. Fragments of Roman buildings are to be found in many places, including the stream which is running

Tuz Gölü, the Great Salt Lake.

through the present-day village of Balhisar.

Pessinos was situated in the middle of the Phrygian plain and historians believe that its people had to move away when the age of invasions began after AD 600. They seem to have moved to present-day Sivrihisar, where there is a Byzantine citadel in the crags behind the town.

There are one or two Ottoman monuments here and also a large 19th-century Armenian church, with an inscription on its front in Armenian script. It now serves as the town's powerstation – you can make out its shape on the north side of the town, as you drive past on the main road.

Eskişehir, the Roman and Byzantine Dorylaeum, lies about another 1½-hour drive west of Sivrihisar. It has always been an important city, but there are few traces of its past in the town one visits today. The walls of the medieval city have vanished, but the circuit can still be traced in hollows on the outskirts of the city. There is a good provincial museum with a good selection of exhibits from all periods.

West of Eskişehir lies the Sakarya valley and a rolling landscape in which the Ottoman Empire was born. The small town of **Söğüt** has the distinction of being the home of the world-famous dynasty which ruled Turkey and much of the Middle East until well into this century. Ertuğrul Gazi, the father of the Sultan Osman I, was a frontier warrior in Söğüt in the late 13th century and his tomb can be visited there today. Outside stand busts of the great rulers of the 17 Turkish states in world history.

Not far away to the south is **Inönü**, the scene of two decisive battles in Turkey's War of Independence against the invading Greeks after World War I.

Further along the road to the west is **Bilecik**, where Osman's wife and his father-in-law, Edibali, lie buried. A few crumbling fragments of wall mark the site of the castle which the first Ottoman war bands captured from the Byzantines. To the north, across the river, is the village of **Mihal Gazi**. Mihal Gazi was a Byzantine Greek local warrior chief who joined forces with Osman and helped him grow into a serious power. His grave, neglected and forlorn, lies in a grassy meadow to the south of the village. It is a reminder of how the first Ottoman ruler made the transition from village raider to self-styled sultan in a single generation.

Northwest of Ankara: The main road from Ankara to Istanbul must be one of the most scenic routes in the country, running through gloriously wooded mountains which often remind the traveler of Switzerland.

Kızılcahaman with its hills and woods is a favorite picnic and resort spot from Ankara. It also boasts a famous Turkish bath and hot-springs spa, and is a favorite area for wild boar hunting with specimens often growing to the size of small cows.

Bolu is famous in Turkey as the home of the country's best cooks. Nearby is **Kartalkaya**, a small winter sports resort. About 20 miles west of Bolu, tucked in the woods is the spa-and-hotel complex of **Abant**. A turn-off north of Bolu

Wheat plains on the high plateau.

leads through spectacular scenery to **Yedi Göller Milli Park**, or Seven Lakes National Forest. Although the drive alone is worth it, the promised lakes are really only small ponds, so you might be disappointed.

The least commonly taken road northwest from Ankara leads through a succession of small towns which have preserved their 19th-century appearance. They are **Beypazarı**, **Nallıhan**, and **Göynük**. To the north is another small town, **Güdül**, which is also worth visiting for its architecture.

These are small mountain or hill communities where life changes only slowly, even in the late 20th century. But each of them boasts a semblance of Byzantine or Ottoman splendor. **Mudurnu**, for instance, has one of the finest of all early Ottoman mosques.

Göynük in particular deserves to be better known than it is. The road there is a lonely winding track through the mountains, so go fully prepared. In Göynük, you can visit the **Tomb of Akşemsettin**, the first *hodja* to give the call to prayer

from Haghia Sophia in 1453 after the Turkish conquest of Istanbul. It is lavishly maintained with gifts from the Muslim world.

At the far end of the mountain road, lie **Taraklı**, **Gölpazarı** (with a most unusual early Ottoman caravansarai) and **Geyve**.

North of Ankara: The landscape becomes much more hilly and wooded not far from the Turkish capital. **Kalecik**, about 50 miles (80 km) away, has a Roman castle with medieval additions and an old Ottoman bridge over the Kızılırmak River.

Further north lie seldom visited towns such as **Kastamonu** (where Atatürk announced the banning of the *fez*), **Tosya**, **Çankırı** and **Osmancık** – each town lying in steep and thickly wooded valleys around the remains of medieval castles.

The most frequently visited town north of Ankara is **Safranbolu**, whose quaint wattle and daub houses are the most perfect surviving examples of Ottoman provincial domestic architecture.

Below, winterscape in central Anatolia. Right, wooden mosque in Kastamonu.

CAPPADOCIA

"...Our eyes were astounded. I remember those valleys in the searingly brilliant light, running through the most fantastic of all landscapes."

So wrote Pere Guillaume de Jerphanion, the French Jesuit scholar who discovered the rock churches of Cappadocia almost by chance during a journey on horseback across Anatolia in the summer of 1907.

What we call "Cappadocia" today, if only for simplicity, is only a small part of the Hellenistic Kingdom and subsequent Roman province which bore that name. The original size of the province stretched for hundreds of miles further east and west.

Even now, when the valleys around the town of Ürgüp are relatively easy to reach (it takes about 3 or 4 hours by car from Ankara, or a similar time from the Mediterranean coast at Mersin), Cappadocia still seems like a lost world to the arriving traveler. It took the 20th century – and perhaps the invention of photography – to make people appreciate the landscape around Ürgüp. Several of the most important fathers of the early Church lived in this district, but none of them mentions what it looked like.

A 10th-century history tells us that its inhabitants were called troglodytes "because they go under the ground in holes, clefts, and labyrinths, like dens and burrows." In the 18th century, a French traveler thought he saw pyramids being used as houses, and weird statues of monks and the Virgin Mary.

Ancient upheavals: The reality is both more straightforward and more bizarre. The region is dominated by the 12,700-ft (3,916-meter) **Erciyes Dağı**, the ancient Mount Argaeus and the third highest mountain in Anatolia. The Romans believed that anyone who managed to climb to the top of its eternally-snowy summit would be able to see not only the Black Sea but also the blue Mediterranean.

Millions of years ago, Erciyes convulsed the surrounding landscape with a torrent of lava, smothering hundreds of miles in what must have been one of the greatest upheavals on the planet. Later, floods, rain, and wind sawed away at the table of lava, creating deep valleys and fissures; slopes turned into cones and columns.

Though the white dust from the rocks looks like sand, it is in fact much more fertile than the soil of the surrounding Central Anatolian steppelands. Trees, vines, and vegetables grow easily in it, attracting a dense population of farmers from the earliest times.

And the first men in these parts quickly discovered that the stone of the rock valleys is as magical as it looks. For it is soft until it comes in contact with the air, making it a perfect medium for carving entire buildings, sculpted out of living rock. Generations of local people have carved innumerable doorways and rooms in the rocks over an area of several hundred square miles. Some were homes for farmers, others were dovecotes or stables. Some may have been

Left, Cappadocia – fairy chimneys and devil's cones.

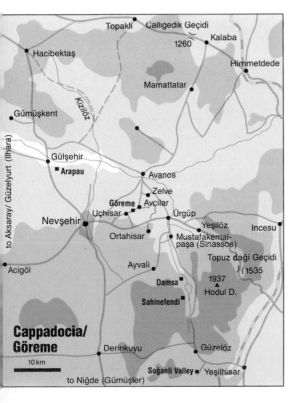

the quarters of the Byzantine Army, and many were used as chapels, cells, and refectories for monks and hermits. Many people still live today in the rock formations, which are cool in the summers.

The result is a fairy-tale landscape, a child's delight, where dwarves, elves, fairies and other supernatural beings seem to have just stepped round the corner, or perhaps gone indoors through the little doorway in the rock you are standing beside.

Three thousand rock churches: Many visitors only make a brief excursion to the cones and rock churches of Göreme, and an hour or two in perhaps Zelve or Ihlara. That's a pity because Cappadocia is best explored in a leisurely fashion by car or even on horse. Several local firms are now hiring out horses for trekking expeditions lasting up to 8 days. No matter how often you go, no two trips need ever be the same. There are an estimated three thousand rock churches in the area between Kayseri, Niğde, Gülşehir, and Ihlara valley. New caves, new "underground cities" and even churches are still being discovered from time to time.

Things to see fall into several categories. There are rock valleys with churches of which **Göreme** is only the most famous. Its chief rival is the magnificent canyon of **Ihlara Valley**, a much better place for a walk or a picnic. Other valleys include **Zelve** (where there was a village until the late 1950s) and **Soğanlı** which is about 50 minutes' drive south of the town of Ürgüp. The scenery along the way is delightful and mysterious but its churches – with the exception of **St Barbara** (good paintings) and **Belli Kilise** (magnificent cone) – do not really compare with those of Göreme or Ihlara.

Other churches are isolated. One of the very best as far as wall painting goes is at **Eski Gümüş** in Gümüsler village, just north of Niğde. A long detour via Mustafapaşa and Soğanlı will take you there, and if you are a Byzantine art buff, it is well worth it.

The church, which was restored by British archaeologists in the 1960s, has **Waiting for a customer.**

a completely preserved courtyard (the only one to survive in its entirety) and solemn frescoes in its interior which deserve to be better known. A room upstairs springs a surprise: a smoky wall covered with non-religious pictures, mostly from Aesop's fables. What it is doing in this monkish place is anyone's guess.

The other isolated but outstanding church of the region is much closer to Ürgüp. Drive out east along the Kayseri road until you see a sign on the right to the **Church of St Theodore**. You will drive about 6 miles (10 km) along a village road, going through first the village of **Karain,** whose people have been decimated by cancer caused by xeolite, the mineral, and then on to the village which used to be known as Tagar and is now called **Yeşilöz**.

Ask for the keeper (*bekçi*) to unlock the church for you. The church, built in a form known to architects as a triconch, has a central dome and unique 11th-century frescoes.

Who built these churches? The his-tory books don't tell us, but there are one or two clues in the paintings on the wall and sometimes in the remains of tombs set into the floor. The **Church at Çavuşin**, between Zelve and Göreme, for instance – you see its entrance high up on a metal ladder as you drive along the road – has a picture of Melias the Magister, a Byzantine-Armenian general who died a prisoner of the Arabs in Baghdad in 974. On the left, you face his altar and beside him a Byzantine Emperor, identified in recent years as John Tzimiskes (968–972), riding a white horse.

You may already have guessed from the large numbers of soldier saints on the walls that this is the land of a warrior aristocracy, the Byzantine frontiersmen who kept the Arabs at bay. Churches where all the saints are in civilian court dress – there are a few of these, notably in the fabulous Ortahisar Valley – are thought to come from the 50-year period in the 11th century when the bureaucrats had effectively ousted the army.

The erosion of time and the hand of man.

After the Battle of Manzikert (1071) and the Turkish conquest of this part of Anatolia, the Byzantine landowners were able to survive for another couple of centuries.

The Church of **Kırkdam Altı Kilisesi** (St George), for example, was reendowed by a Greek nobleman in the last decade of the 13th century. But he was a Greek nobleman who wore a turban (as the frescoes show) and served the Seljuk Sultan Mesut II at Konya. Kırkdam Altı Kilisesi is best approached, not from the steps at the top of Ihlara Valley, but about three or four miles downstream, on the northeast, near the village of **Belisirama**. You will need assistance from the local children to find it.

Another church which postdates Byzantine rule is **Karşi Kilise** or the Church of St John, near Gülşehir. An inscription records that it was established in the year 1214. Guillaume de Jerphanion found it still in use when he visited the district before World War I.

Hacıbektaş: Not everything in Cappadocia is Byzantine, however – one of the most impressive of all the antiquities of this region requires only about a 20-minute journey to the north of Gülsehir, at **Hacıbektaş**.

Hacıbektaş was the mother convent of the Bektaşi order of dervishes who served as the chaplains of the Janissaries, the storm troops of the Ottoman Empire. They were so widespread that 200 years ago it was said that no corner of the Empire was more than half a day's journey from a Bektaşi lodge.

The Bektaşis were a free-thinking, tolerant community. Where else in the world will you see a mosque with a drawing of man in it – something normally regarded as taboo in Islam? At the tomb of the founder of the order, **Hacı Bektaş Veli**, you will usually see a group of local women praying. In a separate shrine nearby is the **Tomb of Ballum Sultan**.

Hacıbektas has an annual feast day on August 14th, when followers of the Bektaşi cult from all over Turkey gather

Tectonic masterpieces.

in the town. This is the last remnant of a great tradition. Rooms in the convent tell their own story: the communal eating hall, with its great cauldrons still hanging by the fireplace, and the meeting room where the "fathers" of the order met in the evenings. This is rather like a Western charterhouse. Each of the senior dervishes had his own special places, marked out by an animal fur. The meeting room contains one rather sad reminder of the past – a photograph of the last August 14th meeting of the Turks in Crete in 1924. Soon after it was taken, these people – who a generation earlier had been more than 35 percent of the island's population – were uprooted in the great population exchange between Greece and Turkey. At the same time, the local Greeks in the towns and villages of Cappadocia were sent to Greece – a land most of them had never seen before.

There are still those who remember their former homes in Crete and other parts of Greece with nostalgia and welcome those Greeks who from time to time revisit the places in Cappadocia where they were born – towns such as **Gelveri**, now officially renamed Güzelyurt near Ihlara, and Mustafapaşa, famous a century ago as **Sinassos**, south of Ürgüp.

Sinassos – A town of paintings: Towns like Gelveri and the larger and more magnificent counterpart, Sinassos, never really recovered from the blow they received when the Ottoman Empire collapsed.

A *bekçi* in the town will take you to see the 19th-century decorations in the rock-church of **St Basil** in a meadow above a hauntingly pretty gorge outside the town. The furnishings have vanished but the church looks much as it did the day the congregation left it. Inside the town, go into the **Hotel Sinassos** and ask to be shown its rooms which are decorated more or less exactly as the 19th-century owners of the house left it. Painted on the wall over the front door is also an extraordinary picture which dates from 1893 but seems to have more to do with the Russian-Japanese war.

Every house has its own stone-sculptured balcony and windows. Inside many of them are late 19th-century frescoes, some with the eyes scoured out by the pious Muslim farmers who inherited these houses in the 1920s. If you can persuade the local people to let you see them, you will be shown a succession of paintings of more or less unique interest: a couple of young lovers dallying on a swing; the judgement of St Paul at Ephesus; 19th-century London as a Cappadocian artist imagined it, with a train running past St Paul's Cathedral; Napoleon fighting Arabs in the desert.

Alas, most of these unique paintings and the beautiful houses which contain them are doomed. The houses are too large for the farmers who are therefore fast replacing them wherever possible with modern-style houses, while the pictures are literally crumbling as you look at them.

In 10 or 20 years, and Mustafapaşa will probably be just another drab and architecturally anonymous central Anatolian town with a few of the new hotels to cater to tourists.

Potter at work in Avanos.

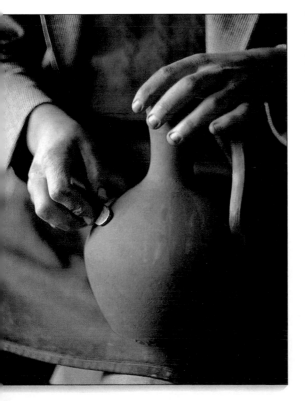

THE NORTHEAST

The Central plateau extends bleak and lonely for miles east of Ankara. Patchy wheatfields alternate with bald hills which centuries of soil erosion have fashioned into spooky forms. Brown and ochre predominate, except when the brief glory of May covers the land with grass and wildflower. The land has little to offer other than the solitude and the magnificence of its daybreaks.

Towns of the region are mostly nondescript: **Yozgat** retains few traces of the mighty Çapanoğlu dynasty, whose writ ran higher than the Ottomans in central Anatolia during the 17th and 18th centuries. **Sivas**, the Sebastia of Romans and Byzantines, deserves a stop for its thriving handicrafts bazaar and its classic monuments of Seljuk architecture. The four theological and medical colleges of **Gök**, **Çifte Minareli**, **Şifahiye** and **Bürüciye Medrese** are all 13th-century foundations of the Seljuk

and Mongol governors of the town, while the Ulu Cami dates from the 12th century. The small iron-mining town of **Divriği** houses, possibly, the most significant work of pre-Ottoman Turkish architecture in Turkey, and certainly calls for a detour. The **Mosque** and **Hospital complex** of the **Ulu Cami** was founded in 1228 by the Mengücük dynasty which ruled the area as vassals to the Seljuks.

Erzincan is a modern-looking city which was entirely rebuilt after the devastating earthquake of 1939. Beyond it lies the wild canyon of the Upper Euphrates, which gradually emerges into the high plateau of the northeast – the Roman province of Armenia Major – at **Aşkale**. Aşkale's only claim to fame derives from its military camp where most Christian and Jewish males of Istanbul were briefly interned in 1942 in keeping with spirit of the times.

Across the mountains: An alternative way to the northeast, which is along the main branch of the ancient Silk Route coming from the seaport of Trabzon of

Preceding page, Ishak Pasha Sarayı near Mount Ararat. **Below**, map of North East Turkey.

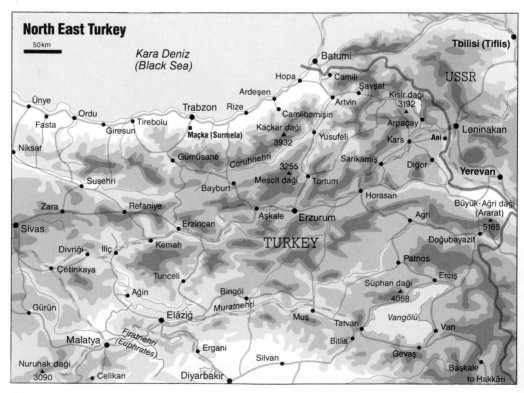

North East Turkey

50km

Kara Deniz (Black Sea)

Tbilisi (Tiflis)

USSR

Batumi

Hopa · Camili · Şavşat
Ardeşen · Artvin · Kisir dağı 3192
Ünye · Ordu · Trabzon · Rize · Camlihemişin · Arpaçay · Leninakan
Fasta · Tirebolu · Giresun · Maçka (Surmela) · Kaçkar dağı · Yusufeli · Kars · Ani
Niksar · 3932
Gümüsane · Coruhnehri · Sarikamiş · Digor · Yerevan
Suşehri · Bayburt · Mescit dağı · Tortum
Zara · Refaniye · Horasan · Büyük-Ağri dağı (Ararat) 5165
Sivas · Erzincan · Aşkale · Erzurum · Agri
Divriği · Iliç · Kemah · TURKEY · Doğubayazit
Çetinkaya · Patnos
Tunceli · Erciş
Ağin · Bingöl · Süphan dağı 4058
Gürün · Elâziğ · Muratnehri · Mus · Tatvan · Vangölü · Van
Malatya · Firatnehri (Euphrates) · Ergani · Bitlis
Nuruhak dağı 3090 · Celikan · Diyarbakir · Silvan · Gevaş · Başkale · to Hakkâri

the Black Sea, also reaches the highlands in Aşkale. From the seashore, it rises to the spectacular heights of the Zigana Pass. The verdant landscape of the **Pontic Mountains** changes rapidly on the descent inland. One enters, first, the pretty apple and apricot orchards of the **Torul** and **Gümüşhane** region, only to realize that it is surrounded by the dry, rocky mountains of the Harsit valley.

Connoisseurs of the altogether out-of-the-way and the unexplored will enjoy the lush mountain valley of **Yağmurdere**, reached by a somewhat reasonably good 25-mile (40-km) road off the left, 11 miles (18 km) past Gümüşhane. It offers the adventurous superb scenery, cold springs and fairly well-preserved Greek churches (though none of major architectural interest) in half a dozen villages, testimony to the Greek population who formed the majority in this area until 1924. A barely drivable road crosses the mountains at an enormous altitude back into the valley of the Sumela Monastery and Trabzon.

Somewhere before **Bayburt** the traveler passes the geographical boundary between Black Sea and the plateau, as well as the ancient historical boundary between the Pontic-Greek and Armenian cultural zones. An outward sign of the change may be noted in the attires of women, who now wear the distinctive brown "sack" covering them fully from head to toe. Variations of the sack fashion continue to dominate through **Erzurum** and eastward until near **Kars** and **Ağrı**. It is one of the more visible manifestations of the extremely conservative, and perhaps, somewhat xenophobic culture of the region of Erzurum.

Bayburt is dominated, besides the walking sacks, by a stupendous fortress which was first built by Justinian, rebuilt by the Bagratids, fortified by a Turkish lord in the 13th century, and destroyed by the Russian army in 1828. After Bayburt, the road climbs to the bleak grandeur of the **Kop Pass** [7,900 ft (2,400 meters)], commanding a panorama of several of the high mountain ranges of the East.

The plateau lying below leads to Aşkale, and thence to Erzurum, the largest and the most important city in eastern Turkey.

The High Plateau: Higher than the central Anatolian basin by about 3,000 ft (1,000 meters) the Northeastern plateau is broken by the gigantic masses of the Kop, Palandöken, Soğanlı and Allahuekber ranges, which give it a vast and terrifying aspect, and finally the single, overwhelming peak of Ararat. Snow buries all for a good half of the year, cutting many villages off from the rest of the world.

Then the endless pastures break into an orgy of grass and wildflowers, in a long spring that lasts well into July. Enormous herds of brown sheep and cattle cover the landscape and underpin the regional economy.

Historically, the plateau has formed the natural route of access between Asia Minor and the greater continent. The ancient east-west trade route crossed the border into the Roman-Byzantine world here: caravans carrying silk and

Çifte Minareli Medrese at Sivas – poetry in stone.

the other riches of Asia from China, through the Taklamakan desert and the bazaars of Bukhara and Samarkand, Nishapur and Tabriz, and the skirts of Erzurum, then either continued westward to Sebastea and Caesarea, or crossed the Zigana Pass to the seaport of Trebizond. They formed the bases of the prosperity of the Armenian kingdoms that straddled this borderland between the Byzantine and Persian realms. Xenophon came back from Persia along the same route with his 10,000 mercenaries in 400 BC. Marco Polo went the same route, in the other direction, as one of the earliest Westerners to seek a slice of the China trade.

Being on an access route proved to be a mixed blessing, though, as wave after wave of invaders broke into Anatolia through the northeast, leaving ruin and desolation in their wakes. Between 1828 and 1918, the region was the scene of at least four wars with Russia, in each of which Czarist armies succeeded in breaching Turkish defenses as far as Erzurum.

In the war of 1877–78 Russia occupied – and held until 1919 – the provinces of Artvin and Kars as far as Sarıkamış. Then, in the winter of 1914, the last of the Turkish dreams of an empire came to grief as several hundred thousand soldiers under Enver Pasha froze to death in the Allahuekber Mountains near Sarıkamış – a melancholy tale commemorated by a monument outside that town.

The short-lived Armenian republic was destroyed in 1920 in battles near Kars. To this day, the military significance of the region has not changed much. The Turkish Third army, one of the most important frontline units of NATO, is based in Erzurum while Sarıkamış and Kars both maintain strong garrisons.

Erzurum: The ancient Theodosiopolis, after Emperor Theodosius the Great who fortified it in the 4th century – is not distinguished for its prettiness. It is a somber, sad city, whose outward aura is somehow reflected in the countenance of its inhabitants. It has been perhaps

Left, these "wraps" are worn by women as symbols of their piety and modesty. And **right**, skin-eating fish in hot springs near Tokat.

best described as a city that has never recovered from winter. Still, it calls for a sojourn for several reasons: its awesome setting in the shadow of the giant **Palandöken Mountain** is one. A superb ski-run overlooking the city, the best in Turkey despite primitive facilities, awaits the hardy soul who will venture out here in winter.

The city also offers quite an array of historical monuments, which survived despite a history of constant warfare and destruction, not to mention the earthquakes of 1939 and 1983. All existing works are of Islamic origin, as Christian monuments that survived the depredations of World War I – including the Cathedral – were sadly subsequently razed.

The three **Kümbets**, or at least one among them, is the oldest historical building in town. It is ascribed to Emir Saltuk, the feudal lord whose dynasty dominated Erzurum for a century after the Turkish conquest. The **Ulu Cami** was built in 1179 by a grandson. The architectural masterpiece of the **Çifte**

Minareli Medrese was built, like the Gök Medrese in Sivas, under the Seljuk ruler, Alaaddin Keykubat II. The Mongols, in their turn, built the **Yakutiye Medrese** in 1310, named after the local governor of Ogeday, a grandson of Gengis Khan who held court in Tabriz. The Ottomans then rebuilt and resettled the city, and among others, contributed the graceful mosque of **Lala Paşa** in 1563 – shortly after the 1555 treaty with Persia which finalized Ottoman rule in the East.

In more recent times, Erzurum served as the setting for the congress of July 1919, which, along with the Sivas Congress of the following month, marked the beginning of the resistance movement that eventually led to the forming of Republic. The Congress of Eastern Notables met under the aegis of General Karabekir, who had effectively ruled here since taking the town from retreating Russian armies in 1918. It resolved to resist Armenian claims in the northeast, and gave crucial support to the efforts of Mustafa Kemal.

Ottoman bridge near Horasan.

Journey to Ararat: From Erzurum, the ancient caravan route continues eastward, carrying perpetual convoys of intercontinental trucks, which have replaced the camels, to Iran, Afghanistan and beyond. At **Pasinler**, a brief detour reveals **Hasankale**, a mighty Armenian fortress which, in the 15th century, served as base for the ephemeral empire of Uzun Hasan, chief of the nomadic tribe of the Akkoyunlu or White Sheep. In Çobandede, a graceful Ottoman bridge spans the Aras river on the right and remains functional after 400 years of service.

Beyond **Horasan**, the **Sarıkamış** and **Kars** road branches off to the left, while the Iran transit road continues through **Eleşkirt** and **Ağrı** toward the spectacular sights of **Mount Ararat** and the palace of Ishak Pasha. The region is now inhabited by mountain Turks, as indicated by the lustier mustaches of men, and the markedly different appearance of women who wear the colorful garb and headgear of the mountain Turkish tribes. There is not much left, however, to attest to the rich past of the land, one of the centers of medieval Armenian culture, and what is left is fast disappearing – thus, the remains of the 7th century patriarchal church in Diyadin which was pulled down recently to provide stone for a new mosque.

Somewhere before **Doğubeyazıt**, the unwary traveler is jolted by the stupendous apparition of Ararat on the horizon. The grandeur of the view is hard to capture in prose and harder in photographs; there is no substitute to actually experiencing it. The volcanic peak – *Ağrı Dağı* in Turkish – stands, at 16,700 ft (5,100 meters), taller than any point in Europe. Its relative elevation over the surrounding plain – over 13,000 ft (4,000 meters) in the north – makes it one of the sheerest profiles in the world, comparable to Colombia's Sierra de Santa Marta or New Guinea's Mount Carstensz. This is then enhanced by the incomparable impact of its single, symmetrical, conical mass. On a typical hazy day, the base of the mountain will blend into the blue sky, leaving an enormous white cap of snow hovering eerily above the horizon.

The search for the remains of Noah's Ark has been a growth business even since the French nobleman Pitton de Tournefort first scaled the mountain in 1707. In recent years search activity has increased with several dozen groups attempting the feat each year. A large number of pieces of rotten timber and indefinite shapes sighted under the ice cap have, thus far, been unable to provide conclusive evidence of any boat on the mountain. In recent years, the former astronaut James Irwin has initiated several efforts to vindicate the Bible, despite the periodic obstruction of skeptical Turkish officials. Turkish opinion regards the Ark-raiders, in general, with much suspicion – their general consensus is that the "arkologists" are either sick, suborning the Kurds or CIA types engaged in setting up devilish devices against the Soviet Union. For those simply interested in climbing the peak, formalities are long, and best dealt with through local adventure travel agencies

like Trek Travel well in advance. For those who want to see the "Ark" without climbing the mountain, another group of bible-pushers say they have found the world's first ocean liner in the hills around Terçeker. Others say it is a big clump of mud.

The palace of **Ishak Pasha**, nested in a high valley above Doğubeyazıt, was built in the 18th century. Not much is known about the family except that they held the title of Ottoman governors at a time when Istanbul would be quite content to receive an occasional tribute from such distant provinces. The impregnable position of the palace-stronghold, overlooking the caravan route, suggests the source of their wealth. Its style and size, echoing the Topkapı, suggest an effort to imitate and, perhaps, rival the court of Istanbul. The architectural style has been described as "imitation Seljuk, mock-Georgian, neo-Armenian and baroque-Ottoman," which add up to an aesthetically pleasant whole. The 24-room harem would make any man envious.

From the palace it is possible to see the remains of an **Urartian Fortress**, an Ottoman mosque and a large enclosed orchard below the town with the ruins of a monastery. The orchard, a green oasis in a parched landscape, is well worth a visit even though it is privately owned. Local tradition takes it to be the site of the well-known medieval romance of Kerem and Asli, which tells of the impossible love of a Moslem youth and a Christian princess.

The road to Kars: The transit road crosses into Iran at **Gürbulak**, a few miles east of Doğubeyazıt. Holders of an Iranian visa can make a day trip to the magnificent Armenian monastery of **St Thaddeus** just beyond the border. A passable dirt road leads uphill from Doğubeyazıt southward, offering the best views of Mount Ararat from high terrain, to the spectacular lava fields of **Mount Tendürek**. It continues then to Çaldıran, site of the great Ottoman victory over Persia in 1514, and on to Van. The paved northern road crosses an enormous hump of Ararat's lava at 7,200

Spot the Ark in the picture.

ft (2,200 meters) and descends into the fertile lands of the Iğdır plain.

The plain, which **Iğdır** shapes with Vagarshapat and Yerevan – the pre-Christian and post-Russian capitals of Armenia – across the Aras river, is a climatic anomaly. Its low altitude – 2,600 ft (800 meters), relative to the mountains around it guarantees permanently warm weather and permits such local agricultural surprises as cotton, rice and citrus fruit.

The Turkish half of the plain is inhabited by Azeri Turks, immigrants of 1878 and 1920 from Azerbaijan, who form the only properly Shi'ite (as opposed to Alevi) community in Turkey. A visit in the month of *Muharrem* (on the lunar calender) may afford a view of the festivities commemorating the martyrdom of Hasan and Hüseyin, observed here with as much fervor as in Iran.

The Aras, and the road along it, follows the border until past the rock-salt mines of **Tuzluca**, then enters the wildly beautiful canyon that leads to **Kağızman** and **Karakurt**. A few kilometers beyond **Tuzluca**, a bad road to **Digor** branches off at the confluence of the Aras with Arpaçay (Ahuryan), and, a short drive farther on leads to the ruins of the ancient city of **Bagaran** which served as the first capital of Bagratid kings during the 9th century. The remains of another 9th-century Armenian church, near the village of **Çeğilli**, can be reached from **Kağızman** either by a lousy 16-mile (25-km) drive or a 1-hour hike from kilometer 21 of the **Karakurt** road.

After that strenuous pilgrimage, it is time to climb once again to the high plateau on the way to **Kars**. One can take either the shorter Kötek route, or the splendidly scenic road through Karakurt and Sarıkamış.

Sarıkamış, with the surrounding cold, dark *taiga* of giant pines, teeming with wolves and foxes and the endless rows of old Russian barracks, reminds the visitor that he has now crossed the border into what used to be an outpost of the Czarist empire until the end of World War I.

The meadows of the Aras in late spring.

Kars confirms the same impression, with a peculiar aura of being utterly out of place and out of time. One is first struck by the grid layout of the city, unique in Turkey, then by the formerly graceful architecture of the downtown area that seems transposed from turn-of-the-century Vienna or Petersburg and left to gather dust in distant Asia. A tilted Parisian cast-iron balcony here, and a broken art nouveau theater gate there complete the picture. This, of course, owes itself to the fact that the current city center was built by the Russians during their final, 41-year-long occupation after 1877. So does the occasional blond descendant of Russians, Germans, and even Estonians one runs into in the vicinity – particularly in the village of **Karacaören**, just outside the city, which is still partly inhabited by Protestant Germans settled here a century ago by the Czar.

The old city, which served as capital to the Bagratids during the early part of the 10th century, is now a slum clinging to the hillside across the Karş stream. It is dominated by a magnificent fortress of the usual Urartu-Byzantine-Armenian-Turkish-Mongolian-Russian pedigree. It deserves a visit for panoramic views of the town and the plateau beyond. On Thursdays, local folk come up to pay their respects at the **Tomb of Celal Baba**, believed to have been a Muslim martyr of the Mongolian invasion. The other historical work of importance in town is the **Cathedral of the Holy Apostles**, built in AD 937, and used alternately as church and mosque for most of the next 1,000 years. It now continues to be useful but only as a timberyard.

Ani: The skeleton of the medieval metropolis of **Ani**, sprawled across the endless meadows of the high plateau, is one of the most impressive sights of the Near East. It is announced by the mighty row of double walls and round towers that loom in the distance, extending more than a mile on the land side. Inside, at the height of its fortunes, it was a city of 100,000 inhabitants and the legendary 1,000 churches. Now the di-

Troglodyte houses near Kars.

lapidated remains of some 10 churches, one mosque and a royal citadel stand in sad and silent testimony to the city's vanished glory.

A town evidently existed in this location since before the Christian era. The Gamsaragan dynasty of Armenian lords held it for several hundred years, before it was acquired in the 9th century by the Bagratids. It entered the period of its full civic bloom in AD 961, when it was made the capital of the medieval Armenian kingdom at the apogee of its power. For the next 100 years, Kings Ashod III, Smbad II, Gagik I, and John Smbad ruled out of Ani. During the reign of John Smbad, the city was besieged, in succession, by a brother of the King, the Ardzruni ruler of Van, the King of Georgia, a first wave of Turkish raiders and finally the Byzantine Emperor Basil II. In 1045, it was delivered to the Byzantines, who resettled part of its population in Cappadocia. A few years later, Turks came in turn and set up a local chieftain as governor, who built the only mosque in town.

The Pahlavuni and Zakharian families succeeded in reestablishing Armenian rule soon afterwards, this time in vassalage to Georgian kings, and Ani continued to flourish, surprisingly, until the mid-13th century. It finally succumbed to the Mongols and the earthquake of 1319. A travelogue of 1905 mentions a single monk and one Armenian family as the only inhabitants of the deserted ruins.

The city is situated on a triangular promontory bounded on two sides by the steep gorges of the Arpaçay (Ahuryan) and a tributary. The land across the Arpaçay is Georgian territory: one may occasionally glimpse groups of visitors trying to view the ruins from across the chasm. The Turkish and Georgian land border is now open for private travel, the result of which is an influx of former Soviet beauties into the nearby Turkish towns for prostitution or to sell all kinds of products for just a few dollars. Parts of the ruins, including the Citadel and the **Church of the Virgin** which overhangs a wild ravine

A lady in he east.

at the far end of the peninsula, may still be off-limits, though.

Entering the city grounds through the main or Lion's Gate, the path to the left takes one to the massive, quadrangular **Cathedral** (built in AD 989 to 1001), the half-collapsed round dome of the **Church of the Redeemer** (1036), the much better preserved **Church of St Gregory** by the ravine (1215), and the beautiful **Convent of the Three Virgins**, standing on a rocky outcrop lower in the gorge. On the righthand side from the Gate are the remains of a Georgian church (1218), the architecturally significant round Church of St Gregory built by King Gagik I, the **Church of the Holy Apostles** (1013), a **dodecagonal church** of the 9th century dedicated, yet again, to St Gregory, and the **Mosque of Menuchehr** from the 1070s.

Beyond the mosque is the badly ruined **Church of Ashod III**, and several equally ruined temples at the citadel. From the citadel one gets a good view of the many cave dwellings that line the walls of the western gorge. These were supposed to have housed the poorer people of Ani. Should one speculate that those "poor people" were, perhaps, refugees from the war-torn countryside, whose influx fueled the sudden and quite extraordinary growth of the city amid the devastations of the 11th century?

Those captivated by the sad beauty of Ani may want to continue exploring the vicinity to take in more. The region is teeming with churches, monasteries and fortresses of roughly the same period – some of them barely known, others inaccessible for lack of roads, or requiring permissions to be negotiated with military authorities.

About 6 miles (10 km) northeast of Ani, near the new Turco-Soviet dam on the Arpaçay, is the monastery complex of **Horomots**, almost as impressive as Ani but virtually unknown to tourists. It contains three well-preserved churches of the 11th century, and several that lie on the Soviet side. The monastery served as a burial ground for the kings of Ani and functioned as an important religious center until the 18th century.

Ani: Armenian ruins on the Arpaçay.

THE ARMENIANS

The emergence of Armenians in what is now eastern and northeastern Turkey dates to the period after the fall of the Urartus in the 7th century BC. Linguistic evidence suggests a wave of Indo-European immigration from the west, apparently related to the Phrygians. A system of powerful and often warring local lords developed in the area bounded by current-day Erzincan, the Çoruh valley, Lake Sevan in the Armenian Republic, Lake Urmia in Iran and Lake Van. It subsisted, with periods of unification under the royal dynasties, until after the Turkish and Mongolian invasions in the 11th and 13th centuries.

The first recorded unification of Armenian princes under a monarchy occurred around 190 BC. King Tigran the Great (95–55 BC) took part in the struggles of his father-in-law, Mithridates of Pontus, against the Romans, and briefly forged an empire extending to Syria and the Mediterranean which survived until the 5th century as a buffer between the Roman-Byzantine and the Persian worlds.

Christianity was adopted in AD 301 during the reign of King Trdad (Tiridates) by the efforts of St Gregory the Illuminator. The Armenian alphabet – which is still in use – was devised in AD 407 by the scribe Mesrob, heralding a period of literary, scholastic and theological ferment in the 5th century. This so-called "golden age" came to an end with the Persian occupation, schism with the Byzantine orthodox church, and a gradual reversion to the dominance of petty regional dynasties.

One such dynasty, the Bagratids of the Çoruh valley and Kars region, succeeded in establishing its dominance over most Armenian princes during the 9th century. The Bagratid kingdom, centered first in Kars, then in Ani, lasted for almost 200 years. It was characterized by an extraordinary architectural activity – with monuments that still dot the landscape in northeastern Turkey and Caucasia.

The Bagratid kingdom was brought to an end by the eastward drive of the Byzantine empire, shortly before the Turkish invasion, in the early 11th century.

The route of the Byzantine army in 1071 near Malzgirt by Turks was no doubt facilitated by the unsettled state of Armenia after the fall of the Bagratids. In fact, some Armenian princes not only welcomed the Turks as a counter to the Byzantines, but actually converted to Islam and participated in the subsequent wars of conquest.

Nevertheless, the Turkish hold on Armenia did not develop into an organized political dominion until the 15th or 16th centuries. Shortly after 1071, Armeno-Georgian dynasties reappeared in the Ani region and ruled until the Mongolian devastation. Semi-independent Armenian towns and chieftains coexisted with marauding Turkish, Kurdish and Arab Beys, as well as tribal coalitions, bandit chiefs and adventurers of unknown origin – in a state of perpetual anarchy and cultural retrogression – until as late as the Ottoman conquest of 1514.

By the end of the 19th century, roughly one-third of the population of the region remained in various degrees Christian and Armenian. The disintegration of the Ottoman Empire in the 19th century led to calls for regional reform, and eventually to notions of Armenian autonomy. Russia and England entered the fray with a view to their conflicting interests in the region.

During World War I, fearing the imminent collapse of its Eastern front under a Russian offensive, the Ottoman government attempted to effect a radical solution to the problem by deporting most of its Armenian population to camps in Mesopotamia.

Since the 1920s, at least officially, no Armenians exist in Eastern Turkey. One may find an occasional village or valley which maintains traces of an Armenian past, but the passing tourist is unlikely to run into one, and Turkish opinion is very sensitive about any perceived attempt to revive a history that it prefers to discreetly forget.

ARTVIN

Several roads lead from Karş to Artvin. The usual route via Göle is scenically the less interesting. The more northerly routes – to Ardahan past the spectacular blue and green scenery of the icy Çildir Lake, then across the mountains to either Şavsat or Ardanuç – lead through idyllic meadowlands to burst into verdant Alpine landscape. The road, however, is rough, and travel on it requires a four wheel drive.

Georgians have inhabited southern Caucasia and the Kura and Çoruh valleys for as long as anyone recalls. Their non-Indo-European language suggests they may have been here before the Hittites and the Urartu. During the centuries of Greek and Roman expansion, a Georgian kingdom (which Greeks called Iberia) held sway in Caucasia, while the ancestors of today's Laz, close relatives of Georgians, ruled in the lesser kingdom of Colchis by the Black Sea. The king of Georgia adopted Christianity shortly after his Armenian counterpart did, but unlike Armenians, Georgians never broke with the Eastern Orthodox church, and managed to maintain their independence in the face of Roman, Byzantine, Persian, Arab and Turkish incursions.

The region around the historic fortresses of Ispir, Oltu and Ardanuç was the scene of a major flourish of medieval Georgian culture following the 8th century. This occurred under the Bagratids, the princely dynasty which also acquired the Armenian crown in the next century. A branch of the family ruled in Tbilisi until the Russian occupation in 1811. The Artvin region was governed by Ottomans through indigenous tributary lords. Islam took root only within the last century, and the Georgian language, though fast vanishing, is still spoken in the distant valleys of Posof, Meydancık (Imerhev), and Camili (Macahel).

The little town of **Artvin** is perched in an almost perpendicular position on a

Ishan: Georgian churches in spectacular settings.

mountainside, some 1,500 ft above the narrow Çoruh river and valley where rafting trips are fast becoming popular with Turkish and foreign sports adventurers. The land is covered with forests, broken by walnut, apple, cherry, and mulberry orchards. The view through the layers of cloud, which may be positioned either above or below the town, is astonishing.

The visitor is likely to fall in love with this little-known corner and overstay his or her intended sojourn. This is facilitated by the presence of **Hotel Karahan**, one of the better hotels east of Ankara. The young Karahan brothers, not only operate the hotel with personal care and an almost shy politeness, but also advise travelers, organize hunting expeditions, maintain mountain lodges, discover hard-to-reach Georgian monuments, and provide a wealth of otherwise unavailable information about the region. One needs an English translator, however, to communicate with them.

Beside its setting and its mild-mannered inhabitants, the principal attraction of the town is the popular festival held at **Kafkasör** late in June each year. This is one of the few truly popular traditional festivities to be found in Turkey, and is attended by tens of thousands from all over the region. They set up a veritable city of ramshackle tents in the high meadows around Kafkasör, with much drinking and merrymaking, during the days leading up to the highlight of the festival: the bullfights held among bovine champions arriving from each village, town, county and district around Artvin.

Exploring the region: Trunk roads follow the arid Çoruh canyon bed where an occasional rickety dirt-and-rock path is seen to go up the sidewall and disappear overhead. Driving up one of them at random – for example, at Demirkent on the way to Yusufeli, or Pirnalli on the Şavşat road – with a sturdy car or preferably a jeep, will invariably reveal a mountain valley which gets greener as it ascends, leading to the main village set in a garden paradise, with waterfalls, orchards, and babbling brooks of clear

water teeming with trout. Another 3,300 ft (1,000 meters) or so higher, one will find, amid a Swiss-postcard landscape, the *yayla* where many villagers keep their beloved summer homes.

The forests beyond the *yayla* offer opportunities for hunting bear, wild boar and ibex. And hidden somewhere within the valley is probably one of the several stupendous Georgian churches of the Bagratid era which dot both southern and eastern parts of the province.

A southern circuit through **Oltu** and **Yusufeli** will cover the churches of Ishan, Bana, Hahuli, Ösk-vank, Dörtkilise and Barhal. A trip up the Imerhevi valley to **Ardanuç** and **Şavşat** will add Dolishane, Opiza, Porta, Tbeti and Yeni Rabat (Satberdi). Allow not less than two days to enjoy either journey, with overnight stays in charming Yusufeli or Şavşat.

Ishan is a good place to lead off with: a 4-mile (6-km) climb from the parched canyon base reveals a veritable oasis, with the mind-blowing mass of the 140-ft (40-meter) tall, red-domed church built in 828 sitting in the backyard of the quaint, village schoolhouse with delicate stone carvings on the outer walls.

The 10th century complex of **Hahuli** (Haho), 6 miles (9 km) up westward from the southern end of Lake Tortum, used to be the most celebrated of Georgian monasteries, and is now one of the best preserved and most impressive. It has served as the local mosque since the 17th century.

Gigantic **Ösk-vank**, another 10th-century work a little further north, also owes its preservation, save a partly collapsed dome, to being used as a mosque. Now partially filled with debris from the construction of a new mosque, the interior is still spacious enough for the occasional volleyball tournament.

Barhal, whose strangely "modern" angular mass belies a history of 10 centuries, is reached by a jolting 2-hour drive from Yusufeli through ever-deepening forest and ever-wilder streams. Devote the rest of the day to trout fishing and bathing under roaring cascades, or use Barhal as a base to climb the *yaylas* of the snowcapped Kaçkar range.

THE BLACK SEA COAST

"Thalassa! The sea!" So shouted the weary remnants of Xenophon's 10,000 adventurers when they caught their first glimpse of the Euxine Sea from a height of 7,000 ft above Trebizond on the return from their ill-fated Persian expedition. The modern-day traveler is bound to share their joy and awe when the azure sea suddenly reveals itself below a dozen ranges of thickly forested mountains and tea plantations, whether on the descent to Hopa at the eastern end, or at any one of the spectacular passes that breach the mountains of the Black Sea coast.

The Hospitable Sea – Pontus Euxinus of antiquity – now suffers from a misnomer: the Black Sea is in fact as blue, or rather as azure, green, turquoise, and indigo as the Mediterranean. It also has crystal-clear waters, and excellent beaches spread along its 745 mile coastline. For the sun and sea seeker, it is handicapped only by its rather short summers and, especially as one moves eastward, by its often rainy climate.

That climate, though, accounts for the biggest attraction of the region – a green landscape utterly unlike the rest of Turkey, rivaled only in range of tone by tropical rain forests. East of Rize, where it rains on the average every other day, the forest acquires a distinctly jungle-like aspect, with tall moss-covered trees rising over a wild undergrowth of ivy.

The coast is lined with countless ancient fishing and trading towns, and punctuated with torrential streams that come down from the humid mountains. Following any one of these streams into the hills and valleys of the hinterland reveals a world of spectacular beauty. Villages, unlike the concentrated huddles of inner Anatolia, spread far – horizontally and vertically – in a succession of spacious farmhouses and intensively cultivated fields, with an occasional grouping of a few shops and a mosque serving as "the downtown." The inhabitants are independent, assertive, hospitable and little acquainted with the arts of bamboozling the tourist.

Humpbacked stone bridges of 16th- to 19th-century vintage span the streams; less picturesque but more efficient are the one-man crank cable cars (platforms really) that span the wilder stretches. The scenery gets greener and grander as one goes further up. Evergreens replace leaf trees, rising clouds wrap all in mist for most of the day. The summer pastures (*yayla*) are reached above the clouds at somewhere past 6,000 ft (2,000 meters). Drivable roads – many of them unmapped – go on up to pass inland, except in Hemşin, where the snow-capped peaks of the Kaçkar range block the path.

The Laz People: The five townships of Hopa, Arhavi, Fındıklı, Ardeşen and Pazar at the eastern end of the coast are home to an idiosyncratic race of people. The Laz, most of them blond and blue-eyed, speak a language akin to Georgian and trace their roots to the ancient king-

dom of Colchis, where Jason and his Argonauts came to rob the Golden Fleece.

Surprisingly for anyone acquainted with the quicksilver mind of the Laz, Jason and his men managed to carry it away, though with the help of Medea – the Colchian princess who eloped with Jason only to be betrayed and deserted by him later on. Her descendants distinguish themselves by a flair for personal independence, an energetic style, and a dry sense of humor – qualities not so immediately discernible elsewhere in Turkey. They also emulate her style of seeking their fortunes away from home; they have come to own most of the real estate and contracting business in Turkey, not to mention bakeries and much of the restaurant trade.

Fish and tea dominate the Laz economy at home. The former becomes palpable with the legendary 101 ways of preparing *hamsi*, the local variety of anchovies. The latter, of which the Rize region produces enough to satisfy the national addiction, adds an almost Southeast Asian look to the already lush landscape.

It turns a random drive through the backcountry in late summer into a feast for the senses; teafields bloom with flocks of Laz women, wearing all colors of the rainbow, picking teabuds, and the many processing plants soak the land with an intoxicating aroma.

The Hemşin Valleys: A tour of the Black Sea will be incomplete without an expedition into the unique world of the **Hemşin valleys**. Hemşin lies in the rain forest above the Laz country of Ardesen and Pazar. It is inhabited by descendants of the Georgians who seeped across the mountains and settled in these inaccessible valleys, living in virtual independence until the last century. Many Hemşinlis now live in Istanbul and Ankara (and Moscow), where they dominate the pastry trade, but return each summer for the annual pilgrimage to the *yayla*.

The forest town of **Çamlıhemşin** comes alive in June, with women clad in the traditional mountaineers' woolen

Çamlıhemşin – passage to a unique and verdant world.

socks and black-and-orange headgear and men rounding up the cattle and provisions for the long trek. Large quantities of *rakı* are consumed along the way, and merry-making goes on through the summer with each *yayla* taking turns to host an endless round of *vartavar* festivities.

The traveler arriving in Hemşin is advised to seek out Savaş Güney, a delightful intellectual-turned-rustic who lives with his German wife in a farm across the roaring waters of the Fırtına River 4 miles above Çamlihemşin. He offers first-rate accommodations on the farm, and acts as a drinking companion and guide to the mountaineer, fisherman, whitewater canoer or just the plain tourist. Güney can also help to organize a camping expedition into the spectacular alpine passes and glacier lakes of the Kaçkar range, or simpler trips to the thermal baths at Ayder, or to the wildly romantic fortress of **Zil Kalesi**, rising above the mist-covered forest atop a crag overhanging the thunderous Fırtına.

The towers of Trebizond: The pleasant port of **Rize** marks the historic limit of Greek colonization on the Pontic coast, thus, also, the eastern border of the medieval empire of Trebizond. From Rize to Ünye and Samsun, the native population was first Hellenized then Islamized over the centuries, traveling far from its Laz roots while still keeping the epithet. Coming from Pazar, one can note the subtle cultural boundary, as usual, through the changing attire of women who now wear the psychedelic white-red-and-black cotton body shawl of the region.

Sürmene (Kastel) detains the traveler for the exceptionally fine 18th-century mansion of the local lords. A trip to the backcountry reveals some of the best-preserved examples of the traditional timber-and-stucco architecture of the Black Sea. Some of the shrewdest entrepreneurs in Turkey originated here, including "Banker Kastelli" who built a fabulous financial empire that came close to controlling half the total savings in the country before its spectacu-

Folklorists at work and play.

lar collapse in 1982.

Commercial acumen also formed the basis of the fabled wealth of the ancient city of Trebizond. From its founding as a Greek colony in the 6th century BC. till earlier this century, its port served as the meeting point of the caravans of Persia and Peking with the fleets of Constantinople and Venice; its merchants dealt in bank shares and bills of lading when the world around them burned in conquest and pillage.

The city held a strange fascination for both the western and the oriental imagination: the great travelers Strabo, Marco Polo and Evliya Çelebi sought it out; Don Quixote dreamt of himself as Emperor of Trebizond; Napoleon went further and claimed descent from the Comneni; Rose Macaulay rhapsodized "the towers of Trebizond shimmering on a far horizon in luminous enchantment."

The city reached the peak of its glory after 1204, when a branch of the imperial Comneni dynasty appointed it as the seat of a Pontic empire after the fall of Constantinople to the Crusaders.

The empire prospered, to the point of goldplating the domes of the imperial palace and cathedral of **Panagia Chrysocephalos** (now the Fatih Mosque), thanks in part to a judicious diplomatic balancing act – which included marrying Comneni princesses into virtually every European and Asiatic ruling family of the age. It lived beyond the retaking of Constantinople by the Palaeologi to outlast Byzantium by 18 years. Keeping in character, it negotiated an orderly transfer of power with Mehmet the Conqueror, and even provided a princess to be married to his son Beyazıt.

Modern **Trabzon**, despite its rapid growth, retains much of its genteel charm, and many traces of a fabulous past. The old port dates from Emperor Hadrian; the grandiose city walls, culminating in the citadel which houses the ruins of the imperial palace with a breathtaking view over the city, are the work of Justinian. Later Byzantine monuments include, beside the Chryso-

Tea plantation near Rize.

cephalos, the **Church of St Eugenius** (Yeni Cuma Mosque since 1461) and the hilltop **Panagia Convent** which was occupied by nuns until 1923. The classic 13th-century **Hagia Sophia** is by far the most significant cultural sight in the city. It houses some of the finest examples of Byzantine painting in the world, painstakingly restored by a British team after centuries of lying under layers of whitewash.

The charming mosque and *türbe* of **Gülbahar Hatun** – Lady Springrose – commemorate the Comneni princess who married Sultan Beyazıt II, then returned to her native city with her Greek-speaking son (later Selim I, the Grim) as the Viceroy of Trabzon.

A more recent example of old Pontic opulence can be seen at the **Atatürk House**, high on the Soğuksu hill where the Trebizondite bourgeoisie used to keep their summer residences. The misleadingly renamed house is in fact the splendid art nouveau mansion of one of the leaders of the town's former Greek oligarchy, built at a time when many were toying with the idea of a revived Pontic Republic in Trabzon. Such dreams came to a rude end in 1923, when Greeks were expelled from Trabzon after their 2,500-year sojourn there, and the confiscated mansion of the would-be president of Pontus fell to the leader of the newly formed Republic of Turkey.

Monasteries of the valley: Other poignant reminders of the Greek past of Trabzon are to be found in the valleys that lead up to the **Zigana Pass**, along the old caravan route toward Erzurum and Asia. A large number of ruined monasteries lie hidden in the mountains there. Only one of them – admittedly the most important and the most scenic – is well-known by tourists. Others await discovery.

The **Monastery of the Black Virgin** at **Sumela** compares with Mount Athos and the Meteora (not to mention Delphi) for the Greek flair for selecting the eeriest and most spectacular settings to contemplate divinity. The enormous 7-story monastery is perched on a ledge

Anchovy catch – a way of life for the Laz.

halfway between heaven and the earth on a 1,200-ft sheer rock face, far in the depths of an uninhabited forest valley. Monks came up here as early as the 4th century, and the place soon developed into the most renowned monastic commune in Asia Minor. It participated in the many politico-religious conflicts of Byzantine times, exercised political clout during the empire of Trebizond, and remained an influential institution right up to 1923.

The present buildings probably date from the 12th century; frescoes that once covered every surface come in three layers dating from 1710, 1740 and 1860. The monastery is in a vandalized state, but no degree of ruin seems enough to detract from the unforgettable effect of the site.

Sumela is reached from Maçka by a paved road, along one of the loveliest of the Black Sea valleys, then a panting 40-minute climb up a forest path. Afterwards one can walk a little farther up valley for a delightful chain of cascades and pools in which to bathe or fish for trout. So refreshed, one can regain the energy for at least two more monasteries, those of **Peristera** and **Vazelon**. Both are virtually unknown by tourists, but almost rival Sumela in age, historic wealth, power and spectacular setting. The former is reached by a bad road from the village of Esiroğlu below Maçka; the latter is across the valley at Küçük Konak 9 miles (15 km) past Maçka. Both require a lot of walking and climbing, but amply reward the effort. Those continuing inland can recover with the customary rice pudding and corn bread of alpine Hamsiköy just below the Zigana; those who make the descent certainly deserve a bottle of *rakı* at one of the seaside fish restaurants of Trabzon.

The green coast: An unbroken succession of towns, descendants of ancient Greek colonies, line the mountainous coast from Trabzon to Samsun and Sinop. With exceptions like Tirebolu and Giresun, they have lost much of their former charm: by dint of the ghastly coastal highway that cuts towns from the sea and the haphazard development which has all but wiped out the distinctive old architecture of the region. Good examples of that architecture can still be seen in the beautiful upper quarter of Akçaabat. **Tirebolu** (former Tripolis) has a Genoese fortress, a relic of the 14th-century trade wars between Venice and Genoa. Along the way there are countless valley routes waiting to be explored. One leads to **Tonya**, a charming mountain town above Vakfıkebir, and the hazelnut country behind Espiye, where several spectacular waterfalls can be discovered up valley.

Giresun is very much a copy of Trabzon, but on a smaller scale, less developed, and more pleasant. It has a parallel history, and just about the same mix of churches and mosques and citadels, again on more modest dimensions. The fortress holds one of the loveliest parks in Turkey, with bird's-eye views over the city and surrounding mountains covered with hazelnut and cherry trees. The last item, by the way, derives its English name from *Cerasus*, the original form of Giresun, whence Lucullus first brought the exotic fruit to Rome. The city is the center of Turkey's flourishing trade in hazelnuts.

Ordu is a staging point for the unforgettable excursion to the spectacular beach-encircled crater lake at **Cambaşı** about 45 miles (70 km) southward. Beyond **Perşembe**, a sad, deserted church stands guard at **Cape Yasun**, where in older times a pagan temple celebrated the cult of Jason. In quaint **Bolaman**, a grand seaside castle recalls the former glories of the once powerful Haznedaroğlu, lords of Pontus in the 18th and 19th centuries.

The formerly proud merchant town of **Fatsa** in the middle of hazelnut country now is chiefly distinguished by the fact that it was a "liberated area" by Turkish Marxists in the late 1970s, with a local tailor elected as mayor. The army soon moved in and arrested thousands, with Marxist mayor later dying in custody.

Farther down the coast is **Ünye**, which offers some of the best beaches of the Black Sea coast, with seaside promenades complete with restaurants and campsites, frequented mainly by the residents of nearby Samsun. **Samsun** itself holds little interest for the traveler except for the old residential quarters uphill, and the fact that it was here, on May 19, 1919, that Mustafa Kemal landed to start the national resistance that culminated in the forming of the Turkish Republic about 4 years later.

The Western Black Sea: The coastal road continues west from Samsun across the great tobacco growing plains of Bafra toward **Sinop**, a peculiar town built at the narrowest point of a peninsula with a seaport at each side.

The city was first settled as a colony of distant Miletus on the southern Aegean, and true to the philosophical traditions of its mother-city, it produced Diogenes, the inventor of Cynicism. Unlike the myth circulated by his detractors, he never lived in a tub and never met Alexander the Great. Sinop also served as the capital of the later kings of Pontus; Mithridates VI (The Great) was born here, and built his birthplace into a fantastic showpiece

with marble avenues, gymnasia and colonnaded agoras. But all that remains today of his city are the strange harbor walls that cut the neck of the peninsula. The hilltop citadel now houses a US military base which explains the unusual number of Americans one meets in Sinop, as well as amenities like good restaurants and the only jogging lane in Turkey along the seashore drive that leads to the beaches at the end of the peninsula.

The wildly scenic 200 miles of coastline west of Sinop is among the least traveled parts of Turkey, mainly because no good road existed here until recently. No road has also meant that cozy fishing towns like **Abana**, **Inebolu**, and **Kurucasile** have fallen behind with the kind of "development" that has marred the Eastern Black Sea – though they are catching up fast, with the help of a third of the population that works in Germany. There are not many specific sights to see; just an endless series of visual feasts at each bend of the corniche and some unspoiled beaches.

The picturesque port of **Amasra** crowns the coast with a perfect castle sitting atop a tiny rocky peninsula. The place used to be a Genoese colony until 1461. Now families of the managers from the coalmining region of **Zonguldak** have replaced the Genoese, and thanks to them it is possible to have a lovely dinner by moonlight at the expense of tax payers in one of the company restaurants along the seaside promenade.

Veni Vidi Vici: Another route back to Istanbul from the Black Sea is to return to Samsun from Sinop and follow the Yesilirmak ("Green River") inland to **Amasya**, possibly the loveliest town in the Anatolian interior. The river bisects the town, its banks lined with the stately houses of the 19th-century rich, the massive rock tombs of the kings of Pontus looming overhead. Rickety cafés on the embankment shaded by chestnuts and weeping willows remind one (with some stretching of the imagination) of the banks of the Seine. One of the riverside mansions has been tastefully restored as

a museum, offering a glimpse of the grace and wealth of the Anatolian *burgher* before the upheavals of the early 20th century.

The town was an important center through Hellenistic, Byzantine and Turkish times. A couple of Byzantine and Ottoman monarchs as well as the geographer, Strabo, were born here, and a rich complement of monuments remains from the Danişmend (the marble *türbe* of **Halifat Gazi**), Seljuk (the **Gök Medrese** and the **Tomb of Torumtay**), Mongol (the remarkable asylum of 1308) and Ottoman periods. The **Complex of Beyazıt II** precedes the mosque of the same name in Istanbul, and is one of the earliest examples of the classical style of Ottoman architecture.

The most impressive piece of history in Amasya, though, is the **citadel** with the five **royal tombs** which are below it. They belong to the strange phenomenon known as the Kingdom of Pontus which emerged in Amasya towards 280 BC, around one Mithridates who might have been a Greek adventurer or a scion of the old Persian provincial aristocracy. His descendants led the final, desperate resistance of semi-Hellenized Anatolian rulers against Roman expansionism. Mithridates VI fought for 25 years against Roman legions. His incredible saga of conquests and collapses, shifting alliances, shipwreck, poisoning, escape, and guerrilla warfare ended with his suicide in 63 BC.

His son, Pharnaces, tried to stage a comeback, but proved an easy foe for Julius Caesar, who noted his unexpected victory at Zela – now **Zile**, south of Amasya – with a telegraphic despatch to his mistress:

"*Veni, vidi, vici,*" or "I came, I saw, I conquered."

The traveler, too, might echo Caesar's words on the way back home, but with a slight grammatical twist reflecting the experiences of his or her first journey to the Asia Minor: "*Veni, vidi, victus sum,*" or "I came, I saw and I was conquered" by the matchless beauty of the land, the boundless hospitality of the people and endless allure that is Turkey.

Left, a day's bag of brown trout for the intrepid or patient. **Right**, Sumela Monastery outside Trabzon.

So, you're getting away from it all.

Just make sure you can get back.

AT&T Access Numbers
Dial the number of the country you're in to reach AT&T.

Country	Number	Country	Number	Country	Number
*ANDORRA	19◊-0011	GERMANY**	0130-0010	*NETHERLANDS	06-022-9111
*AUSTRIA	022-903-011	*GREECE	00-800-1311	*NORWAY	050-12011
*BELGIUM	078-11-0010	*HUNGARY	00◊-800-01111	POLAND†◆²	0◊010-480-0111
BULGARIA	00-1800-0010	*ICELAND	999-001	PORTUGAL†	05017-1-288
CROATIA†◆	99-38-0011	IRELAND	1-800-550-000	ROMANIA	01-800-4288
*CYPRUS	080-90010	ISRAEL	177-100-2727	*RUSSIA† (MOSCOW)	155-5042
CZECH REPUBLIC	00-420-00101	*ITALY	172-1011	SLOVAKIA	00-420-00101
*DENMARK	8001-0010	KENYA†	0800-10	SPAIN	900-99-00-11
*EGYPT† (CAIRO)	510-0200	*LIECHTENSTEIN	155-00-11	*SWEDEN	020-795-611
*FINLAND	9800-100-10	LITHUANIA◆	8◊196	*SWITZERLAND	155-00-11
FRANCE	19◊-0011	LUXEMBOURG	0-800-0111	*TURKEY	9◊9-8001-2277
*GAMBIA	00111	*MALTA	0800-890-110	UK	0800-89-0011

Countries in bold face permit country-to-country calling in addition to calls to the U.S. *Public phones require deposit of coin or phone card.
**Western portion. Includes Berlin and Leipzig. ◊Await second dial tone. †May not be available from every phone. ◆ Not available from public phones. ¹Dial "02" first, outside Cairo. ²Dial 010-480-0111 from major Warsaw hotels. ©1993 AT&T.

Here's a travel tip that will make it easy to call back to the States. Dial the access number for the country you're visiting and connect right to AT&T **USADirect**® Service. It's the quick way to get English-speaking operators and can minimize hotel surcharges.

If all the countries you're visiting aren't listed above, call **1 800 241-5555** before you leave for a free wallet card with all AT&T access numbers. International calling made easy—it's all part of **The *i* Plan.**℠

AT&T

IMPORTANT NOTE

As of January 1, 1994, the telephone numbering system in Turkey was replaced with a new and more sophisticated one. Now all numbers throughout the country have 7 digits, and all area codes have 3 digits. The access code for **long distance calls** is (**0**) and for **international calls** (**00**). Throughout the following listings the area codes of each town or village are provided.

Istanbul, which is larger and more crowded than the capital Ankara, sits on two continents: Europe and Asia. The city's new telephone codes are (212) for the European side, and (216) for the Asian side when you're calling from other parts of the country and from overseas. When in Istanbul, you have to dial (216) first if you're on the European side calling a number on the Asian side, and (212) when calling the European side from the Asian continent. No codes are needed within the same side of the city.

GETTING THERE BY AIR

Most international airlines have regular direct or connecting flights to Istanbul's Atatürk International Airport from major European cities and the US. Some also fly to international airports at Ankara, Izmir, Antalya and Dalaman. Turkish Airlines (THY) flies to and from 30 European destinations, as well as Alma Ata, Amman, Abu Dhabi, Bahrain, Baku, Bangkok, Beirut, Benghazi, Bombay, Cairo, Damascus, Dubai, Jeddah, Karachi, Kuwait, Moscow, New York, Nicosia, Riyadh, Singapore, Tashkent, Tehran, Tel Aviv, Tripoli, Tokyo and Tunisia.
Istanbul Atatürk International Airport, Yeşilköy. Tel: (212) 5748300
Major Turkish Airlines (THY) offices in Istanbul:
Atatürk Airport. Tel: (212) 5748200
Sirkeci. Tel: (212) 5228888
Taksim. Tel: (212) 2521106
THY overseas offices:
Amsterdam: Stadhouderskade 2. Tel: (020) 6853801
Athens: 19 Filellinon Street. Tel: (01) 3222569
Barcelona: Paseo de Gracia 49-1. Tel: (343) 4875349
Berlin: Budapester Strasse 8. Tel: (030) 2624033
Brussels: 51 Cantersteen. Tel: (32) (2) 5117676
Cairo: Moustafa Kamal Square 3. Tel: (20) (2) 3908960
Copenhagen: Ved Vesterport 6. Tel: (33) 144499

Dublin: Aer Lingus Dublin Airport. Tel: (3531) 370011
Frankfurt: Saseler Strasse 35-37. Tel: (069) 27300720
London: 11-12 Hanover Street. Tel: (071) 4994499
Madrid: Plaza de España 18 Torre de 7/7. Tel: (34) (1) 5416426
New York, 821 UN Plaza, 4th floor. Tel: (1) (212) 9865050
Paris: 2 Rue de L'Echelle. Tel: (1) 42602808
Rome: Plaza della Republica 55. Tel: (039) (06) 4819535
Stockholm: Vasagatan 7. Tel: (08) 218534
Sydney: American Express Tower 1602, 388 George Street. Tel: (02) 2211711
Tel Aviv: Hayarkon Street 78. Tel: (03) 5172333
Vienna: Operngasse 3.Tel: (222) 5862024
Zurich: Tal Strasse 58. Tel: (1) 2111070

International airline offices in Istanbul *serving direct flights to*:
Aeroflot, Taksim. Tel: 2523997. *Moscow*
Air France, Taksim. Tel: 2564356. *Paris*
Alitalia, Elmadağ. Tel: 2313391. Rome, *Milan*
American Airlines, Taksim. Tel: 2372003. *US via London*
Austrian Airlines, Taksim. Tel: 2322200. *Vienna*
British Airways, Elmadağ. Tel: 2341300. *London*
Delta Airlines, Taksim. Tel: 2312339. *New York via Frankfurt*
Egyptair, Harbiye. Tel: 2311126. *Cairo*
El-Al, Nişantaşı. Tel: 2465303. *Tel Aviv*
Finnair, Elmadağ. tel: 2345130. *Helsinki*
Iberia, Elmadağ. Tel: 2551968. *Barcelona, Madrid*
KLM, Nişantaşı. Tel: 2300311. *Amsterdam*
Northern Cyprus Turkish Airlines (KTHY), Elmadağ. Tel: 2670973. *Nicosia*
Lufthansa, Taksim. Tel: 2517180. *Frankfurt, Munich, Dusseldorf, Berlin, Stuttgart*
Olympic Airlines, Elmadağ. Tel: 2465081. *Athens*
Qantas, Elmadağ. Tel: 2405032. *Australia, New Zealand, Fiji Islands*
Sabena, Taksim. Tel: 2547254. *Brussels*
SAS, Elmadağ. Tel: 2466075. *Copenhagen*
Singapore Airlines, Harbiye. Tel: 2323706. *Singapore, Amsterdam, Manchester*
Swissair, Taksim. Tel: 2312844. *Zurich*
Tour European Airways, Karaköy. Tel: 2525497. *Charter flights to major European destinations*
Tunisair, Elmadağ. Tel: 2417096. *Tunis*
TWA, Elmadağ. Tel: 2345327. *US via major European cities*

BY SEA

During the summer there are regular ferry-boats between Izmir and Venice, leaving Izmir's Çesme port on Wednesday, 6pm arriving in Venice on Saturday morning. The return to Izmir leaves on Saturday, 8pm. For further information contact:
Turkish Maritime Lines (TML), Istanbul. Tel: (212) 2499222.

TML Izmir. Tel: (232) 4211484 (domestic lines) and 4210094 (overseas).
TML Antalya. Tel: (242) 2425376.

There are also ferry-boats sailing between the Turkish ports of Izmir, Çesme (Izmir), Kuşadası, Bodrum, Ayvalık, Marmaris and the Greek islands of Rhodes, Cos, Samos, Chios, Lesbos, and from Çeşme to Ancona (Italy) in summer. For ticket reservations, contact travel agencies. **Minoan Lines** (Karavan Tourism in Izmir, tel: (232) 4219572 and 4215996) organizes boat cruises to Italy, Crete and other Greek islands. **Topas Maritime Lines** (Gaziosmanpaşa Boulevard 9, Esen Ishanı, Izmir, tel: (232) 4898093, 4848809) operates ferry-boats between Çeşme and Ancona in Italy, departing from Çeşme on Wednesday and from Ancona on Saturday.

Turkish Maritime Lines operate an all-year-round service between Istanbul and Izmir leaving Istanbul on Friday 5.30pm and arriving Saturday 11.30am. (For other destinations inside Turkey, see *Water Transport, Getting Around.*)

BY RAIL

The Istanbul Express has daily departures for Istanbul from Munich, Vienna and Athens, with connecting services in Belgrade and Sophia. There are also weekly departures for Istanbul from Buda-pest, Bucharest and Moscow. Reductions are available for students and people under 26.

BY ROAD

By Coach: Bus coach services also operate from the major European cities as well as from Iran, Iraq, Jordan, Saudi Arabia, Kuwait and Syria.
The following bus companies have offices in European cities:
Bosfor Turizm: in Munich, Paris, Vienna, Geneva, Milan and Venice.
Varan Turizm: in Berlin, Strasbourg, Vienna, Salzbourg, Innsbruck, Zurich and Den Haag.
Ulusoy Turizm: in Karlsruhe, Frankfurt, Rotterdam and Brussels.
By Car: It is possible to drive to Turkey via Bulgaria or Greece in Europe, or through Iran, Iraq and Syria. The roads leading to or from Russia are, however, more problematic.
Approximate distance between London and Istanbul is 3,000 km (1,860 miles).

TRAVEL ESSENTIALS

VISAS & PASSPORTS

Provided that they have a valid passport, nationals of the following countries do not need a visa for visits of up to three months: Australia, Bahamas, Fiji Islands, Finland, France, Gambia, Germany, Gibraltar, Greece, Hong Kong, Iran, Iceland, Jamaica, Japan, Kenya, Kuwait, Mauritius, Morocco, Norway, Netherlands, New Zealand, Oman, Saudi Arabia, Seychelles, Singapore, Switzerland, Trinidad and Tobago, Tunisia, Uganda, United Arab Emirates, and the United States.

Nationals of South Korea, Portugal, Romania, and Yugoslavia do not require a visa for visits of up to two months (again provided they have a valid passport) and nationals of Malaysia may only stay up to 15 days under the same conditions.

British citizens have been required to obtain visas since November 1, 1989, in retaliation for a recent British move that require visas of all Turks. Tourist visas cost £5 and are valid for three months. They are available at consulates and at entry points into Turkey. Nationals of any other countries must obtain a visa from their nearest Turkish consulate.

MONEY MATTERS

The monetary unit is the Turkish lira (TL), and exchange rates are published every day. There is no limit on the amount of foreign currency that you can bring into Turkey, but you are not allowed to take more than $5,000 worth of Turkish lira in and out of the country. Traveler's checks can easily be cashed at most banks.

BANKS
Banks are everywhere in Turkey. The big retail banks all have ATMs, some of which give cash advances. The major names are Akbank, Garanti, Pamukbank, Işbank, Yapı Kredi and Ziraat. Several foreign banks also have branches in Istanbul but most of them provide corporate services only.

BUREAUX DE CHANGE
In you want to change money outside banking hours, foreign exchange offices are available which usually charge commission rates below hotel norms.
Here are a few:
In Istanbul: (dialing code: 212)
Aktif, Şişli. Tel: 2301961
Bamka Döviz, Taksim. Tel: 2535500

Dere Döviz, Nişantaşı. Tel: 2317897
In Izmir: (dialing code: 232)
Bamka Döviz, Çankaya (inside the old flea market).
Tel: 4415859
Izmir Döviz, Çankaya. Tel: 4418886
Kaynak Döviz, Konak. Tel: 4890474

CREDIT CARDS

All major credit cards are now widely accepted in
tourist destinations around the country. The following have offices in Istanbul, Izmir and Ankara:
American Express. Tel: Istanbul (212) 2244363,
2246020; Izmir (232) 4224753; Ankara (312)
4677334.
Diners' Club. Tel: Istanbul (212) 2750515; Izmir
(232) 4217314; Ankara (312) 4390048.
Mastercard, Eurocard and **Visa**. Tel: Istanbul (212)
2506070; Izmir (232) 4252965; Ankara (312)
4314100.

HEALTH

As a rule, health precautions are not necessary, but
if you plan to visit central or eastern Anatolia,
cholera or typhoid injections and a tetanus booster
are a good idea. Similarly, malaria tablets are
recommended when in the Adana area.

Tap water throughout the country is heavily
chlorinated, but it is still not safe enough to drink
because much of the distribution network is worn-
out, and the drinking water can be contaminated.
So, before the on-going renewal of the whole
network is totally complete, vistors are advised to
use bottled water which is inexpensive and available
everywhere, or boil tap water before drinking.

WHAT TO WEAR

Dress according to the area you wish to visit. In
summer, light, cotton clothing for the Marmara,
Aegean and Mediterranean areas is sufficient, but
include some warmer clothing for the Black Sea, and
central and eastern Anatolia where the evenings can
be cool. Comfortable shoes are a must for visiting the
many historical and archaeological sites, and some
form of head covering (eg a scarf) for women when
visiting mosques. Don't forget sun screen lotion as
the sun can be very fierce. Although Turkey is often
regarded as a "Middle Eastern" country and thus
hot, winter travelers will soon discover that it has
as much snow and ice as most of Europe.

CUSTOMS

You are allowed to bring into the country up to 400
cigarettes, 50 cigars, 200g tobacco, and up to 5g
(100cc) or 7 (70cc) bottles of spirit, of which only
three can be of the same brand. Gifts must not exceed
US$500 in value. Antiques and electronic equipment
will be registered in the owner's passport on arrival,
and checked on exit. It is strictly forbidden to take
antiques out of the country. For this reason, if you

purchase a carpet, it is necessary to obtain a
certificate from a museum as proof that it is not an
antique. Possession of any narcotics is treated as a
very, very serious offence.

GETTING ACQUAINTED

GOVERNMENT & ECONOMY

Following many years of economic recession, labor
strife, ineffective government and extremist violence,
a bloodless, military coup occurred in 1980. In
1983, elections were held again for a 400-member
Grand National Assembly. Turkey now has a multi-
party political system which is largely democratic in
nature. In recent years, a competitive free market
orientation has been effective in stimulating economic growth. The advantages of greater foreign
trade, rapid industrial growth and investment are
now being balanced against continuing low wages,
rising inflation and rising consumer expectations.
Turkey is a member of several international bodies
including the United Nations, the Organization for
Economic Cooperation and Development, the Council of Europe and the North Atlantic Treaty
Organization, The Islamic Conference Organization,
as well as an associate member of the European
Economic Community.

The ruling government is a coalition of the
liberal, center-right wing True Path Party (DYP)
and the Social Democratic People's Party (SHP), led
by Tansu Çiller – Turkey's first female prime
minister, and deputy prime minister Murat Karayalçın.

GEOGRAPHY

Turkey is a vast area of 780,000 sq. km (300,000 sq.
miles), of which three percent is in Europe and 97
percent is in Asia. These two continents are divided
by the Bosphorus, the Sea of Marmara, and the
Dardanelles in the northwest of the country.

To the north of Turkey lies the Black Sea, to the
south, the Mediterranean, and to the west the
Aegean; altogether making a total of approximately
8,000 km (5,000 miles) of coastline. The countries
bordering Turkey are Greece and Bulgaria in the
northwest, Georgia and Armenia to the northeast,
Iran to the east and Iraq and Syria to the southeast.

There are many mountains – the Black Sea
Mountains run parallel to the sea, as do the Taurus
Mountains on the south coast. This is the largest

TRAVELLING IN HUNGARY

ADVENTURE IN STYLE

PART OF THE ART

swatch+
automatic

swatch+
SCUBA 200

POP
swatch

swatch+
C-H-R-O-N-O

swatch+

SWIS
made

mountain chain, which turns into the Antitaurus Mountains near Malatya. Anatolia is a plateau getting progressively higher eastwards, culminating at Mount Ararat, the highest mountain at 5,000 meters (16,000 ft). Other peaks are Erçiyes near Kayseri, Suphan Dag overlooking Lake Van, Kaçkar near Rize on the Black Sea, and Cilo in Hakkâri. Several clubs and travel agencies specialize in the growing interest in alpine sports.

The four major cities are Istanbul, Ankara, Izmir and Adana. Ankara is the capital, and the country is divided into 74 provinces. The population of the country in 1990 was 57 million.

TIME ZONES

Turkish Standard Time is 7 hours ahead of Eastern Standard Time and 2 hours ahead of Greenwich Mean Time.

CLIMATE

This varies, depending on the area. The Marmara, Aegean and Mediterranean coasts have a typical Mediterranean climate with hot summers and mild winters, the temperatures becoming a little cooler farther north. The Black Sea coasts have warm summers, mild winters and relatively high rainfall. The central and eastern Anatolian regions have hot, dry summers and cold winters.

Average temperatures (in degrees Celsius) for each quarterly periods of the year in the following regions of the country are:

Region	Jan	Apr	Jul	Oct
Marmara (Istanbul)	7	16	28	19
Aegean (Izmir)	9	20	30	21
Mediterranean (Antalya)	11	22	32	23
Black Sea region (Trabzon)	8	16	16	13
Central Anatolia (Ankara)	4	15	30	18
Eastern Anatolia (Erzurum)	9	6	20	12

CULTURE & CUSTOMS

Turkish attitudes toward women are restrictive in small provincial towns, more relaxed in villages and liberal in big towns. The emphasis is on the family, but although men are seemingly the decision-makers, Turkish women have a strong say in the family as in many cases they are the major bread-winners both in rural and urban areas.

Women in rural regions cover their heads with scarves more as a means of protecting their hair from dust and dirt than for religious conservatism, although religious fundamentalism has prevailed among certain groups in recent years. In big cities women wear Western-style dress, are increasingly well-educated and hold important positions in the professions.

There is little interference in the personal lives of foreigners as they are treated as a law unto themselves. Women visitors should not be afraid to travel alone, or go out at night, though provocative dress may create problems. The major cities in Turkey are very safe places compared with those in other countries – leers and suggestions may be common, but instances of rape and mugging are rare.

WEIGHTS & MEASURES

Turkey uses the metric system for its weights and measures much like those implemented in most European countries.

ELECTRICITY

The electricity in Turkey is of the 220 volt, 50-cycle variety. The two-prong round European plug will usually work here.

BUSINESS HOURS

Offices in Turkey generally operate from Monday to Friday from 9am to 6pm with a one-hour lunch break. They are closed on Saturday and Sunday. Shops in general are closed on Sunday, but more and more large stores are staying open all week.

HOLIDAYS

Apart from the national holidays listed below, there are two religious holidays whose dates move forward by 12 days each year on the Gregorian calender: the Şeker Bayram (the Candy Festival), a three-day holiday when special sweets are eaten to celebrate the end of Ramadan fast; and the four-day Kurban Bayram when sacrificial sheep are slaughtered and their meat distributed to the poor, following the Haj, or Muslim pilgrimage. The Şeker Bayram falls in 12–14 March and the Kurban Bayram in 20–23 May.

January 1	New Year's Day
April 23	National Sovereignty and Children's Day
May 19	Atatürk's Commemoration Youth and Sports Day
August 30	Victory Day
October 29	Republic Day

FESTIVALS

Major festivals take place at the same time every year:

JANUARY

16–17: Selçuk (Izmir) Camel Wrestling Festival.

APRIL

3–18: Istanbul International Film Festival.
4–May 7: Ankara International Arts Festival.
12: Birecik (Urfa) *Kelaynak* (rare bird species) Festival.
19–25: Manisa *Mesir* (traditional sweet) Fete.

MAY

First week: Sultanhisar (Aydın) Culture and Arts Festival.
8–14: Marmaris International Yachting Festival
6–10: Eskişehir Yunus Emre Festival. (Yunus Emre was a 13th-century humanitarian poet and mystic.)
19–June 5: Istanbul International Theater Festival.
20–23: Aksu (Giresun) Culture and Arts Festival.
20–26: Silife (İçel) Music and Folklore Festival.
27–31: Anamur (İçel) Tourism Festival.

JUNE

First week: Bartın Strawberry Festival.
Second week: Bursa International Tourism Festival.
Third week: Traditional Kafkasör Culture and Arts Festival (in Artvin).
2–7: Bandırma "Bird Paradise" Culture and Tourism Festival.
7–13: Bergama International Fair.
8–10: Nasreddin Hodja Festival (in Sivrihisar/ Eskişehir).
9–17: Marmaris International Festival.
17–20: Rize International Tea and Tourism Festival.
28–July 4: Traditional Kırkpınar Wrestling Festival (in Edirne).
20–July 20: Istanbul International Culture and Arts Festival.
June–July: Izmir International Culture and Arts Festival.

JULY

First week: Çeşme Sea Festival and International Song Contest.
3–4: Ihlara (Aksaray) Tourism and Culture Festival.
5–9: Iskenderun Culture and Tourism Festival.
5–10: Akşehir (Konya) Nasreddin Hodja Festival.
13–15: Kütahya Traditional Tile-making and Ceramics Festival.
14–24: Hittite Festival (in Çorum).
19–28: Samsun International Folk Dancing Festival.
21–23: Antakya (Hatay) Tourism and Culture Festival.
27–29: Abana (Kastamonu) Sea Festival.
July–August: Devrek (Zonguldak) Walking Stick and Culture Festival.

AUGUST

Avanos (Nevşehir) Handicrafts and Tourism Festival.
1–8: Dikili (Izmir) Culture and Arts Festival.
2–4: Mengen (Bolu) Traditional Turkish Cooking and Chefs Festival.
4–12: Insuyu (Burdur) Festival.
13–16: Foça Music, Folklore and Water Sports Festival.
10–18: Troy International Festival.
13–16: Ören Culture and Arts Festival.
Fourth week: Antalya International Folk Music and Dancing Festival.

SEPTEMBER

Second week: Ürgüp International Wine Festival.
Third week: Istanbul Tüyap Arts Fair.
Fourth week: Antalya Golden Orange Film Festival.
4–6: Konya International Food Festival.
8–20: Izmir International Fair.
12–October 12: Mersin International Festival.
15–October 15: Diyarbakır Culture and Arts Festival.
15–October 15: Gaziantep (GAP) Culture and Arts Festival.
21–24: Eskişehir Meerschaum (White Gold) Festival.
22–24: Yağcıbedir (Sındırgı) Carpet Festival.
25–26: Turkish Javelin Games.

OCTOBER

First week: Istanbul International Jazz Festival
26–28: Bozburun (Izmir) International Goulet Sailing Festival.

NOVEMBER

1–6: Marmaris International Yacht Races.
Third week: Istanbul International Arts Bienniale. (Organized every two years since 1988.)

DECEMBER

4–8: Demre (Kaş) St Nicholas Festival.
10–17: Konya Mevlana Festival.

RELIGION

Turkey is officially a secular state, although 99 percent of the population are Muslims. There are Jewish, Armenian and Greek minorities, however, who are concentrated in Istanbul and Izmir. Due to its vast history of mixed races and cultures, the country boasts hundreds of non-Muslim places of worship which have now become places of historical interest. But the three biggest towns of Turkey, namely Istanbul, Ankara and Izmir still have many functioning churches and synagogues. Here are just a few:

ISTANBUL
(dialing code 212)

ANGLICAN
St Helena's Church, British Consulate, Galatasaray. Tel: 2447540.
Crimean Memorial, Serdarı Ekrem Sokak 82, Tünel (behind the Swedish Consulate). Now Christ Church, it was designed by the British Victorian architect C.E. Street.

ARMENIAN
Surp Yerrortutyun, Beyoğlu. Tel: 2441382.
Patriarchate, Kumkapı. Tel: 5170970.

GREEK ORTHODOX
Aya Triada (Holy Trinity), Taksim. Tel: 2441358.
Patriarchate, Fener. Tel: 5259193.

JEWISH
Ashkenazy Synagogue, Karaköy. Tel: 2442975.
Neve Shalom Synagogue, Beyoğlu. Tel: 2441576.
Chief Rabbinate, Tünel. Tel: 2448794.

NON-DENOMINATIONAL
Dutch Chapel, Beyoğlu. Tel: 2445212.

PROTESTANT
German Protestant Church, Beyoğlu. Tel: 2503040.

ROMAN CATHOLIC
St Antoine, Beyoğlu. Tel: 2440935. The biggest functioning church in the city.
St Esprit, Harbiye. Tel: 2480910.
St Louis des Français, Beyoğlu. Tel: 2441075.

IZMIR
(dialing code 232)

ANGLICAN
St John's, Talatpaşa Bulvarı, Alsancak. Tel: 4636608.

CATHOLIC
Notre Dame de St Roserie, 1481 Sokak, Alsancak. Tel: 4216666.
Santa Maria, Halit Ziya Bulvarı 67. Tel: 4848632.
St Polycarpe, Gaziosmanpaşa Bulvarı 18 (across from Büyük Efes Hotel). Tel: 4848436. The oldest church in the city dedicated to a mid-first century saint crucified in Izmir.

JEWISH
Bet Israel, Mithatpaşa Caddesi 265, Karataş. Tel: 4251628.
Hevra, 937 Sokak 4/17. Kemeraltı, Konak.
Shaar Ashamayam, 1390 Sokak 4, Alsancak. Tel: 421083.

ORTHODOX
Orthodox Church, 1374 Sokak 24, Alsancak. Tel: 4833601.

PROTESTANT
St Mary Magdelena, Hürriyet Caddesi 18, Bornova. Tel: 3880915.

ANKARA
(dialing code 312)

ANGLICAN
St Nicholas, Şehit Ersan Caddesi 46/A, Çankaya (in the grounds of the British Embassy). Tel: 4401931.

BAPTIST
Baptist Church International, Best Hotel, Atatürk Bulvarı 195. Tel: 286 59 95.

CATHOLIC
French Embassy Church, Kardeşler Sokak 15, Ulus. Tel: 3110118.
Vatican Embassy Church, Italian Embassy, Atatürk Bulvarı 118, Kavaklıdere. Tel: 4265460.

JEWISH
Jewish Synagogue of Ankara, Birlik Sokak 8, Samanpazarı. Tel: 3116200.

PROTESTANT
Protestant Church International, Hürriyet Caddesi 56, Dikmen.

COMMUNICATIONS

MEDIA

Turkey has been enjoying a near revolution in information media in recent years. Not only has the range of Turkish print media, TV and radio expanded enormously, Turkish audiences now have access to international satellite and cable TV networks in many languages.

Television: From a single state-run TV channel in the beginning of 1980s, Turkey now has 12 channels, the majority of which are privately owned. Although mediocre entertainment programmes, soap operas and games-shows basically dominate the screens, almost all channels also show good foreign films (unfortunately for foreigners, dubbed in Turkish), sports and the latest western music clips. Through satellite and cable networks, the leading European channels including the BBC and CNN can be viewed at homes and at larger hotels. **TRT Channel 2** broadcasts the news in English and German at 10pm.

Radio: Private radio channels were a nationwide issue until in early 1993. Before then only state-run stations broadcast, which were inclined to be more soporific than stimulating. Suddenly dozens of private radio stations sprung up throughout the country and were enthusiastically welcomed, especially by young music lovers. A few months later, despite big protests from Turkish people, they were banned for being illegal. When the new prime minister took office in June 1993, one of the first things she did was to encourage private broadcasters. Today Istanbul alone has more than 30 private stations playing Western pop and rock, with news broadcasts thrown in between. The most popular, which offer English speaking DJs on certain programs, are **Power** (FM 100.0), **Energy** (FM 102.0), **Metro** (FM 97.2), **Show** (FM 89.9) for younger audiences. **Radio Blue** (FM 98.0) and the good old state channel **TRT3** (FM 88.2) appeal to more sophisticated listeners with jazz, latin and classical music. TRT3 also broadcasts news in English, French and German following the Turkish bulletin at 9am, 12am, 5pm and 9pm.

Travelers with shortwave radios can pick up broadcasts from China to Canada, including the BBC, Voice of America, Voice of Germany, Voice of Moscow and others.

Newspapers and **magazines**: *Sabah* and *Hürriyet* are Turkey's best selling national newspapers and leading public opinion makers with good news coverage and lots of colour pictures. The left wing *Cumhuriyet* with a modest circulation of 130,000 is considered the most respected and serious newspaper. *Milliyet* is also a dependable, well-established, liberal paper. All major international newspapers and many magazines are also available a day late and rather expensive. The only English-language paper, the *Turkish Daily News* is being published in Ankara and provides coverage of local and international events. *Aktüel* and *Tempo* are popular weekly news magazines, while *Atlas* and *Globe* are monthly quality travel magazines with English text summaries.

Istanbul has an inspiring city guide magazine, the bi-monthly *The Guide Istanbul*, which offers visitors all practical information from the latest events to listings of the best restaurants and places of interest. Another good English-language magazine is *Cornucopia*, which features Turkish arts, history and culture with beautiful pictures.

POSTAL SERVICES

The Turkish mail service is rather erratic but reliable. There is a fixed postage rate for letters abroad (TL 4,000 for Europe and TL 6,000 for the US), and cheaper rates for postcards. Main post offices (PTT) have long opening hours, from 8am–midnight, Monday–Saturday; and 9am–7pm on Sunday. The smaller post offices keep government office hours but are not open on Sunday.

TELEPHONES

Public telephones take tokens which can be bought from any post office or sometimes from booths in the street. Local and international calls can usually be made with no problems at all. The tokens (*jetons*) come in three sizes: small for local calls, large for international calls, and medium which can be used for either. It is useful to note the **dialing codes** for the major towns and tourist destinations:

Ankara	312
Antalya and Alanya	242
Bodrum and Marmaris	252
Istanbul European side: 212	Asian side: 216
Izmir and Kuşadası	232

You will find a complete list of the above on the wall inside phone booths. Other useful numbers for visitors are:

International operator:	115
Directory assistance:	118
Telegrams by phone:	141
Wake-up call:	135

The **international codes** for outgoing country calls include:

Australia	61
Austria	43
Belgium	32
Canada	1
Denmark	45
Egypt	20
France	33
Germany	49
Great Britain	44
Greece	30
Holland	31
Hong Kong	852
Ireland	353
Italy	39
Japan	81
Spain	34
Sweden	46
Switzerland	41
United States	1

TELEGRAMS, TELEX & FAX

Telegrams can be sent from any post office. The number of words and speed required determines the cost. There are three speeds: normal, *acele* (urgent) and *yıldırım* (flash).

Telefax facilities can be found at all larger post offices and hotels while telex is fast becoming redundant.

THE WORLD IS FLAT

Its configuration may not be to Columbus' liking but to every other traveller the MCI Card is an easier, more convenient, more cost-efficient route to circle the globe.

The MCI Card offers two international services—MCI World Reach and MCI CALL USA—which let you call from country-to-country as well as back to the States, all via an English-speaking operator.

There are no delays. No hassles with foreign languages and foreign currencies. No foreign exchange rates to figure out. And no outrageous hotel surcharges.

If you don't possess the MCI Card, please call the access number of the country you're in and ask for customer service.

The MCI Card. It makes a world of difference. **MCI**

No-one appreciates the special needs of business travellers more than Thai. We were, after all, the first Asian airline to offer a business class.

Thai's Royal Executive Class fulfils every wish of the business traveller. From bigger, wider seats to more leg room between your seat and the one in front.

This extra room gives you generous space to wo or relax. And, of course, Thai's fabled inflight servi is always at your beck and call.

Our Royal Executive Class passengers savo

ially selected champagnes and vintage wines from kling crystal. Meals are served from fine china on table linen.

Speedy check-ins at special Royal Executive s counters together with lounge facilities at most airports are yours for just a small premium over the full economy fare.

Where business takes you, Thai probably can too. In fact, for business travel that's smooth as silk, it's really an open and shut case.

TH

as silk

OYSTER GLX

◆ Samsonite*
Our Strengths Are Legendary*
*Trademarks of Samsonite Corporation

EMERGENCIES

TELEPHONE NUMBERS

Ambulance: 112
Police: 115
Fire: 110
Gendarme (in rural areas): 156
Car rescue (in Istanbul): Touring and Automobile Club. Tel. (212) 2778339.

MEDICAL SERVICES

Though some doctors and dentists in the cities do speak English or German, and may have been trained abroad, unless it is an emergency, it is better to wait until you return home for treatment. Hospitals do not meet Western standards though some are better than others, and can be useful in an emergency. Here are some good private services. They expect you to pay immediately, have some cash or a credit card available.

ISTANBUL
(dialing code 212)

Amerikan Hastane (has an ambulance service), Güzelbahçe Sokak, Nişantaşı. Tel: 231 4050.
Florence Nightingale Hastane, Abidei Hürriyet Caddesi 290, Çağlayan, Şişli. Tel: 2244950.
Alman Hastane (German ambulance service), Sıraselviler Caddesi 119, Taksim.Tel: 2517100.
International Hastane (ambulance service), Yeşilyurt. Tel: 5747802.

ANKARA
(dialing code 312)

Kavaklıdere Tıp Merkezi (emergency service), Şimsek Sokak 6, Kavaklıdere. Tel: 4255615.
Bahçelievler Tıp Merkezi, Yedinci Cadde 11/1, Bahçelievler. Tel: 2124940.
Esat Özel Sağlık Merkezi, Küçükesat Caddesi 103/4. Tel: 4371300.

IZMIR
(dialing code 232)

Hayat Hastane, 452 Sokak, Konak. Tel: 4847200.
Sağlık Hastane, 1399 Sokak 25, Alsancak. Tel: 4218620.

A variety of medicines are available without prescription at drugstores (*eczane*), and in the case of minor ailments, it is better to go directly there and ask for assistance.

Hospitals used to dealing with visitors
Ankara: (dialing code 312)
American Hospital, Badgat. Tel: 1391680
Hacettepe Medical Faculty, Ulus. Tel: 3242240

Istanbul: (dialing code 212)
Admiral Bristol American Hospital. Tel: 1314050
Balıklı Greek Hospital. Tel: 5827330
Cerrahpasa Medical Faculty. Tel: 5884800
French Pasteur Hospital. Tel: 1484756
German Hospital. Tel: 1517100
Italian Hospital. Tel: 1499751
Jewish Hospital. Tel: 5258996

SECURITY & CRIME

Turkey has an enviable record of low instances of crime. In Istanbul, with a population of over 8 million, has only 0.7 murders and 10 thefts are committed per day. This low crime rate reflects Turkish society: restricted access to guns, low incidence of drug use, respect for law and order, and most important of all, close-knit communities and enduring family ties.

Crime is rare in Turkey except, perhaps, for pickpocketing which is on the increase in crowded places like the Covered Bazaar in Istanbul. When getting insured, make sure that your medical as well as holiday insurance cover you for both the European and Asian sides of Turkey.

Drugs: The film *Midnight Express* gave Turkey a very bad image. Although the script may have been exaggerated, heavy penalties are given to anyone found in possession of drugs. A foreigner on a narcotics charge can expect long-term imprisonment. However, visitors are very well-treated and it is very, very unlikely that you will be whipped off for a body search the second you reach customs.

GETTING AROUND

DOMESTIC TRAVEL

BY AIR

There is a good network of domestic flights serviced by Turkish Airlines (THY) and fares are, on the whole, reasonable. Although flights are usually fully booked well in advance and the ground facilities at Istanbul's single international airport, Atatürk Airport at Yeşilköy, often falls short of meeting the ever-increasing passenger traffic, Turkish Airlines enjoys a good reputation for punctuality as well as for its on-flight services. You can fly direct to the following cities from Istanbul: Adana, Ankara, Antalya, Bursa, Dalaman, Denizli, Diyarbakır, Erzurum, Gaziantep, Izmir, Kayseri, Konya, Malatya, Samsun, Trabzon, and Van. For many of the Anatolian destinations, it is necessary to fly via Ankara. Security at the airports is very strict and you will be asked to point out your baggage before it is put onto the plane.

Recently, private jets, small aircraft and helicopters servicing small cities and resorts ranging from Bodrum to Uludağ, outside Bursa, have been permitted. You can make enquiries at the offices listed below:

Turkish Airlines (THY)
Adana, Stadyum Caddesi 1. Tel: (322) 4537247, 4543143.
Ankara, Hipodrom Caddesi, Garyanı. Tel: (312) 3124900, 3090400.
Antalya, Cumhuriyet Caddesi, Özel İdare İshanı altı. Tel: (242) 2412830, 2415238, 2423432.
Bodrum, Touralpin Travel Agency, Yeniçarsı Altıncı Sokak 6. Tel: (252) 31633 25, 3168733.
Bursa, Çakırhamam, Temiz Caddesi 16/B. Tel: (224) 2221866, 2211167.
Dalaman. Tel: (252) 6925291.
Denizli, Istiklal Caddesi 27/B. Tel: (258) 2648651, 2648661.
Diyarbakır, Kültür Sarayı Sokak 15. Tel: (412) 2240428, 2243366.
Istanbul (See major THY offices in Istanbul under *Getting There*).
Izmir, Büyük Efes Hotel. Tel: (232) 4258280.
Kayseri, Sahabiye Mahallesi, Yıldırım Caddesi 1. Tel: (352) 2311001, 2313947.

Konya, Alaaddin Caddesi 22. Tel: (332) 3512000, 3512032.
Malatya, Kanalboyu Caddesi 10. Tel: (422) 3211920.
Marmaris, Atatürk Caddesi 30/B. Tel: (252) 4123751.
Trabzon, Kemerkaya Mahallesi, across from Meydan Park. Tel: (462) 3222219.

BY ROAD

LONG-DISTANCE BUSES

Turkey has excellent bus services, both inter- and intra-cities. Not surprisingly, this is the preferred method of long distance travel as it is cheap, reliable, and generally comfortable. For instance, you can leave Ankara at 10pm and be at the south coast at 8am the following morning. To meet increasing demand, many new bus companies have been established, and tickets are thus very easy to obtain. These buses depart from the main bus station (*otogar*) in each town. For city buses, see *Public Transport*.
Major inter-city bus companies:
Kamil Koç (Istanbul, western and southern destinations and Ankara):
  Istanbul, Taksim. Tel: (212) 2492510
  Ankara, Kızılay. Tel: (312) 4257735
  Izmir, Basmane. Tel: (232) 4895910
  Antalya. Tel: (242) 2419292
  Bodrum. Tel: (252) 3164971
Mersin Seyahat (Istanbul, Mersin and Ankara):
  Istanbul, Taksim. Tel: (212) 2497756
  Ankara, Kızılay. Tel: (312) 4254629
Nevtur (Istanbul, Ankara, Kayseri, Cappadocia):
  Istanbul, Taksim. Tel: (212) 2497961
  Ankara, Kızılay. Tel: (312) 4172254
Pamukkale (Istanbul, western and southern destinations):
  Istanbul, Taksim. Tel: (212) 2492791
  Ankara, Kızılay. Tel: (312) 4333007
  Antalya. Tel: (242) 2417236
  Izmir, Basmane. Tel: (232) 4833585; Konak. Tel: 4838112;
  Bodrum. Tel: (252) 316376.
Ulusoy (Istanbul, Ankara, Black Sea region, Izmir and the Aegean region, Antalya and the Mediterranean region):
  Istanbul, Merter. Tel: (212) 5011145, 504839
  Ankara, Kızılay. Tel: (312) 4182013
  Izmir, Alsancak. Tel: (232) 4223602
  Antalya. Tel: (242) 2421303
Varan (Istanbul, Ankara, western and southern destinations, including non-stop executive service and good rest-stops with cafeteria, shop and clean toilets):
  Istanbul, Taksim. Tel: (212) 2517481
  Ankara, Kızılay. Tel: (312) 4172526
  Izmir, Alsancak. Tel: (232) 4255921
  Antalya. Tel: (242) 2426123
  Bodrum. Tel: (252) 3163103

In the cities, there are two types of buses: orange and blue. They usually follow the same, fixed routes, the only difference being that you pay on the municipality-run blue buses, but for the state administration's (IETT's) orange buses you must buy your ticket from one of the many bus ticket booths. Fares are cheap but the journey is slow, and it is advisable not to travel during rush hours (which in Istanbul, tend to be all hours from 8am to 8pm) as the buses get incredibly crowded. There are also private minibuses, also blue, which are faster but not advisable for people of a nervous disposition.

DOLMUS

Another method of traveling around a city or to a neighboring town is by *dolmus*, literally "full" (of passengers). This is a kind of shared taxi which, in some cities, takes the form of a large car, such as a convertible 1950s vintage American car in Istanbul, a Skoda station wagon in Adana, or a regular taxi or minibus in other towns. The *dolmus* travels along a fixed route for a fixed fare and passengers get on and off whenever they want. A few words of Turkish are necessary here to be able to tell the driver when you want to get out.

TAXIS

These tend to be cheap and plentiful. In the cities and big towns, it is often unnecessary to look for taxis; they will find you. A note of caution: make sure the taxi meter is switched on (one red light on the meter for day rate and two red lights for evening rate), for long distances, arrange a price beforehand.

TRAINS

All major cities and many places between are connected by rail. Although cheap, travel is very slow and not always comfortable. There is one "better" class of train – the overnight or express between Ankara and Istanbul which has a dining car and couchettes, as well as sleepers. This is a fun way to travel if you have the time. However, buses are generally faster, cheaper and more comfortable.

Within Turkey, the following trips can be of special interest to tourists: the sleeper express to Pamukkale (famous town of the stalactites and hot springs) which departs from Istanbul's Haydarpaşa station daily at 5.30pm, arriving at 8am the next morning and returning to Istanbul the following day at 8.30am. The Fatih Express leaves for Ankara from Haydarpaşa at 10.30am and allows a panoramic view of the Bolu mountains and the Anatolian plain. This trip takes 8 hours. Purchase tickets and reserve seats in advance. For reservations and enquiries:
Haydarpaşa train station (on the Asian side). Tel: (216) 3360475, 3488020.
Sirkeci train station (on the European side). Tel: (212) 5270051.

WATER TRANSPORT

In Istanbul: Bosphorus cruises can be a lovely way to view the beautiful banks of this narrow channel that parts Europe from Asia. Public ferry-boats leave every day from the Eminönü jetty at 10.30am and 1.30pm, and go all the way to Anadolu Kavak where a lunch break is given before the return journey. The round trip costs TL 35,000. Tel: (212) 2444233 for further information. Fast catamaran sea-buses also ply between Kabatas and Bostancı (on the Asian side) and Büyükada (the largest of the Prince's Islands). They are excellent, though more expensive. Tel: (212) 2491558 for schedules.

Around Turkey: Turkish Maritime Lines operates weekly ferry-boats between Istanbul and Izmir. They leave Istanbul on Friday 5.30pm and arrive next day at 11.45am. The return voyage begins at 2pm on Sunday, arriving in Istanbul at 9pm next morning. The Maritime Lines also serve the ports of the Black Sea region from May to October. Departure from Istanbul is on Monday at 2.30pm, with stops at Zonguldak, Sinop and Samsun on Tuesday, and Giresun, Trabzon and Rize on Wednesday. The return is on Thursday with stops at Ordu, Samsun and Sinop, arriving back in Istanbul on Friday at 1.30pm.
Turkish Maritime Lines (TML), Istanbul. Tel: (212) 2499222.
TML Izmir. Tel: (232) 4211484 (domestic lines), and 4210094 (overseas lines).
TML Antalya. Tel: (242) 2425376.

PRIVATE TRANSPORT

CAR RENTAL

These services are available in most cities and tourist areas. It is best to shop around as prices, conditions and quality may vary considerably. If you hire from one of the international companies, it is often possible to return the car to a different point for no extra charge.

AVIS
Istanbul, Airport. Tel: (212) 6630646; Taksim. Tel: (212) 2417896; also at the Hilton Hotel.
Ankara, Kavaklıdere. Tel: (312) 4672314.
Izmir, Airport. Tel: (232) 2511211, Alsancak. Tel: (232) 4414417; also at the Hilton Hotel.
Antalya. Tel: (242) 2416693.
Bodrum. Tel: (252) 3162333.

BUDGET
Istanbul, Airport. Tel: (212) 5741635; Taksim. Tel: (212) 2430343.
Ankara, Kavaklıdere. Tel: (312) 4175952.
Izmir, Airport. Tel: (232) 2513086.
Antalya. Tel: (242) 2426220.
Bodrum. Tel: (252) 3163038.

EUROPCAR
Istanbul, Airport. Tel: (212) 6630746; Taksim. Tel: (212) 2547788.

Ankara, Küçükesat. Tel: (312) 4183877.
Izmir, Airport. Tel: 232) 2513074; Alsancak. Tel : (232) 4254698.
Bodrum. Tel: (252) 3162309.

HERTZ
Istanbul, Airport. Tel: (212) 5746948; Harbiye. Tel: (212) 2487101.
Ankara, Şili Meydanı. Tel: (312) 4269459.
Izmir, Airport. Tel: (232) 2513481; Alsancak. Tel: (232) 4217002.
Antalya. Tel: (242) 2429929.

LET'S
(also caravans)
Istanbul, Airport. Tel: (212) 5734502; Taksim. Tel: (212) 2552431.
Izmir, Airport. Tel: (232) 2514009; Alsancak. Tel: (232) 4848053.
Antalya. Tel: (242) 2425309.
Bodrum. Tel: (252) 3166649.

THRIFTY
Istanbul, Kızıltoprak (on the Asian side). Tel: (216) 3450102.
Ankara, Gaziosmanpaşa. Tel: (312) 4360606.
Izmir, Alsancak. Tel: (232) 4899383.

Caravan hire:
Anadolu Caravan, Istanbul. Tel: (212) 2601480.
Hewa Caravan, Istanbul. Tel: (212) 2612349; Ankara. Tel: (312) 2230302.

MOTORING ADVICE

Turkish highways are extensive and generally well-maintained, but dangerous due to the large number of buses and trucks. Inter-city highways, especially on the Ankara to Istanbul expressway, tend to be very busy.

Driving at night is certainly not advisable as roads are not well lit, nor well-signposted. Speed limits are 50 kph (30 mph) in urban areas and 99 kph (60 mph) outside them.

WHERE TO STAY

Accommodations in Turkey comes in all conceivable forms, from the deluxe Hilton down to the humble cottage. As is the norm everywhere, larger cities and tourist resorts offer more accommodation choices than the small undiscovered towns and villages. Due to the recent heightening of Turkey's popularity as a tourist destination, the government has launched a campaign designed to double the country's accommodation capacity.

Hotels and Resorts: The following is a list of hotels and resorts rated in terms of their excellence according to a star rating which the prospective guest might find helpful.

ISTANBUL & THE MARMARA REGION

FIVE-STAR HOTELS

Price range: $110–320 for a single room and $150–360 for a double.

ISTANBUL

(Dialing code for the majority of these hotels on the European side is 212; those on the Asian side are indicated as 216 where necessary.)

Büyük Tarabya, Tarabya. Tel: 2621000. Overlooking the Bosphorus in a pretty bay, this hotel has magnificent views but is not too far away from the city center. Turkish bath, indoor and outdoor swimming pools, casino.

Çınar, Yeşilköy. Tel: 5732900. Set on the sea-shore in a pleasant area near the airport, this 35-year-old hotel was recently refurbished. Indoor and outdoor swimming pools, casino.

Çırağan Palace Hotel Kempinski, Beşiktaş. Tel: 2583377. Set in a restored Ottoman palace on the European bank of the Bosphorus. Fairy-tale-like view, spacious rooms, gourmet restaurants, a fabulous outdoor swimming pool, a well-equiped fitness center, Turkish bath, and casino. The most expensive hotel in the city.

Conrad Istanbul, Beşiktaş. Tel: 2273000. Excellent Italian restaurant, French patisserie, luxurious health club with indoor and outdoor swimming pools, nightly jazz in the bar, and casino. The biggest hotel in the city.

Dedeman, Esentepe. Tel: 2748800. Functional and well-located in the commercial district of the city, favored by Anatolian businessmen. Indoor and outdoor swimming pools, casino.

Divan, Taksim. Tel: 2314100. One of the oldest 5-star hotels in the city, featuring a most distinguished Turkish restaurant. Very centrally located.

Hilton, Harbiye. Tel: 2314650. Built in the mid-1950s, the granddaddy of luxury hotels in Turkey. Excellent service. Centrally located but away from the streets on extensive grounds with a beautiful view of the Bosphorus. Indoor and outdoor swimming pools, Turkish bath, casino.

Holiday Inn Crown Plaza, Ataköy. Tel: 5604110. The newest luxury hotel in the city, adjacent to the Ataköy Marina. Facilities include seaside jogging track, tennis courts, indoor and outdoor swimming pools.

İstanbul Polat Renaissance, Yeşilyurt. Tel: 6631700. Another new deluxe hotel near the airport, opened in 1993.

Klassis, Silivri, (65 km/40 miles west of Istanbul; 50 km/30 miles from the airport). Tel: (212) 7274050. More a resort than a city hotel, known for its pretty eclectic architecture and pleasant seaside setting with large gardens. Excellent health club, indoor and outdoor swimming pools, and a casino.

Mövenpick, Maslak. Tel: 2850900. Set in the developing business center, famous for its ice-cream patisserie and pleasant shopping center with a small cinema. Famous guests include Michael Jackson. Has a good Turkish restaurant, fitness and beauty center, indoor swimming pool, Turkish bath and casino.

Ramada, Laleli. Tel: 5139300. In the heart of the old city, close to the Covered Bazaar, enchanting architecture in a restored historic apartment building, and one of the best Chinese restaurants in town.

Sheraton, Taksim. Tel: 2312121. Well-established, centrally located, elegantly appointed with splendid views. Its traditional Ottoman cuisine restaurant, Revan, is one of the best in the city. The dazzling view from its roof-top bar is not to be missed.

Swissotel, Maçka. Tel: 2590101. Wonderful views, great sports facilities, excellent Japanese, French and Swiss restaurants.

The Marmara, Taksim. Tel: 2514696. In the very heart of the city, The Marmara has been the base for international celebrities participating at the Istanbul Festival. Its roof-top Panorama Restaurant offers a unique and breathtaking view of the Bosphorus and the whole city, and high quality food.

FOUR-STAR HOTELS

Price range: $55–160 for a single room and $65–187 for a double.

Aden, Rıhtım Caddesi, Kadıköy (on the Asian side). Tel: (216) 3451000. One of the few good hotels on the Anatolian side, situated near the ferry-boat pier and convenient for the Haydarpaşa train station.

Ataköy Holiday Village, Ataköy. Tel: 5596000. Convenient for the marina and the airport.

Dilson, Sıraselviler Caddesi 49, Taksim. Tel: 2521307. An older hotel that has been upgraded. Good central location.

Eresin, Topçu Caddesi 34, Taksim. Tel: 2560803. A centrally located, modern hotel.

Holiday Inn, Sahilyolu, Ataköy. Tel: 5604110. American-style comfort on the Marmara Sea close to the marina.

Kalyon, Sahilyolu, Sarayburnu (Seraglio Point). Tel: 5174400. On the Marmara Sea coastal road, this older hotel is a perennial favorite of visitors, convenient for the major sights of the old Istanbul.

Kervansaray, Şehit Muhtar Caddesi 61, Taksim. Tel: 2355000. A modern hotel in the city center.

Maçka, Eytam Caddesi 35, Maçka. Tel: 2343200. Excellent location in one of the city's most fashionable districts.

Parksa Hilton, Bayıldım Caddesi 12, Maçka. Tel: 2585674. Well-appointed and managed hotel with some rooms with Bosphorus view. Good bar with live jazz.

Pera Palace, Tepebaşı. Tel: 2514560. The grand, century-old hotel of Agatha Christie and countless other international celebrities. Turn-of-the-century decor and appealing views of the Golden Horn. Not to be missed, at least for its charming, historic patisserie and bar.

President, Tiyatro Caddesi 25, Beyazıt. Tel: 5166980. Located in the crowded tourist area of the city, convenient for the Covered Bazaar and historic sights.

Pullman Etap, Mesrutiyet Caddesi, Tepebaşı. Tel: 2514646. A modern, high-rise hotel close to most consulates and with good views of the city.

Richmond, Istiklal Caddesi 445, Beyoğlu. Tel: 2525460. On the pedestrianized shopping and entertainment street of the historic Istiklal Caddesi, this is a new hotel set in a 19th-century building. Has an old-established, now renovated patisserie, Lebon.

Rıhtım, Kadıköy (on the Asian side). Tel: (216) 3498941. A modern hotel with good facilities and an attractive view of the Kadıköy harbor.

THREE-STAR HOTELS

Price range: $40–75 for a single room and $60–95 for a double.

Büyük Londra, Meşrutiyet Caddesi 117, Tepebaşı, Beyoğlu. Tel: 2491025. Built in mid-19th century, the hotel has a feel of faded grandeur. Comfortable rooms with modern bathrooms. Front rooms have a view of the Golden Horn.

Elan, Meşrutiyet Caddesi 213, Tepebaşı, Beyoğlu. Tel: 2525449. Good location near Istiklal Caddesi and consulates. Air-conditioning, room service and view of the Golden Horn.

Fantazia, Klodfarer Caddesi 33, Sultanahmet. Tel: 6380707. Small but comfortable hotel near the Blue

Mosque. Good view from the terrace cafe. Air-conditioning and private bath.

Pierre Loti, Piyerloti Caddesi 5, Çemberlitaş. Tel: 5185700. A small, pretty hotel close to Haghia Sophia, Topkapı Palace and the Covered Bazaar. Air-conditioning.

SPECIAL-LICENCE HOTELS

Special licence hotels are housed in historic buildings in old, tourist-attractive neighborhoods, and offer most of the amenities of five-star hotels but with a limited number of rooms. First introduced by Çelik Gülersoy of Istanbul's Touring and Automobile Club, an untiring writer, conservationist and renovator of Istanbul's historical and cultural heritage, these hotels may be a unique experience for visitors and should be booked well in advance.

Price range: $40–80 for a single room, $65–110 for a double.

Ayasofya Pansiyonlar (run by the Touring Club), Sultanahmet. Tel: 5133660. A pretty street of brightly-painted old wooden houses, rebuilt and furnished with period pieces, located right behind Haghia Sophia. 57 rooms, 4 suites, a Turkish bath, restaurants and cafés.

Citadel, Kennedy Caddesi 32, Ahırkapı. Tel: 5162313. Situated on the coast road in a restored wooden building. 31 rooms, six suites, restaurant and bar.

Fuat Paşa Hotel, ‹Çayırbası› Caddesi 238, Büyükdere. Tel: 2429860. One of the few hotels on the upper shore of the Bosphorus on the European side. Housed in an old seaside mansion with 51 rooms, restaurant and Turkish bath.

Halı, Klodfarer Caddesi 20, Çemberlitaş, Sultanahmet. Tel: 5162170. Beautifully restored old building close to the main tourist attractions. 35 rooms.

Hippodrome, Mimar Mehmetağa Caddesi 17, Sultanahmet. Tel: 5176889. An Ottoman house transformed into a small hotel with a pleasant terrace. Only 17 rooms.

Ibrahim Pasa, Terzihane Sokak 5, Sultanahmet. Tel: 5180394. A small hotel in a charming old house, tucked away in a corner of the Hippodrome. 19 rooms.

Kariye, Kariye Cami Sokak, Edirnekapı. Tel: 5348414. Right next to the Kariye (Chora) Museum near the ancient city walls, this atmospheric hotel housed in a beautiful, old wooden building has 22 rooms, three suites, a gourmet Ottoman food restaurant, and a secluded café.

Khedive's Palace (run by the Touring Club), Çubuklu (on the Asian side of the Bosphorus). Tel: (216) 3312651. Set high on a thickly-wooded hill, this turn-of-the-century Art Nouveau palace of the Ottoman Egyptian governor is a cozy hide-away with 14 rooms. Full of charm with a large, pretty park and cafe where classical music is played.

Küçük Ayasofya, Şehit Mehmetpaşa Sokak 25, Sultanahmet. Tel: 5161988. A rebuilt Ottoman house with a nice view of the Marmara Sea from the back. 14 rooms.

Poem, Terbıyık Sokak 12, Sultanahmet. Tel: 5176836. An intimate, prettily decorated hotel with only 9 rooms, some with excellent sea views.

Sokullu Paşa, Şehit Mehmetpaşa Sokak 5/7, Sultanahmet. Tel: 518 17 90. Housed in an 18th century wooden mansion with 37 rooms. Has a garden with a fountain, a restaurant in a Byzantine wine cellar, and an original Turkish bath.

Sümengen, Amiral Tafdil Sokak 21, Sultanahmet. Tel: 5176875. Elegant period decor in a restored 19th century Turkish house with views of the Marmara sea. 30 rooms, restaurant and café.

Vardar, Sıraselviler Caddesi 54, Taksim. Tel: 2522896. The only special licence hotel in the very center of the city, Vardar is a block away from Taksim Square. Built 100 years ago, restored into a modern and functional hotel. 40 rooms.

Yesil Ev (run by the Touring Club), Kabasakal Caddesi 5, Sultanahmet. Tel: 5176785. The oldest special licence hotel in the area, housed in a pretty, old mansion. Period decor, charming rear garden and restaurant, good service.

THE PRINCE'S ISLANDS/ ISTANBUL, MARMARA SEA

Splendid Palace (special licence), Büyük Ada (the largest Prince Island). Tel: (216) 3826950. English *Elle* magazine headlined this venerable Art Nouveau hotel among the world's most romantic hotels. Founded in 1908, the hotel has been updated without spoiling its charm. 70 rooms, 4 suites, outdoor swimming pool.

Princess Hotel (special licence), Büyük Ada. Tel: (216) 3821628. 24 rooms with bathroom, phone, air-conditioning, music, satellite TV, balcony with view, plus swimming pool and restaurant.

Halki Palace (special licence), Heybeli Ada (the second largest on Prince Island). Tel: (212) 2319550. A recently restored hotel in an old building. 43 rooms, restaurant, swimming pool.

NORTHERN AEGEAN REGION

ASSOS/BEHRAMKALE

AYVACİK
(dialing code: 286)

In general, hotel room prices are lower outside Istanbul and Ankara. Five-star accommodation is often over $150; four-star $60–$150 and three-star $30–60.

Eden Beach (☆☆), Kadırga Koyu. Tel: 7217039. On a pebbled beach with 68 rooms with phone, central heating, music. Restaurant, bar, and watersports.

Kadırga Motel (Bayram'ın Yeri), Kadırga Koyu. Tel: 7217041. Friendly, peaceful and comfortable facilities. 30 rooms with private bathroom and hot water. Restaurant with delicious food and fresh fish, plus camping site.

Yıldız Pansiyon (pension), Behramkale İskele. Tel: 7217025, 7217169. A cozy place with only 10 rooms, some with village-type fireplaces in winter and appetizing meals in all seasons.

Assos Kervansaray (special licence), Behramkale İskele. Tel: 7217093. The biggest hotel in the village with 50 rooms, all with bathroom, phone, central heating. Nice restaurant and cafe/bar. Hunting and fishing opportunities.

Behram Hotel (special licence), Behramkale İskele. Tel: 7217016. One of the oldest decent hotels in the resort, it has 20 comfortable rooms with bathroom, phone, and a sea-side fish restaurant.

Nazlıhan (special licence), Behramkale İskele. Tel: 7217064. Newly restored from an early 20th century stone mansion, it houses 37 rooms with balconies and private bathrooms.

AYVALİK
(dialing code: 266)

Kaptan, Balıkhane Sokak. Tel: 3129630. Clean, basic yet comfortable, this is probably the best in the town. 13 rooms, 2 suites.

Haus Anette (pension), Nese Sokak 12. Tel: 3125971. A large old house tucked away on a side street. Clean and nicely decorated.

Taksiyahis (pension), Maraşal Fevzi Çakmak Caddesi 71. Tel: 3121494. Run by an Austrian-Turkish couple, this is a large, restored old house with terraces offering wonderful views. Five rooms, shared bathroom and kitchen, a Turkish bath.

Yalı (pension), behind the PTT building, No. 25. Tel: 3122423. A beautiful 150-year-old Greek building restored with period decor. Shaded waterfront garden with a small pier. Five bedrooms, shared bathrooms and kitchen.

THE DARDANELLES

ÇANAKKALE
(dialing code: 286)

Akol (☆☆☆☆), Kordonboyu, Çanakkale. Tel: 2179456.

Anafartalar (☆☆☆), İskele Meydanı, Çanakkale. Tel: 2174454.

Anzac House (pension), Cumhuriyet Meydanı 61, Çanakkale. Tel: 2170156. Best for young backpackers, providing basic facilities. 20 rooms with shared bathrooms.

Yellow Rose (pension), Yeni Sokak 5, Çanakkale. Tel: 2173343. Basic but clean and well-cared for.

GELİBOLU
(dialing code: 286)

Abide, Alçıtepe village, Eceabat, Gelibolu. Tel: 8446158. A charming family-run hotel. The best in the area. Open July–September only.

TRUVA (Troy)
(dialing code: 286)

Hisarlık, Tevfikiye Köyü. Tel: 2831992. A small hotel (11 double rooms, each named after a Trojan hero) serving to individual clients only. Good Turkish meals.

FOÇA
(dialing code: 232)

(Not to be confused with Yeni Foça which has nothing interesting.)

Club Mediterranee Foça Holiday Village. Tel: 8121607.

Hanedan Holiday Village, next to Club Mediterranee. Tel: 8122441.

Hanedan (☆☆), Sahil Caddesi. Tel: 8121515.

Evim Pansiyon (special licence), 216 Sokak 40. Tel: 8121360. Renovated old house with seven rooms and a beautiful garden.

Karaçam (special licence), Sahil Caddesi 70. Tel: 8121416. A charming old Greek house with 24 rooms.

Amphora (special licence), İsmetpaşa Mahallesi, 208 Sokak 7. Tel: 8122806. 27 rooms.

SOUTHERN AEGEAN REGION

BODRUM
(dialing code: 252)

Club Hotel M ☆☆☆☆☆, Değirmen Mevkii, Bodrum. Tel: 3166100.

Karia Princess ☆☆☆☆☆, Canlı Dere Sokak 15, Bodrum. Tel: 3168971.

Club Marverde ☆☆☆☆, Meselik Köyü, Kuyucak, Milas. Tel: 3745400.

Samara ☆☆☆☆, Kaynak Mevkii. Tel: 3167500.

Atrium ☆☆☆, Farabi Sokak 21, Bodrum. Tel: 3162181.

Bantur ☆☆☆, Dr Mümtaz Ataman Caddesi, Bodrum. Tel: 3163548.

Blue ☆☆☆, Neyzen Tevfik Caddesi, Bodrum. Tel: 3162269.

Club Amarissa ☆☆☆, Bitez. Tel: 3431793. A charming, family-run hotel.

Ece Resort ☆☆☆, Gölköy. Tel: 3577389. Famous for its delicious and creative Turkish cuisine.

Şamdan ☆☆☆, Yalıkavak. Tel: 3854424. A favorite spot of İstanbul's socialites.

Manastır Hotel Karaincir ☆☆☆, Akyarlar. Tel: 3936187.

Mandalinci ☆☆☆, Turgutreis. Tel: 3823087.

Eldorador TMT, Atatürk Caddesi 134, Bodrum. Tel: 3161232.
Gökçe Club Armonia, Akyarlar. Tel: 3936481.
Milta Torba, Torba. Tel: 3162343.

Club Mediterranee Kuşadası, Arslanburnu Mevkii. Tel: 6141135.
Pine Bay, Çam Limanı. Tel: 6149370.
Sunset View, Gazibeğendi. Tel: 6144502.

ÇEŞME/IZMIR
(dialing code: 232)

Altınyunus Holiday Resort (holiday village), Boyalık. Tel: 7231250.
Framissima, Boyalık Beach Hotel ☆☆☆☆, Boyalık. Tel: 7127081.
Çeşme Marin ☆☆, Hürriyet Caddesi, Çeşme. Tel: 7127579.
Kervansaray (special licence), Çeşme. Tel: 7127177. 32 rooms and two suites, some with sea view.
Deniz Kızı (pension), Boyalık. Tel: 7126551. Close to the beach with 10 rooms.
Büyük Efes ☆☆☆☆☆, Gaziosmanpaşa Bulvarı 1, Alsancak. Tel: 4844300.
Grand Hotel Plaza ☆☆☆☆☆, Sakarya Caddesi 156, Balçova. Tel: 2592781.
Izmir Hilton ☆☆☆☆☆, Gaziosmanpaşa Bulvarı 7, Alsancak. Tel: 4416060.
Pullman Etap Izmir ☆☆☆☆☆, Cumhuriyet Bulvarı 138, Alsancak. Tel: 4894090.
Kaya Prestige ☆☆☆☆, Şair Esref Bulvarı 1371 Sokak 7, Çankaya. Tel: 4259594.
Marla ☆☆☆☆, Kazım Dirik Caddesi 7, Pasaport. Tel: 4414000.
Pullman Etap Konak ☆☆☆, Mithatpaşa Caddesi 128, Konak. Tel: 4891500.
Aksan ☆☆☆, Gaziler Caddesi 214, Kapılar. Tel: 4417061.
Atlantis ☆☆☆, Gazi Bulvarı 128, Basmane. Tel: 4835548.
Balçova Thermal ☆☆☆, Balçova. Tel: 2590102.
Izmir Palace ☆☆☆, Vasıf Çınar Bulvarı 2, Alsancak. Tel: 4215583.

KUŞADASİ
(dialing code: 256)

Ayma International ☆☆☆☆☆, Kadınlar Denizi, Kuşadası. Tel: 6149041.
Imbat ☆☆☆☆☆, Kadınlar Denizi, Kuşadası. Tel: 6142000.
Adakule ☆☆☆☆, Bayraklı Mevkii. Tel: 6149270, 6143640.
Batıhan ☆☆☆☆, Ilıca. Tel: 6331423.
Grand Özçelik ☆☆☆☆, Yavansu Mevkii. Tel: 6144601.
Hotel Club Akdeniz ☆☆☆, Karaova Mevkii. Tel: 6146971.
Martı ☆☆☆, Kadınlar Denizi. Tel: 6143650.
Zinos ☆☆☆, İçmeler. Tel: 6147399.
Kervansaray (Special licence), Atatürk Bulvarı 2, Kuşadası. Tel: 6144115. A 300-year-old landmark in the town center with 24 rooms. Turkish entertainment with belly-dancer every night.

PAMUKKALE
(dialing code: 258)

Hotel Pamukkale, Pamukkale. Tel: 2722024. Right on the site of the Sacred Pool.
Ergür ☆☆☆☆, Karahayıt Köyü, Pamukkale. Tel: 2714170.
Thermal Colossea ☆☆☆☆, Karahayıt Köyü, Pamukkale. Tel: 2714156.
Hieropolis Thermal (holiday village), Karahayıt. Tel: 2714105.
Aspava (pension), Pamukkale. Tel: 2722090. 14 rooms with bathroom. Thermal water swimming pool.
Kervansaray (pension), Pamukkale. Tel: 2722209. 14 rooms, open air thermal water swimming pool. Delicious Turkish breakfast.

SELÇUK (EPHESUS)
(dialing code: 232)

Ephesus Princess ☆☆☆☆☆, Pamucak Mevkii. Tel: 8914790.
Hitit ☆☆☆☆, Şarapcı Kuyu Mevkii. Tel: 8926007.
Kalehan (special licence), Atatürk Caddesi 49, Selçuk. Tel: 8926154. The prettiest hotel in the area, within walking distance to Ephesus, St John's Church, Selçuk Museum and Artemission. 50 rooms, small swimming pool and good food.

WESTERN MEDITERRANEAN REGION

ANTALYA
(dialing code: 242)

Falez ☆☆☆☆☆, Konyaaltı Mevkii. Tel: 2485000.
Sheraton Voyager ☆☆☆☆☆, Yüz Yıl Bulvarı. Tel: 2432432.
Talya ☆☆☆☆☆, Fevzi Çakmak Caddesi. Tel: 2486800.
Club Hotel Orange ☆☆☆☆, Lara Yolu, Şirinyalı Mevkii. Tel: 3230892.
Prince ☆☆☆☆, Lara Yolu, Karpuzkaldıran Mevkii. Tel: 3233070.
Antares ☆☆☆, Lara Caddesi, 1537 Sokak 16. Tel: 3232244.
Olbia ☆☆☆, Akdeniz Bulvarı, Konyaaltı Plajı. Tel: 2290500.
Turist ☆☆☆, Örnekköy Mevkii, Lara. Tel: 3491414.

SPECIAL LICENCES
Most of the following hotels are restored historic buildings located in around the Kaleiçi, the old town of Antalya near the marina.

Abad, Hesapçı Sokak, Kaleiçi. Tel: 2474466. 13 rooms, restaurant, swimming pool.
Aspen, Kaledibi Sokak 16, Kaleiçi. Tel: 2477178. 40 rooms, 4 suites, inner courtyard with swimming pool, restaurant.
Marina, Mermerli Sokak 15, Kaleiçi. Tel: 2475490. A luxurious conversion of three Ottoman houses, first class food, swimming pool. 43 rooms.
Turban, Kaleiçi. Tel: 2418066. Old warehouse, 28 rooms, restaurant and swimming pool.
Tütav, Mermerli Sokak 2, Kaleiçi. Tel: 2486591. Fabulous location on the city ramparts, period furniture, courtyard with swimming pool, terrace restaurant with sunset view, 20 rooms.
Tuvana, Karanlık Sokak 18, Kaleiçi. Tel: 2476015. 15 rooms, restaurant, swimming pool.

PENSIONS
Doğan, Kılıçarslan Mahallesi, Mermerli Banyo Sokak 5. Tel: 2418842. Friendly owners, comfortable, well-decorated.
Frankfurt, Kılıçarslan Mahallesi, Zeytin Çıkmazı. Tel: 2476224. Quiet and modern.
Villa Mine, Kılıçarslan Mahallesi, Hıdırlık Sokak. Tel: 2476269. New, but has an antique style. Restaurant, gift shop and garden café.

ASPENDOS/BELEK
(dialing code: 242)

Between the main highway east of Antalya and the famous ancient theater of Aspendos there are many large hotels, restaurants and shops.
Paradise Albeach Golf ☆☆☆☆☆, Belek. Tel: 7254076. The biggest hotel golf school in Europe, offers a Championship Course in April.
Club Mega Saray (holiday village), Çamlık Mevkii, Belek. Tel: 7254026.

DEMRE/FINIKE
(dialing code: 242)

Şahin (special licence), Müze Caddesi, Kale/Demre. Tel: 8715686. 30 rooms with private bathroom.
Bahar, Cumhuriyet Caddesi, Finike. Tel: 8552020, 8551474. 24 clean, quiet rooms; excellent service.
Sedir, Cumhuriyet Caddesi 37, Finike. Tel: 8551183.

FETHIYE & OLÜDENIZ
(dialing code: 252)

Pırlanta ☆☆☆☆, Karagözler Mevkii, Fethiye. Tel: 6144959.
Asena ☆☆☆, Hisarönü Köyü, Fethiye. Tel: 6166713.
Sesel ☆☆☆, Foça Mahallesi, Barbaros Sokak 81, Fethiye. Tel: 6131454.
Meri ☆☆, Ölüdeniz. Tel: 6166060.
Robinson Club Lykia Holiday Village, Ölüdeniz. Tel: 6166010.
Besik Pension, Çalış Yolu, Barbaros Sokak, Fethiye. Tel: 6131418

KALKAN
(dialing code: 242)

Club Patara/Patara Prince Hotel ☆☆☆. Tel: 8443920, 8443338. Upmarket holiday village and summer homes. 5 km (3 miles) from Kalkan. 54 rooms, 15 suites, swimming pool, watersports, disco, Turkish bath, restaurants.
Pirat ☆☆☆, Kalkan Marina. Tel: 8443178. Clean, classy amenities including restaurant, swimming pool, superb location.
Kalamar ☆☆, Kalkan. Tel: 8443190. 68 rooms with mountain or sea views, private beach, swimming pool, restaurant with outstanding view.
Dionysia, Cumhuriyet Caddesi, Kalkan. Tel: 8443681. Attractive and clean. 23 rooms, swimming pool, restaurant.
Diva (pension), Cumhuriyet Caddesi, Kalkan. Tel: 8443175. 17 rooms, restaurant, terrace with excellent view.
Oasis (pension), Kalamar Yolu. Tel: 8443086. 18 very clean rooms, terrace with superb view.

KAŞ
(dialing code: 242)

Aqua-Park ☆☆☆☆, Çukurbağ Peninsula. Tel: 8361901.
Club Hotel Phellos ☆☆☆, Doğru Yol Sokak, Kaş. Tel: 8361953.
Bolel ☆☆, Çukurbağ Peninsula. Tel: 8361428.
Kekova ☆☆, Milli Güvenlik Caddesi, Kaş. Tel: 8361950.
Mimosa ☆☆, Elmalı Caddesi, Kaş. Tel: 8361272.

KEMER
(dialing code: 242)

Favori Aqua Resort ☆☆☆☆☆, Çamyuva. Tel: 8246214.
Ramada Renaissance Resort ☆☆☆☆☆, Beldibi. Tel: 8248131.
Club Akman ☆☆☆☆, Çamyuva. Tel: 8246997.
Ifa Tekirova Beach ☆☆☆☆, Kemer. Tel: 8214032.
Centrum ☆☆☆, Merkez Mahallesi, Deniz Caddesi 42, Kemer. Tel: 8144780.
Fame ☆☆☆, Anafartalar Caddesi 1/2, Kemer. Tel: 8141833.

HOLIDAY VILLAGES
Champion, Beldibi. Tel: 8248380.
Club Calimera Hydros Village, Kemer. Tel: 8141133.
Club Mediterranee, Kemer, Tel: 8141009.
Club Turtle's Marco Polo, Çamyuva. Tel: 8246336.
Robinson Club Çamyuva, Kemer. Tel: 8246384.

MARMARIS
(dialing code: 252)

Aqua ☆☆☆☆☆, İçmeler. Tel: 4553633.
Grand Azur ☆☆☆☆☆, Kenan Evren Bulvarı 11, Marmaris. Tel: 4128201.

Paradise Elegance ☆☆☆☆☆, Uzunyalı Caddesi 130, Marmaris. Tel: 4128101.
Chateau de Ville ☆☆☆☆, Kayabal Caddesi, İçmeler. Tel: 4552122.
Iberotel Marmaris Palace ☆☆☆☆, Pamucak Mevkii, İçmeler. Tel: 4553467.
Turunç Hotel ☆☆☆☆, Turunç Köyü. Tel: 4767024.
Blue Bay ☆☆☆, Kenan Evren Bulvarı, Marmaris. Tel: 4124427.
Flamingo ☆☆☆, Siteler Mahallesi 51, Marmaris. Tel: 4124000.
Mavi ☆☆☆, Atatürk Caddesi 72, Marmaris. Tel: 4123618.

HOLIDAY VILLAGES
Iberotel Marmaris, Pamucak Mevkii, İçmeler. Tel: 4553434.
Magic Life Der Club Marmaris, Yalancı Boğazı. Tel: 4120700.
Martı La Perla, İçmeler. Tel: 4553388.

EASTERN MEDITERRANEAN REGION

ADANA
(dialing code: 322)

Büyük Sürmeli ☆☆☆☆☆, Özler Caddesi 175, Kuruköprü. Tel: 3523600.
Inci ☆☆☆☆, Kurtulus Caddesi 40, Kuruköprü. Tel: 4358234.
Rasit Ener Tesisleri (motel), Girne Bulvarı 138. Tel: 3212758. 16 rooms, good service, large garden, swimming pool, good restaurant, plus camping site.

ALANYA
(dialing code: 242)

Most of the following large hotels in and around Alanya are on the seaside or have direct access to the beach. All have swimming pools.
Ananas ☆☆☆☆☆, Karasaz Mevkii. Tel: 5138616.
Serapsu ☆☆☆☆☆, Konaklı Köyü. Tel: 5651476.
Atlanta ☆☆☆☆, Kargıcak Mevkii. Tel: 5262384.
Club Alantur ☆☆☆☆, Dimçayı Mevkii. Tel: 5181740.
Incekum Alaaddin ☆☆☆☆, Avsallar, Incekum. Tel: 5171491.
Rubi ☆☆☆☆, Avsallar, Incekum. Tel: 5171992.
Syedra Princess ☆☆☆☆, Mahmutlar. Tel: 5283060.
Alara ☆☆☆, Yeşilköy, Avsallar. Tel: 5171146. Situated on a charming, quiet peninsula next to a rock shore and sandy beach.
Banana ☆☆☆, Karasaz. Tel: 5134394.
Elysee ☆☆☆, Ahmet Tokus Caddesi, Obayolu Kavsağı. Tel: 5127400.
Riviera ☆☆☆, Saray Mahallesi, Güzelyalı Caddesi. Tel: 5137597.

HOLIDAY VILLAGES
Hamdullah Pasa, Konaklı. Tel: 5651520.
Oasis Beach, Konaklı. Tel: 5651440.

MERSIN (IÇEL)
(dialing code: 324)

Hilton ☆☆☆☆☆, Adnan Menderes Bulvarı. Tel: 3265000.
Ramada ☆☆☆☆☆. Tel: 3361010. The tallest building in Turkey.
Mersin ☆☆☆☆, Gümrük Meydanı. Tel: 2321640
Damlaca ☆☆, Fasih Kayabalı Caddesi 6. Tel: 3363267.

SIDE
(dialing code: 242)

Most of the following large hotels in and around Side are situated on the seaside or have direct access to the beach. All have swimming pools.
Cesars Hotel and Casino ☆☆☆☆☆, Kumköy. Tel: 7532480.
Grand Prestige ☆☆☆☆☆, Titreyengöl. Tel: 7569060.
Seven Seas Resort ☆☆☆☆, Titreyengöl. Tel: 7569001.
Turquoise Novotel Evasion ☆☆☆☆, Sorgun. Tel: 7569330.
Acanthus ☆☆☆☆, Side. Tel: 7533050.
Defne ☆☆☆☆, Selimiye. Tel: 7531905.
Excelsior Corinthia ☆☆☆☆, Titreyengöl. Tel: 7569110.
Iberotel Side Palace ☆☆☆☆, Sorgun. Tel: 7569321.
Sol Selin ☆☆☆☆, Çolaklı, Manavgat. Tel: 7636680.

HOLIDAY VILLAGES
Club Aldiana, Titreyengöl. Tel: 7569260.
Robinson Club Pamfilya, Sorgun. Tel: 7569350.
Sidelya, Çolaklı, Manavgat. Tel: 7636370.
Turtel Side, Selimiye. Tel: 7532024.

EAST & SOUTHEAST REGION

DIYARBAKİR
(dialing code: 412)

Demir ☆☆☆☆, Izzetpasa Caddesi. Tel: 2212315.
Turistik ☆☆, Ziya Gökalp Bulvarı. Tel: 2247550.

ERZURUM
(dialing code: 442)

Büyük Erzurum Hotel ☆☆☆, Ali Ravi Caddesi 5. Tel: 2186528.
Oral ☆☆, Terminal Caddesi 3. Tel: 2189740.

HATAY (ISKENDERUN, ANTAKYA & HARBIYE)
(dialing code: 326)

Büyük Antakya ☆☆☆☆, Atatürk Caddesi 8, Antakya. Tel: 2135869.
Hataylı ☆☆, Osmangazi Caddesi, Iskenderun. Tel: 6121551.

CENTRAL ANATOLIAN REGION

ANKARA
(dialing code: 312)

Ankara Hilton ☆☆☆☆☆, Kavaklıdere. Tel: 4682888.
Büyük Sürmeli ☆☆☆☆☆, Sıhhiyet. Tel: 2317660.
Grand Hotel Ankara ☆☆☆☆☆, Atatürk Bulvarı, Bakanlıklar. Tel: 4256655.
Sheraton Hotel & Towers ☆☆☆☆☆, Kavaklıdere. Tel: 4685454.
Best ☆☆☆☆, Kavaklıdere. Tel: 4670880.
Dedeman ☆☆☆☆, Bakanlıklar. Tel: 4176200.
Içkale ☆☆☆☆, Maltepe. Tel: 2317710.
Pullman Etap Mola ☆☆☆☆, Kızılay. Tel: 4178585.
Alfin ☆☆☆, Menekse Sokak 11, Kızılay. Tel: 4178425.
Bulvar Palas ☆☆☆, Atatürk Bulvarı 141, Bakanlıklar. Tel: 4175020.
Seğmen ☆☆☆, Büklüm Sokak 13, Kavaklıdere. Tel: 4175374.

BOLU
(dialing code: 374)

Koru Hotel ☆☆☆, Ömerler Köyü, Bakırlı Mevki. Tel: 2152528. On the main Istanbul-Ankara road, but still secluded and surrounded with woods. Excellent meals.
Turban Abant Hotel ☆☆☆, Lake Abant. Tel: 2245033. Delightful setting, delicious meals.
Kartalkaya Mountain Hotel, Kartalkaya, Bolu. Tel: 35724. A well-organized ski center with pricy bed, indoor swimming pool and sauna. Advanced booking is essential.

CAPPADOCIA
(dialing code: Aksaray 382; Nevşehir 384)

AKSARAY
Motel Ağaçlı, at the junction to Nevşehir on the Adana road (E-90). Tel: 2134910. A large complex with swimming pool, restaurants.
AVANOS (NEVŞEHIR)
Altınyazı ☆☆☆☆, Kappadokya Caddesi. Tel: 5112010.
Kotas Avanos Irmak ☆☆☆, Hasankale Mevkii. Tel: 5114317.
Venessa ☆☆☆, Kenan Evren Caddesi. Tel: 5113570.

NEVŞEHIR
Altınöz ☆☆☆☆, Rakıp Üner Caddesi 23. Tel: 2135305.
Orsan ☆☆☆☆, Yeni Kayseri Caddesi 15. Tel: 2132115.
Viva ☆☆☆, Yeni Kayseri Caddesi 45. Tel: 2131760.

ESKIŞEHIR
(dialing code: 222)

Büyük Otel ☆☆☆, 27 Mayıs Caddesi 40. Tel: 2311246.
Emek ☆☆, Yunus Emre Caddesi, next to the Bus Station. Tel: 2312940.
Has Termal Otel (thermal spa), Hamam Yolu Caddesi 7. Tel: 2319191.

KAYSERI
(dialing code: 352)

Almer ☆☆☆, Osman Kavuncu Caddesi. Tel: 3207970.
Hattat ☆☆, Osman Kavuncu Caddesi 1. Tel: 2319331.

KONYA
(dialing code: 332)

Balıkçılar ☆☆☆, Mevlana Karsısı 1. Tel: 3509470
Özkaymak ☆☆☆, across from the bus station. Tel: 2333770.
Selçuk ☆☆☆, Alaaddin Caddesi. Tel: 3532525.

BLACK SEA REGION

AMASRA/BARTİN
(dialing code: 378)

Timur ☆☆☆, town center. Tel: 3152589. Largest and most comfortable hotel in town. Terrace with panoramic view.
Kurucasile Hotel, Kurucasile. Tel: 5181463. Outside of town, a decent hotel owned by the town council.

GIRESUN
(dialing code: 454)

Kit-Tur ☆☆☆, Arifbey Caddesi 2. Tel: 2120245.
Giresun ☆☆, Atatürk Bulvarı 103. Tel: 2123017.

ORDU
(dialing code: 452)

Belde ☆☆☆, Kiraz Limanı. Tel: 2143987.
Turist Hotel ☆☆, Atatürk Bulvarı. Tel: 2149115.

SAMSU
(dialing code: 362)

Yafeya ☆☆☆, Cumhuriyet Meydanı. Tel: 4351131.
Dolfin ☆☆, Sümbül Sokak, Atakent. Tel: 4377255.

TRABZON
(dialing code: 462)

Usta ☆☆☆, Telgrafhane Sokak 3, Trabzon. Tel: 3212195.

Aksular ☆☆, Uzunkum Mevkii, Trabzon. Tel: 2297653.

Best T Hotel ☆☆☆, Besikdüzü, Trabzon. Tel: 8713944.

Büyük Liman Tesisleri ☆☆☆, Sahil Caddesi, Vakfıkebir, Trabzon. Tel: 8415725.

FOOD DIGEST

WHAT TO EAT

The Turks take great pride in their cooking. Turkish food, in fact, is a very delicious mixture of Arabic, Greek, Eastern European and European influences. Though fast food is on the increase, you will not be disappointed with the traditional fare.

Meze (hors d'oeuvres) can be eaten as a starter or as a meal by itself, if you don't eat much. You will be presented with a tray of 10 or so dishes and expected to choose about four or five. These are dishes such as fried liver (*arnavut cigerı*, white cheese), fried lamb's brains (*beyin tavası*), *börek* (small cheese or vegetable pastry rolls), *dolma* (stuffed vegetables), *cacık* (cucumber and yogurt garlic) and various salads.

If you want to continue eating after all these *meze*, you can try one of the excellent Turkish soups (*çorba*), for instance, *iskembe*, which is a tripe soup containing a lot of garlic.

Main courses consist of fish or meat dishes. Fish tend to be expensive when out of season, but delicious, particularly in Istanbul or on the coasts. The most common fish on the menu are *kılıç* (swordfish), *kalkan* (turbot), *levrek* (sea bass) *palamut* (tunny fish) and *lüfer* (bluefish). Meat courses are usually lamb (*kuzu*), chicken (*piliç*), or beef (*dana*), cooked with various vegetables; there's also the famed *sis kebabı* – meat grilled on skewers. Pork is available in most large hotels and holiday villages, as well as in upmarket grocery stores.

Acı (a-je) is a useful word to know; it means spicy hot, a characteristic of a lot of Turkish food. Ask for *acısız* (aji-siz) if you don't want it to be spicy. There are also other terms to note:

VEGETABLES

sebze	vegetable
havuç	carrot
patlican	eggplant/aubergine
kabak	zuchini/courgette
bamya	okra
biber	peppers
fasuliye	beans
sogan	onion

FRUIT

meyve	fruit
portakalelma	apple
kayisi	apricot
kiraz	cherry
incir	fig
üzüm	grapes
kavun	melon
seftali	peach
armut	pear
erik	plum
çilek	strawberry
karpuz	watermelon

The Turks pride themselves on their sweets which are very tasty. Here are a few that you will find on the menu:

Asure	pudding made with nuts, cereals and raisins
Baklava	flaky pastry soaked in syrup
Dondurma	ice cream
Kabak Tatlisi	pumpkin slices in syrup
Lokum	Turkish Delight
Muhallebi	milk pudding
Sütlaç	rice pudding

WHERE TO EAT

There are many different types of eating places to be found in Turkey, including some foreign restaurants such as Italian or Chinese. All vary in standards and prices. Don't assume that fancy decor and well-dressed waiters mean good food; often, you will find the simpler restaurants give you better service and more delicious food.

Price guide for a full course meal per person without drinks:

$ = **Inexpensive $5–15**
$$ = **Moderate $15–25**
$$$ = **Expensive $25 plus**

ANKARA
(dialing code: 312)

Les Ambassadeurs, Merit Altınel Hotel, Tandoğan. Tel: 2317760. Good French cuisine and live music, overlooking Tandoğan Square, which is famous for its monumental sculpture. $$$

K P M

KÖNIGLICHE
PORZELLAN
MANUFAKTUR
Berlin

BERLIN MASTERPIECES

ROCAILLE,
Breslauer Stadtschloß
The unusual reliefs and
opulent embellishments
of this rococo design
places extremely high
demands on the artistic
abilities of the craftsmen.

SCHINKEL Basket
Design: app. 1820
by Karl Friedrich Schinkel.

KURLAND, *pattern 73*
The first classicistic service
made by KPM was created
around 1790 by order of
the Duke of Kurland.

KPM BERLIN · Wegelystraße 1 · Kurfürstendamm 26a · Postal address: Postfach 12 21 07, D-10591 Berlin · Phone
(030) 390 09 - 226 · Fax (030) 390 09 - 279 · U. K. AGENCY · Exclusif Presentations, Ltd. · 20 Vancouver Road
Edgware, Middx. HA8 5DA · Phone (081) 952 46 79 · Fax (081) 951 09 39 · JAPAN AGENCY · Hayashitok Co., Ltd.
Nakano-Cho. Ogawa. Marutamachi · Nakagyo-Ku. Kyoto 604 · Phone (075) 222 02 31 / 231 22 22 · Fax (075) 256 45 54

GlobalAccess

GlobalAccess means just what its name says: instant access to your money, wherever and whenever you need it. 24 hours a day. In over 60 countries around the world.

At HongkongBank's ATM network throughout Asia and the Middle East, you can conduct all your usual ATM transactions. You can also withdraw cash and make balance enquiries at Midland Bank ATMs in the UK, and Marine Midland Bank ATMs in the USA. Simply look for the GlobalAccess logo. And, of course, you can get cash from the Plus ATM network worldwide.

It's easy, it's instant and it's fast becoming indispensable for anyone who travels.

For more details on GlobalAccess contact your nearest HongkongBank office. Then you can keep in constant contact with your cash, no matter how far you are from home.

HongkongBank
The Hongkong and Shanghai Banking Corporation Limited

Our history could fill this book, but we prefer to fill glasses.

When you make a great beer, you don't have to make a great fuss.

Ankara Sofrası, Hosdere Caddesi 76, Yukarı Ayrancı. Tel: 4273535. A cozy Turkish restaurant that serves traditional dishes such as *yaprak sarma*, *mantı* and *börek*. $$

Belpa, Bahçelievler Son Durak. Tel: 2222291. Part of the large ice rink and recreation facilities of the city council, this restaurant serves Turkish and international dishes. $$

La Boheme, Köroğlu Caddesi 96/A, Gaziosmanpaşa. Tel: 4363101. Intimate ambience with a French touch. Has a fireplace in winter. $$$

Boyacızade Konağı (Kale Restaurant), Berrak Sokak 9, Samanpazarı. Tel: 3102525. Lovely old house in the citadel. Good wine, home-made bread and other Turkish dishes. $$$

Cengiz Kaan, Köroğlu Caddesi 37/A, Çankaya. Tel: 4375101. A vast menu of excellent Chinese dishes. $$$

Chez Le Belge, on the Konya highway, by the Lake Gölbası, 20 km from the city center. Tel: 4841478. A 15-year-old gourmet restaurant serving French and Belgian cuisine. Reserve. Closed Monday. $$$

Dede, Tunalı Hilmi Caddesi 99/B-5. Tel: 4261365. Serves inexpensive and good Turkish pastry and *mantı* ravioli. $

Greenhouse, Hilton Hotel, Kavaklıdere. Tel: 4682888. International dishes. Special Turkish meals on Tuesday and Chinese cuisine on Friday. $$$

Hacı Arif Bey, Güniz Sokak 48/1, Kavaklıdere. Tel: 4676730. One of the oldest and best meat restaurants in the city. $$

Kınacılar Evi, Kale Kapısı 28, Ulus (near the old citadel). Tel: 3111010. Well-established Turkish restaurant in a restored mansion. Delicious *mezes*. $$

Körfez, Bayındır Sokak 24/A. Tel: 4311459. Very good Turkish food. $$

Mangal 2, Kuloğlu Sokak 29, Asağı Ayrancı. Tel: 4391650. Housed in a restored Turkish building with a fountain. Good Turkish meat dishes. $$

Marco Polo, Hilton Hotel, Kavaklıdere. Tel: 4682888. A gourmet French restaurant. $$$

Milka, Atatürk Boulevard. 185, Kavaklıdere. Tel: 4254048. Turkish and international meat and fish dishes in a restored house with pleasant garden. Closed Sunday. $$$

Pembe Ev, Tunalı Hilmi Caddesi 82/A, 2nd floor. Tel: 4267425. Good, simple Turkish food. $

Pupee Donen, Atakule. Tel: 4407412. Atop a modern tower with an exciting view of the city. $$$

Rıhtım, Iran Caddesi, Buğday Sokak 2/A, Kavaklıdere. Tel: 4272432. Serving Turkish and international dishes. Closed Sunday. $$

RV, Atatürk Boulevard. 243/D, Kavaklıdere. Tel: 4270376. Long-established restaurant offering international cuisine. $$$

Schnitzel Unlimited, Tahran Caddesi 5, Kavaklıdere. Tel: 4685400. A Viennese-style restaurant serving many types of schnitzel and salad. $$

Şömine, Dosteli Sokak 4, Gaziosmanpaşa. Tel: 4378060. Housed in a pretty villa, this restaurant serves French dishes and live violin music. Has a fireplace in winter, and garden open in summer. $$$

Ülker, Yunus Nadi Sokak 21, Çankaya. Tel: 4383297. Top quality home-made dishes served in a restored Turkish house. Closed Sunday. $$

Washington, Bayındır Sokak 22, Kızılay. Tel: 4312218. Turkish food and delicious *mezes*. Popular with politicians and journalists. $$

Yahya, Filistin Sokak 28, Gaziosmanpaşa. Tel: 4368464. International cuisine. "Yahya" meat dish is the specialty. $$

Yakamoz Niyazi's, Tunalı Hilmi Caddesi 114, Kavaklıdere. Tel: 4263752. Good sea food. $$

ANTALYA
(dialing code: 242)

Blue Parrot's Cafe, Kaleiçi, Izmirli Ali Efendi Sokak 10. Tel: 2470349. A pretty Turkish house and garden with orange trees. Serves international dishes. $$$

Club 29, Kaleiçi. Tel: 2416260. A smart, gourmet restaurant and disco after hours, with a commanding view of the harbor. $$$

Club Sazak, Lara Yolu, Şirinyalı Mahallesi. Tel: 3233590. Seafood and Turkish cuisine with live music and splendid view. $$$

Develi, Kenan Evren Bulvarı. Tel: 2412979. Traditional Turkish meat dishes of the southern region. $$

Geyik Bayırı, Çakırlar Mevkii (23 km/14 miles from Antalya). Tel: 4394338. Popular trout restaurant. $$

Hisar, Kaleiçi (entered from Cumhuriyet Caddesi). High in the city walls, good food served in a gracious atmosphere. $$

Kral Sofrası, Kaleiçi. Tel: 2412198. An old wooden house with a warm ambience, *mezes* and meat dishes are especially good. Booking essential. $$$

Küçük Cennet, Selçuk Mahallesi, Iskele Caddesi 13, Kaleiçi. Tel: 2411089. Recommended for its *gözleme*, a local pasta specialty. $

Oda, Sanayi ve Ticaret Odası Binası, 6th floor. Table d'hote meals and a wonderful view. $$

Tütav Hotel, Kaleiçi. Tel: 2486591. Terrific view, European and Turkish dishes. $$$

Yesterday's Chinese Restaurant, Iskele Caddesi, Kaleiçi. Tel: 2470229. $$

ISTANBUL

EUROPEAN SIDE
(dialing code: 212)

Ali Baba (Bosphorus), Kireçburnu Caddesi 20, Kireçburnu. Tel: 2620889. Delicious fish and *mezes* in a garden with a sea view. $$–$$$

Les Ambassadeurs (Bosphorus), Cevdet Pasa Caddesi 113, Bebek. Tel: 2633002. This formal restaurant looks out on the sea and serves fine Turkish and Russian dishes. $$$

Asır, Kalyoncu Kulluk Caddesi 94/1 (off Tarlabası Caddesi, next to the police station), Beyoğlu. Tel: 2500557. A *meyhane* (Turkish tavern) very popular with the locals. A large selection of *meze* and good fish. $$

Asitane, Kariye Hotel, Edirnekapı. Tel: 5348414. Ottoman cuisine accompanied by classical Turkish music in a historic setting. $$–$$$

Beyti, Osman Sokak 8, Florya. Tel: 6632990. An established restaurant, not far from the airport, serving superb meat grills. $$

Borsa, Sirkeci (opposite the train station). Tel: 5118079. One of the oldest restaurants in the city offering many, now rare, Turkish dishes. Has a branch in Osmanbey. Tel: 2324200. $$

Cafe Caliente, Iskele Caddesi 3, Ortaköy. Tel: 2609608. A new but already popular Mexican restaurant. Reserve. $$–$$$

Çiçek Pasajı, Istiklal Caddesi, Galatasaray, Beyoğlu. A charming, historic and and rather bawdy street of small *meyhanes* (taverns) offering drinks, fish and *mezes*. $

Darüzziyafe, Şifahane Caddesi 6, Süleymaniye. Tel: 5118414. Housed within the Süleymaniye Mosque complex, this atmospheric restaurant serves authentic Ottoman cuisine around a courtyard with a pool. No alcoholic drinks. $$

Deniz Park Gazinosu (Bosphorus), Daire Sokak 9, Yeniköy. Tel: 2620415. A genuine, unambitious fish restaurant owned by one of the few remaining Greek families in Istanbul. Its summer terrace has a breathtaking view. $$

Develi, Balıkpazarı, Gümüsyüzük Sokak 7, Samatya. Tel: 5851189. A meat restaurant serving the specialties of southeastern Anatolia since 1912. $$

Divan, Divan Hotel, Taksim. Tel: 2314100. A refined and long-established restaurant serving some of the best Turkish and international dishes in the city. $$$

Dynasty, Ramada Hotel, Laleli. Tel: 5139300. Arguably the best Chinese restaurant in Istanbul. Glamorous setting. $$$

Ece (Bosphorus), Kamacı Sokak 10, Arnavutköy. Tel: 2659600. Delicious, creatively prepared Turkish food with an emphasis on beans and vegetables, served in a pretty restored house. Loud live music on the upper floors. $$–$$$

Façyo (Bosphorus), Kireçburnu Caddesi 13, Tarabya. Tel: 2620024. One of the best fish restaurants on the Bosphorus. A wide range of *mezes*. $$$

Fisher, Inönü Caddesi 51, Taksim. Tel: 2452576. Serves Middle European specialties like schnitzel, strudel, and great pork chops. $$

Four Seasons, Istiklal Caddesi 509, Tünel, Beyoğlu. Tel: 2458941. A large menu of international dishes. An established restaurant close to the consulates, with a European atmosphere. $$

Hacı Abdullah, Sakızağacı Caddesi 19 (off Istiklal Caddesi), Beyoğlu. Tel: 2448561. Old, modest Turkish *lokanta* serving delicious home-style food. $–$$

Hacıbaba, Istiklal Caddesi 49, Beyoğlu. Tel: 2441886. A typical Turkish restaurant with a large selection of tasty dishes. Has a balcony in summer overlooking the courtyard of a Greek church in Taksim. $$

Hamdi Et Lokantası, Tahmis Caddesi, Kalçın Sokak, Eminönü. Tel: 5280390. An unpretentious place for good grilled meats in the old part of the city. $

Han (Bosphorus), Yahya Kemal Caddesi 10, Rumeli Hisar. Tel: 2652968. A rustic fish restaurant. Terrace. $$–$$$

Hasan Balıkçılar, Yat Limanı, Rıhtım Sokak 8, Yeşilköy. Tel: 5738300. A large, featureless restaurant serving some of the best fish dishes in Istanbul. Its baked quince and cream dessert is memorable. Located in the pretty suburban town of Yeşilköy, near the airport. $$$

Istiridye, Mumhane Caddesi 45-47, Karaköy. Tel: 2491772. A small restaurant famous for its fish. Occupies part of a former church. $–$$

Japan Club, Mürbasan Sokak, Koza Is Merkezi A Blok, Balmumcu. Tel: 2661423. The best and the most pricy sushi and teppanyaki in town. $$$

Kallavi, Kallavi Sokak 20 (off Istiklal Caddesi), Beyoğlu. Tel: 2511010. A new *meyhane* serving tasty *mezes* and kebabs. Live Greek folk music Wednesday and Friday. $$

Karaca (Bosphorus), Yahya Kemal Caddesi 1/C, Rumeli Hisar. Tel: 2659720. A perennial favorite for fish and *mezes*, though without much of a view. $$–$$$

Konyalı (Sultanahmet). Tel: 5139697. Set in the grounds of Topkapı Palace, Konyalı is a very long-established Turkish restaurant serving consistently good food. Lunch only. $$

Küçük Hüdadad, Şapçı Han, Kömür Bekir Sokak 2/4, across from Yeni Cami, Eminönü, (no sign outside). A traditional tradesmen's restaurant serving home-style dishes. $

Marmit, Yeşilköy. Tel: 5738581. An original bistro serving Mexican food in an interesting ambience. Reserve. $$–$$$

Memo's (Bosphorus), Salhane Sokak 10/2, Ortaköy. Tel: 2618304. An ambitious bar/restaurant popular with the fast set. Delightful terrace in summer overhanging the sea. Disco after midnight. $$$

Mey (Bosphorus), Rumeli Hisarı Caddesi, Bebekli Apt. 122, Bebek. Tel: 2652599. International fish restaurant with stylishly plain decor and up-market clientele. Reservations essential. $$$

Pandeli, Mısır Çarsısı, Eminönü. Tel: 5273909. A landmark of old Istanbul inside the Spice Market, with delicious traditional Turkish dishes and beautiful wall tiles. Lunch only. $$

Park Şamdan, Mim Kemal Öke Caddesi 18/1, Nişantası. Tel: 2250710. A stylish restaurant popular with well-heeled locals. $$$

Pera Palas, Pera Palas Hotel, Tepebası. Tel: 2514560. The prince of turn-of-the-century Istanbul with venerable interiors, a fine patisserie and café. The restaurant is not very distinguished. $$

THE COLOUR OF LIFE.

A holiday may last just a week or so, but the memories of those happy, colourful days will last forever, because together you and Kodak Ektachrome films will capture, as large as life, the wondrous sights, the breathtaking scenery and the magical moments. For you to relive over and over again.

The Kodak Ektachrome range of slide films offers a choice of light source, speed and colour rendition and features extremely fine grain, very high sharpness and high resolving power.

Take home the real colour of life with Kodak Ektachrome films.

LIKE THIS?

OR LIKE THIS?

A KODAK FUN PANORAMIC CAMERA
BROADENS YOUR VIEW

The holiday you and your camera have been looking forward to all year; and a stunning panoramic view appears. "Fabulous", you think to yourself, "must take that one".

Unfortunately, your lens is just not wide enough. And three-in-a-row is a poor substitute.

That's when you take out your pocket-size, 'single use' Kodak Fun Panoramic Camera. A film and a camera, all in one, and it works miracles. You won't need to focus, you don't need special lenses. Just aim, click and... it's all yours. The total picture.

You take twelve panoramic pictures with one Kodak Fun Panoramic Camera. Then put the camera in for developing and printing.

Each print is 25 by 9 centimetres. Excellent depth of field. True Kodak Gold colours.

The Kodak Fun Panoramic Camera itself goes back to the factory, to be recycled. So that others too can capture one of those spectacular phooooooooootooooooooooooos.

Rami (Sultanahmet), Utangaç Sokak 6. Tel: 5176593. Located next to the Blue Mosque in a restored building with Ottoman decor. Good Turkish cooking served at candle-lit tables. $$

Rejans, Emir Nevruz Sokak 17 (off Istiklal Caddesi, Galatasaray, Beyoğlu. Tel: 2441610. Once the smartest restaurant in the city, Rejans serves authentic Russian cuisine with deadly lemon vodka in a rustic, unambitious atmosphere. Strongly recommended for all visitors. Reservations essential for dinner. $$

Revan, Sheraton Hotel, Taksim. Tel: 2312121. A great view and outstanding Turkish cuisine at this roof-top restaurant. Dinner only. $$$

Ristorante Italiano, Cumhuriyet Caddesi 6/B, Elmadağ. Tel: 2478640. The pioneer of Italian restaurants in town, serving since 1966. $$

Russian Restaurant, Inönü Caddesi, Palas Apt 77/A, Gümüssuyu. Tel: 2434892. A small and established restaurant offering specialties such as *borsht* soup, *kievski*, *stragonoff* and *strudel*. $$

"S" Restaurant, Vezirköskü Sokak 2, Bebek. Tel: 2638326. Elegance above a petrol station. Candle-lit setting and distinguished Turkish and French nouvelle cuisine. One of the most stylish and expensive restaurants in the city. $$$

Sultanahmet Köftecisi (Sultanahmet), Divanyolu Caddesi 28. Tel: 5262782. A modest restaurant, very famous for its meat balls. A favorite of the locals. $

Sultan Pub (Sultanahmet), Divanyolu Caddesi, Şeftali Sokak 2. Tel: 5266347. One of the better places around Sultanahmet. Restaurant, cafe and bar with a warm atmosphere. $$

Süreyya (Bosphorus), Istinye Caddesi 26, Istinye. Tel: 2775886. One of the city's gastronomic landmarks. Marvelous Russian, Turkish and European cuisine. $$$

Tonoz (Bosphorus), Insirah Yokusu 48, Bebek. Tel: 2570419. Unique setting in a historic Genoese cellar with garden. Tasty Turkish food. $$

Ümit (near Sultanahmet), Nuruosmaniye, Alibaba Türbe Sokak 35, Cağaloğlu. Tel: 5129094. Clean and attractive, serving traditional Turkish dishes. Lunch only. $

Urcan (Bosphorus). Tel: 2420367. A renowned fish restaurant, one of the best in town, where fish is chosen from a tank. Near the charming fish market, with a great sea view. $$$

Yakup 2, Asmalımescit Sokak 35, Tünel, Beyoğlu. Tel: 2492925. A genuine *meyhane* popular with artists, journalists and academics. Casual and noisy. $$

Yedi Gün (Bosphorus), Rumeli Kavak. Tel: 2423798. At the northernmost permitted area on the Bosphorus, Yedi Gün, together with several other good fish restaurants, is located in a genuine village atmosphere. $$

Yesil Sandalyeler, Sıraselviler Caddesi 69, Taksim. Tel: 2433049. Famous for *Iskembe Çorbası* (tripe soup), the late favorite of tipsy Turks. $

THE ASIAN SIDE
(dialing code: 216)

Anadolu Kavak. The northernmost residential area on the Anatolian side of the Bosphorus, this charming fishermen's village has dedicated itself to food: excellent, if simple, fish restaurants, pavement vendors selling ice cream and waffles, mussels and meat balls. Most easily reached by ferry-boat. $–$$

Asude, Perihan Abla Sokak 4, Kuzguncuk. Tel: 3344414. A family restaurant with a homely atmosphere serving tasty dishes; fixed menu. $$

Birtat (Prince's Island) Gülistan Caddesi 10, Büyükada. Tel: 3826841. Good food and pleasant atmosphere. Located on the largest of the Prince's Islands. $$

Çamlıca Cafe, Sefa Tepesi, Çamlıca. Tel: 3298191. Ottoman-style pavilions set on Istanbul's highest hill. Turkish olive oil dishes and recorded Turkish classical music. Superb view of the European side. Avoid weekends when it's too crowded. $$

Club 29, Pasabahçe Yolu 24, Çubuklu. Tel: 3223888. Restaurant and swimming pool in one of the most beautiful settings on the Bosphorus. It has its own boat to take you across from Istinye on the European side. $$$

Hasır, Beykoz Korusu, Beykoz. Tel: 3222001. One of the best Turkish restaurants of Istanbul, set in a lovely garden overlooking the Bosphorus from a wooded park. Its *keskek kebab* is a must. Has a branch in Nişantası. Tel: (212) 2301484. $$–$$$

Hıdiv Kasrı, Çubuklu. Tel: 3312651. Housed in a palace built in early 1900s for the Egyptian governor, this restored building, set amongst one of the most thickly wooded hills on the Bosphorus, offers Turkish specialties accompanied by classical music. Its cafe in the beautiful park is worth a visit. $$–$$$

Huzur, Salacak Iskelesi, 20, Üsküdar. Tel: 3333157. A long-established, modest fish restaurant with a wonderful view of the European side at sunset. $$

Kadife Chalet, Kadife Sokak 29, Bahariye, Kadıköy. Tel: 3478596. A charming restaurant/cafe housed in a 19th century wooden house. Turkish dishes with home-grown vegetables. $$

Kız Kulesi Deniz Restaurant, Salacak Sahil Yolu, Üsküdar. Tel: 3410403. Delicious sea food and a great view of the old city on the European side. $$

Koço, Moda Caddesi 265, Moda. Tel: 3360795. One of the oldest fish restaurants in the city, with a vast, peaceful view of the Marmara Sea. Its fish dishes and *mezes* are outstanding. $$

Körfez, Körfez Caddesi 78, Kanlıca. Tel: 4134314. A very smart restaurant set in a secluded, romantic bay, offering wonderful fish dishes and *mezes*. Its Sea Bass cooked in salt is famous. Has a private boat to take you across from Rumeli Hisar. $$$

Leonardo, Polonezköy, Beykoz. Tel: 4323082. Set in the historic village of the Istanbul Polish community, this new restaurant offers tasty dishes in a country atmosphere. $$

Romantika, Fenerbahçe Parkı, Kalamış, Fenerbahçe. Tel: 3363828. Decorated with flowers and birds, within a large conservatory. Turkish cuisine, and a peaceful view of the Marmara Sea. $$

IZMIR
(dialing code: 232)

1888 (Bin Sekizyüz Seksen Sekiz), Cumhuriyet Bulvarı 248, Alsancak. Tel: 4216690. An elegant restaurant worth trying as it offers tasty Mediterranean dishes. Named after the year this Greek mansion was built, it has Art Nouveau decor and an exotic garden. $$$

Altınkapı, 1444 Sokak 14, Alsancak. Tel: 4222648. Famous for its *döner*. $

Arirang Korean Restaurant, Yalı Caddesi 12, Alaybey, Karsıyaka. Tel: 3657263. Korean and Chinese dishes. Reservation is essential. $$$

Bergama, Atatürk Caddesi 296, Alsancak. Tel: 4634829. A good fish and *meze* restaurant on the seaside Kordon Avenue. $$

Boğaziçi Ocakbası, Cengiz Topel Caddesi 38/B, Bostanlı. Tel: 3300013. A good meat restaurant with a sea view. $$

Çiçek Pasajı, Atatürk Caddesi, Pasaport. A down-to-earth street of taverns to go for fish, *mezes*, *raki*, Turkish music, and friendly people. $

Deniz, Atatürk Caddesi 188, Alsancak. Tel: 4220601. Izmir's best fish restaurant. Reservations essential. $$–$$$

Golden & Martı, Atatürk Caddesi 314, Alsancak. Tel: 4214914. A joint venture of the city's two well-established restaurants by the sea on Kordon Avenue. Sea food and some French dishes. $$$

Hanımağa, Yalı Caddesi 422, Karsıyaka. Tel: 3687662. Popular for its *mantı* (ravioli) and *gözleme* (a stuffed pastry). $

Kemal'in Yeri, 1453 Sokak 20/A, Alsancak. Tel: 4223190. A 50-year-old restaurant and tavern which has awards from the Association of Turkish Restaurateurs. Its specialty is fish cooked in milk (*Sütlü Balık*). $$

Parmak Yalatan, 1391 Sokak 4/A, Alsancak. Tel: 4226858. Chicken dishes only. $

Pastavilla, Kıbrıs Şehitleri Caddesi, Alsancak. A chain restaurant serving only spaghettis. $

Pizza Ristorante Italiano, Şehit Nevres Bulvarı 5/A, Alsancak. Tel: 4633105. Italian dishes and a good salad bar. $$

Sultan Sofrası, Çiniliköy, Kemalpasa (on the road to Torbalı). Tel: 8781461. A very good meat and *döner* restaurant near a pretty village, outside Izmir. $$

Vegetarian Restaurant, 1375 Sokak 11/1, Alsancak. Tel: 4217558. A small Turkish vegetarian restaurant. $

Despite the fact that Turks are Muslims, beer and wine do a booming trade here. The national drink is *rakı*, a very strong aniseed liquor which is drunk mixed with water or on the rocks. Turkish wine is certainly acceptable, the best ones being *Kavaklıdere*, *Villa Doluca* and *Karmen*.

Turkish coffee (*kahve*) has a muddy consistency and is drunk out of a tiny cup. The waiter will ask whether you want it *sade* (without sugar), *orta* (medium), or *sekerli* (sweet). Tea (*çay*) is drunk in vast quantities, again out of tiny, tulip-shaped glasses.

Ayran is a combination of yogurt and water, a drink of which the Turks are very fond. It is a very refreshing drink in the summer. Fresh fruit juice is always available, but the fruit depends on the season. Bottled water can be bought everywhere.

To make yourself really popular with your hosts, try saying *serefe* (sh-e-re-feh) or "cheers", or *afiyet olsun* (ah-fih-yet ol-sun) that is, "bon appetit!"

THINGS TO DO

Turkey is a tourist's paradise. Whatever your interest, you will find it here – archaeology, architecture, religion, folklore, history, mountains, boats or beaches.

Here are a few examples of places not to be missed in Istanbul:

Covered Bazaar: the main shopping center.
Dolmabahçe Palace: mid-19th century Sultan's palace.
Topkapı Palace: 15th- to 19th-century Sultan's palace.
Sultan Ahmet Mosque: known as the Blue Mosque due to its blue interior.
Aya Sophia: ancient basilica.
Archaeological Museums: excellent collection of antiquities.
Çamlica: affords an amazingly grand view over the city.
Yıldız Park: beautiful tea houses in a very peaceful setting.
Underground Palace: 6th-century Byzantine cistern.
The Bosphorus and the Prince's Islands

COUNTRY

Within Turkey, there are numerous historical as well as modern sites.

Classical	Modern
Adrianople	Edirne
Antioch	Antakya
Constantinople	Istanbul
Daphne	Harbiye
Edessa	Urfa
Gallipoli	Gelibolu
Halicarnassus	Bodrum
Nicaea	Iznik
Pergamum	Bergama
Sardis	Foça
Smyrna	Izmir
Trebizond	Trabzon

Besides the above, there are also major archaeological sites worth a visit, such as:

Aspendos: very well-preserved Roman amphitheater.
Bogazköy: ancient Hittite capital.
Ephesus: very well-preserved Roman city.
Perge: ruins of a city of the classical age.
Side: Pamphilian city ruins.
Termessos: not excavated, but very well-preserved ruins of an ancient city.

TOURS

Most travel agencies and large hotels will offer you a wide choice of worthwhile tours. English-speaking guides are always provided. Tours vary from half-a-day for part of a city, to a couple of weeks to cover more areas of interest.

Tours visiting parts of Istanbul include "Byzantine Art Tours" with visits to Byzantine churches such as Hagia Sophia, walls and aqueducts; and "Ottoman Art Tours" which includes visits to the Blue Mosque, the Sultans' palaces etc. There are many full and half-day trips to see the many sights of Istanbul as well as sailing tours to the Princes' Islands. You may also join a Bosphorus cruise if you fancy a night on the Bosphorus.

Tours of the Aegean include visits to such interesting places as Ephesus, Sardis, Pergamum, Aphrodisias and Izmir, plus the beautiful resorts of Bodrum, Fethiye and Marmaris. Similarly on the Mediterranean, you can visit the ancient ruins of Perge, Aspendos, Alanya, Antalya, Side, Termessos, and the beaches of Kas, Silifke etc. You may be interested in taking a long tour to cover a greater area such as a tour along the Aegean and Mediterranean coasts, Anatolia, which includes Ankara and Cappadocia, and eastern Turkey.

Specialized tours to less well-known places (with offices in Istanbul):
Alternatif Turizm (Asian side). Tel: (216) 3456650, 34984 9. Trekking, mountain biking, rafting, parapenting and canoing trips in the country.

"Before The Sunset" Travels. Tel: (212) 2592084. Organized walks around less well-known parts of Istanbul, including Anastasia Walls along Black Sea and Kızılcaköy caves in Şile.
Fest Turizm. Tel: (212) 2582589, 2582573. Specialized tours organized by the history magazine, *Tarih ve Toplum*.
Plan Tours, Cumhuriyet Caddesi 131/1, Elmadağ. Tel: (212) 2302272. Tours to Gallipoli war graves, Bursa, Troy, and Pergamum; regular yacht cruises on the Bosphorus.
Positive Tours, Şisli. Tel: (212) 2319054. Trips to Safranbolu, Assos and Pamukkale.
Trek Travel. Tel: (212) 2358230, 2546706. Trekking trips to the Taurus Mountains (southern Turkey), Cappadocia, and Kaçkar Mountains (Black Sea region).

CULTURE PLUS

MUSEUMS

The country boasts more than 150 museums. Here are the most interesting:

ISTANBUL

Archaeological Museum, Sultanahmet. Tel: 5207740. Closed Monday.
Atatürk Museum, Şisli. Tel: 2406319. The house of Turkey's greatest hero and founder of the Republic. Closed Monday and Tuesday.
Asiyan Museum, Bebek. Tel: 2636986. The historic wooden house of Tevfik Fikret, a 19th century poet, in a wonderful setting on the Bosphorus. Closed Monday and Tuesday.
Aya Sofya Museum, Sultanahmet. Tel: 5221750. Closed Monday.
Basilica Cistern (Yerebatan Sarayı), Sultanahmet. Tel: 5221259.
Beylerbeyi Palace Museum, Beylerbeyi (on the Asian side). Tel: 3219320. Closed Monday and Tuesday.
Calligraphy Museum (Hat Sanatları Müzesi), Beyazıt Square. Tel: 5275851. Closed Sunday and Monday.
Caricature Museum, Fatih. Tel: 5211264. Closed Sunday.
Carpet & Kilim Museum, Sultanahmet. Tel: 5181330. Closed Sunday and Monday.
Dolmabahçe Palace Museum, Besiktas. Tel: 2585544. Closed Monday.

Galata Tower, Şishane. Tel: 2451160.

Kariye Camii Museum, Edirnekapı. Tel: 5233009.

Maritime Museum (Deniz Müzesi), Besiktas. Tel: 2610040. Closed Monday and Tuesday.

Military Museum (Askeri Müze), Harbiye. Tel: 2406255.

Mosaic Museum, Sultanahmet. Tel: 5119700.

Sadberk Hanım Museum, Büyükdere Caddesi, Sarıyer. Tel: 2423813. A private museum housing ethnographical and archaeological collections in two handsome old mansions on the Bosphorus. Closed Wednesday.

Topkapı Palace Museum, Sultanahmet. Tel: 5120480. Closed Tuesday.

Museum of Turkish and Islamic Arts, Sultanahmet. Tel: 5181385. Closed Monday.

Yıldız Palace Chalet Kösk, Besiktas. Tel: 2583080.

Yapı Kredi Bank's Museum, Galatasaray. Tel: 2452041. A large collection of ancient coins.

ANKARA

Museum of Anatolian Civilizations, Ulus (below the Citadel). Tel: 3243160. One of the largest and most important archaeological museums in Turkey.

Ethnography Museum, Talat Pasa Bulvarı. Tel: 3113007.

Roman Baths, Çankırı Yolu, Ulus. Extensive Roman baths dating from 3rd century. Closed Monday.

Railway Museum, Gar Alanı (near the main station). Tel: 3090515.

ELSEWHERE IN TURKEY

Adana Archaeological Museum, Seyhan Caddesi. Tel: (322) 4543855.

Afrodisias Museum, Karacasu Ilçesi, Geyre Köyü, Aydın. Tel: (256) 4488003. Fantastic sculptures from the Roman period.

Afyon Archaeological Museum, Kurtulus Caddesi. Tel: (272) 2151191.

Ağrı, Ishak Pasha Palace, Doğubeyazıt.

Amasya Museum, Atatürk Caddesi. Tel: (358) 2124513.

Alanya Museum, Saray Mahallesi. Tel: (242) 5121228.

Anamur Museum, Atatürk Caddesi. Tel: (324) 8161677.

Antalya Museum, Konyaaltı Caddesi. Tel: (242) 2414528. One of the largest. Closed Monday.

Aydın Museum, Hasan Efendi Mahallesi. Tel: (256) 2252259.

Bergama Archaeological Museum, Cumhuriyet Caddesi. Tel: (232) 6331096.

Bodrum Underwater Archaeology Museum, Bodrum Castle. Tel: (252) 3161095.

Bursa Archaeological Museum, Kültür Park. Tel: (224) 2202029.

Bursa Osmanlı Evi Museum, Murat Mahallesi. Tel: (224) 2220868. A 17th-century Ottoman house with beautiful wood carvings.

Bursa Museum of Turkish and Islamic Arts, Yesil Medrese Caddesi. Tel: (224) 3277679. Houses some wonderful Iznik tiles from 13th–18th centuries, and ethnographic pieces.

Bursa Iznik Museum, Müze Caddesi. Tel: (224) 7571027. Hellenistic, Roman, Byzantine, Seljuk and Ottoman pieces and tile-making furnaces.

Çanakkale Archaeological Museum, Izmir Caddesi. Tel: (286) 2173252.

Çorum Alacahöyük Museum, Alacahöyük village. Tel: (364) 4117420. A collection of late Bronze, Hittite, Frigian, Roman and Byzantine period pieces.

Çorum Boğazköy Museum, Boğazkale village. Tel: (364) 4522006. Hattusas and Yazılıkaya temples.

Diyarbakır Archaeological Museum, Ziya Gökalp Bulvarı. Tel: (412) 2217013.

Diyarbakır Cahit Sıtkı Tarancı House, Camii Kebir Mahallesi. A beautiful 18th-century building which was the home of one of Turkey's most popular 20th century poets.

Edirne Archaeology and Ethnography Museum, beside the Selimiye Mosque. Tel: (284) 2251120.

Efes Museum, Selçuk. Tel: (232) 8926010.

Elazığ Archaeology and Ethnography Museum, Mimarlık Fakültesi Kampüsü. Tel: (424) 2122970.

Erzurum Archaeological Museum, Yenişehir Caddesi. Tel: (442) 2181406.

Eskişehir Archaeological Museum, Akarbası Mahallesi. Tel: (222) 2301371.

Eskişehir Lüle Tas› Museum, Kültür Sarayı. Tel: (222) 2330582. Meerschaum-making tools.

Eskişehir Kilim Museum, Ertuğrul Gazi Mahallesi. Tel: (222) 2316613.

Gaziantep Museum, Istasyon Caddesi. Tel: (342) 2313371.

Giresun Museum, Sokakbası. Tel: (454) 2121322.

Hatay (Antakya) Museum, Gündüz Caddesi. Tel: (326) 2146167.

Isparta Museum, Kenan Evren Caddesi. Tel: (246) 2239403.

Içel (Mersin) Museum, Atatürk Caddesi. Tel: (324) 2319618.

Izmir Archaeological Museum, Konak. Tel: (232) 4254929.

Izmir Atatürk Museum, Atatürk Caddesi 248, Alsancak. Tel: (232) 4217026.

Izmir Ethnographic Museum, Konak (across from the Archaeological Museum).

Izmir Kayseri Archaeological Museum, Kısla Caddesi. Tel: (352) 2222149.

Konya Archaeological Museum, Larende Caddesi. Tel: (332) 3513207.

Konya Mevlana Museum. Tel: (332) 3511215.

Konya Turkish and Islamic Arts Museum, Larende Caddesi. Tel: (332) 3518958.

Kütahya Museum, Cumhuriyet Caddesi. Tel: (274) 2236990.

Malatya Museum, Dernek Mahallesi. Tel: (422) 3213006.

Manisa Museum, Murad Caddesi. Tel: (236) 2311071.

Mardin Museum, Meydanbası. Tel: (482) 2127797.
Milet Museum, Yenihisar, Aydın. Tel: (256) 8755038.
Nevşehir Museum. Tel: (384) 2131447.
Niğde Museum. Tel: (388) 2323390.
Pamukkale Archaeological Museum, Denizli. Tel: (258) 2722034.
Side Museum. Tel: (242) 7531006.
Silifke Museum, Tasucu Caddesi. Tel: (234) 7142852.
Trabzon Ayasofya Museum. Tel: (462) 2233043.
Ürgüp Museum. Tel: (384) 3414082.

ART GALLERIES

The major cities have many small art galleries, most of which double up as bars, and are one of the best places to meet local people. The cultural centers have art displays, and for major exhibits, see the local press. A few of the leading art galleries:

ISTANBUL

Aksanat, Istiklal Caddesi 16, Beyoğlu. Tel: 2523500.
Baldem, Akkavak Sokak 22, Nişantası.
Tel: 23240 81.
Baraz, Kurtulus Caddesi 191, Kurtulus. Tel: 2404783.
Is Sanat, Meselik Sokak, Yürekli Han, Taksim. Tel: 2442021.
Nev, Maçka Caddesi 33, Maçka. Tel: 2316782.
Tem, Orhan Ersek Sokak 44/2, Nişantası, 2470899.
Urart, Abdi Ipekçi Caddesi 21, Nişantası. Tel: 2412183.
Vakko, Istiklal Caddesi 123, Beyoğlu. Tel: 2514092.
Yapı Kredi, Istiklal Caddesi 285, Galatasaray, Beyoğlu. Tel: 2524700.

ANKARA

Ars, Attar Sokak 9/15, Gaziosmanpaşa. Tel: 4277731.
Nev, Horasan Sokak 14, Gaziosmanpaşa. Tel: 4379300.
State Painting and Sculpture Museum, Ulus. Tel: 4332026.
Urart, Cinnah Caddesi 43/A, Çankaya. Tel: 4381647.
Vakko, Atatürk Bulvarı 113, Kızılay. Tel: 4252285.
Z, Kırkpınar Sokak 5/B, Çankaya. Tel: 4399417.

CONCERTS & BALLETS

Each major city has its own ballet company, orchestra, theater, etc. Some are better than others, but do not expect them to be up to the same standard as the Royal Ballet or the Bolshoi. Exceptions to this are the annual Istanbul and Izmir festivals where international performers such as Michael Jackson, Sting, London Symphony Orchestra, Lauri Anderson, Monserrat Caballe, etc. have recently topped the bill.

MOVIES

There are many movie theaters in the major cities, often showing original English versions even if the title has been translated into Turkish. The best cinemas in Istanbul are collected on a single street, Istiklal Caddesi, in Beyoğlu. Check local papers for details. Some good cinemas in Ankara and Izmir are:

ANKARA

Akün, Atatürk Boulevard. 227, Kavaklıdere. Tel: 4277656.
Çankaya, Paris Caddesi, Çankaya. Tel: 4280780.
Kavaklıdere, Tunalı Hilmi Caddesi 105, Kavaklıdere. Tel: 4267379.
Metropol, Selanik Caddesi 76, Kızılay. Tel: 4257478.

IZMIR

Çınar, SSK Blokları, Konak. Tel: 4844861.
Karaca, 1379 Sokak, Alsancak. Tel: 4839354.
Konak, Anafartalar Caddesi 20, Kemeraltı, Konak. Tel: 4832191.
Şan, Şan Pasajı, Konak. Tel: 4837511.

BOOKSHOPS

English language books are not especially hard to find but are very expensive. The following is a listing of the more reputable bookshops in the major cities.

ISTANBUL

ABC, Istiklal Caddesi 461, Beyoğlu. Tel: 2416550.
Dünya, Istiklal Caddesi 469, Beyoğlu, tel: 2491006; Narlıbahçe Sokak 15, Cağaloğlu, tel: 5120190; Tesvikiye Caddesi 164, Nişantası, tel: 2470590; Cevdetpasa Caddesi 232. Also at Conrad, Hilton, Mövenpick, Sheraton hotels and Swissotel.
Pandora, Büyük Parmakkapı Sokak 3 (off Istiklal Caddesi), Beyoğlu. Tel: 2451667.
Net, Galleria Shopping Mall, Ataköy. Tel: 5590950; Ramada Hotel. Tel: 5136431.

ANKARA

ABC, Selanik Caddesi 1/A, Kızılay. Tel: 4343842.
Dünya, Tunalı Hilmi Caddesi 82A, Kavaklıdere, tel: 4671633; Konur Sokak 10A, Kızılay, tel: 4186864; Sheraton Hotel, Kavaklıdere, tel: 4270956.

IZMIR

Dünya, Cumhuriyet Bulvarı 143/G, Alsancak. Tel: 4636877.
Haset, fiair Nevres Bulvarı, Kızılay Is Merkezi 3/B. Tel: 4219831.
Konak, Belediye Pasajı P-16, Konak. Tel: 4259395.
Net, Cumhuriyet Bulvarı 142/B, Alsancak. Tel: 4212632.

NIGHTLIFE

Nightlife revolves around *meyhane*, a type of tavern, restaurants, casinos or *paviyons*. Discos are available in the major cities and tourist resorts. Entertainment fads change fast and often, so what may be fashionable this month may not even exist next month.

Certain areas of Istanbul (e.g. Beyoğlu) and Ankara (e.g. Maltepe) have hundreds of seedy establishments with dancing girls to titillate visitors. They tend to be expensive and disappointing, but are worth looking in on for the experience.

Nearly every Turkish town of any size has a legalized brothel district called *genelev*, or "common house". Ask any taxi driver where they are. An experience best reserved for the adventurous.

SHOPPING

Shopping in Turkey is a delight. Don't be afraid to haggle – the shop owners expect it and often you can get items down to a very reasonable price over a glass or two of tea. Fashionable clothes can be bought very cheaply, as Turkey has a booming cotton industry. But avoid buying shoes – for although it is able to make very nice bags, wallets, etc., the leather industry seems to have failed miserably regarding footwear. It is hard to find a good bargain in the tourist areas; try to shop in the more out-of-the-way villages and towns where you will probably find better quality at a better price.

Turkish carpets and flat woven *kilims* can be found almost anywhere – the design corresponds to the area in which it was made; each region has its own specialty. You will find many wonderful things made of hand-beaten copper or brass, samovars, lunch boxes, pots and pans, cauldrons – the craftsmanship is excellent.

Other ancient crafts still survive allowing the visitor to purchase ornate Meerschaum pipes (from

the white stone quarried in the Eskişehir region), green or gold onyx bowls, vases and ornaments, lace-edged scarves and beautifully embroidered cotton blouses. Bursa is famous for its excellent towels and bathrobes.

SHOPPING AREAS

The **Covered Bazaar** in Istanbul is the place to go. It is a veritable labyrinth of shops, selling every imaginable product. Similarly excellent **flea markets** can be found in the **Kuledibi, Çarsıkapı, Üsküdar** and **Topkapı** areas. If you prefer more sophisticated shops, you will find the area around **Istiklâl, Caddesi** and **Cumhuriyet Caddesi** in **Taksim** and **Rumeli Caddesi** in **Nişantası** more to your taste. (Refer to section on customs regulations regarding antiques). The recently-opened **Galleria** in Istanbul is a modern, American-style shopping center with hundreds of clothing, leatherware, and carpet shops. It also has recreational facilities such as ice-skating and fast food outlets.

SPORTS

The national obsession is soccer; the fortunes of favorite teams are closely followed with much celebration after a victory.

Ball Games: Youths play volleyball or basketball, but there is a general dearth of facilities. Tennis is popular with the upper class, and remains an elitist game played in private clubs which are quite expensive.

Skiing: This is becoming more popular but is generally overpriced and underequipped; there are more hotels than ski lifts. Skiing facilities are at Uludağ near Bursa, Kartakaya near Bolu, and Erciyes near Kayseri. At Beydagi Mountains near Antalya in March and April, you can ski in the morning and swim in the Mediterranean in the afternoon, if slushy slopes followed by cold water are your idea of a good time.

Mountaineering: Climbing Mount Ararat is especially popular. There are specialist clubs which deal with this kind of outdoor adventure. You can contact them through the travel agencies.

Swimming: Who needs a swimming pool when there is so much ocean? However, if you are adamant about swimming in pools, they are available in hotels and can also be found in the bigger cities, at a price.

LANGUAGE

Atatürk's great language reform took place in the 1930s, when the Turks changed over from Arabic to Latin characters, and many Persian and Arabic words were replaced by new Turkish ones. The language belongs to the Ural-Altaic group, but do not be put off – it is wonderfully logical and the pronunciation is phonetic. The vowels are pronounced as in German, and the consonants as in English but without the dipthongs. Each syllable is pronounced with equal stress.

c is pronounced like "dj" as in *jump*
ç is pronounced like "ch" as in *chill*
s is pronounced like "s" as in *sleep*
ş is pronounced like "sh" as in *sharp*
g is pronounced like "g" as in *good*
ğ is silent, often elongating the previous vowel
a is pronounce like "a" as in *father*
e is pronounced like "ai" as in *available*
i with a dot is pronounced "ee" as in *see*
ı without a dot is a shawh sound, like the vowels in *ever*
o is pronounced like "o" as in *over*
ö is like the German "oe" as in *Woerten* or the English *words*
u is pronounced like "oo" as in *you*
ü is like the German "ue" as in *Ueber*

There are no dipthongs in Turkish, nor is there a "th" sound usually mispronounced in foreign words as either "t" or "z".

In the East, "h" as in "horse" is usually transformed into a semi-gutteral "khorse", as is the crisp "k" sound in words like "Turk", which ends up sounding like "Turkh". Such pronounciation in good circles drives Turks wild and identifies the speaker as a country bumpkin.

Other regional variations can be just about mutually unintelligible: "k" becomes "ch" in the eastern Black Sea, but a "g" in the south, and at times even "q". Kurds in the east have trouble with the umlaut vowels, as well as the thin "v" of standard Turkish, which becomes "w" when they speak.

None of this is bound to affect the traveler over much, but it is advisable to learn at least a few phrases from the following list to wow new friends and make more new ones.

SOME USEFUL TURKISH

Hello	*Merhaba* (mer-ha-ba)
Good morning/ Good day	*Günaydin* (gun-ahy-din)
Good night	*Iyi geceler* (eey gej-e-ler)
Good evening	*Iyi aksamlar* (eey ak-sham-lar)
Good bye	*Allahaısmarlardık* (ala-is-mal-adik)
Please	*Lütfen* (Lut-fen)
Thank you	*Tesekkür ederim* (tesh-e-kur e-derim) *sagol* (sa-ol) or *mersi*
Yes	*Evet* (e-vet)
No	*Hayır* (high-ir)
Excuse me	*Affedersiniz* (Af-eder-sin-iz)
How are you?	*Nasılsınız?* (Na-sil-sin-is?)
I don't speak Turkish	*Türkçe bilmiyorum* (Tur-che bil-mi-yor-um)
Do you speak English?	*Ingilizce biliyor-musunuz?* (ing-liz-je bil-ior-mus-un-us)
What time is it?	*Saat Kaç?* (saaht kach?)
At what time?	*Saat kaçta?* (saaht kach-ta?)
Beat it!	*Defol!* (def-ol!)

SHOPPING

I would like...	*...Istiyorum* (ee-sti-yor-um)
There isn't any	*Yok*
How much is it?	*Ne kadar?* (ne ka-dar?)
Cheap	*Ucuz* (u-jzooz)
Expensive	*Pahalı* (pa-ha-leh)
Old	*Eski*
New	*Yeni*
Very nice/beautiful	*Çok güzel* (Chok gu-zel)
How many?	*Kaç tane?* (kach tah-neh?)
This	*Bu*
That	*Su* (shoo)

TRAVELING/VISITING

Where is the...	*...nerede* (ne-re-deh)
Here	*Burada* (boo-ra-dah)
There	*Surada* (shoo-ra-dah)
Near	*Yakın* (ya-kun)
Far	*Uzak* (oo-zak)
When?	*Ne zaman?* (ne za-man)
City	*Sehir* (sh-e-hir)
Village	*Köy* (koy)
Forest	*Orman* (or-man)
Sea	*Deniz* (de-niz)
Lake	*Göl* (gurl)
Farm	*Çiftlik* (chift-lik)
Church	*Kilise* (kil-ee-seh)
Mosque	*Cami* (jar-mi)
Post Office	*Postane* (pos-ta-neh)
Bus station	*Otogar* (oto-gar)
Train station	*Gar* or *Istasyon* (is-tas-yon)
Airport	*Havaalanı* (hava-alaneh)
Port	*Liman* (lee-man)
Quay	*Iskele* (is-ke-leh)
North	*Kuzey* (ku-zeh)

South	*Güney* (gu-neh)
East	*Dogu* (do-u)
West	*Batı* (ba-teh)

DAYS OF THE WEEK

Monday	*Pazartesi* (pa-zar-tes-i)
Tuesday	*Salı* (sar-leh)
Wednesday	*Carsamba* (char-sham-bah)
Thursday	*Persembe* (Per-shem-beh)
Friday	*Cuma* (ju-ma)
Saturday	*Cumartesi* (ju-mar-te-sih)
Sunday	*Pazar* (pa-zar)

MONTHS OF THE YEAR

January	*Ocak* (oj-ak)
February	*Subat* (shu-bat)
March	*Mart*
April	*Nisan*
May	*Mayıs* (ma-yis)
June	*Haziran* (hahzi-ran)
July	*Temmuz* (tem-muz)
August	*Agustos* (ah-ust-os)
September	*Eylül*
October	*Ekim* (eh-kihm)
November	*Kasım* (kahsihm)
December	*Aralık* (ah-ra-lihk)

NUMBERS

1	*bir* (beer)
2	*iki* (eek-ee)
3	*üç* (ooch)
4	*dört* (dirt)
5	*bes* (besh)
6	*altı* (al-tih)
7	*yedi* (ye-dih)
8	*sekiz* (seh-kihz)
9	*doduz* (doh-kuz)
10	*on*
11	*onbir* (onbeer)
12	*oniki* (on-eek-ee)
20	*yirmi* (yir-mih)
21	*yirmibir*
22	*yirmiiki*
30	*otuz* (o-tooz)
40	*kırk*
50	*elli*
60	*altmıs* (alt-mish)
70	*yetmis* (yet-mish)
80	*seksen*
90	*doksan*
100	*yüz* (yooz)
200	*ikiyüz*
1,000	*bin*
2,000	*ikibin*
1,000,000	*milyon*

USEFUL ADDRESSES

TOURIST INFORMATION

There are tourist information bureaus to assist the traveler in most cities, as follows:

Adana, Atatürk Caddesi No. 13. Tel: (322) 4311323

Adiyaman, Atatürk Bulvarı 184. Tel: (416) 2131008

Afyon, Dumlupinar Mah. Ordu Bul. 22. Tel: (272) 2135447

Agrı, Cumhuriyet Ilkokuluarkasi. Tel: (472) 2153730

Aksaray, Ankara Caddesi, Dinçer Apt. 2/2. Tel: (382) 2132474

Alanya, Çarsi Mahalesi Kalearkarsı Cad. Tel: (242) 5121240

Ankara, Gazi Mustafa Kemal Bulvarı 121, Tandoğan. Tel: (312) 4887007

Antalya, Mermerli Sokak, Kaleiçi. Tel: (242) 2470541

Ayvalık, Yat Limani Karsısı. Tel: (266) 3122122

Bergama, Zafer Mah. Izmir Yolu Uzeri 54. Tel: (232) 6323368

Bodrum, 12 Eylül Mey. Tel: (252) 3161091

Bursa, Ulu Cami Parkı. Tel: (224) 2212359

Çanakkale, Hükümet Konağı, 1st floor. Tel: (286) 2175012

Çesme, Iskele Meydanı 8. Tel: (232) 7126653

Datça, Hükümet Binası. Tel: (252) 7123646

Diyarbakır, Kültür Sarayı, 6th floor. Tel: (412) 2217840

Edirne, Talatpasa Asfatı 76/A. Tel: (284) 2121490

Eğridir, Sahil Yolu 13. Tel: (246) 3122098

Erdek, Hükümet Caddesi, Birinci Sokak 2. Tel: (266) 8351169

Fethiye, Iskele Mey. 1. Tel: (252) 6141527

Foça, Atatürk Mah. Foça Girisi. Tel: (232) 8121222

Ipsala, (Greece border), Edirne. Tel: (284) 6161577

Iskendurun, Atatürk Bulvarı 99/B. Tel: (326) 6132879

Istanbul, Sultanahmet Square. Tel: (212) 5181802; Karaköy Sea Port. Tel: 2495776; Mesrutiyet Caddesi 57, Galatasaray. Tel: 2432928

Izmir, Atatürk Caddesi 418, Alsancak. Tel: (232) 4220207; Büyük Efes Hotel arcade, Alsancak. Tel: 4899278

Kapıkule, Hudut Sahası Girisi Uniteleri. Tel: (284) 2382019

Karş, Lise Cad. No. 4. Tel: (474) 2122300

Kaş, Cumhuriyet Mey. 6. Tel: (242) 8361238

Kemer, Belediye Binasi. Tel: (242) 8141536

Köyceğiz, Kordon Gölpark 1. Tel: (252) 2624703

Kuşadası, Iskele Mey. Tel: (256) 6141103

THE KODAK GOLD GUIDE TO BETTER PICTURES.

Good photography is not difficult. Use these practical hints and Kodak Gold II Film: then notice the improvement.

Move in close. Get close enough to capture only the important elements.

Frame your Pictures. Look out for natural frames such as archways or tree branches to add an interesting foreground. Frames help create a sensation of depth and direct attention into the picture.

One centre of interest. Ensure you have one focus of interest and avoid distracting features that can confuse the viewer.

Use leading lines. Leading lines direct attention to your subject i.e. – a stream, a fence, a pathway; or the less obvious such as light beams or shadows.

Maintain activity. Pictures are more appealing if the subject is involved in some natural action.

Keep within the flash range. Ensure subject is within flash range for your camera (generally 4 metres). With groups make sure everyone is the same distance from the camera to receive the same amount of light.

Check the light direction. People tend to squint in bright direct light. Light from the side creates highlights and shadows that reveal texture and help to show the shapes of the subject. If shooting into direct sunlight fill-in flash can be effective to light the subject from the front.

CHOOSING YOUR KODAK GOLD II FILM.

Choosing the correct speed of colour print film for the type of photographs you will be taking is essential to achieve the best colourful results.

Basically the more intricate your needs in terms of capturing speed or low-light situations the higher speed film you require.

Kodak Gold II 100. Use in bright outdoor light or indoors with electronic flash. Fine grain, ideal for enlargements and close-ups. Ideal for beaches, snow scenes and posed shots.

Kodak Gold II 200. A multipurpose film for general lighting conditions and slow to moderate action. Recommended for automatic 35mm cameras. Ideal for walks, bike rides and parties.

Kodak Gold II 400. Provides the best colour accuracy as well as the richest, most saturated colours of any 400 speed film. Outstanding flash-taking capabilities for low-light and fast-action situations; excellent exposure latitude. Ideal for outdoor or well-lit indoor sports, stage shows or sunsets.

INSIGHT GUIDES

COLORSET NUMBERS

160 Alaska	135F Düsseldorf	158 Netherlands
155 Alsace	204 East African	100 New England
150 Amazon Wildlife	Wildlife,	184E New Orleans
116 America, South	149 Eastern Europe,	184F New York City
173 American Southwest	118 Ecuador	133 New York State
158A Amsterdam	148A Edinburgh	293 New Zealand
260 Argentina	268 Egypt	265 Nile, The
287 Asia, East	123 Finland	120 Norway
207 Asia, South	209B Florence	124B Oxford
262 Asia, South East	243 Florida	147 Pacific Northwest
194 Asian Wildlife,	154 France	205 Pakistan
Southeast	135C Frankfurt	154A Paris
167A Athens	208 Gambia & Senegal	249 Peru
272 Australia	135 Germany	184B Philadelphia
263 Austria	148B Glasgow	222 Philippines
188 Bahamas	279 Gran Canaria	115 Poland
206 Bali Baru	169 Great Barrier Reef	202 Portugal
107 Baltic States	124 Great Britain	114A Prague
246A Bangkok	167 Greece	153 Provence
292 Barbados	166 Greek Islands	156 Puerto Rico
219B Barcelona	135G Hamburg	250 Rajasthan
187 Bay of Naples	240 Hawaii	177 Rhine
234A Beijing	193 Himalaya, Western	127A Rio de Janeiro
109 Belgium	196 Hong Kong	172 Rockies
135A Berlin	144 Hungary	209A Rome
217 Bermuda	256 Iceland	101 Russia
100A Boston	247 India	275B San Francisco
127 Brazil	212 India, South	130 Sardinia
178 Brittany	128 Indian Wildlife	148 Scotland
109A Brussels	143 Indonesia	184D Seattle
144A Budapest	142 Ireland	261 Sicily
260A Buenos Aires	252 Israel	159 Singapore
213 Burgundy	236A Istanbul	257 South Africa
268A Cairo	209 Italy	264 South Tyrol
247B Calcutta	213 Jamaica	219 Spain
275 California	278 Japan	220 Spain, Southern
180 California,	266 Java	105 Sri Lanka
Northern	252A Jerusalem-Tel Aviv	101B St Petersburg
161 California,	203A Kathmandu	170 Sweden
Southern	270 Kenya	232 Switzerland
237 Canada	300 Korea	272 Sydney
162 Caribbean	202A Lisbon	175 Taiwan
The Lesser Antilles	258 Loire Valley	112 Tenerife
122 Catalonia	124A London	186 Texas
(Costa Brava)	275A Los Angeles	246 Thailand
141 Channel Islands	201 Madeira	278A Tokyo
184C Chicago	219A Madrid	139 Trinidad & Tobago
151 Chile	145 Malaysia	113 Tunisia
234 China	157 Mallorca & Ibiza	236 Turkey
135E Cologne	117 Malta	171 Turkish Coast
119 Continental Europe	272B Melbourne	210 Tuscany
189 Corsica	285 Mexico	174 Umbria
281 Costa Rica	285A Mexico City	237A Vancouver
291 Cote d'Azur	243A Miami	198 Venezuela
165 Crete	237B Montreal	209C Venice
184 Crossing America	235 Morocco	263A Vienna
226 Cyprus	101A Moscow	255 Vietnam
114 Czechoslovakia	135D Munich	267 Wales
247A Delhi, Jaipur, Agra	211 Myanmar (Burma)	184C Washington DC
238 Denmark	259 Namibia	183 Waterways
135B Dresden	269 Native America	of Europe
142B Dublin	203 Nepal	215 Yemen

You'll find the colorset number on the spine of each Insight Guide.

Marmaris, Iskele Meydanı 92. Tel: (252) 4121035
Mersin (İçel), Inönü Bulvarı Liman Giris Sahasi. Tel: (324) 2312710
Muğla, Belediye Atapark Sitesi. Tel: (252) 2143127
Nevşehir, Yeni Kayseri Cad. Hastane Yan 22. Tel: (384) 2133659
Selçuk, Atatürk Mah. Efes Muzesi Karsisi 23. Across from the museum. Tel: (232) 8922945
Side, at the entrance to the town. Tel: (242) 7531265
Silifke, Atatürk Caddesi 1/2. Tel: (324) 7141151
Trabzon, Vilayet Binası, 4th floor. Tel: (462) 2235833
Ürgüp, Kayseri Caddesi 37. Tel: (384) 3411059

TOURIST INFORMATION BUREAUS ABROAD

Austria, Singer Strasse 2/8, 1010 Vienna. Tel: (0222) 5122128/9
Belgium, Rue Montoyer 4, 1040 Brussels. Tel: (02) 5138230-9
Denmark, Vesterbrogade 11A 1620, Copenhagen V. Tel: (01) 223100, 228374
Federal Republic of Germany, Baseler Strasse 37, 6, Frankfurt MI, tel: (0611) 233081/2; Karlplatz 3/1, 8000 Munich 2, tel: (089) 594902, 594317
France, 02, Champs-Elysees, 75008 Paris. Tel: (1) 45 62 78 68
Italy, Piazza della Republica, 56-00185, Rome. Tel: (6) 462957, 4741697
Japan, Turkish Embassy 33-6, 2 Chome Jingumae Shibuya-Ku, Tokyo. Tel: (03) 4706380, 4705131
Netherlands, Herengracht 451, 1017 BS Amsterdam. Tel: (020) 266810
Saudi Arabia, Turkish Embassy Medina Road Kilo 6, Al Arafat Street, Jeddah. Tel: 6654578
Spain, Plaza de España, Torre de Madrid, Planta 13 Of: 3 Madrid 28008. Tel: 248014, 2487114
Sweden, Kungsgatan 3, S-111 43 Stockholm. Tel: (08) 218620-30
Switzerland, Talstrasse 74, 8001 Zurich. Tel: (01) 2210810
United Kingdom, 170-173 Piccadilly (First Floor), London W1. Tel: (071) 7348681/2
United States, 821 United Nations Plaza, New York, NY 10017, tel: (212) 6872194; 2010 Massachusetts Strasseenue, NW, Washington DC 20036, tel: (202) 8338411, 4299844

TRAVEL AGENCIES

ADANA
(dialing code: 322)

Adalı Turizm, Stadyum Caddesi 37/C. Tel: 4537440
Günes Turizm, Ziyapasa Bulvarı 42. Tel: 4533033

ANKARA
(dialing code: 312)

Atak, Arjantin Caddesi 25, Gaziosmanpaşa. Tel: 4671394, 4679585
Efor Tour, Cinnah Caddesi 46/2, Çankaya. Tel: 4407927
Konvoy Tur, Atatürk Boulevard 233/8, Kavaklıdere. Tel: 4267624, 4263110
Saltur, Atatürk Boulevard 199/G, Bakanlıklar. Tel: 4255973
Tempo, Izmir Caddesi 57/15, Kızılay. Tel: 4251279

ANTALYA
(dialing code: 242)

ATT Tourism, Cumhuriyet Caddesi 80/602. Tel: 2423224
Attalos Travel, Cumhuriyet Caddesi, Yıldız Ishanı 80/1. Tel: 2412542. Helicopter trips to Cappadocia and Pamukkale.
Ekin, Fevzi Çakmak Caddesi 26/A. Tel: 2429929
Metro Tours, Fevzi Çakmak Caddesi, 1314 Sokak, Elif Apt. Tel: 2415925
Pamfilya, 30 Ağustos Caddesi 57/B. Tel: 2431500
Tantur, Atatürk Caddesi, Üçkapılar. Tel: 2429397

BURSA
(dialing code: 224)

Esperanto Turizm, Inönü Caddesi 15/1. Tel: 2216456
Nartur, Çekirge Caddesi 41. Tel: 2200016

ISTANBUL
(dialing code: 212)

Art Tours, Valikonağı Caddesi 77/3, Polat Apt., Nişantası. Tel: 2310487
Bosfor Turizm, Mete Caddesi 14/3, Taksim. Tel: 2499921
Duru Turizm, Cumhuriyet Caddesi 243, Harbiye. Tel: 2319000
Genç Tur, Yerebatan Caddesi 15/3, Sultanahmet. Tel: 5205274
Irem Tur, Nispetiye Caddesi, Şirin Apt 48/11, Etiler. Tel: 2658405
National Tour, Rumeli Caddesi, Ogan Apt 16/7, Nişantası. Tel: 2527725
Plan Tours, Cumhuriyet Caddesi 131/1, Elmadağ. Tel: 2302272, 2308118
Tantur, Gazeteciler Sitesi, Yazarlar Sokak 17, Esentepe. Tel: 2724974
Ten Tour, Halaskargazi Caddesi, Küçükbahçe Sokak, Samanyolu ıs Merkezi, 3/1, Şisli. Tel: 2328135
Türk Ekspress, Cumhuriyet Caddesi 91/1, Şakir Pasa Ishanı, Elmadağ. Tel: 2301515
Vip Turizm, Cumhuriyet Caddesi 269/2, Harbiye. Tel: 2416514
Visitur, Cumhuriyet Caddesi 129/8, Elmadağ. Tel: 2414040
Vista Travel, Cumhuriyet Caddesi 233/4, Harbiye. Tel: 2300056

IZMIR
(dialing code: 232)

Bodrum Tour, Şair Esref Bulvarı 18/203, Alsancak. Tel: 4412228
Egetur, Talatpasa Bulvarı 2/B, Alsancak. Tel: 4217921
Pamfilya, Atatürk Caddesi 270, Alsancak. Tel: 4215873
Setur, Atatürk Caddesi 194/A, Alsancak. Tel: 4215595

KUŞADASİ
(dialing code: 256)

Akdeniz Turizm, Atatürk Bulvarı 25. Tel: 6141140, 6141010
Azim-Tur, Liman Caddesi, Yayla Pas. 1. Tel: 6141553
Diana Turizm, across from the marina. Tel: 6144900
Eray Turizm, Ismet Inönü Bulvarı 38/D. Tel: 6141214
Turkuaz Turizm, Kahramanlar Caddesi 98/B. Tel: 6141392

MERSIN (IÇEL)
(dialing code: 324)

Güney Turizm, Istiklal Caddesi, 107 Sokak 4/10. Tel: 2330208
Soli-Tur, Ismet Inönü Bulvarı 31. Tel: 2354406

BODRUM
(dialing code: 252)

Admiral Turizm, Neyzen Tevfik Caddesi 78. Tel: 3161781
Flama Tour, Neyzen Tevfik Caddesi 222. Tel: 3161842
Gündüz Turizm, Dr Alim Bey Caddesi 2. Tel: 3161551
Karya Tur, Mendirek, Belediye Dükkanları. Tel: 3161914
Tussock Turizm, Neyzen Tevfik Caddesi, Saray Sokak 2. Tel: 3162236

FETHIYE
(dialing code: 252)

Bigtur, Atatürk Caddesi 28. Tel: 6143456
Megri-tur, Atatürk Caddesi 34. Tel: 6144444

MARMARIS
(dialing code: 252)

Air Tour, Kenan Evren Bulvarı, Manolya Sokak. Tel: 4123915, 4121557
Esin Turizm, Kemeraltı Mahallesi, Atatürk Caddesi 12. Tel: 4122001, 4122328
Euro Tour, Ismet Kamil Öner Caddesi 8. Tel: 4124388
Gino Tour, Hacı Sabri Sokak 24/1. Tel: 4126380

NEVŞEHIR (CAPPADOCIA
(dialing code: 384)

Magic Valley Cappadocia, near the bus terminal, Ürgüp. Tel: 3412145, 3413730

EMBASSIES & CONSULATES

ANKARA
(dialing code: 312)

Australia, Nenhatun Caddesi 83, Gaziosmanpaşa. Tel: 4361240
Austria, Atatürk Boulevard. 189, Kavaklıdere. Tel: 4342172
Belgium, Nenhatun Caddesi 109, Gaziosmanpaşa. Tel: 4366520
Canada, Nenehatun Caddesi 75, Gaziosmanpaşa. Tel: 4361275
Denmark, Kırlangıç Sokak 42, Gaziosmanpaşa. Tel: 4275258
Finland, Galip Dede Sokak 1/19, Çankaya. Tel: 4264964
France, Paris Caddesi 70, Kavaklıdere. Tel: 4681154
Germany, Atatürk Boulevard. 114, Kavaklıdere. Tel: 4265465
Greece, Ziya Ürrahman Caddesi 9-11, Çankaya. Tel: 4368860
Israel, Farabi Sokak 43, Kavaklıdere. Tel: 4264993
Italy, Atatürk Boulevard. 118, Kavaklıdere. Tel: 4265460
Japan, Resit Galip Caddesi 81, Gaziosmanpaşa. Tel: 4460500
Netherlands, Köroğlu Sokak 16, Gaziosmanpaşa. Tel: 4460470
New Zealand, Kızkulesi Sokak 42/1, Gaziosmanpaşa. Tel: 4460768
Norway, Kelebek Sokak 18, Gaziosmanpaşa. Tel: 4360051
Portugal, Cinnah Caddesi 28/3, Çankaya. Tel: 4461890
Russian Federation, Karyağdı Sokak 5, Asağı Ayrancı. Tel: 4392122
Spain, Vali Doktor Resit Sokak 6, Çankaya. Tel: 4380392
Sweden, Katip Çelebi Sokak 7, Kavaklıdere. Tel: 4286735
Switzerland, Atatürk Boulevard. 247, Kavaklıdere. Tel: 4675555
Turkish Republic of North Cyprus, Incirli Sokak 20, Gaziosmanpaşa. Tel: 4379538
United Kingdom, Şehit Ersan Caddei 46/A, Çankaya. Tel: 4274310
United States, Atatürk Boulevard 110, Kavaklıdere. Tel: 4265470

ISTANBUL
(dialing code: 212)

Australia, Etiler. Tel: 2577050
Austria, Yeniköy. Tel: 2624984

Belgium, Taksim. Tel: 2433300
Canada, Gayrettepe. Tel: 2725174
Denmark, Fındıklı. Tel: 2450385
Finland, Taksim. Tel: 2455880
France, Taksim. Tel: 2431852
Germany, Taksim. Tel: 2515404
Greece, Galatasaray. Tel: 2450596
Israel, Nişantası. Tel: 2464125
Italy, Galatasaray. Tel: 2431024
Japan, Taksim. Tel: 2517605
Netherlands, Tünel. Tel: 2515030
Norway, Karaköy. Tel: 2499753
Portugal, Taksim. Tel: 2511 30
Russian Federation, Tünel. Tel: 2442610
Spain, Tesvikiye. Tel: 2252153
Sweden, Tünel. Tel: 2435770
Switzerland, Tesvikiye. Tel: 2591115
United Kingdom, Tepebası. Tel: 2526436
United States, Tepebası. Tel: 2513602

Further Reading

GENERAL

Akurgal, Ekrem. *Ancient Civilizations and Ruins of Turkey*. 3rd edition. Istanbul: Haset Kitabevi, 1973.

Akurgal, Ekrem. *The Art of the Hittites*. London: Thames and Hudson, 1962.

Aslanapa, Oktay. *Turkish Art and Architecture*. London: Faber and Faber, 1971.

Bean, George. *Aegean Turkey*. London: Ernest Benn, 1966.

Bean, George. *Lycia*. London: Ernest Benn, 1978.

Bean, George. *Turkey Beyond the Maeanders*. London: Ernest Benn, 1971.

Bittel, Kurt. *Hattusa, The Capital of the Hittites*. Oxford University Press, 1970.

Blegen, Carl. *Troy and the Trojans*. London: Thames and Hudson, 1963.

Cook, John. *The Greeks in Ionia and the East*. London: Thames and Hudson, 1962.

Davis, Fanny. *The Palace of Topkapı*. New York: Scribners, 1970.

der Nersessian, Sirapie. *The Armenians*. London: Thames and Hudson, 1979.

Efendi, Evliya. *Narrative of Travels*. New York: Johnson Reprint Co., 1968.

Freely, John. *Stamboul Sketches*. Istanbul: Redhouse Press, 1974.

Goodwin, Godfrey. *A History of Ottoman Architecture*. London: Thames and Hudson, 1971.

Green, Peter. *Alexander of Macedon*. London: Penguin Books, 1970.

Gürney, O.R. *The Hittities*. London: Penguin Books, 1968.

Inalcik, Halil. *The Ottoman Empire: The Classical Age, 1300-1600*. London: Weidenfeld and Nicolson, 1973.

Kinross, Lord. *Atatürk: The Rebirth of a Nation*. London: Weidenfeld and Nicolson, 1964.

Kinross, Lord. *The Ottoman Centuries*. New York: Morrow Quill, 1977.

Krautheimer, Richard. *Early Christian and Byzantine Architecture*. London: Penguin Books, 1965.

Lewis, Bernard. *The Emergence of Modern Turkey*. Oxford University Press, 1968.

Lewis, Raphaela. *Everyday Life in Ottoman Turkey*. London: B.T. Batsford, 1971.

Makal, Mahmut. *A Village in Anatolia*. London: Valentine, Mitchell, 1954.

Mellaart, James. *Catal Höyük*. London: Thames and Hudson, 1967.

Menemencioglu, Nermin. *Turkish Verse*. London: Penguin Books, 1978.

Orga, Irfan. *Portrait of a Turkish Family*. London: Macmillan, 1957.

Ostrogorsky, Georg. *History of the Byzantine State*. Oxford: Blackwell, 1968.

Peters, F.E. *The Harvest of Hellenism*. New York: Simon and Schuster, 1970.

Runciman, Steven. *The Fall of Constantinople, 1453*. Cambridge University Press, 1965.

Shaw, Stanford J. and Ezel Kural Shaw. *History of the Ottoman Empire and Modern Turkey*. London: Cambridge University Press, 1976.

Sumner-Boyd, Hilary and John Freely. *Istanbul: A Brief Guide to the City*. Redhouse Press, 1973.

Vidal, Gore. *Julian*. New York: Signet, 1962.

Williams, Gwynn. *Eastern Turkey: A Guide and History*. London: Faber and Faber, 1972

ART/PHOTO CREDITS

INDEX

A

H

I

N

O

P & Q